Case Studies in Contemporary Criticism

A Companion to
JAMES JOYCE's

Ulysses

Case Studies in Contemporary Criticism
SERIES EDITOR: Ross C Murfin

Case Studies in Contemporary Criticism

SERIES EDITOR: Ross C Murfin, *Southern Methodist University*

A Companion to
JAMES JOYCE's
Ulysses

**Biographical and Historical Contexts,
Critical History, and Essays from
Five Contemporary Critical Perspectives**

EDITED BY

Margot Norris
University of California, Irvine

Bedford Books
BOSTON   ❧   NEW YORK

For Bedford Books
President and Publisher: Charles H. Christensen
General Manager and Associate Publisher: Joan E. Feinberg
Managing Editor: Elizabeth M. Schaaf
Developmental Editor: John Sullivan
Production Editors: Ellen C. Thibault, Deborah Baker
Copyeditor: Lisa Wehrle
Text Design: Sandra Rigney, The Book Department
Cover Design: Richard Emery Design, Inc.
Cover Art: Photograph of the O'Connell Bridge, Dublin, ca. 1902.
Courtesy of the National Library of Ireland.
Composition: Pine Tree Composition, Inc.
Printing and Binding: Haddon Craftsmen, Inc.

Library of Congress Catalog Card Number: 97-74966

Manufactured in the United States of America.

2 1 0 9 8
f e d c b a

For information, write: Bedford Books, 75 Arlington Street, Boston, MA 02116 (617-426-7440)

ISBN: 0-312-11598-9 (paperback)
ISBN: 0-312-21067-1 (hardcover)

Acknowledgments

Jacques Derrida, "Ulysses Gramophone." In *James Joyce: The Augmented Ninth.* Edited by Bernard Benstock, 27–54. Syracuse, NY: Syracuse University Press, 1988.

Wolfgang Iser. "Patterns of Communication in Joyce's *Ulysses*." In *The Implied Reader: Patterns of Communication in Prose Fiction from Bunyan to Beckett.* 1974. Reprinted by permission of the Johns Hopkins University Press.

About the Series

Volumes in the Case Studies in Contemporary Criticism series provide college students with an entrée into the current critical and theoretical ferment in literary studies. Each volume presents critical essays that discuss a classic literary work from different theoretical perspectives, together with the editors' introductions to both the literary work and the critics' theoretical perspectives. Other volumes in the series include the complete text of the classic work under study. This volume, however, does not reprint the text of *Ulysses*, due to its substantial length and ready availability.

The volume editor of each Case Study has written an introduction to the work's biographical and historical contexts, surveyed the critical responses to the work since its initial publication, and when necessary, selected and prepared an authoritative text of the classic work. Thus situated biographically, historically, and critically, the work is examined in five critical essays, each representing a theoretical perspective of importance to contemporary literary studies. These essays, prepared especially for undergraduates by exemplary critics, show theory in praxis; whether written by established scholars or exceptional young critics, they demonstrate how current theoretical approaches can generate compelling readings of great literature.

As series editor, I have prepared introductions, with bibliographies, to the theoretical perspectives represented in the five critical

essays. Each introduction presents the principal concepts of a particular theory in their historical context and discusses the major figures
and key works that have influenced their formulation. It is my hope
that these introductions will reveal to students that effective criticism is
informed by a set of coherent assumptions, and will encourage them
to recognize and examine their own assumptions about literature.
After each introduction, a selective bibliography presents a partially annotated list of important works from the literature of the particular
theoretical perspective, including the most recent and readily available
editions and translations of the works cited in the introduction. Finally, I have compiled a glossary of key terms that recur in these volumes and in the discourse of contemporary theory and criticism. We
hope that the Case Studies in Contemporary Criticism series will reaffirm the richness of its literary works, even as it introduces invigorating
new ways to mine their apparently inexhaustible wealth.

Ross C Murfin
Series Editor
Southern Methodist University

About This Volume

This *Companion to James Joyce's "Ulysses": A Case Study in Contemporary Criticism* differs from the other volumes in the Case Studies series because it does not reprint the text of the work under consideration. The length of *Ulysses*—one of the "big" books among the classics, with 644 pages in the Gabler edition—makes its inclusion impractical. Instead, this volume—with its various introductory discussions of Joyce, *Ulysses*, and contemporary criticism and its critical essays about the novel—can usefully supplement whatever edition of the work is being read.

There is, in effect, no "definitive" edition of *Ulysses*. Joyce's text had a difficult birth: typed by friends when paid typists objected to its obscenity, published by a kindly bookseller who permitted the author to make endless changes and corrections, and printed by French printers daunted by highly experimental prose in a foreign language. *Ulysses* was an editing nightmare from the start. Editorial controversy revisited the book twice—first in the 1980s when argument surrounded the unveiling of a new "corrected text" by Hans Walter Gabler (now known as "the Gabler edition") that was published in 1986 by Vintage Books, a division of Random House. I discuss these editorial difficulties briefly in "A Critical History of *Ulysses*" later in this volume, noting that the Gabler edition enjoys wide use among Joyce critics, including the authors whose original essays appear here. More recently, a new text edited by Danis Rose called *Ulysses: A Reader's Edition* (1997) has aroused argument over its alterations of Joyce's spelling, punctuation, and some words.

The essays by Jacques Derrida and Wolfgang Iser reprinted here cite the 1968 London Penguin edition and the 1937 London Bodley Head edition, respectively. The differences between these earlier editions and the Gabler edition are extensive and significant enough to warrant leaving *Ulysses* citations in the Derrida and Iser essays in their original form. The argument and interpretation of Derrida, in particular, might have been affected by changing his citations to the Gabler edition.

Because of its enormous complexity and difficulty, *Ulysses* poses special challenges both to the novice reader and to an introductory volume like this that attempts to help with the initiation. In response I have tried to give a very basic introduction to the novel's organization and narrative in my discussion of its critical history, complete with the Homeric "titles" for the episodes because these are not part of the text of *Ulysses* itself. I also have attached an expanded bibliography of *Ulysses* that includes many introductory guidebooks and episode-by-episode analyses, which I hope undergraduate students and first-time readers will find valuable.

Ulysses yields a new and rich possibility of meaning to virtually any critical approach applied to it. Theorists developing new approaches are frequently challenged to explore the implications of their assumptions and the usefulness of their methods by testing them against this experimental text. Thus have I enjoyed the unique opportunity to demonstrate deconstructive and reader-response approaches to *Ulysses* by going to their theoretical source in the works of Jacques Derrida and Wolfgang Iser. Inventors and pioneers of deconstruction and reader-response criticism, respectively, Derrida and Iser demonstrate how *Ulysses* illuminates theory at the same time that theory illuminates *Ulysses*. Jacques Derrida has graciously permitted me to reprint a portion of the essay that he presented at the Ninth International James Joyce Symposium in Frankfurt in June 1984. The piece, translated by Tina Kendall with emendations and some notes by Shari Benstock, was published in 1988 in *James Joyce: The Augmented Ninth*, edited by Bernard Benstock. Wolfgang Iser prepared a shortened and simplified version of his essay, "Patterns of Communication in Joyce's *Ulysses*," for this volume. This piece was taken from his seminal study of reader-response theory, *The Implied Reader*. There is much to appreciate in the work of Derrida and Iser: groundbreaking theory, an original and significant contribution to Joyce studies, and their generosity as colleagues and teachers of theory at the University of California, Irvine. The other three essays on *Ulysses* demonstrating feminist, psychoanalytical, and Marxist approaches to the novel were especially prepared for this volume by Vicki Mahaffey, Kimberly Devlin, and Patrick McGee. They reflect the innovative and theoretically sophisticated work these young scholars have contributed to the study of Joyce over the years, as well as their enthusiastic commitment to teach Joyce effectively to undergraduates. I am also grateful to the Case Study series editor, Ross Murfin, for entrusting me with this project, and for providing the essays with insightful critical contexts. Ellen Thibault, Deborah Baker, Lisa Wehrle, and John Sullivan deserve my thanks for their expert editorial work on behalf of Bedford Books.

My own students, both undergraduate and graduate, deserve my warmest gratitude for continually renewing my understanding and appreciation of Joyce's *Ulysses* and for reminding me of the challenges that first-time readers of the novel confront. They have shared with me for a quarter of a century now the strange effect this radically innovative novel has on its readers. First affronting us as an elite artifact, it eventually becomes a living experience—a lifestyle, almost—that knits its readers into sympathetic communities. My wish is that this volume helps bring a new generation of students and readers into our charmed circle.

Margot Norris
University of California, Irvine

Contents

Case Studies in Contemporary Criticism

A Companion to
JAMES JOYCE's

Ulysses

Introduction: Biographical and Historical Contexts

After the extraordinary complexity that James Joyce brought to the telling of life stories in his fiction, any account of Joyce's own life must feel the burden of biography's limitations, biases, and conventionalities. Writing Joyce's biography is complicated further by the problem of maintaining crucial distinctions between his life and his writing. Besides the many autobiographical details that shape Joyce's *A Portrait of the Artist as a Young Man* (1916), hundreds of real people, places, and events are represented in the texts of *Dubliners* (1914), and *Ulysses* (1922). Joyce told his friend Frank Budgen, "I want . . . to give a picture of Dublin so complete that if the city one day suddenly disappeared from the earth it could be reconstructed out of my book" (Budgen 67). This verisimilitude obliges biography writers to resist dual temptations in the case of Joyce: the temptation to read his life *into* his fiction, and the temptation to read his life *out of* his fiction.

Fortunately, we have a range of excellent biographies of Joyce whose emphases balance each other. Richard Ellmann's monumental *James Joyce*, published in 1959 and revised in 1982, offers a compendious and copiously documented record of Joyce's life and work that is generally regarded as definitive, although it clearly follows the heroic contours of the *Künstlerroman*, the novel genre that portrays artistic development. In contrast to Ellmann's Irish artist with immortal longings for greatness, Peter Costello's 1992 *James Joyce: The Years of Growth 1882–1915* draws Joyce's youth in the more prosaic historical rhythms of Irish life suggested by *Stephen Hero* (1944), Joyce's incomplete first version of *Portrait*. Morris Beja's 1992 *James Joyce: A Literary Life* pays special attention to the interplay of his writing and his life to offer the most illuminating blend of biography and criticism we now have. Other biographies of Joyce range from such early works as Herbert Gorman's 1939 *James Joyce*, an "authorized" version commissioned by Joyce in 1930, to Brenda Maddox's scholarly but "unauthorized" *Nora: The Real Life of Molly Bloom* (1988). The latter gives a feminist account of the Joyces' domestic, social, and sexual lives that angered some of Joyce's descendants upon its 1988 publication.

The following account of Joyce's life attempts to emphasize those aspects of the biography and its historical setting most relevant to the scope and complexity of *Ulysses*.

James Joyce was born in Rathgar, a suburb of Dublin, on February 2, 1882, and died in Zurich, Switzerland, on January 13, 1941. His life span, which coincided with that of Virginia Woolf (1882–1941), began in Victorian Ireland and ended in a Europe whose maps were being redrawn by World War II. In his father's time, Ireland's quasi-colonial status gave the country representation in the British Parliament, but very little control over its own affairs. The potato famines of the 1840s had caused many Irish tenant farmers to default on rents and to suffer evictions from their land, which led to strong pressures for agrarian reform and Home Rule in the later nineteenth century. Charles Stewart Parnell (1846–1891), a member of the Protestant Anglo-Irish Ascendancy, or landowning ruling class, became leader of the Home Rule party and allied himself with the more revolutionary Land League. However, his hopes for achieving Irish home rule through parliamentary negotiations with Prime Minister William Ewart Gladstone's government were not realized. He was politically rejected by the electorate when his role in the divorce of his mistress, Kitty O'Shea, and their subsequent marriage aroused the condemnation of the Catholic hierarchy. This was the political climate into which James Joyce was born in 1882, nine years before Parnell died of a heart broken by political betrayal, as it was popularly construed. In *A Portrait of the Artist as a Young Man*, Joyce dramatized how his family enshrined the legend of the martyred Parnell, now deemed Ireland's "uncrowned king."

Joyce's father, John Stanislaus Joyce, came from a well-to-do Cork family related to the Irish patriot, Daniel O'Connell, called "the Liberator." He attended Queen's College in Cork to study medicine but never achieved the degree. Under the aegis of a family coat of arms, he considered himself "a gentleman" in class terms. John Joyce was a boisterous, funny, volatile man of "absolutely unreliable temper," according to his son Stanislaus (35), but with a good tenor voice and a flair for mimicry and storytelling that made him highly popular with the hard-drinking friends that he cultivated after coming to Dublin in 1874 or 1875. In 1880 John Joyce married an even-tempered, cultured woman named Mary Jane (May) Murray, whose family he reviled. He eventually lost his only real job as a tax collector and never developed a career. He attributed this failing (perhaps not entirely unjustly) to political conspiracies and reprisals aimed at him for his support of Parnell (Costello 118). With his wife pregnant nearly every year, John Joyce produced children and mortgages in tandem as he sought to stave off debts to moneylenders that were eroding his inheritance. He failed, and by James's twelfth year in 1894, John Joyce had ten surviving children, eleven mortgages, and no remaining property (Ellmann 21).

As the eldest surviving child, James Joyce keenly felt the decline from the affluence of his infancy—which allowed him briefly to attend a distinguished Jesuit boarding school—to a mean, poverty-stricken adolescence clouded by the death of a much-loved younger brother, George, from typhoid fever. Of James's many siblings, Stanislaus—the brother next in age—became his closest companion and confidante. The many street addresses of Joyce's youth attest to the frequent evictions or threats of eviction that kept the large family on the move to poorer and more urban residences. After forty-four-year-old May Joyce died in 1903 of cancer, the many Joyce children, neglected by an improvident father, fell into desperate disorder and hardship.

Joyce's mother came from a family that valued erudition. Joyce's parents, ambitious for their sons even when their fortunes declined, secured for James what his friend Oliver St. John Gogarty later called "'a miserable background and sumptuous education'" (Maddox 35). The Jesuit schools Joyce attended—Clongowes Wood College (1888–1891), Belvedere College, Dublin (1893–1898), and University College, Dublin (1898–1902)—taught him the Latin classics, trained him in rigorous scholastic thinking, and subjected him to the intellectual authority of the Catholic Church in matters of taste and morality. Patrick Parrinder describes the insular effects of this education: "Virtually every development in European philosophy since the Renaissance was condemned *a priori*, being the product of heretics, atheists, Protestants or Jews" (19). These schools taught Joyce the canons of the British public school curriculum (including cricket as the favored sport) while increasingly pressing the claims of an Irish cultural nationalism. The young Joyce found the latter—especially the recovery of the Gaelic language, occultism, and folklore—parochial and backward-looking. At University College, Dublin, founded by John Henry Newman in 1854, Joyce chose the modern language course of study, regarded as "the Ladies' Course" according to Peter Costello (159).

Joyce supplemented his studies with visits to the Capel Street Library in Dublin, whose new books introduced him to the brilliant Continental literature then published abroad. This reading provided an alternative to the imperialistic inflections of the English poetic tradition as Joyce would later represent it in *Ulysses*. In his essay "Drama and Life," delivered to the university Literary and Historical Society in 1900, he defined the progressive principles of a new realism in Continental drama: "Life we must accept as we see it before our eyes, men and women as we meet them in the real world, not as we apprehend them in the world of faery" (*Critical Writings* 45). These words announce the uncompromising realism that became a crucial aspect of *Ulysses*. Before leaving the university, Joyce had achieved a precocious cosmopolitanism, reading Ibsen's plays in Dano-Norwegian and Dante in the original, translating the plays of Gerhart Hauptmann, and publishing an essay on Ibsen's *When We Dead Awaken* (1899) in the prestigious London *Fortnightly Review*.

"Joyce made a powerful impression on his fellow-students," Patrick Parrinder notes. "For all his celebrated aloofness he wrote, debated, joked, conversed, and plunged into the mêlée as a precocious intellectual and champion of unpopular causes" (21). Joyce moved in an original and witty circle that he supplemented with his father's political and drinking cronies. This allowed him to populate the Dublin of his fictions with lively, verbally gifted, professionally thwarted male characters, whose fates he entwined with colonial politics. Many of Joyce's university colleagues moved on to distinguished, and tragic, careers in Ireland: George Clancy (Davin) was murdered while serving as Mayor of Limerick during the period known as the Troubles; Thomas Cosgrave (Lynch) drowned in the Thames in 1926, a possible suicide; Francis Sheehy-Skeffington (McCann), Joyce's pacifist, socialist, feminist friend, was murdered while trying to prevent looting during the 1916 Easter uprising in Dublin; Thomas Kettle, elected to Parliament on a Home Rule platform, was killed in the Battle of the

Somme in World War I. Only J. F. Byrne (Cranly), Constantine Curran, and Oliver St. John Gogarty (Mulligan) survived to a comfortable maturity: Curran as Registrar of the High Court, and Gogarty as a successful physician, poet, and senator in the Free State. In Joyce's youth, these figures roamed a city small enough in social and political scale to be contained in a large book. Fredric Jameson described this Dublin as "not exactly the full-blown capitalist metropolis, but like the Paris of Flaubert, still regressive, still distantly akin to the village, still un- and underdeveloped enough to be representable" (135).

The cultural life of that "ambitious and intense" city (Ellmann 98) was dominated by an Anglo-Irish intelligentsia whose chief figures included the novelist George Moore, the theosophist George Russell (pseudonym AE), Lady Augusta Gregory (one of the founders of the Abbey Theatre), and the eminent poet W. B. Yeats. Although Joyce represents Dublin's cultural elite as spurning Stephen Dedalus in *Ulysses*, Ireland's leading literati actually gave Joyce considerable help, offering him publication opportunities, hospitality, letters of introduction and recommendation, and outright subsidies. When upon matriculation Joyce decided to study at the Faculty of Medicine in Paris, Lady Gregory gave money for his passage; Yeats met him in London, dined him, lodged him, and introduced him to Arthur Symons, who later arranged to publish Joyce's poems, *Chamber Music* (1907); dramatist John Synge visited him in Paris.

Joyce's Paris sojourn was neither academically nor artistically successful, and it came to a premature end when his mother's terminal illness obliged him to return to Ireland in 1903. Joyce spent the year following his mother's death in desultory activity, writing and trying to publish, taking singing lessons, teaching school. He lived with various relatives, borrowed money, and stayed briefly with Gogarty at the Martello Tower in Sandycove, which became the setting for the opening of *Ulysses*. Joyce was salvaged from this spiritual vagrancy by the unlikely agency (given the ineptitude in romance that drove him to prostitutes in his teens) of love. On June 16, 1904—a day he was to memorialize as the date of the events of *Ulysses*—Joyce went walking with a young Galway woman named Nora Barnacle, who worked at Finn's Hotel in Dublin. A complex intimacy ensued in which the young woman showed her wit and unruffled self-possession as her lover tried to shock her with his various irreverences and apostasies. The relationship culminated in an ill-planned elopement to the Continent that soon found the penniless couple chasing an elusive Berlitz position, which eventually materialized in the Adriatic seaports of

Pola, where they lived for six months, and Trieste. There the couple began a marriage without the benefit of legal sanction that fulfilled the waggish prophecy of Joyce's father, who on hearing Nora's name, joked, "Barnacle? She'll never leave him" (Maddox 9).

As a city, Trieste was a perfect place for what William Johnsen has called "the moment of modernism, when Joyce modernised himself" (6). A largely Italian city under lax Austrian rule since the fourteenth century, Trieste culturally blended East and West in its colorful population of Italians, Austrians, Slovenes, Hungarians, Greeks, Turks, and Jews. This cosmopolitanism blended with traits that made the city similar to Dublin, including a small-town familiarity and much political ferment sparked by the Irredentist movement agitating for the city's freedom from Austrian rule. Joyce took a lively philosophical and ideological interest in the city's socialist and anarchist activity.

As interesting and exciting as Trieste proved to be, Joyce's newly established home life was plagued by cultural isolation and lack of money. The isolation was especially difficult for Nora, who did not speak the language and who soon faced the upheaval of pregnancy and the birth of a new baby, George (Giorgio), in 1905. The birth of a son posed a legal dilemma that Joyce, whose decision not to marry was a rebellion against religious and governmental authority, may have solved with a ruse. To register Giorgio as legitimate without entirely abandoning his principle, Joyce may have married Nora in a civil ceremony in Trieste under an assumed name. The Joyces' domestic situation was soon simultaneously eased and complicated when Joyce's brother Stanislaus joined the young family. For the next decade Stanislaus became the family's mainstay—acting as bank, factotum, superego, muse, and critic for his brother. Meanwhile, Joyce's teaching at the Berlitz school gave him valuable contact with a diverse European clientele including the Austrian-Italian novelist Ettore Schmitz, also known as Italo Svevo. The teaching job was sufficiently flexible that it allowed him time to work on his own writing.

Joyce wrote on two fronts simultaneously: an autobiographical novel entitled *Stephen Hero* that grew to a thousand unpublishable pages and a collection of short stories, *Dubliners*, written in the spare, precise, objective style of Gustave Flaubert's *contes*. Like its successor, the later *Bildungsroman A Portrait of the Artist as a Young Man*, *Stephen Hero* described a young Irishman's university social world and intellectual progress, but in a style less tight, smooth, and aesthetically mannered. The stories of *Dubliners*, on the other hand, already exhibited the polished language Joyce needed to have his countrymen take "one good look at themselves in my nicely polished looking-glass" (Ellmann 222).

Joyce spent much time in 1905 and 1906 negotiating with a publisher, Grant Richards, who, after signing a contract to publish *Dubliners*, requested many changes and deletions in the stories to protect himself and his printer from prosecution for libel and obscenity. Joyce refused and, dismayed and disrupted in his writing, abruptly relocated his wife and infant son to Rome in 1906 to work in the correspondence department of a bank. The family found the city uncongenial and dangerous, and after Joyce had been mugged and robbed by some drinking companions, they returned to Trieste the following year. The sojourn, however, was not totally unproductive: while in Rome, Nora conceived another child, while Joyce conceived ideas for two highly significant pieces of future writing: a story called "The Dead," which eventually became the extravagant finale of *Dubliners*, and a sketch about a Dubliner named Mr. Hunter, which eventually turned into the novel *Ulysses*.

During his next two years in Trieste, Joyce settled down to the business of being a serious writer. Aided by his pupil Roberto Prezioso he began to write articles for the paper *Il Piccolo della Sera*. Later another pupil, Attilio Tomaro, gave him the opportunity to deliver lectures at the Università Popolare. His topic was Ireland under British rule, aimed at a general Triestine audience interested in cities under imperial rule. His negotiations with the publisher Elkin Matthews at last resulted in his first publication at the age of twenty-five: the volume of lovely, lyrical poems called *Chamber Music*. Offers to set the lyrics to music excited and energized Joyce. He began translating Synge's *Riders to the Sea* into Italian and recasting *Stephen Hero* into the clean, taut prose he had been perfecting in *Dubliners*. This period of professional optimism was marred by some severe personal difficulties. Joyce suffered the first of many bouts of eye inflammation, or iritis, and was hospitalized for rheumatic fever at the same time Nora delivered their second child in the pauper's ward. The little girl was named Lucia, meaning *light*, perhaps as a talisman against her father's troubled eyesight (though she herself was born with a disfiguring cast in her eye). But Joyce's writing progressed, and by the time he decided to return to Ireland for a visit with his son Giorgio, he made contact with Maunsel and Company to arrange the publication of *Dubliners*.

Between 1909 and 1912 Joyce made three ill-fated trips to Ireland, which were to be his last despite the wealth of experience they provided for the writing of *Ulysses*. Brenda Maddox believes that the first trip was troubled in advance by Joyce's fears of censure for his son's illegitimacy, which made him defensive and easily offended (87). As a result, when his former classmate Thomas Cosgrave (Lynch in *Portrait*) confided that he had been intimate with Nora before Joyce met her, Joyce fell into a delirium of rage, jealousy, and abjection that he spewed out in a series of brutal letters to Nora. Before Nora replied, Joyce's friend J. F. Byrne (Cranly in *Portrait*) calmed him by declaring the accusation a "blasted lie" (Maddox 92), an exoneration quickly corroborated by Stanislaus, who had once heard Cosgrave complain of being rejected by Nora. Byrne's deliverance of Joyce from his imagined fears of betrayal occurred at 7 Eccles Street in Dublin, the address commemorated as the home of Leopold and Molly Bloom in *Ulysses*. His immense relief at having averted a conjugal crisis was quickly transformed into an erotic obsession that became a series of obscene letters and importunities addressed to Nora. These letters, with an even more explicit set produced during Joyce's second trip to Ireland, comprised the "masturbatory correspondence" (Maddox 103) that so shocked readers when they appeared among the *Selected Letters* edited by Richard Ellmann in 1975. But apart from their private function in bridging the sexual privations of a traumatic marital separation, they served Joyce's apprenticeship in pornographic writing exhibited later in the polymorphously perverse fantasies of the "Circe" and "Penelope" chapters of *Ulysses*.

Joyce returned to Trieste from his first trip to Dublin in September 1909 with one of his sisters, Eva, who inspired another turnaround trip with her delight at the novelty of cinema in Trieste. Backed by several Italian entrepreneurs, Joyce returned to Dublin the next month to open a cinema there. After many problems and added expenses, Cinematograph Volta opened in December 1909. Although the venture soon failed and had to be sold without profit, the conspicuous cinematographic effects in Joyce's later writing attest to his early interest in film. Many years later Joyce discussed the possibility of filming *Ulysses* with the great Russian director, Serge Eisenstein. (A black-and-white film of *Ulysses* was eventually made in 1967 by Joseph Strick.)

Upon Joyce's second return from Dublin, another sister, Eileen, joined the colony of six other family members to form what Brenda Maddox describes as a genial commune:

> It was in many ways a lively place. Giorgio and Lucia made everyone laugh. There was much singing around the rented piano. . . .
> Nora, Eileen, and Eva did the cooking together. Nora roasted

chickens stuffed with mashed potatoes, sauteed onion, and a touch of cinnamon, her specialty. . . . Right in the midst of all their activity in the kitchen sat Joyce. He liked to work there, where the light was best, and would sit there reading, with his feet propped up on the table, or writing, with his papers spread across it. (110)

These were much happier years for Nora, whose successful adjustment to the cultural sophistication of Trieste was abetted by its superb opera, which became one of her lifelong passions. In 1912 Nora took Lucia on her first visit home to Ireland. She was soon joined by Joyce and Giorgio, and the family made a sentimental visit to Ireland's western coast. They visited Nora's family in Galway, the Oughterard cemetery (where Michael Furey—based on Nora's adolescent beau, Michael Bodkin—is buried in "The Dead"), and the Aran Isles. Back in Dublin, Joyce faced increasing resistance from George Roberts, the director of Maunsel and Company, to the publication of *Dubliners*. The controversy ended with Roberts threatening to sue Joyce for delivering a libelous manuscript for publication. Joyce desperately tried to rescue the edition by offering to buy it himself. He was too late: the printer, John Falconer, fearing prosecution for libel and obscenity, had burned the pages and broken the type. Joyce salvaged only the one copy of proofs and the title page, which became the basis of the 1914 edition, and wrote a vengeful poem, "Gas from a Burner," on the back of his violated contract as he returned to Trieste.

While the James Joyces were visiting Ireland, in Trieste brother Stanislaus was unable to prevent yet another eviction for unpaid back rent. The Joyces thus returned to a new and different Triestine address, at which they remained for three years until World War I forced them to evacuate to Switzerland. Soon after his return to Trieste, Joyce resumed work on *Portrait* and began to explore publication options with friends and patrons, including W. B. Yeats. He recast his earlier story of a sensitive Dublin boy into an ironic new version, creating an imitative style that allowed the narrative to enact and parody the boy's mental and artistic development in a corresponding poetic language. These efforts were accompanied by other new and strange projects. Joyce, who was now teaching English at the commercial high school as well as to an enlarged body of private pupils, began to develop a silent and voyeuristic passion for one of the beautiful young women he tutored, whom Ellmann identified as Amalia Popper (342). He transformed his erotic feelings and fantasies into the strange Swinburnean poetic document that was later published as *Giacomo Joyce*

(1914). At the same time, Joyce began making notes for *Exiles* (1918), a play possibly inspired by jealousy and titillation at the idea that his former student and benefactor, Roberto Prezioso, harbored a triangular attraction to Nora and Joyce himself (Maddox 115). These interiorized romantic excitations and adventures find their way into the complicated erotic texture of the Blooms' marital dynamics and imaginings in *Ulysses*.

By the end of 1913 Joyce's luck was turned by the historical tides of modern literary history. That winter American poet Ezra Pound heard of Joyce's talent and publication difficulties from Yeats, with whom Pound was staying at Stone Cottage in England. Pound, who was to help numerous experimental writers of the period get funded and published, wrote Joyce, encouraging him to send some pieces to two literary journals with which he was connected. "The latter can pay a little, the former practically can not pay at all, we do it for larks and to have a place for markedly modern stuff," Pound wrote to Joyce (Ellmann 349). At the same time, Grant Richards re-opened negotiations to publish *Dubliners*. Pound's overture catapulted Joyce at last into publication and public notice. Better than any other writer of the time, Pound understood the difficulty of financing modernistic writing whose formal traits—simple, direct language enriched by resonant international erudition and cultural allusion—made it difficult to market to a general public. His own efforts included intensive fund-raising from a network of affluent friends and supporters of the modern arts.

But a more enduring solution was what Sally Dennison has called "alternative publishing" (3), of which Pound wrote "80% of such literature of my generation (from 1910 to 1930) as has any solid value, has been published only via specially founded 'amateur' publishing houses" (*Pound/Joyce* 247). These publishing ventures included the "little magazines," of which Hoffman, Allen, and Ulrich wrote, "Little magazines are willing to lose money, to court ridicule, to ignore public taste, willing to do almost anything—steal, beg, or undress in public—rather than sacrifice their right to print good material" (2). Joyce sent Pound *Dubliners* and the first chapters of *Portrait* in response to his letter, and one of these "little magazines," *The Egoist*, agreed to begin publishing *Portrait* in serial form. Joyce was especially fortunate that one of the editors of *The Egoist*, which had begun as a feminist journal called *The New Freewoman*, was a politically sensitive, intellectually open-minded, and culturally altruistic young woman named Harriet Shaw Weaver. Weaver eventually became Joyce's patron, making it possible for him to write the most elaborate experimental fiction in twentieth-century literature.

The years 1914 and 1915 were among the most eventful, if disheartening, of Joyce's life, with World War I disrupting the long-awaited onset of success. *The Egoist* was publishing *Portrait* to mixed, but nonetheless encouraging, reviews. Grant Richards, intrigued by this reception, wrote a new contract for *Dubliners* and brought the volume out in June 1914. In August 1914, Great Britain declared war on Austria-Hungary, putting Joyce, who was formally a British subject, in an awkward and dangerous position. "His enemy had been England; now he, as a British subject, was the enemy. Most confusing," Peter Costello writes (314). The uncertainty of the mails made serialization difficult. Joyce's pupils dispersed, and Stanislaus was arrested while on holiday near Trieste and interned by the Austrians for much of the war. Joyce's sister Eileen married one of her brother's pupils, the Czech bank manager Frantisek Schaureck, who many years later was to embezzle funds and commit suicide. In May 1915 Italy declared war on Austria, and the Joyces decided that they must move to safer territory. Joyce's aristocratic pupils, who fortuitously included the sons of the Austrian governor, helped his family secure exit visas. In June 1915, the Joyces moved to Zurich in neutral Switzerland.

In spite of the stress of these two years, Joyce had now completed *A Portrait of the Artist as a Young Man* and begun writing the first three chapters of *Ulysses*. These opening chapters, commonly called the "Telemachiad," reflect Joyce's life during the year after his mother's death. They reverse the triumphant ending of *Portrait* by resuming the story of Stephen Dedalus with his defeated return from flight and exile. *Ulysses*, a modern psychological reenactment of the events of Homer's *Odyssey*, was to interweave the life of the young artist with that of a Jewish-Irish couple, Leopold and Molly Bloom, on a single day in 1904 Dublin. The "style of scrupulous meanness" (*Selected Letters* 83) that Joyce had perfected in *Dubliners* and *Portrait* was abandoned for a richly textured and ever-changing narrative reflecting states of individual consciousness mingled with a variety of public and cultural discourses.

Joyce's move to Zurich at this time was a fortuitous benefit because the city had become an asylum for avant-garde art and theater. Now increasingly recognized as an important new author, Joyce made many friends, including several Greeks with whom he could discuss the *Odyssey*. He met the painter Frank Budgen, who became one of the closest friends of his adulthood. Joyce frequented the Club des

Étrangers, and occasionally visited the headquarters of the Dadaists Tristan Tzara and Hans Arp at the Café Voltaire. He saw all of August Strindberg's plays, became interested in the works of Frank Wedekind, made friends with the actors Claud and Daisy Sykes, and tried to find ways to have *Exiles* produced. Joyce helped found a company called the English Players in the hopes it might eventually stage *Exiles*. They rounded up a cast of professional and amateur actors for their first play, Oscar Wilde's *The Importance of Being Earnest* (1895), a production that subsequently involved Joyce in ridiculous litigation with an English actor named Henry Carr over the price of tickets and a pair of trousers. Tom Stoppard eventually made this incident the absurd center of *Travesties* (1974), his play about the Dada-like convergence of Joyce, Tzara, and Lenin in Zurich during the war.

Joyce worked steadily on *Ulysses*, but in 1917 his writing was interrupted dramatically by attacks of glaucoma, which required an iridectomy and convalescence in Locarno. During his three months in Locarno, Joyce befriended a young, tubercular physician named Gertrude Kaempffer to whom he began to make erotic overtures. She steadfastly declined, but Joyce's brief arousal may have become memorialized in the name of Gerty MacDowell in the "Nausicaa" chapter of *Ulysses*. The following year in Zurich, he initiated another such overture to a young woman with a limp named Marthe Fleischmann. This relationship went much further and in time involved an epistolary exchange that brought Joyce into a violent confrontation with Marthe Fleischmann's guardian. Along with Gertrude Kaempffer, Marthe Fleischmann seems to have contributed her name and characteristics to Leopold Bloom's extramarital dalliances with Gerty MacDowell and Martha Clifford in *Ulysses*. These erotic forays seem not to have ruffled the Joyce marriage.

In 1918, *Little Review*, a little magazine published by the American partners Jane Heap and Margaret Anderson, offered to serialize *Ulysses*. Joyce's writing became easier at this time because two separate, anonymous patrons came forward with generous subsidies that allowed him to abandon teaching for the writing of *Ulysses*. The first of these turned out to be Harriet Shaw Weaver, who donated a large war bond on which Joyce could draw interest. Weaver, who later in life became a member of the Communist Party, felt uncomfortable living on unearned income while Joyce labored incessantly on writing that failed to earn him a living. She eventually endowed Joyce with a bequest that later sustained his family during their years in Paris and beyond. The second patron was later revealed as the wealthy daughter of John D. Rockefeller, Edith McCormick, a philanthropist living in Zurich who supported musicians and artists. She was heavily under the influence of the psychoanalyst Carl Jung. When she abruptly canceled her funding at the end of the war, without offering an explanation, some speculated that it was because Joyce had refused to let Jung psychoanalyze him.

When the war ended in November 1918, the Joyce clan slowly reassembled in Trieste. Eileen and Frantisek Schaureck and their two infant daughters took a large apartment and were soon joined by Stanislaus, at last released from his internment in Austria. Joyce, who had been finishing "Scylla and Charybdis," "Wandering Rocks," "Cyclops," and "Sirens" in Zurich, hesitated for many months before moving Nora and the children back to Trieste, where they were to join Eileen's extended household. During this last period in Zurich, he was trying to find a publisher for *Ulysses*; he was refused by, among others, Leonard and Virginia Woolf's Hogarth Press. Discomfort with the book's indecency, as well as the inadequacy of their hand presses to produce such a large and complex book, may have figured in the Woolfs' refusal. At this same time the Austrian writer Stefan Zweig became fascinated with the psychological complexities of Joyce's play *Exiles* and managed to facilitate its production on the Munich stage in 1919. Unfortunately it opened to largely poor reviews that hastened its closing. The Joyces finally moved back to Trieste, where Joyce worked on the "Nausicaa" and "Oxen of the Sun" chapters of *Ulysses*. But the clan's flat was overcrowded with eleven people, counting the cook and nanny, and the Joyces came not to like postwar Trieste. In May 1919, Joyce at last met Ezra Pound in person in Lago di Garda, where Pound's wife was recuperating from an illness. Pound suggested that Joyce move to Paris. The Joyces arrived in Paris in July 1920, planning to stay only for a few weeks on their way to London. They stayed for twenty years.

Pound helped the family find a tiny apartment on loan from a friend and lined up people to help the always needy Joyces get settled. After commandeering extra beds, furniture, favors, and loans from the literary agent Jenny Serruys, Joyce continued writing the difficult, experimental "Circe" chapter of *Ulysses*. Pound also asked friends to receive the Joyces, and at a party hosted by the poet André Spire, Joyce met two booksellers who were life companions as well as business partners: Adrienne Monnier and Sylvia Beach. Sylvia Beach's Left Bank bookstore, Shakespeare and Company, had become a commercial salon for English language writers where they could pick up mail, read literary magazines, and borrow newly published books from the excellent lending library. Joyce soon joined the writers André Gide, Gertrude Stein, F. Scott Fitzgerald, the musician George Antheil, and many others as one of Sylvia Beach's "bunnies"—"from the word *abonné*: subscriber" (Beach 22). As he had done in Trieste and Zurich, Joyce found good friends and excellent drinking companions in Paris. In time these included Robert McAlmon (husband of the poet H.D.'s companion, "Bryher" Ellerman), Wyndham Lewis, Ernest Hemingway, Valéry Larbaud, Arthur Power (an Irishman who later published his conversations with Joyce), and the avant-garde novelist Djuna Barnes. He met other famous contemporaries, including T. S. Eliot and Marcel Proust. The supper meeting with Proust, after a Stravinsky-Diaghilev ballet, did not go well. According to witnesses, the two novelists chiefly exchanged symptoms—"Joyce said, 'I've headaches every day. My eyes are terrible.' Proust replied 'My poor stomach.'" (Ellmann 508)—and discussed truffles.

Within the year the censorship difficulties of Margaret Anderson and Jane Heap, whose *Little Review* was sued and financially ruined by the New York Society for the Suppression of Vice for serializing *Ulysses*, convinced Joyce that he would not find a commercial publisher for the book. When Sylvia Beach asked Joyce if he would let Shakespeare and Company "have the honor of bringing out your *Ulysses*," he reportedly accepted "immediately and joyfully" (Beach 47). The French printer Maurice Darantière of Dijon agreed to undertake printing the work and, to finance the venture, a prospectus was circulated asking for advance subscriptions. "Ezra Pound made a sensation when he deposited on my table one day a subscription blank with the signature of W. B. Yeats on it. Ernest Hemingway was down for several copies of the book" (Beach 51). But many difficulties delayed the publication process. The French printers had trouble with the unconventional English; Joyce reworked nearly a third of the text with corrections and emendations; the typists were shocked by "Circe." After the husband of one typist threw the pages into the fire, Sylvia Beach's sister, Cyprian, followed by other friends and volunteers, typed "Circe." Joyce suffered another massive iritis emergency while writing "Penelope," but by October 1921, he completed "Ithaca," and *Ulysses* was finished. Always intensely superstitious about his birthday, Joyce desperately wanted the book out by his fortieth, on February 2, 1922. Darantière drove his staff to heroic efforts and had two copies ready to send by mail on February 1. To deliver them on time, he gave them to the conductor of the Dijon-Paris express train, who handed them to

Sylvia Beach when the train pulled into the Paris station at 7 A.M. A ten-minute taxi ride delivered the first copy of *Ulysses* to Joyce's flat; Beach exhibited the second copy to admiring crowds at Shakespeare and Company all day.

Soon after the publication of the book, Nora decided she wanted to visit Ireland again, a plan that greatly perturbed Joyce because, in the wake of a controversial treaty with Great Britain signed in 1921, Ireland was now a Free State on the verge of civil war. The treaty provisions divided Ireland into a republican Catholic south and a British Protestant north and required that the Irish parliament pledge allegiance to the Crown. These provisions created division and conflict within the army factions. Nora planned to travel at Easter, the anniversary of the 1916 Easter uprising in Dublin. When they reached Galway, Nora and her teenage children did indeed get a firsthand glimpse of the Troubles, as this period of upheaval came to be called. Troops that Giorgio contemptuously thought of as "Zulus" taunted the seventeen-year-old, soldiers invaded their boarding house bedroom to set up artillery for firing on Irregulars below, and the train car in which they fled back to Dublin was shot at by both sides. These frightening experiences only confirmed Joyce's cynicism about Irish politics.

By the time the family returned, however, they discovered that they were famous. Brenda Maddox describes the effects of *Ulysses* on Joyce: "If *A Portrait* had made Joyce's reputation, *Ulysses* turned him into a celebrity. People clambered on chairs to get a look at him. They sent notes in restaurants asking him to join them, they rang his doorbell. Journalists crowded in at parties" (211). Joyce's time was now divided between concerns about the advertisement, reviews, editions, and translations of *Ulysses*, and the conception and design of a new, even more outrageously experimental book that was for many years known only as "Work in Progress." Joyce kept the title of this new book, *Finnegans Wake* (1939), secret from everyone but Nora. He began this new work by collecting and sorting many kilos of old stories and unused notes left over from *Ulysses*, recording conversations he heard and overheard, and writing down his dreams. Joyce planned *Finnegans Wake* as a night book, or dream book, exploring unconscious thoughts, wishes, and fears to balance the wakeful day book of *Ulysses*. Dreams, irrationality, and unconscious states had been a chief preoccupation of the Dadaists and Surrealists, whose work he had first encountered in Zurich. During the two years after the publication of *Ulysses*, Joyce's concentration was fragmented by trips to the Côte d'Azur and Bognor Regis in Sussex and enervated by iritis and dental problems. He nevertheless managed to sketch the first eight chapters of *Finnegans Wake* before the end of 1923.

The 1920s in Paris were a heady, troubled time for Joyce. At the center of modern art in its heyday, he nonetheless felt himself awash in complex and contradictory critical currents. At the very time the genius of *Ulysses* became gradually indisputable, the avant-gardism of *Finnegans Wake* met increasing skepticism. In August 1922, Joyce at last met his great benefactor, Harriet Shaw Weaver, and Maddox suspects she was as disturbed by Joyce's profligacy as she was later alarmed by his drinking. "Within hours she witnessed 'her' money flying in all directions—to waiters, porters, taxi drivers. He tipped proudly and wildly" (213). Although during the years of composing *Finnegans Wake*, Joyce made Weaver his literary confidante, the stylistic extravagance and linguistic impenetrability of the text brought her, at times, close to apostasy: "It seems to me you are wasting your genius," she wrote him in 1927 (Ellmann 590). But she never abandoned her support of him or his family.

Other friends did not remain blindly loyal to this new project. Pound defected with candor and humor. "Nothing so far as I make out, nothing short of divine vision or a new cure for the clapp [sic] can possibly be worth all the circumambient peripherization," he wrote Joyce in November 1926 (Ellmann 584). Wyndham Lewis criticized Joyce in his book *Time and Western Man* (1927). His attack was vicious because it was ad hominem; Ellmann describes it as Lewis treating Joyce "as an Irish *parvenu*" (595). Stanislaus Joyce, his brother's strongest supporter in the early days, was perhaps most unkind, calling *Finnegans Wake* "the beginning of softening of the brain" (Ellmann 577).

Fortunately, new friends and admirers emerged to replace the defectors. The twenty-three-year-old Samuel Beckett turned up in Paris to pay his respects and stayed to serve as translator, scribe, and unpaid secretary to the near-blind Joyce. Eugene and Maria Jolas put their new avant-garde journal *transition* at his disposal to print installments of "Work in Progress." In 1929, a dozen of Joyce's friends including Beckett and William Carlos Williams published a book defending *Finnegans Wake* against the published attacks of Lewis, Rebecca West, and Sean O'Faolain. Published by Shakespeare and Company, the essays in *Our Exagmination Round His Factification for Incamination of Work in Progress* (after a line in *Finnegans Wake*) used Eugene Jolas's call for a "revolution of the word" to place Joyce's poetic experiments in the context of the philosophical avant-garde of the 1920s. An even more dramatic show of support was marshalled by the plight of *Ulysses* in America. Because the United States was not a signatory to the Bern convention that ratified international copyright law, *Ulysses* was not protected by copyright in the United States. An entrepreneurial magazine publisher named Samuel Roth exploited this legal vulnerability to produce pirated installments of *Ulysses* in his magazine *Two Worlds Monthly*. Unable to get a rapid judicial injunction against this piracy, Joyce organized an international petition to protest his legal plight. The 167 signatories of this protest constituted a veritable who's who of modern literature.

The personal lives of the Joyces during the 1920s were marked by stability, fame, and luxury, on the one hand, and by medical problems and family worries on the other. Nora was finally able to furnish a wonderful apartment in the Square Robiac, where she could cook and entertain. The Joyces hosted lively social evenings at home as alternatives to their regular, expensive dining at the restaurant Les Trianons. They dressed like dandies. Holidays were spent in Holland, Sussex, Austria, and many other resort areas, often to allow Joyce to recuperate from his frequent eye operations.

Stanislaus at last became engaged in his early forties, but his marriage to Nelly Lichtensteiger was postponed for a time because he had to help the shattered Eileen Schaureck after her husband's suicide. Nora was diagnosed with cancer that was cured with a hysterectomy. The Joyce children were growing up talented and affectionate but increasingly showed the strains of their nomadic upbringing. They had learned many languages (German, French, and English, in addition to their native "house" language, Italian) and attended many schools. They were bright and interesting, but ill-trained for any profession outside the realm of art. Giorgio had an excellent voice, and Lucia a gift for dance; neither had the discipline and emotional stamina needed to sustain a career. Giorgio began to attach himself to a married socialite named Helen Fleischman, who was eleven years older than his twenty years and the mother of a son. Joyce became obsessed with promoting the career of an Irish opera singer named John Sullivan, claiming the connection would help him foster Giorgio's singing career. Lucia gave up her dancing and became increasingly unfocused, aimless, and erratic in her behavior. In 1930, Giorgio and Helen Kastor Fleischman married, with Joyce delighted at his acquisition of an extended Jewish family. His son's marriage increased pressure to legitimate his own children. To secure the inheritance rights of Giorgio's progeny, Joyce married Nora in July 1931, in London, in the glare of much unwanted publicity. (The earlier Triestine marriage under an assumed name would not have served legal purposes.) In the following year Joyce wrote the poem "Ecce Puer" to express how the birth of his grandson, Stephen James Joyce, consoled him for the death of his own father.

During the 1930s, Joyce labored on *Finnegans Wake* while his vision deteriorated into near blindness and his daughter's symptoms worsened into full-blown madness. He also provoked an estrangement from the two women who had been his most loyal and trusted supporters, Sylvia Beach and Harriet Shaw Weaver. Beach, exhausted by Joyce's importunings for services and money, was angry and bitter when Joyce, through friends, pressured her into reducing the inflated asking price by which she hoped to repel bids to sell her interest in *Ulysses*. She eventually reverted the rights to Joyce, but the "separation was a painful one" (Banta and Silverman, 162). Joyce needed an American publisher to stop Roth's piracy of *Ulysses* in the United States. Bennett Cerf of Random House offered him a contract and hired an attorney, Morris Ernst, to argue the case of *Ulysses* in an obscenity trial before Judge John M. Woolsey of the United States District Court in New York. On December 6, 1933, a favorable decision was handed down, and Joyce was soon featured in *Time* magazine. Joyce's friendship with Sylvia Beach was destroyed by these professional complications.

Joyce's friendship with Harriet Shaw Weaver was destroyed later in the decade by familial complications. Beginning soon after her parents' marriage, Lucia Joyce's adolescent idiosyncrasies metamorphosed into a serious mental illness. A series of obsessional or contrived romances with young men, including Alexander Calder and Samuel Beckett, aggravated rather than relieved her symptoms. On Joyce's fiftieth birthday, February 2, 1932, Lucia threw a chair at her mother and became so violent that she was carried off to a mental clinic by her brother. During the next several years, as her behavior became increasingly bizarre and dangerous, she was bundled from doctor to doctor, treatment to treatment. She spent time at the posh sanitarium, Prangins, near Geneva, where Zelda Fitzgerald was also treated, and in Zurich saw Carl Jung. Joyce's friends and family members across several countries—including his widowed sister, Eileen Schaureck, Maria Jolas, and Harriet Shaw Weaver—were pressed into service as nurses and jailers to keep Lucia from turning on gas jets and setting fires. Joyce, frantic and helpless in the face of Lucia's catastrophic decline, blamed her difficulties on doctors and keepers, including the saintly Miss Weaver. Lucia was hospitalized permanently in the mid-1930s and spent the last thirty years of her life at St. Andrew's Hospital in Northampton, England, where she died in 1982.

Joyce continued to work on *Finnegans Wake* during this tragic time and managed to produce some of his sunniest, most playful writing, including "The Mime of Mick, Nick, and the Maggies," his pantomime of children's games, dances, songs, and riddles in Book II of *Finnegans Wake*. Nora complained that Joyce kept her awake nights by laughing at his own writing; she reported she had to tell him, "Now, Jim, stop writing or stop laughing" (Maddox 324). The funny writing may have served as a shoring of fragments against an increasingly horrifying world in which there was little to laugh about. Lucia's illness was to be followed some years later by the growing illness of Giorgio's wife, whose manic-depressive condition worsened with a failing marriage. Samuel Beckett was stabbed in Paris and seriously wounded. With Hitler's annexation of Austria in 1938, the Joyces became worried about the safety of Jewish family and friends. Joyce finished *Finnegans Wake* as signs of impending war alarmed Europe. Joyce's daughter-in-law Helen was miraculously well enough to throw a lavish celebration for the book's publication on Joyce's fifty-seventh birthday, February 2, 1939. But by Christmas of that year, Joyce and Nora, like many of their friends, had left Paris. They were desperately worried about their family: a daughter and daughter-in-law both hospitalized for psychosis, a nearly blind paterfamilias, a dazed son, and a rather lost young grandson. They stayed for a time in a village in Burgundy, while their loyal friend Paul Léon returned to their abandoned Paris flat to rescue Joyce's papers. Léon was later arrested during a Gestapo roundup of Parisian Jews and was killed on a forced march in 1942.

The Joyces returned to Zurich at the outbreak of World War II, as they had done at the outbreak of World War I. Lucia had been denied a visa to leave France, and unable to get access to their London funds, the Joyces had an anxious scramble to raise money for the entry deposit required of refugees by Switzerland. They arrived in Zurich in mid-December 1940; less than a month later, Joyce was dead. The stomach pains he had suffered for years had been unrecognized as the symptoms of an ulcer, whose perforation required emergency surgery on January 10. Joyce survived the surgery, but peritonitis followed, and he died on January 13, 1941. He was buried two days later in Fluntern Cemetery in Zurich. Nora Joyce lived on in Zurich for another decade, dying there in 1951.

Margot Norris

WORKS CITED

Banta, Melissa, and Oscar A. Silverman, eds. *James Joyce's Letters to Sylvia Beach, 1921–1940.* Bloomington: Indiana UP, 1987.

Beach, Sylvia. *Shakespeare & Company.* Lincoln: U of Nebraska P, 1991.

Beja, Morris. *James Joyce: A Literary Life.* Columbus: Ohio State UP, 1992.

Budgen, Frank. *James Joyce and the Making of "Ulysses."* Bloomington: Indiana UP, 1973.

Costello, Peter. *James Joyce: The Years of Growth 1882–1915.* London: Kyle Cathie, 1992.

Dennison, Sally. *(Alternative) Literary Publishing.* Iowa City: U of Iowa P, 1984.

Ellmann, Richard. *James Joyce.* Rev. ed. New York: Oxford UP, 1982.

Gorman, Herbert. *James Joyce.* New York: Rinehart, 1948.

Hoffman, Frederick J., Charles Allen, Carolyn F. Ulrich. *The Little Magazine.* Princeton: Princeton UP, 1947.

Jameson, Fredric. "*Ulysses* in History." *James Joyce and Modern Literature.* Ed. W. J. McCormack and Alistair Stead. London: Routledge, 1982. 126–41.

Johnsen, William A. "Joyce's *Dubliners* and the Futility of Modernism." *James Joyce and Modern Literature.* London: Routledge, 1982.

Joyce, James. *The Critical Writings of James Joyce.* Ed. Ellsworth Mason and Richard Ellmann. Ithaca: Cornell UP, 1989.

———. *Selected Letters.* Ed. Richard Ellmann. New York: Viking, 1975.

Joyce, Stanislaus. *My Brother's Keeper.* New York: Viking, 1958.

Maddox, Brenda. *Nora: The Real Life of Molly Bloom.* Boston: Houghton, 1988.

Manganiello, Dominic. *Joyce's Politics.* London: Routledge, 1980.

Parrinder, Patrick. *James Joyce.* Cambridge: Cambridge UP, 1984.

Pound/Joyce: The Letters of Ezra Pound to James Joyce. Ed. Forrest Read. New York: New Directions, 1967.

A Critical History of
Ulysses

I

Perhaps every novice reader of *Ulysses* is doomed to reenact the frustrations of its first generation of readers, who found the great novel—considered by some the greatest novel written in English—obscured by a pyrotechnic display of stylistic devices, arcane erudition, and an immense symbolic superstructure. Yet Joyce himself provided help with the technical difficulties even before the book's publication. In 1920 he sent his Italian translator Carlo Linati a complex scheme of Homeric and other parallels, with the following explanation:

> I think that in view of the enormous bulk and the more than enormous complexity of my damned monster-novel it would be better to send him a sort of summary—key—skeleton—scheme (for home use only). . . . It is the epic of two races (Israel-Ireland) and at the same time the cycle of the human body as well as a little story of a day (life). The character of Ulysses has fascinated me ever since boyhood. . . . My intention is not only to render the myth *sub specie temporis nostri* but also to allow each adventure (that is, every hour, every organ, every art being interconnected and interrelated in the somatic scheme of the whole) to condition and even to create its own technique. (*Selected Letters* 271)

Although this description also buries the realism of the plot ("a little story of a day") under a mass of allusion and allegory, Joyce here clarifies his intention to have novel, style, myth, and symbolism work together organically.

When Joyce advised his aunt Josephine Murray (an excellent example of a common reader) that she should buy a copy of Charles Lamb's *Adventures of Ulysses* (1808) for help with *Ulysses* (*Selected Letters* 293), he was by no means condescending. Lamb's redacted version of Homer's *Odyssey* had introduced him to the classic at age twelve, and he continued to receive his Homer in translation (Butcher and Lang), scholarship (Samuel Butler), and interpretations that shaped his use of the myth (for example, Victor Bérard [*Les Phéniciens et l'Odyssée*, 1902–1903], whose theory on the Semitic origins of the *Odyssey* contributed to Joyce's decision to make his Ulysses a Jew [Seidel]). By exploring life in modern day Dublin through a classical text, Joyce situated himself at the heart of the early-twentieth-century Anglo-American literary movement known as Modernism. Like T. S. Eliot's great poem *The Waste Land* (published in 1922, the same year as *Ulysses*) Joyce's novel was imbued with a revisionary classicism that began to revitalize modern thinking in the late nineteenth century. This classical pulse quickened in archaeology with Heinrich Schliemann's discovery of the historical Troy and coursed through the diverse fields of philosophy (Friedrich Nietzsche's "The Birth of Tragedy," 1872), anthropology (Jessie Weston's *From Ritual to Romance*, 1920; Sir James Frazer's *The Golden Bough*, 1890), and psychoanalysis (Freud's classical typologies, such as the Oedipus complex). Joyce's contemporaries freely invested their writing with classical reference and mythology—Ezra Pound in "Homage to Sextus Propertius," W. B. Yeats in "Leda and the Swan," H.D. in "Eurydice," "Helen," and "Cassandra," Rainer Maria Rilke in "Sonnets to Orpheus," and Eugene O'Neill in *Mourning Becomes Electra*, to name only a few. In his 1923 essay, "*Ulysses*, Order, and Myth," T. S. Eliot pays tribute to Joyce's *Ulysses*—"I hold this book to be the most important expression which the present age has found" (175)—and attributes its greatness to what he called "the mythical method" (178). For Eliot the function of myth in the novel is nothing less than to restore meaning to the chaos of the modern world. "It is simply a way of controlling, of ordering, of giving a shape and a significance to the immense panorama of futility and anarchy which is contemporary history. . . . It is, I seriously believe, a step toward making the modern world possible for art" (177).

Hugh Kenner reminds us that Joyce had access not to a single Homer, but to many Homers. He suggests that the Homers that Joyce privileged served less the aims of transcendence, as Eliot would have it, than those of novelization. Kenner writes of Samuel Butler's Homer (whom Butler identified, in his *The Authoress of the "Odyssey,"* 1897, as a woman): "Butler's was simply the first creative mind— Joyce's was the second—to take the archaeologist's Homer seriously: to consider what it might mean to believe that the *Odyssey* was composed by a real person in touch with the living details of real cities, real harbors, real bowls and cups and pins and spoons, real kings, real warriors, real houses" ("Homer's Sticks and Stones" 293). In other words, *Ulysses* may have served to domesticate the *Odyssey* as much as to mythologize the modern world. Kenner's is one of many attempts to confound what Michael Groden describes as the two predominant sides of "*Ulysses*' many dualisms—the 'novelistic' story and the 'symbolistic' pattern of parallels and correspondences" (4). Harry Levin also argues that *Ulysses* is best read with myth and map, that is, the *Odyssey* in one hand and *Thom's Dublin Directory* in the other. *Ulysses* retains such meticulous historical grounding that it is difficult to tell its historical realism from its fictional realism: "the Gold Cup races were run off at Ascot. At New York, when the *General Slocum* exploded in the East River, five hundred lives were lost. From the Orient came news of Russo-Japanese conflict over Port Arthur. . . . At the Gaiety Theatre Mrs. Bandman Palmer was appearing in *Leah*. . . . Clery's was advertising a summer sale; sandwich-men, bearing the more or less consecutive letters of H. E. L. Y. S., filed through the streets" (Levin 69). Years later, Phillip Herring did research in Gibraltar that rescued Molly Bloom from her overmythification as earth goddess by filling in the mysterious parentage and sketchy childhood of a "historical Molly Bloom" (*Joyce's Uncertainty Principle* 117–40) as though she had been a living personage rather than a fictional creation.

Before turning to a more systematic account of *Ulysses* criticism over the last seventy years, it may be helpful to summarize the novel briefly in a way that glosses at least some of the Homeric parallels, sketches in the major outlines of the plot, and indicates some of the stylistic strategies and experiments in the text. Its chief Greek intertext is the *Odyssey*, Homer's epic poem that recounts the adventures of Odysseus, king of Ithaca, as he attempts to return home after fighting in the Trojan War. His journey is delayed for twenty years by many obstacles, including storms and shipwrecks; seduction by goddesses; the narcosis of lotus-eaters; encounters with cannibals, one-eyed giants, and sirens; a journey to the underworld; and navigation past treacherously moving rocks, monsters, and maelstroms. During Odysseus' long absence, his wife Penelope staves off insolent suitors for her hand and for Odysseus' vacant throne by weaving and unweaving a shroud, while her nearly grown son Telemachus searches for his father. Upon his return, Odysseus kills the suitors in a bloody battle and reunites with his family and his people.

Joyce's *Ulysses* is divided into three sections, conventionally called "The Telemachiad," "The Wanderings of Odysseus," and "Nostos" or "The Homecoming." These three sections are comprised of eighteen chapters or *episodes*, as they are commonly called, named after Homeric parallels Joyce assigned to each chapter in schema he drew up as guides to the novel for his friends Stuart Gilbert and Carlo Linati:

I. Telemachiad

1: Telemachus
2: Nestor
3: Proteus

II. The Wanderings of Odysseus

4: Calypso
5: Lotus-Eaters
6: Hades
7: Aeolus
8: Lestrygonians
9: Scylla and Charybdis
10: Wandering Rocks
11: Sirens
12: Cyclops
13: Nausicaa
14: Oxen of the Sun
15: Circe

III. Nostos

16: Eumaeus
17: Ithaca
18: Penelope

The novel is set in Dublin on June 16, 1904, and traces the activities, convergences, and thoughts of three people: Stephen Dedalus (Telemachus), Leopold Bloom (Odysseus), and Molly Bloom (Penelope)—amid the busy commercial, cultural, and political life of a modern city.

"The Telemachiad" describes the morning activities of Stephen Dedalus, the protagonist of *A Portrait of the Artist as a Young Man* (1916), who has returned from Paris to attend his dying mother. After breakfast with a friend (Buck Mulligan) and a British visitor (Haines) in the Martello Tower in Sandycove ("Telemachus"), Stephen goes on to teach at the school of the anti-Semitic Mr. Deasy ("Nestor"). He then walks toward Dublin along Sandymound strand, lost in philosophical meditations revealed through the technique of "stream-of-consciousness," which Joyce credited to Édouard Dujardin's 1888 novel *Les Lauriers sont coupés* ("Proteus"). Like Telemachus in the *Odyssey*, whose home and security are threatened by suitors in his father's absence, Stephen's state is one of dispossession: his birthright squandered by his father and his place as an Irish poet usurped by Trinity and Oxford students with better claims as "gentlemen," he is forced to collude in inculcating imperialistic ideologies (Roman history and English poetry) into the minds of Irish scions. Having refused to pray at his mother's deathbed, he is racked by guilt like another literary mourning and dispossessed son, Hamlet.

The second section of *Ulysses*, "The Wanderings of Odysseus," begins at the home of the Irish-Jewish couple Leopold and Molly Bloom at 7 Eccles Street in Dublin. Bloom's enactment of Odysseus' amorous and dangerous adventures take chiefly psychological and social form. He serves his wife breakfast in bed and cooks himself a pork kidney ("Calypso"), picks up a clandestine pornographic letter at the post office on his way to the Turkish baths ("Lotus-Eaters"), and attends a funeral at the cemetery in Glasnevin ("Hades"). There he enacts Odysseus' journey to the underworld by confronting the general topic of death in its most intimate form by thinking of his father's suicide and the mysterious death of his newborn son eleven years before. Bloom's job as an advertising canvasser takes him to Dublin newspaper offices ("Aeolus") and, after a modest lunch at Davy Byrne's eatery ("Lestrygonians"), to the National Library, where Stephen Dedalus is informally lecturing on Shakespeare. "Aeolus" metaphorically enacts its Homeric parallel (Aeolus was lord of the winds) with windy rhetoric and mimics its newspaper setting by writing in the typographic layout of newspaper columns and headlines: "SOPHIST WALLOPS HAUGHTY HELEN SQUARE ON PROBOSCIS. SPARTANS GNASH MOLARS. ITHACANS VOW PEN IS CHAMP" (*U* 7.1032). Stephen's attempt at the library to establish his artistic credentials among influential literati requires him to steer a tricky course between the conceptual predilections and artistic investments of his interlocutors, like Odysseus trying to maneuver his ship between a six-headed monster ("Scylla") and a deadly whirlpool ("Charybdis").

After a chapter depicting all of Dublin on the move ("Wandering Rocks"), Bloom sees his wife's impresario, Hugh "Blazes" Boylan, drinking and flirting before keeping what Bloom fears (correctly) will be an adulterous tryst with Molly at 7 Eccles Street. Odysseus' temptation by the music of the Sirens (which he hears tied to his mast) is thematically recapitulated as flirtation and operatic performance, and stylistically by writing that resembles an orchestral fugue ("Sirens"). Stopping in Barney Kiernan's pub to meet friends, Bloom is assaulted by a fiercely nationalistic and anti-Semitic citizen, who, prejudiced and xenophobic like the one-eyed Cyclops throwing rocks, tosses a biscuit tin after him ("Cyclops"). The gigantism of "Cyclops" is stylistically represented as hyperbolic and inflated rhetoric.

Calming himself on Sandymount strand, where three young women are minding three little boys, Bloom catches sight of the underclothes of one of the girls and becomes incited to masturbation. The episode narrates the romantic fantasies of Gerty Mac-Dowell ("Nausicaa") in the prose of ladies' magazines, advertising, and sentimental novelettes. Bloom stops at the Holles Street Maternity Hospital to inquire about the prolonged labor of a friend, Mrs. Purefoy, and ends up joining a group of roistering medical students ("Oxen of the Sun"). Their brutish humor regarding human reproduction signifies the "crime against fecundity" committed by Odysseus' men when they slaughtered the sacred oxen of the sun god. "Oxen of the Sun" stylistically recapitulates the embryonic gestation of English prose style in pastiches ranging from Anglo-Saxon to modern slang. Worried about the drunken Stephen Dedalus carousing with the medicals, Bloom paternally decides to follow him and his friends to Nighttown, the Dublin red-light district ("Circe"). There, in Bella Cohen's brothel, Bloom turns metaphorically into a pig (Circe turns Odysseus' men into swine) as masochistic fantasies are triggered by his day's casual pornographic reading (*Sweets of Sin*) and fears of cuckoldry. This episode of magical enchantment and disenchantment is narrated through the transmogrifications of Expressionist drama. "Circe" ends with Stephen breaking a lamp while striking at a hallucinated image of his mother with his stick and with Bloom narrowly saving him from arrest for getting into a fight with two British soldiers. In "Eumaeus" Bloom takes Stephen to a cabman's shelter (analogous to the safe hut of the swineherd Eumaeus in the *Odyssey*) where they hear the incredible yarns of a sailor who identifies himself as W. B. Murphy. This chapter, about disguises and trust, prepares the way for the return home ("Nostos") to the "Ithaca" of Bloom's house at 7 Eccles Street. There Bloom offers Stephen cocoa, friendship, and a home, which he declines, in a chapter structured in the factitious question-and-answer format of the Catholic catechism. After Stephen wanders off into the night, Bloom returns to his wife's bed of adultery having worked through the "antagonistic sentiments" of "Envy, jealousy, abnegation, equanimity" (*U* 17.2155), like Odysseus who alone knows the secret of his marriage bed. Penelope ends the book with the long, unpunctuated sentences of Molly Bloom's thoughts in bed: her suitors (old boyfriends, Boylan, fantasized lovers including Stephen) slain as her own marital equanimity returns her to thoughts of her husband's romantic courtship and first lovemaking. "Then he asked me would I yes to say yes my mountain flower and first I put my arms around him yes and drew him down to me so he could feel my breasts all perfume yes and his heart was going like mad and yes I said yes I will Yes" (*U* 18.1605).

II

Because *Ulysses* was serialized in the *Little Review*, criticism of the text preceded its single-volume publication in 1922. The book's reception throughout the 1920s and 1930s was strongly colored by controversy about its form (or rather its "formlessness") and its putatively obscene content. The strongest early objections to the book came from British writers and critics, who read its vulgarity as a mark of the author's class inferiority and found its form nowhere visible within the British novel tradition. Stanley Sultan reports that "Alfred Noyes, England's 'unofficial poet laureate,' spoke on *Ulysses* before the Royal Society of Literature. 'There is no foulness conceivable to the mind of madman or ape that has not been poured into its imbecile pages,' he said" (3). Virginia Woolf wrote in her diary, "I finished *Ulysses* and think it a mis-fire. Genius it has, I think; but of the inferior water. The book is diffuse. It is brackish. It is pretentious. It is underbred, not only in the obvious sense, but in the literary sense" (48). Even his fellow Irishman, George Moore, supposedly said of *Ulysses*, "How can one plow through such stuff? I read a little here and there, but, oh my God, how bored I got! Probably Joyce thinks that because he prints all the dirty little words he is a great novelist. . . . Joyce, Joyce, why he's nobody—from the Dublin docks: no family, no breeding" (qtd. in Ellmann, *James Joyce* 529). Edmund Gosse, a translator of Ibsen, who at Yeats's request had secured a subsidy from the Royal Literary Fund for Joyce during the war, stridently urged Louis Gillet in 1924 to refuse to review *Ulysses* in *Revue des Deux-Mondes*. "You could only expose the worthlessness and impudence of his writing," he insisted, calling Joyce "a literary charlatan of the extremest order" and "a sort of Marquis de Sade, but does not write so well." He called *Ulysses* "an anarchical production, infamous in taste, in style, in everything" and deplored its "perfectly cynical appeal to sheer indecency" (qtd. in Ellmann, *James Joyce* 528).

These pedigreed hostilities to *Ulysses* stimulated the urgency and occasional defensiveness of many of the early tributes to the work's genius. Ezra Pound's praise was blunt and unequivocal: "All men should 'Unite to give praise to *Ulysses*'; those who will not, may content themselves with a place in the lower intellectual orders," he wrote in the opening of his famous "Paris Letter" published in *The Dial* in June 1922 (*Pound/Joyce* 194). He brushed aside the obscenity issue as a monstrous hypocrisy. "And the book is banned in America, where every child of seven has ample opportunity to drink in the details of the Arbuckle case" (200), he wrote, referring to the lurid rape and manslaughter trial of the silent film star Fatty Arbuckle. He praised the novel's perfectly crafted form and language by placing it squarely in the tradition of Gustave Flaubert. "Joyce has taken up the art of writing where Flaubert left it. . . . *Ulysses* has more form than any novel of Flaubert's" (194). This restoration of Joyce to a Continental novel tradition became the most effective strategy for justifying its form. Joyce's friend and admirer, the novelist Valéry Larbaud, recognized Dujardin's influence on Joyce's stream of consciousness technique and employed it in his own 1923 novel *Amants, heureux amants*. Another friend of Joyce, Stuart Gilbert, countered the charges of formlessness levied against the novel by stressing (with the help of the Homeric schema supplied by Joyce) the novel's complex mythic and structural organization (ix).[1]

---

[1] In 1972, Richard Ellmann's *Ulysses on the Liffey* revisited the novel's structure with an aesthetically nuanced scheme modeled on the schema Joyce had given Gilbert and Linati (see p. 24).

A year later, the American critic Edmund Wilson related Joyce's writing to the poetics of French Symbolism and French fiction and described the structure of *Ulysses* as "symphonic rather than narrative" (209). Wilson's essay, which Jeffrey Segall calls "a crucial document in the history of Joyce criticism" (94), introduced *Ulysses* sympathetically to an intellectual American audience attuned to the ideological debates about modern literature between humanists and Marxists throughout the 1930s.[2] Joyce would be criticized and defended by both sides during this period, most strongly in 1934 at the First International Writers' Congress in Moscow, where Karl Radek sharply attacked *Ulysses* for lacking a social conscience, while Wieland Herzfelde defended the significance of its representational innovations. Other commentaries on the social value of Joyce's work, positive and negative, were written during the 1930s by Paul Elmer More and Alick West. Joyce reportedly complained to Eugene Jolas about the harsh Marxist criticisms of his work by noting "I don't know why they attack me. Nobody in any of my books is worth more than a thousand pounds" (Ellmann, *James Joyce* 5).

By 1941—the year of Joyce's death—his academic respectability was consolidated in America when Harry Levin, a Harvard professor of comparative literature, published the first U.S. full-length critical study of Joyce's work. Levin's *James Joyce: A Critical Introduction* maintained Larbaud's and Wilson's powerful strategy of reading *Ulysses* through the philosophical preoccupations of Continental fiction. Levin used Thomas Mann's "dialectical pattern of *Künstler* versus *Bürger*" (66) to argue that "Joyce's work commemorates the longstanding quarrel between the bourgeois and the bohemian" (133).[3] Informed by the ideological debates of his colleagues in the 1930s, Levin read *Ulysses'* protest against a Philistine culture as a doomed gesture of liberalism.

[2]In addition to the social preoccupations of criticism in the 1930s, the arts—particularly the highly experimental visual arts—provided a more aesthetic lens for the reading of *Ulysses*. In 1932 Joseph Beach wrote an article, "Post-Impressionism: Joyce," and the psychoanalyst Carl Jung described in his essay, "*Ulysses:* A Monologue," the "new consciousness" produced by cubistic practices in the novel.

[3]The practice of reading Joyce intertextually by exploring literary, artistic, and philosophical influences in *Ulysses* has become a long-standing tradition in Joyce criticism. Studies on the influence of Aquinas (William Noon), Shakespeare (William Schutte), and Catholicism (J. Mitchell Morse) all appeared in the 1950s, and Virginia Mosely's study of Joyce and the Bible was published in the 1960s. In later decades, these intertextual approaches were sophisticated with more complex philosophical arguments by such critics as Robert Boyle and Beryl Schlossman on Joyce's Catholicism and

In reaction to the vexed ideological debates of the 1930s, the so-called New Criticism that came into fashion in the 1940s and 1950s inaugurated critical practices of close reading and textual analysis that put the external determinants of biography and history aside. During this period, *Ulysses* received rigorous scholarly scrutiny that neutralized earlier complaints of vulgarity and lack of discipline by focusing on the work's poetic craft and verbal texture. Richard M. Kain's 1947 book-length study of the novel, *Fabulous Voyager: James Joyce's "Ulysses,"* inaugurated meticulous attention to the naturalistic detail and stylistic precision of the text. Close reading, carefully glossed allusions, and heavy symbolic allegory made *Ulysses* readily accessible to common readers in William York Tindall's 1959 *A Reader's Guide to James Joyce.* Such other well-known writers of the New Criticism as R. P. Blackmur and William Empson also wrote essays on *Ulysses* during this time.

The publication of Hugh Kenner's *Dublin's Joyce* in 1956 was a major critical event in Joyce studies. The strategies of this book, refined and elaborated during the next four decades, consisted of meticulously close reading supplemented by noting significant interventions that are operative in the text by their *absence*: the subtle effects and changes produced by intonation, idiom, and other qualities of voice; the irony produced by unstated incongruities, significant errors, omissions, and silences ("we ought to observe how much silence pervades such of their conversation as we do hear" [Kenner, *Ulysses* 51]). For the next several decades, Kenner refined his complex close readings of the Joycean text at the same time that he consolidated his influence as the premier critic of Modernism. He published his ambitious study of modernist poetics, *The Pound Era*, in 1971. In his 1978 work, *Joyce's Voices,* he articulated the "Uncle Charles Principle": *"the narrative idiom need not be the narrator's"* (18). His 1980 edition of *Ulysses* elaborated the myriad ways the text stimulates the reader's interpretive creativity with the questions it embeds.

Mary Reynolds on Joyce and Dante. More broadly conceived studies of philosophical influence on Joyce's text were written by Jackson Cope and Theoharis Constantine Theoharis, and in 1982 Umberto Eco published *The Aesthetics of Chaosmos: The Middle Ages of James Joyce.* In 1987 Phillip Herring's *Joyce's Uncertainty Principle* inflected Joyce's philosophy with theories of relativity and uncertainty in modern science. The influence of Continental drama, fiction, and opera on *Ulysses* were explored by Bjorn Tysdahl (Ibsen), Richard Cross (Flaubert), Peter Egri (Mann), Breon Mitchell (the German novel), and Timothy Martin (Wagner). In 1976 Michael Seidel reexamined Joyce's poetic and philosophical inspiration by the *Odyssey* in *Epic Geography: James Joyce's "Ulysses."* More recently, Martha Black's study of Joyce and Shaw and Scott Klein's on Joyce and Wyndham Lewis continue this tradition.

While New Criticism dominated American literary practice, British criticism extended an Arnoldian tradition of promoting high culture and moral seriousness into midcentury, largely through the influential thinking of F. R. Leavis. Leavis expelled Joyce from his *The Great Tradition* for failing to write, like D. H. Lawrence, from a "depth of religious experience." He complained that

> there is no organic principle determining, informing, and controlling into a vital whole, the elaborate analogical structure, the extraordinary variety of technical devices, the attempts at an exhaustive rendering of consciousness, for which *Ulysses* is remarkable, and which got it accepted by a cosmopolitan literary world as a new start. It is rather, I think, a dead end. (25–26)

Leavis, unprepared for the revolution in critical theory that would come to dominate literary study for the last quarter of the twentieth century, could not have been more wrong. He failed to see that it was precisely the absence of an "organic principle" in *Ulysses*—indeed, the text's questioning the concept and validity of an "organic principle"— that for the next thirty years made *Ulysses'* open form create the multiplicity of interpretive possibilities that transformed it into a poetic chameleon, a text for all critical seasons.

The need to find the vision or telos behind the novel's technical complexity stirred critical creativity in the 1960s. S. L. Goldberg's 1961 *The Classical Temper: A Study of James Joyce's "Ulysses"* answered Leavis most directly by elevating the novel to a high moral plane on the basis of the "classical temper" of its humanistic objectivity. In the following year, Robert Martin Adams' *Surface and Symbol: The Consistency of James Joyce's "Ulysses"* (1962) probed Joyce's strategy in a controversial, but fascinating, analysis of the interplay between the novel's factual and fictional materials and their narrative and symbolic effects. A few years later Arnold Goldman's 1966 *The Joyce Paradox: Form and Freedom in His Fiction* addressed the problem of the text's propensity to produce conflicting readings with an ambitious argument that related its interpretive openness to the paradoxes inherent in all of Joyce's texts. The *Ulysses* critics of the 1960s defeated the early charges against the text's formlessness with mounting evidence of precise craft[4]

---

[4]A. Walton Litz's *The Art of James Joyce* (1961) inaugurated a tradition of genetic research into Joyce's composition practices that eventually informed editorial principle and expertise while contributing a scholarly underpinning to Joyce's design. This work

at the same time that they deflected pressure to link its technical virtuosity to a single origin, function, or purpose.

The 1970s and 1980s brought an explosion of criticism and scholarship to the study of *Ulysses* that was increasingly colored by the mounting translations and importations of French and German critical theory into the American academy. The influence of Continental theory produced two important effects on the study of Joycean texts. First, poststructuralism and deconstruction stressed the metaphysics of language by exploring its performativity, its freeplay, its rhetorical productivity, and its self-referentiality. This highly theoretical approach to language validated Joyce's avant-garde linguistic experiments (which had first been celebrated in the 1930s) with greater technical and logical insight. Although some examples of this approach appeared as early as 1972—Sally Purcell's translation of Hélène Cixous's *The Exile of James Joyce*, for example—most deconstructive approaches to Joyce appeared later in the decade and initially focused on *Finnegans Wake*, such as Margot Norris's 1976 *The Decentered Universe of "Finnegans Wake."* In addition, Continental theory encompassed methods and insights from a variety of disciplines—especially linguistics, philosophy, psychoanalysis, and anthropology. As a result, criticism assumed a highly interdisciplinary focus during the 1970s and 1980s, as exemplified in Colin MacCabe's *James Joyce and the Revolution of the Word* (1978), which used structuralist, psychoanalytic, and Marxist theories to argue for the philosophically revolutionary potential of Joyce's most radical formal experiments.

One of the earliest effects of Continental theory was found in linguistically informed attention to the nature of narrative, which

---

was continued in the 1970s by Phillip Herring, who edited the British Museum notesheets for the last seven chapters of *Ulysses*, and Michael Groden, whose 1977 *"Ulysses" in Progress* used a meticulously researched composition history to represent the novel as a palimpsest of Joyce's creative development. Groden identifies Joyce's three experimental compositional phases as the interior monologue, the parodies and imitative styles, and the final strategy of compositional self-reflection. The 1960s also saw the first readers' guides and research tools for *Ulysses*. Stanley Sultan, Harry Blamires, and Clive Hart's studies were designed to help readers with the generic and narrative progress of the novel. Weldon Thornton's *Allusions in "Ulysses": An Annotated List* appeared in 1968 and was the first reference guide to offer annotations for the numerous allusions in the work. This text was followed in 1974 by an even more comprehensive guide: Don Gifford and Robert Seidman's *Notes for Joyce,* which were issued in a revised and expanded version as *"Ulysses" Annotated* in 1988.

produced increasingly sophisticated speech act theory, rhetorical analysis, and reception theory. One of the earliest narratological approaches was David Hayman's *"Ulysses": The Mechanics of Meaning* (1970), which analyzed the book's techniques, structures, and styles to postulate the influential notion that point of view in *Ulysses* may be controlled by an "Arranger," rather than a narrator or groups of narrators. A decade later, Karen Lawrence's 1981 *The Odyssey of Style in "Ulysses"* argued that the increasingly radical narrative and stylistic experiments of the later episodes in the novel function self-reflexively, to make style itself a performative activity in the novel. Two other studies appeared in the 1980s oriented, like Lawrence's, toward effects on the reader of *Ulysses*. Brook Thomas's 1982 *James Joyce's "Ulysses": A Book of Many Happy Returns* used the premises of reader-response criticism—including the notion that the text constructs the reader—to focus on the self-revealing textual consciousness at work in the novel's telling. John Paul Riquelme's *Teller and Tale in Joyce's Fiction: Oscillating Perspectives* (1983) challenged the notion of Joyce's impersonal narration in *Ulysses*. On a more technical level of language, Roy Gottfried's *The Art of Joyce's Syntax in "Ulysses"* (1980) argued that Joyce creates deliberate tensions between order and freedom in the text by transgressing traditional rules of syntax. Finally, in the mid-1980s two important collections of essays on Joyce's language at last brought together the work of the eminent Swiss Joyce scholar, Fritz Senn. Senn's *Nichts Gegen Joyce: Joyce Versus Nothing*, published in Zurich in 1983, includes several important essays on *Ulysses*, including "Dynamics of Corrective Unrest" in which Senn argues that the novel is "probably the first consistently autocorrective work of literature" (121). A year later, John Paul Riquelme edited Senn's *Joyce's Dislocutions: Essays on Reading as Translation*, in which Senn uses the trope of translation to explore Joyce's creation of shifting and multivalent meanings through a polyglot's sense of language.

The disciplinary diversity of critical theory, which explored literary language through the lenses of various "human sciences," expressed itself in a Joycean criticism increasingly inflected by methodologies drawn from other fields. The interiorized nature of *Ulysses*, whose language portrays and exposes a complex variety of psychic states and mechanisms, made Joyce's work a particularly rich subject for psychoanalytic criticism. Mark Shechner's 1974 *Joyce in Nighttown: A Psychoanalytic Inquiry into "Ulysses"* appeared as the first significant Freudian study of the novel, tracing the psychoanalytic strategies that transformed biographical material into fictional complications in the text.[5] In 1980 Sheldon Brivic's *Joyce Between Freud and Jung* offered a psychoanalytically balanced and eclectic overview of Joyce's fictional development with attention to *Ulysses*. More than a decade later, psychoanalytic criticism—under the influence of Jacques Lacan, who was himself influenced by Joyce—significantly turned its focus toward the performative nature of writing and textuality. Mature explorations of the role of language in the construction of the subject as a self-divided creation of cultural discourses emerged in the 1990s, notably in Kimberly Devlin's analysis of the "uncanny" Joycean text in her 1991 *Wandering and Return in "Finnegans Wake": An Integrative Approach to Joyce's Fictions*. A year earlier, Suzette Henke's *James Joyce and the Politics of Desire* used the psychoanalytic theories of Freud, Jacques Lacan, and Julia Kristeva to explore gendered gestures of textual performativity in Joyce's works. This same attention to psychoanalytically performative language may be found in the essays by Joseph Boone, Marilyn Brownstein, and Ellen Carol Jones in Susan Stanford Friedman's 1993 collection of essays, *Joyce: The Return of the Repressed*.

Politics in a broad sense—including Marxist criticism, Frankfurt School criticism, cultural study, postcolonial criticism, and feminism—began to dominate *Ulysses* studies in the late 1980s and early 1990s.[6] The inaugural text for this trend was Dominic Manganiello's 1980 *Joyce's Politics*, whose focus on the biographical restoration of Joyce's interest in political theories and issues laid the groundwork for the later studies of postcolonialism and culture study in *Ulysses*. Franco Moretti's 1983 *Signs Taken for Wonders* contains a provocative essay, "The Long Goodbye: *Ulysses* and the End of Liberal Capitalism," that argues for the homology between the novel and Britain's capitalist crisis in the early twentieth century. Cheryl Herr's *Joyce's Anatomy of Culture* (1986) looks specifically at the ideologies Joyce imported into his texts by using Irish popular discourses, particularly the newspaper, the sermon, and the music-hall stage. Herr's analysis of "Circe" is

---

[5]Three works that are not explicitly psychoanalytical but that nonetheless focus on the function of metamorphosis and transformation in *Ulysses* are books by Elliott Gose, John Gordon, and Lindsey Tucker. Tucker's work focuses specifically on the body and alimentation as tropes of creativity in *Ulysses*.

[6]During the 1970s, Bernard Benstock, John Garvin, and C. H. Peake all contributed studies of Joyce's relationship to Ireland. Patrick Parrinder's 1984 study for advanced students contains excellent chapters on five chapters in *Ulysses*, with many interesting glosses on the political issues they raise.

greatly enriched by her discovery of intriguing source materials from the popular culture of turn-of-the-century Ireland. Patrick McGee's 1988 *Paperspace: Style as Ideology in Joyce's "Ulysses"* resists the textualist impulse to treat Joyce's radical stylistic experiments in the novel as autonomous in favor of restoring them to the realm of the historical and the social.

Following Seamus Deane's 1985 *Celtic Revivals: Essays in Modern Irish Literature*, the Irish Field Day Theatre Company sponsored a book of three essays by noted Marxist critics Terry Eagleton, Fredric Jameson, and Edward Said called *Nationalism, Colonialism, and Literature* (1990); Eagleton and Jameson's essays contain specific reference to *Ulysses*. Jeffrey Segall uses *Ulysses* to cast "a beam under which we may scrutinize a period in American cultural history when polemics dominated literary debate" (8) in his 1993 *Joyce in America: Cultural Politics and the Trials of "Ulysses."* Enda Duffy's 1994 *The Subaltern "Ulysses"* makes even greater revolutionary claims for the novel: "I want to reclaim *Ulysses* in these terms for Irish readers as *the* text of Ireland's independence . . . a novel preoccupied . . . with both the means by which oppressed communities fight their way out of abjection and the potential pitfalls of anticolonial struggles" (1). Vincent Cheng's 1995 *Joyce, Race, and Empire* contains chapters on *Ulysses* that focus particularly on the "ethnography of Irishness and . . . perspectives of racial and ethnic otherness in the novel" (xvi). Finally, at the other spectrum of politics, James McMichael is concerned with how the novel educates and enlarges our sense of human responsibility to others through its ethics of reading (*"Ulysses" and Justice*, 1991).

Feminist approaches to *Ulysses* reflect many of the ideological shifts and theoretical inflections that invigorated the sophistication of feminist criticism in the 1970s and 1980s. Moving away from querulous complaints that Joyce failed to make women sufficiently strong, heroic, independent, or intellectual (in the work of Sandra Gilbert, Susan Gubar, Carolyn Heilbrun, and other American feminist critics), later feminist criticism complicated both misogynistic and gyneolatrous readings of Molly Bloom with historical considerations. In Winter 1981, the *James Joyce Quarterly* published Mary Power's essay, "The Discovery of *Ruby*," which located and identified the novel *Ruby. A Novel. Founded on the Life of a Circus Girl* as the source of the text Molly Bloom reads in bed in *Ulysses*. Power's discovery led to an important reconsideration of the role of pornography in the novel and stressed the importance of historical research for achieving an accurate grasp of the text's sexual politics. Bonnie Kime Scott's 1984 *Joyce and*

Feminism corrected general misperceptions about Joyce's attitudes and experiences with respect to historical feminism and his relationship with women in his familial and professional life. Both Scott's book and Suzette Henke and Elaine Unkeless's 1982 *Women in Joyce* contain discussions of *Ulysses*. Richard Brown's 1985 *James Joyce and Sexuality* supplies a broad historical context for Joyce's engagement with the philosophical, scientific, and social sexologies prominent in early twentieth-century thought. Mary Lowe-Evans is more pointedly indebted to the approaches of new historicism in excavating the discourses of population control that shape many ideological issues in the Joycean text. Her 1989 *Crimes Against Fecundity: Joyce and Population Control* contains an important chapter on "Oxen of the Sun."

The figure of Molly Bloom alone has generated an impressive body of scholarship. David Hayman's "The Empirical Molly" in Staley and Benstock's *Approaches to "Ulysses"* (1970), and Phillip Herring's "Toward an Historical Molly Bloom" (1978) treat Molly as a complex character, on a par with Stephen Dedalus and Leopold Bloom. James Van Dyck Card's 1984 *An Anatomy of "Penelope"* displays Molly's contradictions as products of careful author intention, given the archival evidence of manuscripts, typescripts, and proofs. Richard Pearce's collection of essays, *Molly Blooms: A Polylogue on "Penelope" and Cultural Studies* contains provocative sections on "Molly and the Male Gaze," "Molly in Performance," "Negotiating Colonialism," "Molly as Consumer," and "Molly as Body and Embodied." Another excellent selection of essays on Molly Bloom, "Feminist Readings of Joyce," appeared in the 1989 special issue of *Modern Fiction Studies,* guest edited by Ellen Carol Jones.

A series of books that in the late 1980s and early 1990s explored problems of authority in the Joycean text fruitfully use gender issues as a trope for problems of legitimacy and power. Although her discussion of *Ulysses* merely caps her exploration of the British novel tradition, Christine van Boheemen's 1987 *The Novel as Family Romance: Language, Gender, and Authority from Fielding to Joyce* contributes an influential exploration of gender in the novel with an approach theoretically inflected by Continental deconstruction. Vicki Mahaffey's 1988 *Reauthorizing Joyce* uses Molly Bloom and "Penelope" to typologize a multiple and collective alternative to the more oppressive authorities associated with other figures, styles, and institutions in *Ulysses.* Frances Restuccia's 1989 *Joyce and the Law of the Father* uses chiefly psychoanalytic theories, in which resistance is typologized by the trope of the perverse (sadism, fetishism, the phallic mother, prohibition, and so forth), to explore the fate of authority in the Joycean text. Jean-Michel Rabaté's 1991 *James Joyce, Authorized Reader* likewise uses Derridian and Lacanian premises to explore the figure of paternity in delineating problems of authorization in the compact between author and reader. Even though deconstructive criticism gravitated more readily toward *Finnegans Wake* than the earlier works, Derek Attridge and Daniel Ferrer's 1984 *Post-structuralist Joyce* includes two interesting essays on *Ulysses*: André Topia's "The Matrix and the Echo: Intertextuality in *Ulysses*" and Daniel Ferrer's psychoanalytically explored "Circe, Regret, and Regression." Derek Attridge's 1988 *Peculiar Language: Literature as Difference from the Renaissance to James Joyce* conducts a Derridian exploration of the language of *Ulysses* in its chapter 6, "Literature as Deviation: Syntax, Style, and the Body in *Ulysses*." Robert Scholes' 1992 *In Search of James Joyce* contains a series of important essays on *Ulysses*, including "*Ulysses*: A Structuralist Perspective," and a fascinating chapter on "Circe" and modern painting, entitled "In the Brothel of Modernism: Picasso and Joyce."

The flood of new studies on *Ulysses* is not abating in the 1990s. They include some works on teaching *Ulysses* that augment the large number of introductory studies, chapter-by-chapter discussions, and collections of essays[7] that have accumulated over the years. In 1993, the Modern Language Association published Kathleen McCormick and Erwin Steinberg's *Approaches to Teaching Joyce's "Ulysses"*, which attempts to introduce students to background materials and various theoretical approaches to the text. In 1996 Robert Newman published a collection of essays on teaching *through* or *with Ulysses* under the title *Pedagogy, Praxis, "Ulysses": Using Joyce's Text to Transform the Classroom.*

This summary of the critical history of *Ulysses* is inevitably incomplete. New introductory guides like Vincent Sherry's and other research tools continue to augment the large number of older directories and companion studies with important new material on *Ulysses*. Fortunately, there are a series of excellent bibliographical aids available for finding much additional *Ulysses* scholarship that is here omitted, although these are inevitably limited by their publication dates. The

---

[7]Among the most useful introductory guides for students are the episode-by-episode discussions of Harry Blamires and Suzette Henke (*Joyce's Moraculous Sindbook*) and the collection of essays focused on each episode edited by Clive Hart and David Hayman. Single volume introductory discussions of the novel are found in Clive Hart, Vincent Sherry, and Patrick McCarthy. The studies of Stanley Sultan and Daniel Schwarz are somewhat more complex. Some other excellent collections of essays are edited by Thomas Staley (*"Ulysses": Fifty Years*, which contains Hugh Kenner's provocative essay on "Molly's Masterstroke") and by Staley and Bernard Benstock.

most comprehensive of these, if not the most recent, is Thomas Jackson Rice's *James Joyce: A Guide to Research* (1982). Thomas Staley's user-friendly *An Annotated Critical Bibliography of James Joyce* (1989) is more up to date. Sidney Feshbach and William Herman offer a compact "History of Joyce Criticism and Scholarship" in Zack Bowen and James F. Carens's 1984 *A Companion to Joyce Studies*. And recently, the *James Joyce Quarterly* 32 (Winter 1995) published a thirty-year index listing the contents of the journal's first thirty volumes that is beautifully organized and indexed for easy retrieval of virtually anything published on *Ulysses* in its pages.

The future of *Ulysses* scholarship will be enriched by two landmark publishing events of 1978 and 1984. The first was the astonishing production of *The James Joyce Archive*, an event whose significance Phillip Herring described as "galactic" (Review 86). Sixty-three oversized volumes collect a facsimile of virtually Joyce's entire workshop, which includes most of the available notes and notebooks, holograph drafts, manuscripts, typescripts, and text proofs for his published work. Using *The James Joyce Archive*, Joyce scholars can now check the evolution of the chapters of *Ulysses* from early notes through successive drafts and galley proofs in the comfort of their own university libraries.

The second seismic event in the field of *Ulysses* scholarship was the 1984 publication of a critical and synoptic edition of *Ulysses*, edited by Hans Walter Gabler with Wolfhard Steppe and Claus Melchior. In 1986, Random House published a trade edition of Gabler's text that called itself "The Corrected Text," which made the work available in paperback. Gabler, who was assisted in this editorial enterprise by an international advisory committee that included Richard Ellmann, Clive Hart, A. Walton Litz, and Michael Groden, confronted an unusual array of editorial problems created by the chaotic exigencies of the process leading up to the publication of the 1922 edition. In his introduction, Gabler carefully laid out the editorial premises and procedures he adopted for making difficult decisions on what to retain or change in the 1984 critical and synoptic edition. This exposure of his editorial process provided the information that led to an attack by John Kidd, initially in an essay with the somewhat scurrilous title of "The Scandal of *Ulysses*." The Gabler edition thus became a point of intense controversy that spilled far beyond the confines of the Joyce community.

But while the Gabler edition's flaws have been quite thoroughly explored in Sandulescu and Hart's 1986 *Assessing the 1984 "Ulysses"*, the text has endured with considerable popularity among large numbers of scholars, students, and readers, who appear to trust the judgments behind its corrections. Furthermore, Michael Groden's "Afterword" to the 1993 Bodley Head publication of the Gabler edition of *Ulysses* pointed out that Gabler's presentation of his editing procedures has "lifted the general public, students, literary critics, and scholars—the vast majority of whom are not themselves editors—to a heightened awareness of textual editing" (647). Jerome McGann theorizes the implications of the impossibility of producing a definitive text in his 1985 article "*Ulysses* as a Postmodern Text: The Gabler Edition" in *Criticism*. The Fall 1990 issue of the *James Joyce Quarterly* carried pieces by Michael Groden ("A Response to John Kidd's 'An Inquiry into *Ulysses: The Corrected Text*'" 81–110) and John Kidd ("Gabler's Errors in Context: A Reply to Michael Groden on Editing *Ulysses*") stating and discussing the editorial points in dispute.

The future of *Ulysses* study holds an entirely different and brave new world of editing in its cards. A number of scholars, among whom Michael Groden appears to be in the vanguard, are now at work exploring the possibilities of an electronic hypertext of *Ulysses*—a text enhanced with simultaneous annotations, illustrations, and criticism—made possible by computer technology. At the moment when *Ulysses* scholarship is about to undergo a millennial revolution, Joyce's wonderful novel demonstrates once again its unquenchable vigor as a text for all times and for all critical and scholarly seasons.

Margot Norris

WORKS CITED

Adams, Robert Martin. *Surface and Symbol: The Consistency of James Joyce's "Ulysses."* New York: Oxford UP, 1962.

Attridge, Derek. *Peculiar Language: Literature as Difference from the Renaissance to James Joyce.* Ithaca: Cornell UP, 1988.

Attridge, Derek, and Daniel Ferrer. *Post-Structuralist Joyce: Essays from the French.* Cambridge: Cambridge UP, 1984.

Barrow, Craig Wallace. *Montage in James Joyce's "Ulysses."* Potomac, MD: Studia Humanitatis, 1980.

Beach, Joseph Warren. "Post-Impressionism: Joyce." *The Twentieth-Century Novel: Studies in Technique.* New York: Appleton, 1932.

Benstock, Bernard. *James Joyce: The Undiscover'd Country.* New York: Barnes, 1977.

Benstock, Shari, and Bernard Benstock. *Who's He When He's at Home: A James Joyce Directory.* Urbana: U of Illinois P, 1980.

Black, Martha Fodaski. *Shaw and Joyce: The Last Word in Stolentelling.* Gainesville: U of Florida P, 1995.

Blackmur, R. P. "The Jew in Search of a Son: Joyce's *Ulysses.*" *Eleven Essays in the European Novel.* New York: Harcourt, 1964.

Blamires, Harry. *The Bloomsday Book: A Guide Through Joyce's "Ulysses."* London: Methuen, 1966.

Boheemen, Christine van. *The Novel as Family Romance: Language, Gender, and Authority from Fielding to Joyce.* Ithaca: Cornell UP, 1987.

Bowen, Zack. *Musical Allusions in the Works of James Joyce: Early Poetry through "Ulysses."* Albany: SUNY P, 1974.

Bowen, Zack, and James F. Carens, eds. *A Companion to Joyce Studies.* Westport, CT: Greenwood, 1984.

Boyle, Robert, S. J. *James Joyce's Pauline Vision: A Catholic Exposition.* Carbondale: Southern Illinois UP, 1978.

Brivic, Sheldon R. *Joyce between Freud and Jung.* Port Washington, NY: Kennikat, 1980.

Brown, Richard. *James Joyce and Sexuality.* Cambridge: Cambridge UP, 1985.

Card, James Van Dyck. *An Anatomy of "Penelope."* Rutherford, NJ: Farleigh Dickinson UP, 1984.

Cheng, Vincent J. *Joyce, Race, and Empire.* Cambridge: Cambridge UP, 1995.

Cixous, Hélène. *The Exile of James Joyce.* Trans. Sally A. J. Purcell. New York: Lewis, 1972.

Cope, Jackson I. *Joyce's Cities: Archaeologies of the Soul.* Baltimore: Johns Hopkins UP, 1981.

Cross, Richard K. *Flaubert and Joyce: The Rite of Fiction.* Princeton: Princeton UP, 1971.

Deane, Seamus. *Celtic Revivals: Essays in Modern Irish Literature, 1880–1980.* London: Faber, 1985.

Dent, R. W. *Colloquial Language in "Ulysses": A Reference Tool.* Newark: U of Delaware P, 1994.

Devlin, Kimberly J. *Wandering and Return in "Finnegans Wake": An Integrative Approach to Joyce's Fictions.* Princeton: Princeton UP, 1991.

Duffy, Enda. *The Subaltern "Ulysses."* Minneapolis: U of Minnesota P, 1994.

Eagleton, Terry, Fredric Jameson, and Edward W. Said. *Nationalism,*

Colonialism, and Literature. Minneapolis: U of Minnesota P, 1990.

Eco, Umberto. *The Aesthetics of Chaosmos: The Middle Ages of James Joyce.* Trans. Ellen Esrock. Tulsa: University of Tulsa P, 1982.

Egri, Peter. *Avantguardism and Modernity: A Comparison of James Joyce's "Ulysses" with Thomas Mann's "Der Zauberberg" and "Lotte in Weimar."* Trans. Paul Aston. Tulsa: University of Tulsa P, 1972.

Eliot, T. S. "*Ulysses*, Order, and Myth." *Selected Prose of T. S. Eliot.* Ed. Frank Kermode. New York: Harcourt, 1975. 175–78.

Ellmann, Richard. *James Joyce.* Rev. ed. New York: Oxford UP, 1982.

———. *Ulysses on the Liffey.* New York: Oxford UP, 1972.

Empson, William. "The Theme of *Ulysses.*" *Kenyon Review* 18 (1956): 26–52.

French, Marilyn. *The Book as World: James Joyce's "Ulysses."* Cambridge: Harvard UP, 1976.

Friedman, Susan Stanford, ed. *Joyce: The Return of the Repressed.* Ithaca: Cornell UP, 1993.

Garvin, John. *James Joyce's Disunited Kingdom and the Irish Dimension.* Dublin: Gill, 1976.

Gifford, Don, with Robert J. Seidman. *"Ulysses" Annotated: Notes for James Joyce's 'Ulysses.'* Rev. ed. Berkeley: U of California P, 1988.

Gilbert, Stuart. *James Joyce's "Ulysses": A Study.* London: Faber, 1930.

Gillespie, Michael Patrick. *Inverted Volumes Improperly Arranged: James Joyce and His Trieste Library.* Ann Arbor: UMI Research P, 1983.

Goldberg, S. L. *The Classical Temper: A Study of James Joyce's "Ulysses."* London: Chatto, 1961.

Goldman, Arnold. *The Joyce Paradox: Form and Freedom in His Fiction.* Evanston: Northwestern UP, 1966.

Gordon, John. *James Joyce's Metamorphoses.* Dublin: Gill, 1981.

Gose, Elliott B. *The Transformation Process in Joyce's "Ulysses."* Toronto: U of Toronto P, 1980.

Gottfried, Roy K. *The Art of Joyce's Syntax in "Ulysses."* Athens: U of Georgia P, 1980.

Groden, Michael. Afterword. *Ulysses.* By James Joyce. Ed. Hans Walter Gabler. London: Bodley Head, 1993. New York: Vintage, 1996.

———. "A Response to John Kidd's 'An Inquiry Into *Ulysses: The Corrected Text.*'" *James Joyce Quarterly* 28 (Fall 1990): 81–110.

———. *"Ulysses" in Progress.* Princeton: Princeton UP, 1977.

Hart, Clive. *James Joyce's "Ulysses."* Sydney: Sydney UP, 1968.

Hart, Clive, and David Hayman, eds. *James Joyce's "Ulysses": Critical Essays.* Berkeley: U of California P, 1974.

Hart, Clive, and A. M. Leo Knuth. *A Topographical Guide to James Joyce's "Ulysses."* 2 vols. Colchester, Eng.: Wake Newslitter, 1975.

Hayman, David. "The Empirical Molly." *Approaches to "Ulysses": Ten Essays.* Ed. Thomas F. Staley and Bernard Benstock. Pittsburgh: U of Pittsburgh P, 1970. 103–35.

———. *"Ulysses": The Mechanics of Meaning.* Englewood Cliffs: Prentice-Hall, 1970.

Henke, Suzette A. *James Joyce and the Politics of Desire.* New York: Routledge, 1990.

———. *Joyce's Moraculous Sindbook: A Study of "Ulysses."* Columbus: Ohio State UP, 1978.

Henke, Suzette A., and Elaine Unkeless, eds. *Women in Joyce.* Urbana: U of Illinois P, 1982.

Herr, Cheryl. *Joyce's Anatomy of Culture.* Urbana: U of Illinois P, 1986.

Herring, Phillip F., ed. *Joyce's "Ulysses" Notesheets in the British Museum.* Charlottesville: UP of Virginia, 1972.

———. *Joyce's Uncertainty Principle.* Princeton: Princeton UP, 1987.

———. Rev. of *The James Joyce Archive. James Joyce Quarterly* 19 (Fall 1981): 85–97.

———. "Toward an Historical Molly Bloom." *English Literary History* 45(1978): 501–21.

The James Joyce Archive. Ed. Michael Groden, et al. New York: Garland, 1978–.

Jones, Ellen Carol, guest co-ed. *Modern Fiction Studies* 35 (Autumn 1989). "Feminist Readings of Joyce" issue.

Joyce, James. *Selected Letters.* Ed. Richard Ellmann. New York: Viking, 1975.

———. *Ulysses.* Ed. Hans Walter Gabler, with Wolfhard Steppe and Claus Melchior. New York: Vintage, 1986.

Jung, Carl G. "*Ulysses:* A Monologue." *The Spirit in Man, Art, and Literature.* Trans. R. F. C. Hull. Princeton: Princeton UP, 1966.

Kain, Richard M. *Fabulous Voyager: James Joyce's "Ulysses."* Chicago: U of Chicago P, 1947.

Kelly, Dermot. *Narrative Strategies in Joyce's "Ulysses."* Ann Arbor: UMI Research P, 1988.

Kenner, Hugh. *Dublin's Joyce.* Bloomington: Indiana UP, 1956.

————. "Homer's Sticks and Stones." *James Joyce Quarterly* 6(Summer 1969): 285–98.

————. *Joyce's Voices.* Berkeley: U of California P, 1978.

————. *The Pound Era.* Berkeley: U of California P, 1971.

————. *Ulysses: Revised Edition.* Baltimore: Johns Hopkins UP, 1987.

Kidd, John. "Gabler's Errors in Context: A Reply to Michael Groden on Editing *Ulysses.*" *James Joyce Quarterly* 28(Fall 1990): 111–51.

————. "The Scandal of *Ulysses.*" *The New York Review of Books.* 30 June 1988: 32.

Klein, Scott W. *The Fictions of James Joyce and Wyndham Lewis: Monsters of Nature and Design.* Cambridge: Cambridge UP, 1994.

Lawrence, Karen. *The Odyssey of Style in "Ulysses."* Princeton: Princeton UP, 1981.

Leavis, F. R. *The Great Tradition.* London: Chatto, 1960.

Levin, Harry. *James Joyce: A Critical Introduction.* Norfolk, CT: New Directions, 1941.

Litz, A. Walton. *The Art of James Joyce: Method and Design in "Ulysses" and "Finnegans Wake."* London: Oxford UP, 1961.

Lowe-Evans, Mary. *Crimes Against Fecundity: Joyce and Population Control.* Syracuse: Syracuse UP, 1989.

MacCabe, Colin. *James Joyce and the Revolution of the Word.* London: Macmillan, 1978.

Maddox, James H. *Joyce's "Ulysses" and the Assault upon Character.* New Brunswick: Rutgers UP, 1978.

Mahaffey, Vicki. *Reauthorizing Joyce.* New York: Cambridge UP, 1988.

Manganiello, Dominic. *Joyce's Politics.* London: Routledge, 1980.

Martin, Timothy. *Joyce and Wagner: A Study of Influence.* Cambridge: Cambridge UP, 1991.

McCarthy, Patrick A. *"Ulysses": Portals of Discovery.* Boston: Twayne, 1990.

McCormick, Kathleen, and Erwin R. Steinberg, eds. *Approaches to Teaching Joyce's "Ulysses."* New York: MLA, 1993.

McGann, Jerome J. "*Ulysses* as a Postmodern Text: The Gabler Edition." *Criticism* 27 (1985): 283–306.

McGee, Patrick. *Paperspace: Style as Ideology in Joyce's "Ulysses."* Lincoln: U of Nebraska P, 1988.

McMichael, James. *"Ulysses" and Justice.* Princeton: Princeton UP, 1991.

Mitchell, Breon. *James Joyce and the German Novel, 1922–33.* Athens: Ohio UP, 1976.

More, Paul Elmer. "James Joyce." *On Being Human.* Princeton: Princeton UP, 1936.

Moretti, Franco. *Signs Taken for Wonders: Essays in the Sociology of Literary Forms.* Trans. Susan Fischer, David Forgacs, and David Miller. London: Verso, 1983.

Morse, J. Mitchell. *The Sympathetic Alien: James Joyce and Catholicism.* New York: New York UP, 1959.

Mosely, Virginia. *Joyce and the Bible.* De Kalb: Northern Illinois UP, 1967.

Newman, Robert, ed. *Pedagogy, Praxis, "Ulysses": Using Joyce's Text to Transform the Classroom.* Ann Arbor: U of Michigan P, 1996.

Noon, William T., *Joyce and Aquinas.* New Haven: Yale UP, 1957.

Norris, Margot. *The Decentered Universe of "Finnegans Wake."* Baltimore: Johns Hopkins UP, 1976.

Parrinder, Patrick. *James Joyce.* Cambridge: Cambridge UP, 1984.

Peake, C. H. *James Joyce: The Citizen and the Artist.* Stanford: Stanford UP, 1977.

Pearce, Richard, ed. *Molly Blooms: A Polylogue on "Penelope" and Cultural Studies.* Madison: U of Wisconsin P, 1994.

Pound/Joyce: The Letters of Ezra Pound to James Joyce. Ed. Forrest Read. New York: New Directions, 1967.

Power, Mary. "The Discovery of *Ruby.*" *James Joyce Quarterly* 18(Winter 1981): 115–21.

Rabaté, Jean-Michel. *James Joyce, Authorized Reader.* Trans. Baltimore: Johns Hopkins UP, 1991. Trans. of *James Joyce, Portrait de l'auteur en autre lecteur.* 1984.

Raleigh, John Henry. *The Chronicle of Leopold and Molly Bloom: "Ulysses" as Narrative.* Berkeley: U of California P, 1977.

Restuccia, Frances L. *Joyce and the Law of the Father.* New Haven: Yale UP, 1989.

Reynolds, Mary T. *Joyce and Dante: The Shaping Imagination.* Princeton: Princeton UP, 1981.

Rice, Thomas Jackson. *James Joyce: A Guide to Research.* New York: Garland, 1982.

Riquelme, John Paul. *Teller and Tale in Joyce's Fiction: Oscillating Perspectives.* Baltimore: Johns Hopkins UP, 1983.

Sandulescu, Constantin-George. *The Joycean Monologue.* Colchester, Eng.: Wake Newslitter, 1979.

Sandulescu, C. George, and Clive Hart, eds. *Assessing the 1984 "Ulysses."* Totowa, NJ: Barnes, 1986.

Schlossman, Beryl. *Joyce's Catholic Comedy of Language.* Madison: University of Wisconsin P, 1985.

Schneider, Ulrich. *Die Funktion der Zitate im "Ulysses" von James Joyce.* Bonn: Bouvier, 1970.

Scholes, Robert. *In Search of James Joyce.* Urbana: U of Illinois P, 1992.

Schutte, William M. *Joyce and Shakespeare: A Study in the Meaning of "Ulysses."* New Haven: Yale UP, 1957.

Schwarz, Daniel R. *Reading Joyce's "Ulysses."* London: Macmillan, 1987.

Scott, Bonnie Kime. *Joyce and Feminism.* Bloomington: Indiana UP, 1984.

Segall, Jeffrey. *Joyce in America: Cultural Politics and the Trials of "Ulysses."* Berkeley: University of California P, 1993.

Seidel, Michael. *Epic Geography: James Joyce's "Ulysses."* Princeton: Princeton UP, 1976.

Senn, Fritz. *Joyce's Dislocutions: Essays on Reading as Translation.* Ed. John Paul Riquelme. Baltimore: Johns Hopkins UP, 1984.

———. *Nichts Gegen Joyce: Joyce Versus Nothing.* Zurich: Haffmans Verlag, 1983.

Shechner, Mark. *Joyce in Nighttown: A Psychoanalytic Inquiry into "Ulysses."* Berkeley: U of California P, 1974.

Sherry, Vincent. *James Joyce "Ulysses."* New York: Cambridge UP, 1994.

Staley, Thomas F. *An Annotated Critical Bibliography of James Joyce.* New York: St. Martin's, 1989.

———, ed. *"Ulysses": Fifty Years.* Bloomington: Indiana UP, 1974.

Staley, Thomas F., and Bernard Benstock, eds. *Approaches to "Ulysses": Ten Essays.* Pittsburgh: U of Pittsburgh P, 1970.

Steinberg, Erwin. *The Stream of Consciousness and Beyond in "Ulysses."* Pittsburgh: U of Pittsburgh P, 1973.

Sultan, Stanley. *The Argument of "Ulysses."* Middletown, CT: Wesleyan UP, 1987.

Theoharis, Theoharis Constantine. *Joyce's "Ulysses": An Anatomy of the Soul.* Chapel Hill: U of North Carolina P, 1988.

Thomas, Brook. *James Joyce's "Ulysses": A Book of Many Happy Returns.* Baton Rouge: Louisiana State UP, 1982.

Thornton, Weldon. *Allusions in "Ulysses": An Annotated List.* Chapel Hill: U of North Carolina P, 1968.

Tindall, William York. *A Reader's Guide to James Joyce*. New York: Farrar, 1959.

Tucker, Lindsey. *Stephen and Bloom at Life's Feast: Alimentary Symbolism and the Creative Process in James Joyce's "Ulysses."* Columbus: Ohio State UP, 1984.

Tymoczko, Maria. *The Irish "Ulysses."* Berkeley: U of California P, 1994.

Tysdahl, Bjorn J. *Joyce and Ibsen: A Study in Literary Influence.* New York: Humanitas, 1968.

Van Caspel, Paul. *Bloomers on the Liffey: Eisegetical Readings of Joyce's "Ulysses."* Baltimore: Johns Hopkins UP, 1986.

West, Alick. "James Joyce: *Ulysses.*" *Crisis and Criticism, and Selected Literary Essays.* London: Lawrence, 1975.

Wilson, Edmund. *Axel's Castle.* 1931. New York: Scribner's, 1969.

Woolf, Virginia. *A Writer's Diary.* Ed. Leonard Woolf. New York: Harcourt, 1982.

Deconstruction
and
Ulysses

WHAT IS DECONSTRUCTION?

Deconstruction has a reputation for being the most complex and forbidding of contemporary critical approaches to literature, but in fact almost all of us have, at one time, either deconstructed a text or badly wanted to deconstruct one. Sometimes when we hear a lecturer effectively marshal evidence to show that a book means primarily one thing, we long to interrupt and ask what he or she would make of other, conveniently overlooked passages that seem to contradict the lecturer's thesis. Sometimes, after reading a provocative critical article that *almost* convinces us that a familiar work means the opposite of what we assumed it meant, we may wish to make an equally convincing case for our former reading of the text. We may not think that the poem or novel in question better supports our interpretation, but we may recognize that the text can be used to support *both* readings. And sometimes we simply want to make that point: texts can be used to support seemingly irreconcilable positions.

To reach this conclusion is to feel the deconstructive itch. J. Hillis Miller, the preeminent American deconstructor, puts it this way: "Deconstruction is not a dismantling of the structure of a text, but a demonstration that it has already dismantled itself. Its apparently solid ground is no rock but thin air" ("Stevens' Rock" 341). To deconstruct a text isn't to show that all the high old themes aren't there to be found in it. Rather, it is to show that a text—not unlike DNA with its double helix—can have intertwined, opposite "discourses"—strands of narrative, threads of meaning.

Ultimately, of course, deconstruction refers to a larger and more complex enterprise than the practice of demonstrating that a text can have contradictory meanings. The term refers to a way of reading texts practiced by critics who have been influenced by the writings of the French philosopher Jacques Derrida. It is important to gain some understanding of Derrida's project and of the historical backgrounds of his work before reading the deconstruction that follows, let alone attempting to deconstruct a text.

Derrida, a philosopher of language who coined the term *deconstruction*, argues that we tend to think and express our thoughts in terms of opposites. Something is black but not white, masculine and therefore not feminine, a cause rather than an effect, and so forth. These mutually exclusive pairs or dichotomies are too numerous to list but would include beginning/end, conscious/unconscious, presence/absence, and speech/writing. If we think hard about these dichotomies, Derrida suggests, we will realize that they are not simply oppositions; they are also hierarchies in miniature. In other words, they contain one term that our culture views as being superior and one term viewed as negative or inferior. Sometimes the superior term seems only subtly superior (*speech, cause*), but at other times we know immediately which term is culturally preferable (*presence, beginning*, and *consciousness* are easy choices). But the hierarchy always exists.

Of particular interest to Derrida, perhaps because it involves the language in which all the other dichotomies are expressed, is the hierarchical opposition "speech/writing." Derrida argues that the "privileging" of speech, that is, the tendency to regard speech in positive terms and writing in negative terms, cannot be disentangled from the privileging of presence. (Postcards are written by absent friends; we read Plato because he cannot speak from beyond the grave.) Furthermore, according to Derrida, the tendency to privilege both speech and presence is part of the Western tradition of *logocentrism*, the belief that in some ideal beginning were creative *spoken* words, such as "Let there be light," spoken by an ideal, *present* God.[1] According to logocentric

---

[1]Derrida sometimes uses the word *phallogocentrism* to indicate that there is "a certain indissociability" between logocentrism and the "phallocentrism" (Derrida, *Acts* 57) of a culture whose God created light, the world, and man before creating woman—

tradition, these words can now be represented only in unoriginal speech or writing (such as the written phrase in quotation marks above). Derrida doesn't seek to reverse the hierarchized opposition between speech and writing, or presence and absence, or early and late, for to do so would be to fall into a trap of perpetuating the same forms of thought and expression that he seeks to deconstruct. Rather, his goal is to erase the boundary between oppositions such as speech and writing, and to do so in such a way as to throw the order and values implied by the opposition into question.

Returning to the theories of Ferdinand de Saussure, who invented the modern science of linguistics, Derrida reminds us that the association of speech with present, obvious, and ideal meaning—and writing with absent, merely pictured, and therefore less reliable meaning—is suspect, to say the least. As Saussure demonstrated, words are *not* the things they name and, indeed, they are only arbitrarily associated with those things. A word, like any sign, is what Derrida has called a "deferred presence"; that is to say, "the signified concept is never present in itself," and "every concept is necessarily . . . inscribed in a chain or system, within which it refers to another and to other concepts" ("Différance" 138, 140). Neither spoken nor written words have present, positive, identifiable attributes themselves. They have meaning only by virtue of their difference from other words (*red, read, reed*) and, at the same time, their contextual relationship to those words. Take *read* as an example. To know whether it is the present or past tense of the verb—whether it rhymes with *red* or *reed*—we need to see it in relation to some other words (for example, *yesterday*).

Because the meanings of words lie in the differences between them and in the differences between them and the things they name, Derrida suggests that all language is constituted by *différance*, a word he has coined that puns on two French words meaning "to differ" and "to defer": words are the deferred presences of the things they "mean," and their meaning is grounded in difference. Derrida, by the way, changes the *e* in the French word *différence* to an *a* in his neologism *différance;* the change, which can be seen in writing but cannot be heard in spoken French, is itself a playful, witty challenge to the notion that writing is inferior or "fallen" speech.

In *Dissemination* (1972) and *De la grammatologie* [*Of Grammatology*] (1967), Derrida begins to redefine writing by deconstructing

from Adam's rib. "Phallocentrism" is another name for patriarchy. The role that deconstruction has played in feminist analysis will be discussed later.

some old definitions. In *Dissemination,* he traces logocentrism back to
Plato, who in the *Phaedrus* has Socrates condemn writing and who, in
all the great dialogues, powerfully postulates that metaphysical longing
for origins and ideals that permeates Western thought. "What Derrida
does in his reading of Plato," Barbara Johnson points out in her translator's introduction to *Dissemination,* "is to unfold dimensions of
Plato's *text* that work against the grain of (Plato's own) Platonism"
(xxiv). Remember: that is what deconstruction does, according to
Miller; it shows a text dismantling itself.

In *Of Grammatology,* Derrida turns to the *Confessions* of Jean-
Jacques Rousseau and exposes a grain running against the grain.
Rousseau—who has often been seen as another great Western idealist
and believer in innocent, noble origins—on one hand condemned
writing as mere representation, a corruption of the more natural,
childlike, direct, and therefore undevious speech. On the other hand,
Rousseau acknowledged his own tendency to lose self-presence and
blurt out exactly the wrong thing in public. He confesses that, by writing at a distance from his audience, he often expressed himself better:
"If I were present, one would never know what I was worth,"
Rousseau admitted (Derrida, *Of Grammatology* 142). Thus, Derrida
shows that one strand of Rousseau's discourse made writing seem a
secondary, even treacherous supplement, while another made it seem
necessary to communication.

Have Derrida's deconstructions of *Confessions* and the *Phaedrus*
explained these texts, interpreted them, opened them up and shown us
what they mean? Not in any traditional sense. Derrida would say that
anyone attempting to find a single, homogeneous or universal meaning in a text is simply imprisoned by the structure of thought that
would oppose two readings and declare one to be right and not
wrong, correct rather than incorrect. In fact, any work of literature
that we interpret defies the laws of Western logic, the laws of opposition and noncontradiction. From deconstruction's point of view, texts
don't say "A and not B." They say "A and not-A." "Instead of a
simple 'either/or' structure," Johnson explains, "deconstruction attempts to elaborate a discourse that says *neither* 'either/or' *nor*
'both/and' nor even 'neither/nor,' while at the same time not totally
abandoning these logics either. The word deconstruction is meant to
undermine the either/or logic of the opposition 'construction/
destruction.' Deconstruction is both, it is neither, and it reveals the
way in which both construction and destruction are themselves not
what they appear to be" (Johnson, *World* 12–13).

Although its ultimate aim may be to criticize Western idealism and logic, deconstruction began as a response to structuralism and to formalism, another structure-oriented theory of reading. Using Saussure's theory as Derrida was to do later, European structuralists attempted to create a *semiology*, or science of signs, that would give humankind at once a scientific and a holistic way of studying the world and its human inhabitants. Roland Barthes, a structuralist who later shifted toward poststructuralism, hoped to recover literary language from the isolation in which it had been studied and to show that the laws that govern it govern all signs, from road signs to articles of clothing. Claude Lévi-Strauss, a structural anthropologist who studied everything from village structure to the structure of myths, found in myths what he called *mythemes*, or building blocks, such as basic plot elements. Recognizing that the same mythemes occur in similar myths from different cultures, he suggested that all myths may be elements of one great myth being written by the collective human mind.

Derrida did not believe that structuralists had the concepts that would someday explain the laws governing human signification and thus provide the key to understanding the form and meaning of everything from an African village to Greek myth to Rousseau's *Confessions*. In his view, the scientific search by structural anthropologists for what unifies humankind amounts to a new version of the old search for the lost ideal, whether that ideal be Plato's bright realm of the Idea or the Paradise of Genesis or Rousseau's unspoiled Nature. As for the structuralist belief that texts have "centers" of meaning, in Derrida's view that derives from the logocentric belief that there is a reading of the text that accords with "the book as seen by God." Jonathan Culler, who thus translates a difficult phrase from Derrida's *L'Écriture et la différence* [*Writing and Difference*] (1967) in his book *Structuralist Poetics* (1975), goes on to explain what Derrida objects to in structuralist literary criticism:

> [When] one speaks of the structure of a literary work, one does so from a certain vantage point: one starts with notions of the meaning or effects of a poem and tries to identify the structures responsible for those effects. Possible configurations or patterns that make no contribution are rejected as irrelevant. That is to say, an intuitive understanding of the poem functions as the "centre" . . . : it is both a starting point and a limiting principle. (244)

Deconstruction calls into question assumptions made about literature by formalist, as well as by structuralist, critics. Formalism, or the

New Criticism as it was once commonly called, assumes a work of literature to be a freestanding, self-contained object, its meanings found in the complex network of relations that constitute its parts (images, sounds, rhythms, allusions, and so on). To be sure, deconstruction is somewhat like formalism in several ways. Both formalism and deconstruction are text-oriented approaches whose practitioners pay a great deal of attention to rhetorical *tropes* (forms of figurative language including allegory, symbol, metaphor, and metonymy). And formalists, long before deconstructors, discovered counterpatterns of meaning in the same text. Formalists find ambiguity: deconstructors find undecidability. On close inspection, however, the formalist understanding of rhetorical tropes or figures is quite different from that of deconstruction, and undecidability turns out to be different from the ambiguity formalists find in texts.

Formalists, who associated literary with figurative language, made qualitative distinctions between types of figures of speech; for instance, they valued symbols and metaphors over metonyms. (A metonym is a term standing for something with which it is commonly associated or contiguous; we use metonymy when we say we had "the cold plate" for lunch.) From the formalist perspective, metaphors and symbols are less arbitrary figures than metonyms and thus rank more highly in the hierarchy of tropes: a metaphor ("I'm feeling blue") supposedly involves a special, intrinsic, nonarbitrary relationship between its two terms (the feeling of melancholy and the color blue); a symbol ("the river of life") allegedly involves a unique fusion of image and idea.

From the perspective of deconstruction, however, these distinctions are suspect. In "The Rhetoric of Temporality," Paul de Man deconstructs the distinction between symbol and allegory; elsewhere, he, Derrida, and Miller have similarly questioned the metaphor/metonymy distinction, arguing that all figuration is a process of linguistic substitution. In the case of a metaphor (or symbol), they claim, we have forgotten what juxtaposition or contiguity gave rise to the association that now seems mysteriously special. Derrida, in "White Mythology," and de Man, in "Metaphor (*Second Discourse*)," have also challenged the priority of literal over figurative language, and Miller has gone so far as to deny the validity of the literal/figurative distinction, arguing that all words are figures because all language involves *catachresis*, "the violent, forced, or abusive importation of a term from another realm to name something which has no proper name" (Miller, *Ariadne* 21).

The difference between the formalist concept of literary ambiguity and the deconstructive concept of undecidability is as significant as the gap between formalist and deconstructive understandings of figurative language. Undecidability, as de Man came to define it, is a complex notion easily misunderstood. There is a tendency to assume that it refers to readers who, when forced to decide between two or more equally plausible and conflicting readings, throw up their hands and decide that the choice can't be made. But undecidability in fact debunks this whole notion of reading as a decision-making process carried out on texts by readers. To say we are forced to choose or decide, or that we are unable to do so, is to locate the problem of undecidability falsely within ourselves, rather than recognizing that it is an intrinsic feature of the text.

Undecidability is thus different from ambiguity, as understood by formalists. Formalists believed that a complete understanding of a literary work is possible, an understanding in which ambiguities will be resolved objectively by the reader, even if only in the sense that they will be shown to have definite, meaningful functions. Deconstructors do not share that belief. They do not accept the formalist view that a work of literary art is demonstrably unified from beginning to end, in one certain way, or that it is organized around a single center that ultimately can be identified and defined. Neither do they accept the concept of irony as simply saying one thing and meaning another thing that will be understood with certainty by the reader. As a result, deconstructors tend to see texts as more radically heterogeneous than do formalists. The formalist critic ultimately makes sense of ambiguity; undecidability, by contrast, is never reduced, let alone mastered by deconstructive reading, although the incompatible possibilities between which it is impossible to decide can be identified with certainty.

For critics practicing deconstruction, a literary text is neither a sphere with a center nor an unbroken line with a definite beginning and end. In fact, many assumptions about the nature of texts have been put in question by deconstruction, which in Derrida's words "dislocates the borders, the framing of texts, everything which should preserve their immanence and make possible an internal reading or merely reading in the classical sense of the term" ("Some Statements" 86). A text consists of words inscribed in and inextricable from the myriad discourses that inform it; from the point of view of deconstruction, the boundaries between any given text and that larger text we call language are always shifting.

It was that larger text that Derrida was referring to when he made his famous statement "*there is nothing outside the text*" (*Grammatology* 158). To understand what Derrida meant by that statement, consider the following: we know the world through language, and the acts and practices that constitute that "real world" (the Oklahoma City bombing, the decision to marry) are inseparable from the discourses out of which they arise and as open to interpretation as any work of literature. Derrida is not alone in deconstructing the world/text opposition. De Man viewed language as something that has great power in individual, social, and political life. Geoffrey Hartman, who was closely associated with deconstruction during the 1970s, wrote that "nothing can lift us out of language" (xii).

Once we understand deconstruction's view of the literary text—as words that are part of and that resonate with an immense linguistic structure in which we live and move and have our being—we are in a better position to understand why deconstructors reach points in their readings at which they reveal, but cannot decide between, incompatible interpretive possibilities. A text is not a unique, hermetically sealed space. Perpetually open to being seen in the light of new contexts, any given text has the potential to be different each time it is read. Furthermore, as Miller has shown in *Ariadne's Thread: Story Lines* (1992), the various "terms" and "famil[ies] of terms" we use in performing our readings invariably affect the results. Whether we choose to focus on a novel's characters or its realism, for instance, leads us to different views of the same text. "No one thread," Miller asserts, "can be followed to a central point where it provides a means of overseeing, controlling, and understanding the whole" (21).

Complicating matters still further is the fact that the individual words making up narratives—the words out of which we make our mental picture of a character or place—usually have several (and often have conflicting) meanings due to the complex histories of their usage. (If your professor tells the class that you have written a "fulsome report" and you look up the word *fulsome* in a contemporary dictionary, you will learn that it can mean either "elaborate" or "offensive"; if, for some reason, you don't know what *offensive* means, you will find out that it can equally well describe your favorite quarterback and a racist joke.) "Each word," as Miller puts it, "inheres in a labyrinth of branching interverbal relationships"; often there are "forks in the etymological line leading to bifurcated or trifurcated roots." Deconstructors often turn to etymology, not to help them decide whether a statement means this or that, but rather as a way of revealing the coincidence of several meanings in the same text. "The effect of etymological retracing," Miller writes, "is not to ground the work solidly but to render it unstable, equivocal, wavering, groundless" (*Ariadne* 19).

Deconstruction is not really interpretation, the act of choosing between or among possible meanings. Derrida has glossed de Man's statement that "there is no need to deconstruct Rousseau" by saying that "this was another way of saying: there is always already deconstruction, at work *in* works, especially *literary* works. It cannot be applied, after the fact and from outside, as a technical instrument. Texts deconstruct *themselves* by themselves" (Derrida, *Memoires* 123). If deconstruction is not interpretation, then what is it? Deconstruction may be defined as reading, as long as reading is defined as de Man defined it—as a process involving moments of what he called *aporia* or terminal uncertainty, and as an act performed with full knowledge of the fact that all texts are ultimately unreadable (if reading means reducing a text to a single, homogeneous meaning). Miller explains unreadability by saying that although there are moments of great lucidity in reading, each "lucidity will in principle contain its own blind spot requiring a further elucidation and exposure of error, and so on, ad infinitum. . . . One should not underestimate, however, the productive illumination produced as one moves through these various stages of reading" (*Ethics* 42, 44).

Miller's point is important because, in a sense, it deconstructs or erases the boundary between the readings of deconstructors and the interpretations of more traditional critics. It suggests that all kinds of critics have had their moments of lucidity; it also suggests that critics practicing deconstruction know that their *own* insights—even their insights into what is or isn't contradictory, undecidable, or unreadable in a text—are hardly the last word. As Art Berman writes, "In *Blindness and Insight* de Man demonstrates that the apparently well-reasoned arguments of literary critics contain contradiction at their core; yet there is no alternative path to insight. . . . The readers of criticism recognize the blindness of their predecessors, reorganize it, and thereby gain both the insight of the critics and a knowledge of the contradiction that brings forth insight. Each reader, of course, has his own blindness; and the criticism of criticism is not a matter of rectifying someone else's mistakes" (Berman 239–40).

When de Man spoke of the resistance to theory he referred generally to the antitheoretical bias in literary studies. But he might as well have been speaking specifically of the resistance to deconstruction, as expressed not only in academic books and journals but also in popular magazines such as *Newsweek*. Attacks on deconstruction became more common and more personal some four years after de Man's death in

1983. That was the year that a Belgian scholar working on a doctoral thesis discovered ninety-two articles that de Man had written during World War II for the Brussels newspaper *Le Soir*, a widely read French-language daily that had fallen under Nazi control during the German occupation of Belgium. Ultimately, one hundred and seventy articles by de Man were found in *Le Soir*; another ten were discovered in *Het Vlaamsche Land*, a collaborationist newspaper published in Flemish. These writings, which date from 1941 (when de Man was twenty-one years old), ceased to appear before 1943, by which time it had become clear to most Belgians that Jews were being shipped to death camps such as Auschwitz.

De Man's wartime journalism consists mainly, but not entirely, of inoffensive literary pieces. In one article de Man takes Germany's triumph in World War II as a given, places the German people at the center of Western civilization, and foresees a mystical era involving suffering but also faith, exaltation, and rapture. In another article, entitled *"Les Juifs dans la littérature actuelle"* ["Jews in Present-day Literature"], de Man scoffs at the notion that Jewish writers have significantly influenced the literature of his day and, worse, considers the merits of creating a separate Jewish colony that would be isolated from Europe.

No one who had known de Man since his immigration to the United States in 1948 had found him to be illiberal or anti-Semitic. Furthermore, de Man had spent his career in the United States de-mystifying or, as he would have said, "debunking" the kind of ideo-logical assumptions (about the relationship between aesthetics and national cultures) that lie behind his most offensive Belgian newspaper writings. The critic who in *The Resistance to Theory* (1986) argued that literature must not become "a substitute for theology, ethics, etc." (de Man 24) had either changed radically since writing of the magical integrity and wholeness of the German nation and its culture or had not deeply believed what he had written as a young journalist.

These points have been made in various ways by de Man's former friends and colleagues. Geoffrey Hartman has said that de Man's later work, the work we associate with deconstruction, "looks like a belated, but still powerful, act of conscience" (26–31). Derrida, who like Hartman is a Jew, has read carefully de Man's wartime discourse, showing it to be "split, disjointed, engaged in incessant conflicts" (Hamacher, Hertz, and Keenan 135). "On the one hand," Derrida finds *"unpardonable"* de Man's suggestion that a separate Jewish colony be set up; "on the other hand," he notes that of the four writers de Man praises in the same article (André Gide, Franz Kafka, D. H. Lawrence, and Ernest Hemingway), not one was German, one (Kafka) *was* Jewish, and all four "represent everything that Nazism . . . would have liked to extirpate from history and the great tradition" (Hamacher, Hertz, and Keenan 145).

While friends asserted that some of de Man's statements were unpardonable, deconstruction's severest critics tried to use a young man's sometimes deplorable statements as evidence that a whole critical movement was somehow morally as well as intellectually flawed. As Andrej Warminski summed it up, "the 'discovery' of the 1941–42 writings is being used to perpetuate the old myths about so-called 'deconstruction'" (Hamacher, Hertz, and Keenan 389). Knowing what some of those myths are—and why, in fact, they *are* myths—aids our understanding in an indirect, contrapuntal way that is in keeping with the spirit of deconstruction.

In his book *The Ethics of Reading* (1987), Miller refutes two notions commonly repeated by deconstruction's detractors. One is the idea that deconstructors believe a text means nothing in the sense that it means whatever the playful reader *wants* it to mean. The other is the idea that deconstruction is "immoral" insofar as it refuses to view literature in the way it has traditionally been viewed, namely, "as the foundation and embodiment, the means of preserving and transmitting, the basic humanistic values of our culture" (9). Responding to the first notion, Miller points out that neither Derrida nor de Man "has ever asserted the freedom of the reader to make the text mean anything he or she wants it to mean. Each has in fact asserted the reverse" (10). As for the second notion—that deconstructors are guilty of shirking an ethical responsibility because their purpose is not to (re)discover and (re)assert the transcendent and timeless values contained in great books— Miller argues that "this line of thought" rests "on a basic misunderstanding of the way the ethical moment enters into the act of reading" (9). That "ethical moment," Miller goes on to argue, "is not a matter of response to a thematic content asserting this or that idea about morality. It is a much more fundamental 'I must' responding to the language of literature in itself. . . . Deconstruction is nothing more or less than good reading as such" (9–10). Reading itself, in other words, is an act that leads to further ethical acts, decisions, and behaviors in a real world involving relations to other people and to society at large. For these, the reader must take responsibility, as for any other ethical act.

A third commonly voiced objection to deconstruction is to its playfulness, to the evident pleasure its practitioners take in teasing out all the contradictory interpretive possibilities generated by the words in a text, their complex etymologies and contexts, and their potential to be read figuratively or even ironically. Certainly, playfulness and pleasure are aspects of deconstruction. In his book *The Post Card* (1987), Derrida specifically associates deconstruction with pleasure; in an interview published in a collection of his essays entitled *Acts of Literature* (1992), he speculates that "it is perhaps this *jouissance* which most irritates the all-out adversaries of deconstruction" (56). But such adversaries misread deconstruction's "jouissance," its pleasurable playfulness. Whereas they see it as evidence that deconstructors view texts as tightly enclosed fields on which they can play delightfully useless little word games, Derrida has said that the "subtle and intense pleasure" of deconstruction arises from the "dismantl[ing]" of repressive assumptions, representations, and ideas—in short, from the "lifting of repression" (*Acts* 56–57). As Gregory S. Jay explains in his book *America the Scrivener: Deconstruction and the Subject of Literary History* (1990), "Deconstruction has been not only a matter of reversing binary oppositions but also a matter of disabling the hierarchy of values they enable and of speculating on alternative modes of knowing and of acting" (xii).

Far from viewing literature as a word-playground, Derrida, in Derek Attridge's words, "emphasizes . . . literature as an institution," one "not given in nature or the brain but brought into being by processes that are social, legal, and political, and that can be mapped historically and geographically" (*Acts* 23). By thus characterizing Derrida's emphasis, Attridge counters the commonest of the charges that have been leveled at deconstructors, namely, that they divorce literary texts from historical, political, and legal institutions.

In *Memoires for Paul de Man* (1986), Derrida argues that, where history is concerned, "deconstructive discourses" have pointedly and effectively questioned "the classical assurances of history, the genealogical narrative, and periodizations of all sorts" (15)—in other words, the tendency of historians to view the past as the source of (lost) truth and value, to look for explanations in origins, and to view as unified epochs (for example, the Victorian period, 1837–1901) what are in fact complex and heterogeneous times in history. As for politics, Derrida points out that de Man invariably "says something about institutional structures and the political stakes of hermeneutic conflicts," which is to say that de Man's commentaries acknowledge that conflicting interpretations reflect and are reflected in the politics of institutions (such as the North American university).

In addition to history and politics, the law has been a subject on which deconstruction has had much to say of late. In an essay on Franz Kafka's story "Before the Law," Derrida has shown that for Kafka the law as such exists but can never be confronted by those who would do so and fulfill its commands. Miller has pointed out that the law "may only be confronted in its delegates or representatives or by its effects on us or others" (*Ethics* 20). What or where, then, is the law itself? The law's presence, Miller suggests, is continually deferred by narrative, that is, writing about or on the law which constantly reinterprets the law in the attempt to reveal what it really is and means. This very act of (re)interpretation, however, serves to "defer" or distance the law even further from the case at hand, since the (re)interpretation takes precedence (and assumes prominence) over the law itself. (As Miller defines it, narrative would include everything from a Victorian novel that promises to reveal moral law to the opinion of a Supreme Court justice regarding the constitutionality of a given action, however different these two documents are in the conventions they follow and the uses to which they are put.) Miller likens the law to a promise, "the validity of [which] does not lie in itself but in its future fulfillment," and to a story "divided against itself" that in the end "leaves its readers . . . still in expectation" (*Ethics* 33).

Because the facts about deconstruction are very different from the myth of its playful irreverence and irrelevance, a number of contemporary thinkers have found it useful to adapt and apply deconstruction in their work. For instance, a deconstructive theology has been developed. Architects have designed and built buildings grounded, as it were, in deconstructive architectural theory. In the area of law, the Critical Legal Studies movement has, in Christopher Norris's words, effectively used "deconstructive thinking" of the kind de Man used in analyzing Rousseau's *Social Contract* "to point up the blind spots, conflicts, and antinomies that plague the discourse of received legal wisdom." Critical legal theorists have debunked "the formalist view of law," that is, the "view which holds law to be a system of neutral precepts and principles," showing instead how the law "gives rise to various disabling contradictions," such as "the problematic distinction between 'private' and 'public' domains." They have turned deconstruction into "a sophisticated means of making the point that all legal discourse is performative in character, i.e., designed to secure assent through its rhetorical power to convince or persuade" (Norris, *Deconstruction and the Interests* 17). Courtroom persuasion, Gerald

Lopez has argued in a 1989 article in the *Michigan Law Review*, consists of storytelling as much as argument (Clayton 13).

In the field of literary studies, the influence of deconstruction may be seen in the work of critics ostensibly taking some other, more political approach. Barbara Johnson has put deconstruction to work for the feminist cause. She and Shoshana Felman have argued that chief among those binary oppositions "based on repression of differences with entities" is the opposition man/woman (Johnson, *Critical* x). In a reading of the "undecidability" of "femininity" in Balzac's story "The Girl with the Golden Eyes," Felman puts it this way: "the rhetorical hierarchization of the . . . opposition between the sexes is . . . such that woman's *difference* is suppressed, being totally subsumed by the reference of the feminine to masculine identity" ("Rereading" 25).

Elsewhere, Johnson, Felman, and Gayatri Spivak have combined Derrida's theories with the psychoanalytic theory of Jacques Lacan to analyze the way in which gender and sexuality are ultimately textual, grounded in language and rhetoric. In an essay on Edmund Wilson's reading of Henry James's story *The Turn of the Screw*, Felman has treated sexuality as a form of rhetoric that can be deconstructed, shown to contain contradictions and ambiguities that more traditional readings of sexuality have masked. Gay and lesbian critics have seen the positive implications of this kind of analysis, hence Eve Kosofsky Sedgwick's admission in the early pages of her book *Epistemology of the Closet* (1990): "One main strand of argument in this book is deconstructive, in a fairly specific sense. The analytic move it makes is to demonstrate that categories presented in a culture as symmetrical binary oppositions . . . actually subsist in a more unsettled and dynamic tacit relation" (9–10).

In telling "The Story of Deconstruction" in his book on contemporary American literature and theory, Jay Clayton assesses the current status of this unique approach. Although he notes how frequently deconstructive critics have been cited for their lack of political engagement, he concludes that deconstruction, "a movement accused of formalism and arid intellectualism, participates in the political turn of contemporary culture" (34). He suggests that what began as theory in the late 1960s and 1970s has, over time, developed into a method employed by critics taking a wide range of approaches to literature— ethnic, feminist, new historicist, Marxist—in addition to critics outside of literary studies per se who are involved in such areas as Critical Legal Studies and Critical Race Theory, which seeks to "sustain a complementary relationship between the deconstructive energies of

Critical Legal Studies and the constructive energies of civil rights activism" (58).

Clayton cites the work of Edward Said as a case in point. Through 1975, the year that his *Beginnings: Intention and Method* was published, Said was employing a form of deconstructive criticism that, in Clayton's words, emphasized the "power" of texts "to initiate projects in the real world" (45–46). Said became identified with cultural and postcolonial criticism, however, beginning in 1978 with the publication of his book *Orientalism*, in which he deconstructs the East/West, Orient/Occident opposition. Said argues that Eastern and Middle Eastern peoples have for centuries been stereotyped by the Western discourses of "orientalism," a textuality that in no way reflects the diversity and differences that exist among the peoples it claims to represent. According to Said, that stereotyping not only facilitated the colonization of vast areas of the globe by the so-called West but also still governs, to a great extent, relations with the Arab and the so-called Eastern world. The expansion of Said's field of vision to include not just literary texts but international relations is powerfully indicative of the expanding role that deconstruction currently plays in developing contemporary understandings of politics and culture, as well as in active attempts to intervene in these fields.

Jacques Derrida, the theorist most closely associated with deconstruction, begins the essay that follows, entitled "Ulysses Gramophone" with "*Oui*," a French word that might seem to "quote" or "translate" the last word of Joyce's *Ulysses*. But "*oui*," Derrida suggests in this article written in French and translated by Tina Kendall, may itself be untranslatable. Indeed, Derrida goes on to suggest that *all* words, indeed all languages, defy translation: "according to a distinction I have hazarded elsewhere concerning history and the name of Babel," Derrida writes, "what remains *untranslatable* is at bottom the only thing *to translate*, the only thing *translatable*. What must be translated (*l'à-traduire*) of that which is translatable (*traductible*) can only be the untranslatable (*intraduisible*)."

Having undercut the possibility of writing in French about a novel written in English, and having done so via a characteristically paradoxical statement that seems to equate opposite terms, Derrida subsequently suggests that the slippery associations involved in translation also pertain to "all the genealogical chances that set afloat the notion of legitimate consanguinity in *Ulysses* and no doubt elsewhere." By this he presumably means that when we identify ourselves via our biological lineage or "family tree," or through names determinable due to patriarchal naming practices that conceal more associations than they reveal, we define ourselves via connections at least as questionable and open to contradiction as those between words and their supposed, closest relatives in another language. In *Ulysses*, the encounter between Leopold Bloom and Stephen Dedalus raises questions about whether it is biology and a shared name that makes a relationship paternal or filial, or whether it can be some other connection—involving sympathy, understanding, or shared qualities, for instance.

Derrida then proceeds, via a long digression on lakes, dice, Tokio (in the news in *Ulysses* because of the Russo-Japanese war), and Tokyo (where Derrida says he began writing his essay and shopped for postcards) by applying arguments he made in his book *La Carte Postale* (*The Post Card*) to Joyce's views on published texts. Joyce, Derrida recalls, "speaks of the equivalence of a postcard and a publication," suggesting that both constitute an "open text," an "exhibited surface, . . . an open letter." *Ulysses*, Derrida points out, contains a "trace," or "relay," of this view of the postcard as an "open text"; we can, for instance, follow a "narrative path" that leads from Mr. Reggy Wylie's postcard to Gerty MacDowell to Leopold Bloom's unaddressed postcard to Flynn to the letter Bloom is looking for when he remembers the unaddressed postcard.

For Derrida, that path also leads to the idea of a postcard addressed to a fictitious recipient and bearing no message (*correspondence*), an idea suggested in *Ulysses* by the passage in which a sailor shows Bloom a postcard bearing "a group of savage women in striped loincloths" on one side and only an address on the other. Derrida views *Ulysses* itself as an unaddressed postcard, an open text. Any reader—for it has no addressee—can follow any of an infinite number of paths, or "correspondences," through the novel, much as Homer's Odysseus moved from adventure to adventure. The reader of *Ulysses*, like Odysseus, is an "autobiographic-encyclopedic navigator," which is to say that his or her understanding stems from patterns of association grounded in personal autobiographical (including literary) experience.

Every reader of Joyce's novel is, in a sense, like Derrida, who began his essay on *Ulysses* while in Tokyo looking for postcards, who therefore could hardly help noticing the word Tokio in Joyce's novel, and who subsequently began tracking the correspondences suggested by this noncorrespondence. Every reader of *Ulysses* is also like the reader of Derrida's essay, which is itself "a postcard cast to sea" with no particular addressee or address; that is, the individual members of this essay's audience will follow different traces or tracks through its intentionally meandering argument, full of cross-references and occasions for interpretive "translation," "transfers," and "crossovers" (to use a few of Derrida's recurring terms).

Although it runs against the grain of deconstruction to call any reading "typical of deconstruction" or "typically Derridean," several features of Derrida's essay on Joyce can be traced back to his earlier work. He repeats (albeit with the inevitable *différance*) critical moves made in earlier readings when he indulges in creative wordplay, utilizes false etymologies that nonetheless lead down intellectually stimulating paths, and embeds Joyce's fiction in an autobiographical narrative. By contextualizing *Ulysses* in a story of his own travels from Ithaca (New York) to Oxford (Ohio) to Tokyo, Derrida gives his reading of the novel the metafictional status of a story about—in the double sense of "based on" and "around"—Joyce's story.

In this essay, originally given as an address in French to an audience of Joyce scholars gathered in Frankfurt, Germany, Derrida makes other moves consistent with the strategies of deconstruction. By showing the labyrinthine quality of writing—not just in Joyce's *Ulysses* but in the general text of literature and language in which it participates—he "undermines" the concept of linguistic (and scholarly) "competence" on which learned societies rest. (In Derrida's view, linguistic competence is illusory due to the collapsible nature of the signifier / signified distinction and the fact that each person has his or her own personal, idiosyncratic, associational flows that make any utterance or text untranslatable.) Via a complex discussion of telephones, of the "telephonic 'yes'" or *oui* with which we typically reassure interlocutors that what they have thought and said has been reproduced and "heard" (that is, listened to and understood) at our end of the line, and of what he calls "telephonic spacing" in the text of *Ulysses*, Derrida shows how a scene in the novel involving a professor, a telephone, and Bloom's voice "crosses all the lines in our network, the paradoxes of competence and institution, represented here in the shape of the professor." Subsequently returning to the suspect subjects of genealogy and familial legitimacy raised earlier, Derrida playfully admits to having felt intimidated by the invitation to speak about *Ulysses* in front of Joyce experts—with what, he suggests, will surely be deemed "incompetence"—but also flattered by the opportunity "to be part of this mighty family," to achieve the "legitimation so generously offered."

At several points in "Ulysses Gramophone," Derrida deconstructs the speech/writing opposition and the privilege granted speech over writing in Western metaphysics. He does so in a discussion of his essay's rejected title, which involved a play on *oui* ("yes") and *ouï* ("hear" in the composite word meaning "hearsay"). (The distinction between *oui* and *ouï* is easier to see than to hear, a fact that contradicts the valuative speech-over-writing hierarchy.) Later, Derrida interrogates the privilege granted speech over writing when he says that "The final 'Yes,' the last word, the eschatology of the book, gives itself up only to *reading*, since it distinguishes itself from the others by an inaudible capital letter; what also remains equally inaudible, although visible, is the lateral incorporation of *yes* in *eyes*. Languages of eyes, of ayes." Through the subsequent analysis of a scene involving a typewriter, telephone, and the repeated word "Yes," Derrida refers to a "gramophony" inscribed in *Ulysses*, a speech/writing that "responds, of course, to the dream of a reproduction which *preserves* as its truth the living *yes*, archived into the very quick of the voice" but that "gives way to the possibility of parody, of a *yes* technique that persecutes the most spontaneous, the most giving desire of the *yes*."

                                                                Ross C Murfin

DECONSTRUCTION:
A SELECTED BIBLIOGRAPHY

Writings on Deconstruction

Arac, Jonathan, Wlad Godzich, and Wallace Martin, eds. *The Yale Critics: Deconstruction in America*. Minneapolis: U of Minnesota P, 1983. See especially the essays by Bové, Godzich, Pease, and Corngold.

Berman, Art. *From the New Criticism to Deconstruction: The Reception of Structuralism and Post-Structuralism*. Urbana: U of Illinois P, 1988.

Butler, Christopher. *Interpretation, Deconstruction, and Ideology: An Introduction to Some Current Issues in Literary Theory*. Oxford: Oxford UP, 1984.

Clayton, Jay. *The Pleasure of Babel: Contemporary American Literature and Theory*. New York: Oxford UP, 1993.

Culler, Jonathan. *On Deconstruction: Theory and Criticism After Structuralism*. Ithaca: Cornell UP, 1982.

———. *Structuralist Poetics: Structuralism, Linguistics, and the Study of Literature*. Ithaca: Cornell UP, 1975. See especially ch. 10.

Esch, Deborah. "Deconstruction." *Redrawing the Boundaries: The Transformation of English and American Literary Studies*. Ed. Stephen Greenblatt and Giles Gunn. New York: MLA, 1992. 374–91.

Feminist Studies 14 (1988). Special issue on deconstruction and feminism.

Hamacher, Werner, Neil Hertz, and Thomas Keenan. *Responses: On Paul de Man's Wartime Journalism*. Lincoln: U of Nebraska P, 1989.

Hartman, Geoffrey. "Blindness and Insight." *The New Republic*, 7 Mar. 1988.

Jay, Gregory S. *America the Scrivener: Deconstruction and the Subject of Literary History*. Ithaca: Cornell UP, 1990.

Leitch, Vincent B. *American Literary Criticism from the Thirties to the Eighties*. New York: Columbia UP, 1988. See especially ch. 10, "Deconstructive Criticism."

———. *Cultural Criticism, Literary Theory, Poststructuralism*. New York: Columbia UP, 1992.

Loesberg, Jonathan. *Aestheticism and Deconstruction: Pater, Derrida, and de Man*. Princeton: Princeton UP, 1991.

Melville, Stephen W. *Philosophy Beside Itself: On Deconstruction and Modernism*. Theory and History of Lit. 27. Minneapolis: U of Minnesota P, 1986.

Norris, Christopher. *Deconstruction and the Interests of Theory*. Oklahoma Project for Discourse and Theory 4. Norman: U of Oklahoma P, 1989.

———. *Deconstruction: Theory and Practice*. London: Methuen, 1982. Rev. ed. London: Routledge, 1991.

———. *Paul de Man, Deconstruction and the Critique of Aesthetic Ideology*. New York: Routledge, 1988.

Weber, Samuel. *Institution and Interpretation*. Minneapolis: U of Minnesota P, 1987.

Works by de Man, Derrida, and Miller

de Man, Paul. *Allegories of Reading*. New Haven: Yale UP, 1979. See especially ch. 1, "Semiology and Rhetoric," and ch. 7, "Metaphor (Second Discourse)."

———. *Blindness and Insight*. New York: Oxford UP, 1971. Minneapolis: U of Minnesota P, 1983. The 1983 edition contains important essays not included in the original edition. See especially "Rhetoric of Temporality."

———. "Phenomenality and Materiality in Kant." *Hermeneutics: Questions and Prospects.* Ed. Gary Shapiro and Alan Sica. Amherst: U of Massachusetts P, 1984. 121–44.

———. *The Resistance to Theory.* Minneapolis: U of Minnesota P, 1986.

———. *Romanticism and Contemporary Culture.* Ed. E. S. Burt, Kevin Newmarkj, and Andrzej Warminski. Baltimore: Johns Hopkins UP, 1993.

———. *Wartime Journalism, 1939–1943.* Lincoln: U of Nebraska P, 1989.

Derrida, Jacques. *Acts of Literature.* Ed. Derek Attridge. New York: Routledge, 1992.

———. "Différance." *Speech and Phenomena.* Trans. David B. Alison. Evanston: Northwestern UP, 1973.

———. *Dissemination.* 1972. Trans. Barbara Johnson. Chicago: U of Chicago P, 1981. See especially the concise, incisive "Translator's Introduction," which provides a useful point of entry into this work and others by Derrida.

———. "Force of Law: The 'Mystical Foundation of Authority.'" Trans. Mary Quaintance. *Deconstruction and the Possibility of Justice.* Ed. Drucilla Cornell, Michel Rosenfeld, and David Gray Carlson. New York: Routledge, 1992. 3–67.

———. *Given Time. 1, Counterfeit Money.* Trans. Peggy Kamuf. Chicago: U of Chicago P, 1992.

———. *Margins of Philosophy.* Trans. Alan Bass. Chicago: U of Chicago P, 1982. Contains the essay "White Mythology: Metaphor in the Text of Philosophy."

———. *Memoires for Paul de Man.* Wellek Library Lectures. Trans. Cecile Lindsay, Jonathan Culler, and Eduardo Cadava. New York: Columbia UP, 1986.

———. *Of Grammatology.* Trans. Gayatri C. Spivak. Baltimore: Johns Hopkins UP, 1976. Trans. of *De la grammatologie.* 1967.

———. "Passions." *Derrida: A Critical Reader.* Ed. David Wood. Cambridge: Basil Blackwell, 1992.

———. *The Post Card: From Socrates to Freud and Beyond.* Trans. with intro. Alan Bass. Chicago: U of Chicago P, 1987.

———. "Some Statements and Truisms about Neo-logisms, Newisms, Postisms, and Other Small Seisisms." *The States of "Theory."* New York: Columbia UP, 1990. 63–94.

———. *Specters of Marx.* Trans. Peggy Kamuf. New York: Routledge, 1994.

———. *Writing and Difference.* 1967. Trans. Alan Bass. Chicago: U of Chicago P, 1978.

Miller, J. Hillis. *Ariadne's Thread: Story Lines.* New Haven: Yale UP, 1992.

———. *The Ethics of Reading: Kant, de Man, Eliot, Trollope, James, and Benjamin.* New York: Columbia UP, 1987.

———. *Fiction and Repetition: Seven English Novels.* Cambridge: Harvard UP, 1982.

———. *Hawthorne and History: Defacing It.* Cambridge: Basil Blackwell, 1991. Contains a bibliography of Miller's work from 1955 to 1990.

———. *Illustrations.* Cambridge: Harvard UP, 1992.

———. "Stevens' Rock and Criticism as Cure." *Georgia Review* 30 (1976): 3–31, 330–48.

———. *Typographies.* Stanford: Stanford UP, 1994.

———. *Versions of Pygmalion.* Cambridge: Harvard UP, 1990.

Essays on Deconstruction and Poststructuralism

Barthes, Roland. *S/Z.* Trans. Richard Miller. New York: Hill, 1974. In this influential work, Barthes turns from a structuralist to a poststructuralist approach.

Benstock, Shari. *Textualizing the Feminine: On the Limits of Genre.* Norman: U of Oklahoma P, 1991.

Bloom, Harold, et al., eds. *Deconstruction and Criticism.* New York: Seabury, 1979. Includes essays by Bloom, de Man, Derrida, Miller, and Hartman.

Chase, Cynthia. *Decomposing Figures.* Baltimore: Johns Hopkins UP, 1986.

Cohen, Tom. *Anti-Mimesis: From Plato to Hitchcock.* Cambridge: Cambridge UP, 1994.

Elam, Diane. *Feminism and Deconstruction: Ms. en Abyme.* New York: Routledge, 1994.

Felman, Shoshana. "Rereading Femininity." Special Issue on "Feminist Readings: French Texts/American Contexts," *Yale French Studies* 62 (1981): 19–44.

———. "Turning the Screw of Interpretation." *Literature and Psychoanalysis: The Question of Reading: Otherwise.* Special issue, *Yale French Studies* 55–56 (1978): 3–508. Baltimore: Johns Hopkins UP, 1982.

Harari, Josué, ed. *Textual Strategies: Perspectives in Post-Structuralist Criticism.* Ithaca: Cornell UP, 1979.

Johnson, Barbara. *The Critical Difference: Essays in the Contemporary Rhetoric of Reading.* Baltimore: Johns Hopkins UP, 1980.

———. *A World of Difference.* Baltimore: Johns Hopkins UP, 1987.

Krupnick, Mark, ed. *Displacement: Derrida and After.* Bloomington: Indiana UP, 1987.

Meese, Elizabeth, and Alice Parker, eds. *The Difference Within: Feminism and Critical Theory.* Philadelphia: John Benjamins, 1989.

Sedgwick, Eve Kosofsky. *Epistemology of the Closet.* Berkeley: U of California P, 1990.

Ulmer, Gregory L. *Applied Grammatology.* Baltimore: Johns Hopkins UP, 1985.

———. *Teletheory: Grammatology in the Age of Video.* New York: Routledge, 1989.

Poststructuralist Approaches to Joyce

Attridge, Derek. "Criticism's Wake." *James Joyce: The Augmented Ninth.* Ed. Bernard Benstock. Syracuse: Syracuse UP, 1988.

Attridge, Derek, and Daniel Ferrer, eds. *Post-structuralist Joyce: Essays from the French.* Cambridge: Cambridge UP, 1984.

Boheemen-Saaf, Christine van. "Deconstruction after Joyce." *New Alliances in Joyce Studies.* Ed. Bonnie Kime Scott. Newark: U of Delaware P, 1988. 29–36.

Cixous, Hélène. *The Exile of James Joyce.* Trans. Sally A. J. Purcell. New York: David Lewis, 1972.

Eco, Umberto. *The Aesthetics of Chaosmos: The Middle Ages of James Joyce.* Trans. Ellen Esrock. Tulsa: U of Tulsa, 1982.

Kristeva, Julia. *Desire in Language.* Ed. Leon S. Roudiez. Trans. Thomas Gora, Alice Jardine, and Leon S. Roudiez. New York: Columbia UP, 1980.

Lernout, Geert. *The French Joyce.* Ann Arbor: U of Michigan P, 1990.

MacCabe, Colin. *James Joyce and the Revolution of the Word.* London: Macmillan, 1978.

Norris, Margot. *The Decentered Universe of "Finnegans Wake."* Baltimore: Johns Hopkins UP, 1976.

Roughley, Alan. *James Joyce and Critical Theory: An Introduction.* London: Harvester, 1991.

A DECONSTRUCTIVE PERSPECTIVE

JACQUES DERRIDA

Ulysses Gramophone
Hear say yes in Joyce[1]

Oui Oui, you are receiving me, these are French words.[2]
To be sure, and I do not even need to reinforce my message with
another phrase, all you need is to have heard the first word, *oui*, to
know, that is if you understand enough French, that, thanks to the authorization graciously bestowed on me by the organizers of this James
Joyce Symposium, I shall address you, more or less, in the language
presumed to be mine (*ma langue supposée*), though the last expression
can be almost seen as an anglicism.

But can *oui* be quoted or translated? This is one of the questions I
intend (*j'entends*) to pose during this talk. How can the sentences that
I have just thrown out at you be translated? The one I began with, just
as Molly begins and ends what is too lightly referred to as her monologue, that is, the repetition of a *oui*, is not content just to *mention*, it
uses in its own way these two *ouis*, the ones that I now quote. In my
opening, you could not decide and you are still incapable of deciding
if I was saying *oui* or quoting, or shall we say more generally, if I was
mentioning the word *oui* twice, as a reminder, and I quote, that these
are indeed French words.

In the first case, I affirm, acquiesce, subscribe to, approve, reply, or
make a promise; at any rate, I agree to something and I sign: to take
up again the old *speech act theory* distinction, which is useful up to a
certain point, between *use* and *mention*, the usage of *oui* is always at
least implied when signing takes place.

In the second case, I would rather have quoted or mentioned the
oui, oui. Now if the act of quoting or mentioning also undoubtedly presupposes some signature, some confirmation of the act of mentioning,

---

[1]This text was translated by Tina Kendall, with emendations by Shari Benstock. All
Ulysses quotations are taken from the 1968 London Penguin edition. Footnotes marked
with the initials JD are from the original French text; additional explanatory notes for
the English text are by Shari Benstock and are marked with the initials SB. The footnotes have been renumbered by Margot Norris for this excerpted version of the essay.
[2]The French verb *entendre* includes in its range of meanings "to hear" and "to understand," both of which are implied in the translation "receiving." In its reflexive form
(*s'entendre*), a form also used in this essay, it means to hear each other, to understand
each other, to get along with each other. (SB)

this remains implicit and the implicit *oui* is not to be confused with the quoted or mentioned *oui*.

So you still do not know what I wanted to *say* or *do* when I began with this sentence, "*Oui, oui,* you are receiving me, these are French words." In fact you are not receiving me loud and clear at all.

I repeat the question: how will the sentences that I have just thrown out at you be translated? In so far as they mention or quote *oui,* they repeat the French word, and translation is, in principle, absurd or illegitimate: yes, yes, these are not French words. When at the end of *Discours de la Méthode,* Descartes explains why he had decided to write in the language of his country, the Latin translation of *Discours* simply omits this paragraph. What is the sense of writing a sentence in Latin, the gist of which is: the following reasons illustrate why I am now writing in French? It is true that the Latin translation was the only one violently to erase this affirmation of the French language. For it was not just one translation among many; it alleged, according to the laws of the philosophical society of the time, to bring *Discours de la Méthode* back to what should have been the true original in its true language. But we'll leave that for another lecture.[3] I simply wanted to mark that the affirmation of a language through itself is untranslatable. An act which in one language *remarks* the language itself, and which in this way affirms doubly, once by speaking it and once by saying that it has thus been spoken, opens up the space for a *re-marking,* which, at the same time and in the same double way, defies and calls for translation. According to a distinction I have hazarded elsewhere concerning history and the name of Babel, what remains *untranslatable* is at bottom the only thing *to translate,* the only thing *translatable.* What must be translated (*l'à-traduire*) of that which is translatable (*traductible*) can only be the untranslatable (*intraduisible*).

You have already realized that I have been preparing the ground to speak to you about *oui,* or at the very least, about some of the modalities of *oui,* and I should like to specify straightaway, as a kind of rough outline, that this is in some of the sequences in *Ulysses.*[4]

3To be published. (JD)

4The French verb *s'apprêter* (translated here as "preparing the ground," or, more literally, "preparing myself") is one of some two dozen verb forms used throughout the essay that, in their reflexivity, call attention to self-actions, where grammatically the subject and object of the verb are the same. Thus these verbs echo, underwrite, and call out two of Derrida's major concerns here: (1) the always already implicated affirmative of any statement (which, simultaneously internal and external to her, is articulated in Molly's double "yes"); and (2) the putting into question of the independent status of "subject" and "object," of "sender" and "receiver" in speech act theory. Primary among

To put an end, without further ado, to circulation or to an inter-minable circumnavigation, in order to avoid the aporia with a view to a better beginning, I threw myself in the water, as we say in French, and I decided to open myself, together with you, to a chance encounter.[5] With Joyce, luck is always taken in hand by the law, its sense and its agenda, using overdetermination of figures and ruses.[6] And yet the chance nature (*l'aléa*) of meetings, the randomness of coincidences lends itself to being affirmed, accepted, yes, even approved in all their occurrences. In all their occurrences, that is to say, in all the genealogi-cal chances that set afloat the notion of legitimate consanguinity in

these verbs are *se rappeler* ("to remember," "to recall," "to recollect"—more literally, to call again to oneself), *se lire* ("to read," "be read"—or "to read itself"), and *se donner* ("to give oneself up," "to devote oneself to," "to abandon oneself to"). When possible, the translation has been kept close to the implied self-action of the verb (as a reminder that the verb is calling to itself). The essay also explores the reciprocal nature of certain interchanges, sometimes exploiting simultaneously the reflexive and reciprocal elements in a single term. When it has not been possible to retain the reflexivity, the French verb has been placed in parentheses following the translation.

Derrida also uses a group of verbs whose prefixes suggest repetition, doubling, an action folding back on itself, notably: *retrouver* ("to re-find"), *rappeler* ("to re-call"), *ré-pondre* ("to re-spond," "to answer"), *revenir* ("to come back," "to come again"), *repar-ler* ("to speak again"), *raconter* ("to re-count," "to tell"). Again, it has not always been possible to retain the sense of this repeating and doubling through the translation. And the double sense of certain French words (*fils*, meaning both "son" and "threads") is sometimes lost in the English as are the resonating doubles of the French text, silently attesting to Derrida's argument that what remains "untranslatable" in that which is "translatable" is the only thing to "translate."

Also often lost in the English translation are repetitions of the same word through a variety of contexts, for example: *marquer, la marque; propre; appeler, interpeller; passage; traverser; mémoire; mémoriser; parasiter; correspondance*. (SB)

[5]The "chance encounter" here carries greater risk in French: *l'aléatoire d'une ren-contre*. The Latin, *alea*, translates into French as *un coup de dé* (the title of a Mallarmé text about which Derrida has written elsewhere; *un coup de dés* in English is translated by making the singular *dé* plural: a roll of the dice. Derrida plays on *un coup de dé* at every chance in this text (especially with other strokes of luck, taps and telephone calls, *un coup de téléphone*, or more forceful blows, *à coups de coudes*, elbowing one's way through). Often it has not been possible to retain in seemingly random occurrences. A cer-tain dependence upon luck, chance, and an uncertain outcome has become a game of "chance" in both languages (musically speaking, the "aleatory" are sound sequences played at random or by chance). *Aléa* translates into English as hazardous or risky, car-rying with it the risks of "chance." (SB)

[6]In French, this sentence is: *Avec Joyce, la chance est toujours ressaisie par la loi, le sens et le programme, selon la surdétermination des figures et des ruses*. The verb *ressaisir* means literally "to seize again" (carrying with it the juridical meaning of *saisir*— "a seizure") and to "take control." The English translation, "to take in hand," carries with it both "to seize authoritatively" and to supervise, instruct, control, direct. *Le sens* has multiple meanings (which echo here): "sense" (including in the "figural," which appears as "figures"), "meaning," "signification," "understanding," "direction," and "way." (SB)

Ulysses and no doubt elsewhere. This is all too clear in the encounter between Bloom and Stephen to which I shall return shortly.

To throw oneself in the water, I was saying. I was, to be specific, thinking of the water of a lake. But, knowing Joyce's word, you may have thought that I was referring to the bottle in the sea. But lakes were not so foreign to him, as I shall presently demonstrate.

The throw of the dice (*l'aléa*) to which I said *oui*, deciding in the same way to subject *you* to it too, I give the proper name — Tokyo.

Tokyo: does this city lie on the western circle that leads back to Dublin or to Ithaca?

An aimless wandering, a random trek (*la randonnée d'une "randomness"*) led me one day to the passage (Eumaeus, The Shelter, 1 A.M.) in the course of which Bloom names "the coincidence of meeting, discussion, dance, row, old salt, of the here today and gone tomorrow type, night loafers, the whole galaxy of events, all went to make up a miniature cameo of the world we live in" (*U*, 567). The "galaxy of events" was translated into French by "*gerbe des événements*," which omits the milk and therefore the milky tea that runs through (*irrigue*) *Ulysses*, turning it into a milky way or "galaxy." Allow me one more slight detour, a parenthesis: we were wondering what happens to the *yes* when it is repeated in a *mention* or in a quotation. But what happens when it becomes a trademark, a kind of nontransferable commercial license? And since we are spinning in the milk here, what happens when *yes* becomes, yes, a brand, or a brandname, of yoghurt? I shall come back to Ohio, this place marked in *Ulysses*. Now in Ohio there exists a type of Dannon yoghurt which is simply called *YES*. Underneath the *YES* legible on the lid, we find the slogan: "Bet You Can't Say No to Yes."

"Coincidence of meeting" declares the passage I was in the middle of quoting. A little later the name Tokyo crops up: suddenly, like a telegram or a newspaper heading, *The Telegraph*, which is to be found under Bloom's elbow, "as luck would have it" — as it says at the beginning of the paragraph.

The name Tokyo is associated with a battle. "Great battle Tokio." It is not Troy, but Tokyo, in 1904; the battle with internal Russia. Now, I was in Tokyo just over a month ago, and that is where I began writing this lecture — or rather, I began to dictate the main ideas into a pocket cassette recorder.

I decided to date it like this — and dating is signing — on the morning of 11 May when I was looking for postcards in a sort of news agency in the *basement* of the Okura Hotel. I was looking for postcards that would show Japanese lakes, or let's call them inland seas (*mers intérieures*). It had crossed my mind to follow the edges of lakes in *Ulysses*, to venture out on a grand lakeside tour between the lake of life which is the Mediterranean Sea and the *Lacus Mortis* referred to in the hospital scene, to be exact, and dominated by the symbol of the mother: "they came trooping to the sunken sea, *Lacus Mortis*. . . . Onward to the dead sea they tramp to drink" (*U*, 411). This is, in fact, what I had initially thought of for this lecture on *Ulysses*, to address (*adresser*), as you say in English, the postcard scene, rather the inverse of what I did in *La carte postale*, where I tried to restage the babelization of the postal system in *Finnegans Wake*. You will no doubt know better than I that the whole pack of postcards perhaps hints at the hypothesis that the geography of Ulysses' trips around the Mediterranean lake could have the structure of a postcard or a cartography of postal dispatches. This will gradually be illustrated, but for the moment I should like to take up a remark made by J. J. in which he speaks of the equivalence of a postcard and a publication. Any public piece of writing, any open text, is also offered like the exhibited surface, in no way private, of an open letter, and therefore of a postcard with its address incorporated in the message and hereafter open to doubt, and with its coded and at the same time stereotyped language, trivialized by the very code and number. Conversely, any postcard is a public document, deprived of all privacy and, moreover, in this way laying itself open to the law (*tombe sous le coup de la loi*). This is indeed what J. J. says: "—And moreover, says J. J. [they are not just any initials], a postcard is publication. It was held to be sufficient evidence of malice in the testcase Sadgrove *v*. Hole. In my opinion an action might lie" (*U*, 320). Translated: there would be cause for a certain action to be pursued before the law, to sue, but also that the action itself might lie.

The trace, the relay, of the postcard that we are following can be found in Mr. Reggy Wylie's postcard, "his silly postcard" that Gerty could tear "into a dozen pieces" (*U*, 360). Among others, there is also the "postcard to Flynn" that Bloom remembers, furthermore, having forgotten to address, which underlines the nature of anonymous publicity: a postcard has no proper addressee, apart from the person who acknowledges having received it with some inimitable signature. *Ulysses*, an immense postcard. "Mrs Marion. Did I forget to write the address on that letter like the postcard I sent to Flynn?" (*U*, 367). I refer to these postcards along a discursive path, or more precisely, along a narrative path, which I cannot always trace (*reconstituer*).

There is the ineluctable problem of method to which I shall return in a moment. The postcard without an address does not let itself be forgotten; it recalls itself to Bloom's memory just when he is looking for a misplaced letter: "Where did I put the letter? Yes, all right" (*U*, 365). We can assume that the reassuring "yes" accompanies and confirms the return of memory: the letter has been relocated (*le lieu de la lettre est retrouvé*). A little further, after Reggy's "silly postcard," there is the "silly letter": "Damned glad I didn't do it in the bath this morning over her silly I will punish you letter" (*U*, 366). Let us leave enough time for the bath fragrance to reach us. You could pursue the intensification of derision up to Molly's sarcastic remarks about the man Breen: "now [he's] going about in his slippers to look for £1000 for a postcard up up O Sweetheart May" (*U*, 665).

So I was in the middle of buying postcards in Tokyo, in an underground passage in the Hotel Okura. Now the sequence which, in telegraphic style, mentions the "Great Battle Tokio," after having recalled the "coincidence of meeting," the illegitimate genealogy and erratic seed that links Stephen to Bloom, "the galaxy of events," and so on, is a passage from another postcard. Not this time a postcard without an address but a messageless postcard (*une carte postale sans correspondance*). So one could say a postcard without a text, which could be reduced to the mere association of a picture and an address. Now it so happens that here the address is fictitious too. The addressee of this messageless card is a sort of fictitious reader. Before returning to this question, let us complete the "Tokyo" circle sequence, which I must quote. It follows closely from the extraordinary exchange between Bloom and Stephen on the subject of *belonging, l'appartenance*: "You suspect, Stephen retorted with a sort of half laugh, that I may be important because I belong to the *faubourg Saint Patrice* called Ireland for short" (*U*, 565).

"I would go a step farther, Mr Bloom insinuated" (the French translation, which renders "a step farther" as *un peu plus loin*, and which met the approval of J. J., who co-signed it, lacks among other things the association "stepfather," which superimposes at the bottom of all these genealogical fantasies, with their genetic crossovers and chance disseminations, a dream of legitimation through adoption, and the return of the son or, through marriage, with the daughter. But we can never tell who belongs to whom, what to whom, what to what, who to what. There is no subject of belonging, no more than there is an owner (*propriétaire*) of the postcard: it remains without any assigned addressee).

—But I suspect, Stephen interrupted, that Ireland must be important because it belongs to me.

—What belongs? queried Bloom, bending, fancying he was perhaps under some misapprehension. Excuse me. Unfortunately I didn't catch the latter portion. What was it you? . . .

Stephen speeds things up: "We can't change the country. Let us change the subject" (*U*, 565–66).

But going to Tokyo is not enough to change the country, let alone the language.

A little later, then; the return of the messageless postcard made out to a fictitious addressee. Bloom thinks of the aleatory encounters, the galaxy of events, and he dreams of writing, as I am doing here, of what happens to him, his story, "my experiences," as he puts it, and he wants to keep some kind of chronicle of this, a diary within a diary (*journal*) or a personal newspaper (*journal*), by making free associations without constraint. So here it is, we are drawing close to the postcard in the vicinity of Tokyo: "The coincidence of meeting . . . the whole galaxy of events . . . To improve the shining hour he wondered whether he might meet with anything approaching the same *luck* [my italics] as Mr Philip Beaufoy if taken down in writing. Supposing he were to pen something out of the common groove (as he fully intended doing) at the rate of one guinea per column, *My Experiences*, let us say, *in a Cabman's Shelter*" (*U*, 567).

My Experiences is both my "phenomenology of the mind" in the Hegelian sense of a "science of the experience of the consciousness" and the great circular return, the autobiographic-encyclopedic circumnavigation of Ulysses: there has often been talk of the Odyssey of the phenomenology of the mind. Here the phenomenology of mind would have the form of a diary of the conscious and the unconscious in the chance form of letters, telegrams, of newspapers called *The Telegraph*, for example, long-distance writing, and also of postcards for which sometimes the only text, taken out of some sailor's pocket, merely exhibits a fantasy in the form of an address.

Bloom has just spoken of "My Experiences":

The pink edition, extra sporting, of the *Telegraph*, tell a graphic lie, lay, as luck would have it, beside his elbow and as he was just puzzling again, far from satisfied, over a country belonging to him and the preceding rebus the vessel came from Bridgwater and the postcard was addressed to A. Boudin, find the captain's age, his *eyes* [my italics of the words *eyes*, to which we shall return] went aimlessly over the respective captions which came under his special province, the allembracing give us this day our daily press. First he got a bit of a start but it turned out to be only something about somebody named H. du Boyes, agent for typewriters or something like that. Great battle Tokio. Lovemaking in Irish £200 damages. (*U*, 567)

I am not going to analyze here the statigraphy of the "Tokio battlefield": experts can do that ad infinitum; the limitations of a lecture permit me only to recount to you, like a postcard cast to sea, *my experiences in Tokyo*, and then to pose the question in passing of *yes*, of chance, and of Joycean experience as expertise: but what is an expert, Ph.D. scholar in things Joycean? What of the Joycean institution and what should I think of the hospitality with which it honors me today in Frankfurt?

Bloom juxtaposes the allusion to the postcard to something that already offers a pure associative juxtaposition, the contiguity of which is apparently insignificant and yet this insignificance is underlined: it is the question of the captain's age, which we should guess rather than calculate, after the presentation of a series of facts, the figures of a *rebus*, with no evident connection to the question in hand. Nevertheless, always understood (*sous-entendu*) in the joke is the fact that the captain is the captain of a ship. Now the postcard is in fact the very same one the sailor spoke about, a sea-traveler, a captain who, like Ulysses, returns one day from a long circular voyage around the Mediterranean lake. A few pages earlier, same place, same time: "—Why, the sailor answered, upon reflection upon it, I've circumnavigated a bit since I first joined on. I was in the Red Sea. I was in China and North America and South America. I seen icebergs plenty, growlers. I was in Stockholm and the Black Sea, the Dardanelles, under Captain Dalton, the best bloody man that ever scuttled a ship. I seen Russia . . . I seen maneaters in Peru" (*U*, 545–46).

He has been everywhere except Japan, I said to myself. And here he is taking a messageless postcard out of his pocket. As for the address, it is fictitious, as fictitious as *Ulysses*, and it is the only thing that this Ulysses has in his pocket:

He fumbled out a picture postcard from his inside pocket, which seemed to be in its way a species of repository, and pushed it along the table. The printed matter on it stated: *Choza de Indios. Beni, Bolivia.*

All focused their attention on the scene exhibited, at a group of savage women in striped loincloths. . . . His postcard proved a centre of attraction for Messrs the greenhorns for several minutes, if not more.

• • •

Mr Bloom, without evincing surprise, unostentatiously turned over the card to peruse the partially obliterated address and postmark. It ran as follows: *Tarjeta Postal. Señor A. Boudin, Galeria Becche, Santiago, Chile.* There was no message evidently, as he took particular notice. Though not an implicit believer in the lurid story narrated . . . having detected a discrepancy between his name (assuming he was the person he represented himself to be and not sailing under false colours after having boxed the compass on the strict q.t. somewhere) and the fictitious addressee of the missive which made him nourish some suspicions of our friend's *bona fides*, nevertheless. . . . (*U*, 546–47)

. . . Up until now I have been speaking to you about letters in *Ulysses*, and postcards, about typewriters and telegraphs, but the telephone is missing, and I must relate to you a telephone experience. For a long time, I have thought—and this is still true today—that I would never be ready to give a talk on Joyce to an audience of Joyce experts. But when it comes to Joyce, what is an expert? that's my question. Still just as intimidated and behind schedule, I felt highly embarrassed when, in March, my friend Jean-Michel Rabaté telephoned me to ask for a title. I didn't have one. I only knew that I wanted to discuss *yes* in *Ulysses*. I had even tried casually counting them; more than 222 *yes*es in the so-called original version (and we know better than ever what precautions we must take when we use this expression). I came up with this no doubt approximate figure after an initial counting up, which took into consideration only the *yes*es in their explicit form.[7] I mean the word *yes*, since there are other examples of *yes* without the word *yes*, and indeed, the number of *yes*es is not the same in translation, which is a major problem; the French version adds quite a few. More than a quarter of these *yes*es are to be found in what is so ingenuously termed Molly's monologue: wherever there is a *yes*, whatever break may have taken place in the monologue, the other is hooked up somewhere on the telephone.

[7]Later, in the week following this lecture, a student and friend whom I met in Toronto drew my attention to another counting up of *yes*es. This calculation arrived at a far higher figure, having no doubt included all the *ayes* which I noted only in passing, and which are pronounced like the word *I*, signifying the word *I* (*je*). This counting poses a problem, to which I will return later. There is another estimation, that of Noel

When Jean-Michel Rabaté phoned me, I had, then, already decided to interrogate, if we can put it like that, the *yes*es of *Ulysses* as well as the institution of Joycean experts, as well as to question what happens when the word *yes* is written, quoted, repeated, archived, *recorded*, gramophoned, or is the subject of translation or transfer. But I still had no title, only a statistic and a few notes on a single sheet. I asked Rabaté to wait a second, went up to my room, cast a glance at the page of notes and a title crossed my mind with a kind of irresistible brevity, the authority of a telegraphic order: *hear say yes (oui dire) in Joyce*. So, you are receiving me, saying *yes* in Joyce but also saying it so that the yes *(le oui)* which can be noticed, the *saying yes (le dire oui)*, sallies forth like a quotation or a rumor going about, circumnavigating, as it were, the ear's labyrinth, which is what we know only by hear-say *(oui-dire)*. The play on "hear say yes," *l'oui-dire* and *l'ouï-dire*, can only be fully effective in French, which exploits the obscure, babelian homonymy of *oui* with just a dotted "i," and *ouï* with a diaresis. This untranslatable homonymy can be heard (by *oui dire*, that is) rather than read *with the eyes*, with the last word, *eyes*, noticed in passing, saying *yes* in the passage, giving itself to reading the grapheme *yes* rather than hearing it. *Yes* can only be a mark in *Ulysses*, a mark at once written and spoken, vocalized as a grapheme and written as a phoneme, *yes*, in a word, gramophoned.

So *hear say yes (l'oui-dire)* seemed to me to be a good title, sufficiently untranslatable and potentially capable of captioning what I wanted to say about the *yes*es in Joyce. Rabaté said "yes" to me on the telephone, that this title was fine. . . . All of you are experts and you belong to one of the most remarkable institutions. It bears the name

Riley Fitch in *Sylvia Beach and the Lost Generation: A History of Literary Paris in the Twenties and Thirties* (New York: Norton; London: Penguin, 1983), 109–10. If I quote the whole of the paragraph, it is because it seems to go beyond the mere arithmeticality of the *yes*:

One consultation with Joyce concerned Benoist-Méchin's translation of the final words of *Ulysses*: "and his heart was going like mad and yes I said Yes I will." The young man wanted the novel to conclude with a final "yes" following the "I will." Earlier Joyce had considered using "yes" (which appears 354 times in the novel) as his final word, but had written "I will" in the draft that Benoist-Méchin was translating. There followed a day of discussion in which they dragged in all the world's great philosophers. Benoist-Méchin, who argued that in French the "*oui*" is stronger and smoother, was more persuasive in the philosophical discussion. "I will" sounds authoritative and Luciferian. "Yes," he argued, is optimistic, an affirmation to the world beyond oneself. Joyce, who may have changed his mind earlier in the discussion, conceded hours later, "yes," the young man was right, the book would end with "the most positive word in the language." (JD) of a man who did everything, and admitted it, to make this institution indispensable, to keep it busy for centuries, as though on some new Tower of Babel to *make a name* for himself again. The institution can be seen as a powerful reading machine, a signature and countersignature machine in the service of his name, of his "patent." But as with God and the Tower of Babel, it is an institution for which he did everything he could to make it impossible and improbable in its very principle, to de-construct it in advance, even going as far as to undermine the very concept of competence, upon which one day an institutional legitimacy might be founded, whether we are dealing with a competence of knowledge or know-how. Before returning to this question, that is, of what you and I are doing here, as an exemplification of competence and incompetence, I shall hang on to the telephone for a little longer, before breaking off a more or less telepathic communication with Jean-Michel Rabaté. Up until now we have amassed letters, postcards, telegrams, typewriters, et cetera. We should remember that if *Finnegans Wake* is the sublime babelization of a *penman* and *postman*, the motif of postal difference, of remote control and telecommunication, is already powerfully at work in *Ulysses*. And, as always, this is *remarked en abyme*. For example, in "THE WEARER OF THE CROWN": "Under the porch of the general post office shoeblacks called and polished. Parked in North Prince's street, His Majesty's vermillion mailcars, bearing on their sides the royal initials, E. R., received loudly flung sacks of letters, postcards, lettercards, parcels, insured and paid, for local, provincial, British and overseas delivery" (*U*, 118). This *remote control* technology, as we say of television remote control, is not an element outside of this context; it affects the inside of meaning in the most elementary sense, even so far as the statement or the inscription of practically the shortest word, the gramophony of *yes*. This is why the wandering circumnavigation of a postcard, letter, or a telegram only shifts destinations in the perpetual buzzing of a telephone obsession, or again, a telegramophonic obsession, if you take into account a gramophone or answering service.

If I am not mistaken, the first phone call sounds with Bloom's words: "Better phone him up first" in a sequence entitled "AND IT WAS THE FEAST OF THE PASSOVER" (*U*, 124). A little before, he had somewhat mechanically, like a record, repeated this prayer, the most serious of all prayers for a Jew, the one that should never be allowed to become mechanical, to be gramophoned: *Shema Israel Adonai Elohanu*. If, more or less legitimately (for everything and nothing is legitimate when we lift out segments as examples of narrative metonymy) we subtract this

element from the most obvious narrative frame in the book, then
we can speak of the telephonic *Shema Israel* between God, who is
infinitely removed (*a long-distance call, a collect call from or to the
collector of prepuces*) and Israel. *Shema Israel* means, as you know, call
to Israel, listen Israel, hello Israel, to the address of the name of Israel,
a person-to-person call.[8] The "Better phone him up first" scene takes
place in the offices of *The Telegraph (Le Télégramme)* newspaper (and
not *The Tetragram*) and Bloom has just paused to watch a kind of
typewriter, a composing machine, a typographic womb (*matrice*): "He
stayed in his walk to watch a typesetter neatly distributing type." And
as he first of all reads it backwards ("Reads it backwards first"), composing the name of Patrick Dignam, the name of the father, Patrick,
from right to left, he remembers his own father reading the hagadah
in the same direction. In the same paragraph, around the name of
Patrick, you can follow the whole series of fathers, the twelve sons
of Jacob, et cetera, and the word "practice" crops up twice to scan this
patristic and *perfectly* paternal litany ("Quickly he does it. Must require
some practice that." And twelve lines lower, "How quickly he does
that job. Practice makes perfect.") This comes almost immediately
after we read, "Better phone him up first": "*plutôt un coup de téléphone
pour commencer,*" the French translation says. Let's say that it's better
to begin with a phone call. In the beginning, there must have been
some phone calls.

   In the beginning, there was the telephone. Before the act or the
word, the telephone. In the beginning was the telephone. We can hear
the telephone constantly ringing, this *coup de téléphone* plays on apparently random figures, but about which there is so much to say; we hear
it resonate unceasingly. And it incorporates within itself this *yes* toward
which we slowly, moving in circles around it, return. There are several

---

[8]Elsewhere, in the brothel, it is the circumcised who say the "Shema Israel," and
there is also the *Lactus Morte*, the dead sea: "THE CIRCUMCISED: (*In a dark guttural
chant as they cast dead fruit upon him, no flowers*) *Shema Israel Adonai Elohena Adonai
Echad*" (*U*, 496).
   And while we are speaking of Ulysses, the dead sea, gramophones, and soon the
laugh, there is *Remembrance of Things Past*: "He stopped laughing; I should have liked
to recognize my friend, but, like Ulysses in the Odyssey when he rushes forward to embrace his dead mother, like the spiritualist who tries in vain to elicit from a ghost an answer which will reveal its identity, like the visitor at an exhibition of electricity who cannot believe that the voice which the gramophone restores unaltered to life is not a voice
spontaneously emitted by a human being, I was obliged to give up the attempt." A little
higher up: "The familiar voice seemed to be emitted by a gramophone more perfect
than any I had ever heard." *The Past Recaptured*, trans. Andreas Mayor. New York:
Vintage Books, 1971, pp. 188–89. (JD)

modalities or tonalities of the telephonic *yes*, but one of them, without saying anything else, returns to mark, simply, that we are *here*, present, listening, on the other end of the line, ready to answer but not for the moment responding to anything other than the preparation to answer (hello, yes; I'm listening, I can hear that you are there, ready to speak just when I am ready to speak to you). In the beginning was the telephone, yes, in the beginning a telephone call. A few pages after "*Shema Israel*" and the first telephone call, just after the unforgettable Ohio scene entitled "MEMORABLE BATTLES RECALLED" (you can hear that a voice can trip quickly from Ohio to the Battle of Tokyo), a certain telephonic *yes* resounds with a "Bingbang" which recalls the origin of the universe. A competent professor has just passed by "—A perfect cretic! the professor said. Long, short and long," after the cry "In Ohio!" "My Ohio!" Then, at the beginning of "O, HARP EOLIAN" (*U*, 129), there is the sound of teeth chattering as dental floss is applied (and if I were to tell you that this year, before going to Tokyo, I went to Oxford, Ohio, and that I even bought some dental floss— that is to say, an eolian harp—in a drugstore in Ithaca, you would not believe me. You would be wrong; it is true and can be verified). When "the resonant unwashed teeth" vibrate to the dental floss, we hear "—Bingbang, bingbang." Bloom then asks to ring: "I just want to phone about an ad." Then "the telephone whirred inside." This time the eolian harp is not dental floss but the telephone, the cables of which are elsewhere "the navel cords," which harp back to Eden. "—Twenty eight . . . No, twenty . . . Double four . . . Yes." We cannot tell if this *Yes* is part of a monologue, approving the Other within (yes that's the right number) or if he is already in communication with the other end of the line. We cannot know. The context is cut, end of sequence.

But at the end of the following sequence ("SPOT THE WINNER"), a telephonic "yes" rings again in the same offices of *The Telegraph*: "Yes . . . *Evening Telegraph* here, Mr Bloom phoned from the inner office. Is the boss . . . ? Yes, *Telegraph* . . . To where? . . . Aha! Which auction rooms? . . . Aha! I see . . . Right. I'll catch him" (*U*, 130).

It is repeatedly said that the phone call is *internal*. "Mr Bloom . . . made for the *inner* door" when he wants to ring; then "the telephone whirred *inside*," and finally, "Mr Bloom phoned from the *inner* office." So, a telephonic interiority: for before any appliance bearing the name "telephone" in modern times, the telephonic *tekhnè* is at work within the voice, multiplying the writing of voices without any instruments, as Mallarmé would say, a mental telephony, which, inscribing remoteness, distance, difference, and spacing in sound (*phoné*), institutes, forbids, *and at the same time* interferes with the so-called monologue. At the same time, in the same way (*du même coup*), from the first phone call (*dès le premier coup de téléphone*) and from the simplest vocalization, from the monosyllabilized quasi-interjection of the word *oui*, "yes," "ay." More conclusively, we have the instance of these *yes, yeses* which *speech act* theorists use as an illustration of the performative and which Molly repeats at the end of the so-called monologue, the "*Yes, Yes, I do*," her consent in the marriage ceremony. When I speak of mental telephony, or even of masturbation, I am implicitly quoting "THE SINS OF THE PAST"; "(*In a medley of voices*) He went through a form of clandestine marriage with at least one woman in the shadow of the Black Church. Unspeakable messages he telephoned mentally to Miss Dunne at an address in d'Olier Street while he presented himself indecently to the instrument in the callbox" (*U*, 491–92).

Telephonic spacing is particularly superimposed in the scene entitled "A DISTANT VOICE." The scene crosses all the lines in our network, the paradoxes of competence and institution, represented here in the shape of the professor, and, in every sense of the word, the *repetition* of the word *yes* between *eyes and ears, entre les yeux and les oreilles.* All these telephonic lines can be drawn from one paragraph:

A DISTANT VOICE

—I'll answer it, the professor said going . . .

—Hello? *Evening Telegraph* here . . . Hello? . . .

Who's there? . . . Yes . . . Yes . . . Yes . . .

The professor came to the inner door. [*inner* again]

—Bloom is at the telephone, he said. (*U*, 137–38)

Bloom-is-at-the-telephone. In this way, the professor defines a particular situation at a certain moment in the novel, no doubt, but as is always the case in the stereophony of a text that gives several outlines to each statement, always allowing metonymic extracts to be taken— and I am not the only reader of Joyce to indulge in this pursuit, at once legitimate and abusive, authorized and improper—the professor is also naming the permanent essence of Bloom. This can be read in this particular paradigm: *he is at the telephone*, he is always there, he belongs to the telephone, he is riveted yet destined there. His being is a being-at-the-telephone. He is hooked up to a multiplicity of voices and answering machines. His being-there is a being at the telephone,

in the way that Heidegger speaks of a being for the death of *Dasein*.
And I am not playing with words when I say that: Heideggerian
Dasein is also a being-called, it always is, as we are informed in *Sein
und Zeit*, and as my friend Sam Weber reminded me, a *Dasein* that can
only comply with itself using the Call (*der Ruf*) as a starting point,
a call which has come from afar, which does not necessarily use words,
and which, in a certain way, is not saying anything. To such an analysis, we could apply down to the last detail the whole of chapter 57 of
Sein und Zeit on the subject of *der Ruf*, drawing, for example, on
phrases like the following: *Der Angerufene ist eben dieses Dasein;
aufgerufen zu seinem eigensten Seinkönnen (Sich-vorweg . . .) Und
aufgerufen ist das Dasein durch den Anruf aus dem Verfallen in das
Man . . .* The called one is precisely this *Dasein*; summoned, called
forth, called up toward this possibility of being the most proper (before himself). And in this way the *Dasein* is hailed by this call, called
out to, called out of the collapse of the "one," of anonymity. Unfortunately, we do not have the time to enter further into this analysis over
and above the jargon of *Eigentlichkeit*, which is particularly remembered in this university [Frankfurt].

—Bloom is at the telephone, he said.

—Tell him to go to hell, the editor said promptly. X is Burke's
public house, see? (*U*, 138)

Bloom is at the telephone, hooked up to a powerful network to
which I shall return in an instant. He belongs in his essence to a poly-
telephonic structure. But he is at the telephone in the sense that he is
also being *waited for* on the telephone. When the professor says,
"Bloom is at the telephone," and I shall shortly say, "Joyce is at the
telephone," he is saying: he is waiting for someone to respond to him,
waiting for an answer, which the editor—who must decide the future
of his text, its safekeeping and its truth—does not want to give, and
who at this point sends him to hell, a *Verfallen* then into the hell of
censured books. Bloom is waiting for an answer, for someone to say,
"hello, yes," that is, for someone to say, "Yes, yes," beginning with
the telephonic *yes* indicating that there is indeed another voice, or an
answering machine, on the other end of the line. When, at the end of
the book, Molly says, "yes, yes," she is answering a request, but a request that she requests. She is at the telephone, even when she is in
bed, asking, and waiting to be asked, on the telephone (since she is
alone) to say, "yes, yes." And the fact that she asks "with my eyes"

does not prevent this demand being made by telephone; on the contrary: "well as well him as another and then I asked him with my eyes to ask again yes and then he asked me would I yes to say yes my mountain flower and first I put my arms around him yes and drew him down to me so he could feel my breasts all perfume yes and his heart was going like mad and yes I said yes I will Yes" (*U*, 704).

The final "Yes," the last word, the eschatology of the book, gives itself up only to *reading*, since it distinguishes itself from the others by an inaudible capital letter; what also remains equally inaudible, although visible, is the literal incorporation of *yes* in *eyes*. Languages of eyes, of ayes.

We still do not know what *yes* means and how this small word, if it is one, operates in language and in what we calmly refer to as speech acts. We do not know whether this word shares anything at all with any other word in any language, even with the word *no*, which is most certainly not symmetrical to it. We do not know if a grammatical, semantic, linguistic, rhetorical, or philosophical concept exists capable of this event marked *yes*. Let us leave that aside for the moment. Let us, and this is not merely fiction, act *as if* this would not prevent us, on the contrary, from hearing what the word *yes* governs. We will move on to the difficult questions later, if we have time.

Yes on the telephone can be crossed in one and the same occurrence, by a variety of intonations whose differentiating qualities are potentialized on stereophonic long waves. They may appear only to go as far as interjection, as far as the mechanical quasi signal that indicates either the mere presence of interlocutory *Dasein* at the other end of the line (Hello, yes?) or the passive docility of a secretary or a subordinate who, like some archiving machine, is ready to record orders (*yes sir*) or who is satisfied with purely informative answers (*yes, sir; no, sir*). This is just one example among many. I have deliberately chosen the section where a typewriter and the trade name H.E.L.Y.'s lead us to the last piece of furniture in the hall, or, as a techno-telecommunication type of introduction, to a certain gramophone, and at the same time connects us to the network of the prophet Elijah. So here we are, though of course I have sectioned and selected, filtering away the noise on the line:

> Miss Dunne hid the Capel street library copy of *The Woman in White* far back in her drawer and rolled a sheet of gaudy notepaper into her typewriter.

Too much mystery business in it. Is he in love with that one, Marion? Change it and get another by Mary Cecil Haye.
The disk shot down the groove, wobbled a while, ceased and ogled them: six.
Miss Dunne clicked at the keyboard:
—16 June 1904. [almost eighty years.]
Five tallwhitehatted sandwichmen between Monypeny's corner and the slab where Wolfe Tone's statue was not, eeled themselves turning H.E.L.Y.'S and plodded back as they had come. . . .
The telephone rang rudely by her ear.
—Hello. Yes, sir. No, sir. Yes, sir. I'll ring them up after five. Only those two, sir, for Belfast and Liverpool. All right, sir. Then I can go after six if you're not back. A quarter after. Yes, sir. Twenty-seven and six. I'll tell him. Yes: one, seven, six.
She scribbled three figures on an envelope.
—Mr Boylan! Hello! That gentleman from *Sport* was in looking for you. Mr Lenehan, yes. He said he'll be in the Ormond at four. No, sir. Yes, sir. I'll ring them up after five. (*U*, 228–29)

It is not by accident that the repetition of *yes* can be seen to assume mechanical, servile forms, often bending the woman to her master, even if any answer to the other as a singular other must, it seems, escape it. In order for the *yes* of affirmation, assent, consent, alliance, of engagement, signature, or gift to have the value it has, it must carry the repetition within itself. It must *a priori* and immediately confirm its promise and promise its confirmation. This essential repetition lets itself be haunted by an intrinsic threat, by an internal telephone which interferes (*parasiter*) with it like a mimetic, mechanical double, like its incessant parody. We shall return to this fatality. But we can already hear a gramophony which records writing in the liveliest voice. *A priori* it reproduces it, in the absence of all intentional presence of the affirmer. Such gramophony responds, of course, to the dream of a reproduction which *preserves* as its truth the living *yes*, archived into the very quick of the voice. But in this way it gives way to the possibility of parody, of a *yes* technique that persecutes the most spontaneous, the most giving desire of the *yes*. To meet (*répondre à*) its destination, this *yes* must reaffirm itself immediately. Such is the condition of a signed commitment. *Yes* can only express *itself* by promising itself its own memory. (*Le oui ne peut se dire que s'il se promet la mémoire de soi.*) The affirmation of the word *yes* is the affirmation of memory. *Yes* must preserve itself, reiterate itself, must archive its voice in order to give itself once again to be heard (*la redonner à entendre*).

This is what I call the gramophone effect. *Yes* gramophones itself and, *a priori*, telegramophones itself.

The desire for memory and the mourning implicit in the word *yes* set in motion an anamnesic machine. And its hypermnesic overacceleration. The machine reproduces the quick (*le vif*), it doubles it with its automaton. The example I have chosen offers the privilege of a double contiguity: from the word *yes* to the word *voice* and to the word *gramophone* in a sequence expressing the desire for memory, desire as memory of desire and memory for desire. It takes place in Hades, in the cemetery, at about 11 o'clock in the morning, the time reserved for the *heart* (that is, as Heidegger would put it again, the place reserved for memory that is retained and for truth), here in the sense of the Sacred Heart:

> The Sacred Heart that is: showing it. Heart on his sleeve. . . .
> How many! All these here once walked round Dublin. Faithful departed.
> As you are now so once were we.
> Besides how could you remember everybody? Eyes, walk, voice. Well, the voice, yes: gramophone. Have a gramophone in every grave or keep it in the house. After dinner on a Sunday. Put on poor old greatgrandfather Kraahraark! Hellohellohello amawfullyglad kraark awfullygladaseeragain hellohello amarawf kopthsth. Remind you of the voice like the photograph reminds you of the face. Otherwise you couldn't remember the face after fifteen years, say. For instance some fellow that died when I was in Wisdom Hely's. (*U*, 115–16)[9]

What right do we have to select or interrupt a quotation from *Ulysses*? This is always legitimate and illegitimate, to be made legitimate like an illegitimate child. I could follow the sons of Hely (Bloom's old boss), threading them through all sorts of genealogies. Rightly or wrongly, I judge it more economical here to rely on the association with the name of the prophet Elijah, to whom a good many passages are devoted, or rather whose coming at regular intervals can be foretold. I pronounce *Elie* in the French way, but in the English name for Elijah, Molly's *Ja* can be heard echoing if Molly gives voice to the flesh (*la chair*, hang on to this word) which always says *yes* (*stets bejaht*, Joyce reminds us, reversing Goethe's words). I shall not investigate further the part of the text where it is said, "voice out of heaven,

[9]I am told that James Joyce's grandson is here, now, in this room. This quotation is naturally dedicated to him. (JD)

calling: *Elijah! Elijah!* and he answered with a main cry: *Abba! Abba!* And they beheld Him even Him, ben Bloom Elijah, amid clouds of angels" (*U*, 343).

No, without transition, I give myself up to repetition, to that which is called "the second coming of Elijah" in the brothel. The Gramophone, the character and the voice, if I can put it like this, of the gramophone just shouted:

Jerusalem!
Open your gates and sing
Hosanna . . . (*U*, 472)

In the second coming of Elijah after "the end of the world," Elijah's voice acts as a kind of telephone exchange or marshalling yard. All communication, transport, transfer, and translation networks go through him. Polytelephony goes through Elijah's programophony. But do not forget, whatever you do, that Molly reminds us that ben Bloom Elijah lost his job at Hely's. Bloom had thought at that time of prostituting Molly, of making her pose naked for a very rich man. Elijah is just a voice, a skein of voices. It says, "*C'est moi qui opère tous les téléphones de ce réseau-là*" in the French translation approved by Joyce for "Say, I am operating all this trunk line. Boys, do it now. God's time is 12.25. Tell mother you'll be there. Rush your order and you play a slick ace. Join on right here! Book through to eternity junction, the nonstop run" (*U*, 473). I want to insist (in French) on the fact that seats must be *booked* (*louer*), reserved near Elijah, Elijah must be *praised (louer)* and the *booking* (*location*) of this *praise* (*louange*) is none other than the book which stands in lieu of *eternity junction*, like a transferential and teleprogramophonic exchange.[10] "Just one word more," continues Elijah, who also evokes the second coming of Christ and asks us if we are ready, "Florry Christ, Stephen Christ, Zoe Christ, Bloom Christ," et cetera. "Are you all in this vibration? I say you are"—which is translated into French by "*Moi je dis que oui,*" a problematic though not illicit translation about which we must speak again. And the voice of the one who says "yes," Elijah, saying to those who are in the *vibration* (a key word in my view) that they can call him any time, straightaway, instantaneously, without using any technique or postal system, but going by the sun, by solar

---

[10]The French plays upon both meanings of *louer* ("to book" or "to rent" and "to praise"), of *location* (a "hiring" or "renting"), and of *louange* ("praise" or "commendation") as well as *livre* ("book"). (SB)

cables and rays, by the voice of the sun—we could say photophone or heliophone. He says "by sunphone": "Got me? That's it. You call me up by sunphone any old time. Bumboosers, save your stamps" (*U*, 473). So do not write me any letters, save your stamps, you can collect them, like Molly's father.

We have arrived at this point because I was telling you about my travel experiences, my round trip, and about a few phone calls. If I am telling stories, it is to put off speaking about serious things and because I am too intimidated. Nothing intimidates me more than a community of experts in Joycean matters. Why? I wanted first of all to speak to you about this, to speak to you about authority and intimidation. . . .

I did not feel worthy of the honor that had been bestowed on me, far from it, but I must have been nourishing some obscure desire to be part of this mighty family which tends to sum up all others, including their hidden narratives of bastardy, legitimation, and illegitimacy. If I have accepted, it is mainly for having suspected some perverse challenge in a legitimation so generously offered. You know better than I the concern regarding familial legitimation; it is this which makes *Ulysses*, as well as *Finnegans Wake*, vibrate. I was thinking, in the plane, of the challenge and the trap, because experts, I said to myself, with the lucidity and experience that a long acquaintance with Joyce confers on them, ought to know better than most to what extent, beneath the simulacrum of a few signs of complicity, of references or quotations in each of my books, Joyce remains a stranger to me, as if I did not know him. Incompetence, as they know, is the profound truth of my relationship to this work which I know deep down only indirectly, through hearsay, through rumors, through what people say (*des "on-dit"*), second-hand exegeses, always partial readings. For these experts, I said to myself, the time has come for the deception to burst out (*éclater*), and how best could this be demonstrated or denounced if not at the opening of a large symposium?

So, in order to defend myself against this hypothesis, which was almost a certainty, I asked myself: but in the end what does competence come down to in the case of Joyce? And what can a Joycean institution, a Joycean family, a Joycean international organization be? I do not know how far we can speak of the modernity of Joyce, but if this exists, beyond the apparatus for postal and programophonic technologies, it is linked to the declared project of keeping generations of university scholars at work for centuries of babelian edification, which must itself have been drawn up using a technological model and the division of university labor that could not be that of former centuries. The scheme of bending vast communities of readers and writers to this law, to detain them by means of an interminable transferential chain of translation and tradition, can equally well be attributed to Plato and Shakespeare, to Dante and Vico, without mentioning Hegel and other finite divinities. But none of these could calculate, as well as Joyce did, his feat (*son coup*), by modifying it to certain types of world research institutions prepared to use not only means of transport, of communication, of organizational programming allowing an accelerated capitalization, a crazy accumulation of interest in terms of knowledge blocked in Joyce's name, while he even lets you all sign in his name, as Molly would say ("I could often have written out a fine cheque for myself and write his name on it" [*U*, 702]), but also the modes of archivization and consultation of data unheard of (*inouïes*) for all the grandfathers whom I have just named, omitting Homer. The intimidation holds to this: Joyce experts are the representatives as well as the effects of the most powerful project for programming the totality of research in onto-logico-encyclopedic fields for centuries, all the while commemorating his own, proper signature. A Joyce scholar has rightly at his/her disposal, has the right to dispose of, the totality of competence in the encyclopedic field of the *universitas*. He has at his command the computer of all memory, he plays with the entire archive of culture—at least of what is said to be Western culture, and of what in this returns to itself according to the Ulyssean circle of encyclopedia; and this is why one can always at least dream of writing *on* Joyce and not *in* Joyce from the fantasy of some Far Eastern capital, without, in my case, having too many illusions about it. The effects of this preprogramming, you know better than I, are admirable and terrifying, and sometimes of intolerable violence. One of them has the following form: nothing can be invented *on the subject* of Joyce. Everything we can say about *Ulysses*, for example, has already been anticipated, including as we have seen, the scene about academic competence and the ingenuity of metadiscourse. We are caught in the net. All the gestures sketched in to allow an initiatory movement are already announced in an overpotentialized text that will remind you, at a given moment, that you are captive in a language, writing, knowledge, and *even narration* network. This is one of the things I wanted to demonstrate before, in recounting all these stories, moreover true ones, about the postcard in Tokyo, the trip to Ohio, or the phone call

from Rabaté. We have verified that all this had its narrative paradigm
and was *already* recounted in *Ulysses*. Everything that happened to me,
including the narrative that I would attempt to make of it, was already
foretold and forenarrated, this unusualness being dated, prescribed in
a sequence of knowledge and narration: within *Ulysses*, to say nothing
of *Finnegans Wake*, by a hypermnesis machine capable of storing in
an immense epic work, with the Western memory and virtually all
the languages in the world *including traces of the future*. Yes, everything has already happened to us with *Ulysses* and has been signed in
advance by Joyce. . . .

Reader-Response Criticism
and
Ulysses

WHAT IS READER-RESPONSE CRITICISM?

Students are routinely asked in English courses for their reactions to the texts they are reading. Sometimes there are so many different reactions that we may wonder whether everyone has read the same text. And some students respond so idiosyncratically to what they read that we say their responses are "totally off the wall." This variety of response interests reader-response critics, who raise theoretical questions about whether our responses to a work are the same as its meanings, whether a work can have as many meanings as we have responses to it, and whether some responses are more valid than others. They ask what determines what is and what isn't "off the wall." What, in other words, is the wall, and what standards help us define it?

In addition to posing provocative questions, reader-response criticism provides us with models that aid our understanding of texts and the reading process. Adena Rosmarin has suggested that a literary text may be likened to an incomplete work of sculpture: to see it fully, we must complete it imaginatively, taking care to do so in a way that responsibly takes into account what exists. Other reader-response critics have suggested other models, for reader-response criticism is not a monolithic school of thought but, rather, an umbrella term covering a variety of approaches to literature.

Nonetheless, as Steven Mailloux has shown, reader-response critics *do* share not only questions but also goals and strategies. Two of the basic goals are to show that a work gives readers something to do and to describe what the reader does by way of response. To achieve those goals, the critic may make any of a number of what Mailloux calls "moves." For instance, a reader-response critic might typically (1) cite direct references to reading in the text being analyzed, in order to justify the focus on reading and show that the world of the text is continuous with the one in which the reader reads; (2) show how other nonreading situations in the text nonetheless mirror the situation the reader is in ("Fish shows how in *Paradise Lost* Michael's teaching of Adam in Book XI resembles Milton's teaching of the reader throughout the poem"); and (3) show, therefore, that the reader's response is, or is analogous to, the story's action or conflict. For instance, Stephen Booth calls *Hamlet* the tragic story of "an audience that cannot make up its mind" (Mailloux, "Learning" 103).

Although reader-response criticism is often said to have emerged in the United States in the 1970s, it is in one respect as old as the foundations of Western culture. The ancient Greeks and Romans tended to view literature as rhetoric, a means of making an audience react in a certain way. Although their focus was more on rhetorical strategies and devices than on the reader's (or listener's) response to those methods, the ancients by no means left the audience out of the literary equation. Aristotle thought, for instance, that the greatness of tragedy lay in its "cathartic" power to cleanse or purify the emotions of audience members. Plato, by contrast, worried about the effects of artistic productions, so much so that he advocated evicting poets from the Republic on the grounds that their words "feed and water" the passions!

In our own century, long before 1970, there were critics whose concerns and attitudes anticipated those of reader-response critics. One of these, I. A. Richards, is usually associated with formalism, a supposedly objective, text-centered approach to literature that reader-response critics of the 1970s roundly attacked. And yet in 1929 Richards managed to sound surprisingly *like* a 1970s-vintage reader-response critic, writing in *Practical Criticism* that "the personal situation of the reader inevitably (and within limits rightly) affects his reading, and many more are drawn to poetry in quest of some reflection of their latest emotional crisis than would admit it" (575). Rather than deploring this fact, as many of his formalist contemporaries would have done, Richards argued that the reader's feelings and experiences provide a kind of reality check, a way of testing the authenticity of emotions and events represented in literary works.

Approximately a decade after Richards wrote *Practical Criticism,* an American named Louise M. Rosenblatt published *Literature as Exploration* (1938). In that seminal book, now in its fourth edition (1983), Rosenblatt began developing a theory of reading that blurs the boundary between reader and text, subject and object. In a 1969 article entitled "Towards a Transactional Theory of Reading," she sums up her position by writing that "a poem is what the reader lives through under the guidance of the text and experiences as relevant to the text" (127). Rosenblatt knew her definition would be difficult for many to accept: "The idea that a *poem* presupposes a *reader* actively involved with a *text,*" she wrote, "is particularly shocking to those seeking to emphasize the objectivity of their interpretations" ("Transactional" 127).

Rosenblatt implicitly and generally refers to formalists (also called the "New Critics") when she speaks of supposedly objective interpreters shocked by the notion that a "poem" is something cooperatively produced by a "reader" and a "text." Formalists spoke of "the poem itself," the "concrete work of art," the "real poem." They had no interest in what a work of literature makes a reader "live through." In fact, in *The Verbal Icon* (1954), William K. Wimsatt and Monroe C. Beardsley defined as fallacious the very notion that a reader's response is relevant to the meaning of a literary work:

> The Affective Fallacy is a confusion between the poem and its *results* (what it *is* and what it *does*). . . . It begins by trying to derive the standards of criticism from the psychological effects of a poem and ends in impressionism and relativism. The outcome . . . is that the poem itself, as an object of specifically critical judgment, tends to disappear. (21)

Reader-response critics have taken issue with their formalist predecessors. Particularly influential has been Stanley Fish, whose early work is seen by some as marking the true beginning of contemporary reader-response criticism. In "Literature in the Reader: Affective Stylistics" (1970), Fish took on the formalist hegemony, the New Critical establishment, by arguing that any school of criticism that would see a work of literature as an object, claiming to describe what it *is* and never what it *does*, is guilty of misconstruing the very essence of literature and reading. Literature exists when it is read, Fish suggests, and

its force is an affective force. Furthermore, reading is a temporal
process. Formalists assume it is a spatial one as they step back and sur-
vey the literary work as if it were an object spread out before them.
They may find elegant patterns in the texts they examine and reexam-
ine, but they fail to take into account that the work is quite different to
a reader who is turning the pages and being moved, or affected, by
lines that appear and disappear as the reader reads.

In a discussion of the effect that a sentence penned by the
seventeenth-century physician Thomas Browne has on a reader reading, Fish pauses to say this about his analysis and also, by extension,
about his critical strategy: "Whatever is persuasive and illuminating
about [it] is the result of my substituting for one question—what does
this sentence mean?—another, more operational question—what
does this sentence do?" He then quotes a line from John Milton's
Paradise Lost, a line that refers to Satan and the other fallen angels:
"Nor did they not perceive their evil plight." Whereas more traditional
critics might say that the "meaning" of the line is "They did perceive
their evil plight," Fish relates the uncertain movement of the reader's
mind *to* that half-satisfying interpretation. Furthermore, he declares
that "the reader's inability to tell whether or not 'they' do perceive
and his involuntary question . . . are part of the line's *meaning,* even
though they take place in the mind, not on the page" (*Text* 26).

The stress on what pages *do* to minds (and what minds do in response) pervades the writings of most, if not all, reader-response critics. Stephen Booth, whose book *An Essay on Shakespeare's Sonnets*
(1969) greatly influenced Fish, sets out to describe the "reading experience that results" from a "multiplicity of organizations" in a sonnet
by Shakespeare (*Essay* ix). Sometimes these organizations don't make
complete sense, Booth points out, and sometimes they even seem curiously contradictory. But that is precisely what interests reader-response
critics, who, unlike formalists, are at least as interested in fragmentary,
inconclusive, and even unfinished texts as in polished, unified works.
For it is the reader's struggle to *make sense* of a challenging work that
reader-response critics seek to describe.

The German critic Wolfgang Iser has described that sense-making
struggle in his books *The Implied Reader* (1972) and *The Act of Reading: A Theory of Aesthetic Response* (1976). Iser argues that texts are
full of "gaps" (or "blanks," as he sometimes calls them). These gaps
powerfully affect the reader, who is forced to explain them, to connect
what they separate, to create in his or her mind aspects of a poem or
novel or play that aren't *in* the text but that the text incites. As Iser

puts it in *The Implied Reader*, the "unwritten aspects" of a story "draw the reader into the action" and "lead him to shade in the many outlines suggested by the given situations, so that these take on a reality of their own." These "outlines" that "the reader's imagination animates" in turn "influence" the way in which "the written part of the text" is subsequently read (276).

In *Self-Consuming Artifacts: The Experience of Seventeenth-Century Literature* (1972), Fish reveals his preference for literature that makes readers work at making meaning. He contrasts two kinds of literary presentation. By the phrase "rhetorical presentation," he describes literature that reflects and reinforces opinions that readers already hold; by "dialectical presentation," he refers to works that prod and provoke. A dialectical text, rather than presenting an opinion as if it were truth, challenges readers to discover truths on their own. Such a text may not even have the kind of symmetry that formalist critics seek. Instead of offering a "single, sustained argument," a dialectical text, or self-consuming artifact, may be "so arranged that to enter into the spirit and assumptions of any one of [its] . . . units is implicitly to reject the spirit and assumptions of the unit immediately preceding" (*Artifacts* 9). Whereas a critic of another school might try to force an explanation as to why the units are fundamentally coherent, the reader-response critic proceeds by describing how the reader deals with the sudden twists and turns that characterize the dialectical text, returning to earlier passages and seeing them in an entirely new light.

"The value of such a procedure," Fish has written, "is predicated on the idea of meaning as *an event,*" not as something "located (presumed to be embedded) *in* the utterance" or "verbal object as a thing in itself" (*Text* 28). By redefining meaning as an event rather than as something inherent in the text, the reader-response critic once again locates meaning in time: the reader's time. A text exists and signifies while it is being read, and what it signifies or means will depend, to no small extent, on *when* it is read. (*Paradise Lost* had some meanings for a seventeenth-century Puritan that it would not have for a twentieth-century atheist.)

With the redefinition of literature as something that exists meaningfully only in the mind of the reader, with the redefinition of the literary work as a catalyst of mental events, comes a concurrent redefinition of the reader. No longer is the reader the passive recipient of those ideas that an author has planted in a text. "The reader is *active,*" Rosenblatt insists ("Transactional" 123). Fish begins "Literature in the Reader" with a similar observation: "If at this moment someone were to ask, 'what are you doing,' you might reply, 'I am reading,' and thereby acknowledge that reading is . . . something *you do*" (*Text* 22). Iser, in focusing critical interest on the gaps in texts, on what is not expressed, similarly redefines the reader as an active maker.

Amid all this talk of "the reader," it is tempting and natural to ask, "Just who *is* the reader?" (Or, to place the emphasis differently, "Just who is *the* reader?") Are reader-response critics simply sharing their own idiosyncratic responses when they describe what a line from *Paradise Lost* does in and to the reader's mind? "What about my responses?" you may want to ask. "What if they're different? Would reader-response critics be willing to say that my responses are equally valid?"

Fish defines "the reader" in this way: "*the* reader is the *informed* reader." The informed reader (whom Fish sometimes calls "the *intended* reader") is someone who is "sufficiently experienced as a reader to have internalized the properties of literary discourses, including everything from the most local of devices (figures of speech, etc.) to whole genres." And, of course, the informed reader is in full possession of the "semantic knowledge" (knowledge of idioms, for instance) assumed by the text (*Artifacts* 406).

Other reader-response critics define "*the* reader" differently. Wayne C. Booth, in *A Rhetoric of Irony* (1974), uses the phrase "the implied reader" to mean the reader "created by the work." (Only "by agreeing to play the role of this created audience," Susan Suleiman explains, "can an actual reader correctly understand and appreciate the work" [8].) Gerard Genette and Gerald Prince prefer to speak of "the narratee, . . . the necessary counterpart of a given narrator, that is, the person or figure who receives a narrative" (Suleiman 13). Like Booth, Iser employs the term "the implied reader," but he also uses "the educated reader" when he refers to what Fish called the "informed reader."

Jonathan Culler, who in 1981 criticized Fish for his sketchy definition of the informed reader, set out in *Structuralist Poetics* (1975) to describe the educated or "competent" reader's education by elaborating those reading conventions that make possible the understanding of poems and novels. In retrospect, however, Culler's definitions seem sketchy as well. By "competent reader," Culler meant competent reader of "literature." By "literature," he meant what schools and colleges mean when they speak of literature as being part of the curriculum. Culler, like his contemporaries, was not concerned with the fact that curricular content is politically and economically motivated. And "he did not," in Mailloux's words, "emphasize how the literary competence he described was embedded within larger formations and traversed by political ideologies extending beyond the academy" ("Turns" 49). It remained for a later generation of reader-oriented critics to do those things.

The fact that Fish, following Rosenblatt's lead, defined reader-response criticism in terms of its difference from and opposition to the New Criticism or formalism should not obscure the fact that the formalism of the 1950s and early 1960s had a great deal in common with the reader-response criticism of the late 1960s and early 1970s. This has become increasingly obvious with the rise of subsequent critical approaches whose practitioners have proved less interested in the close reading of texts than in the way literature represents, reproduces, and/or resists prevailing ideologies concerning gender, class, and race. In a retrospective essay entitled "The Turns of Reader-Response Criticism" (1990), Mailloux has suggested that, from the perspective of hindsight, the "close reading" of formalists and "Fish's early 'affective stylistics'" seem surprisingly similar. Indeed, Mailloux argues, the early "reader talk of . . . Iser and Fish enabled the continuation of the formalist practice of close reading. Through a vocabulary focused on a text's manipulation of readers, Fish was especially effective in extending and diversifying the formalist practices that continued business as usual within literary criticism" (48).

Since the mid-1970s, however, reader-response criticism (once commonly referred to as the "School of Fish") has diversified and taken on a variety of new forms, some of which truly *are* incommensurate with formalism, with its considerable respect for the integrity and power of the text. For instance, "subjectivists" like David Bleich, Norman Holland, and Robert Crosman have assumed what Mailloux calls the "absolute priority of individual selves as creators of texts" (*Conventions* 31). In other words, these critics do not see the reader's response as one "guided" by the text but rather as one motivated by deep-seated, personal, psychological needs. What they find in texts is, in Holland's phrase, their own "identity theme." Holland has argued that as readers we use "the literary work to symbolize and finally to replicate ourselves. We work out through the text our own characteristic patterns of desire" ("UNITY" 816). Subjective critics, as you may already have guessed, often find themselves confronted with the following question: If all interpretation is a function of private, psychological identity, then why have so many readers interpreted, say, Shakespeare's *Hamlet* in the same way? Different subjective critics have answered the question differently. Holland simply has said that common identity themes exist, such as that involving an oedipal fantasy.

Meanwhile, Fish, who in the late 1970s moved away from reader-response criticism as he had initially helped define it, came up with a different answer to the question of why different readers tend to read the same works the same way. His answer, rather than involving common individual identity themes, involved common *cultural* identity. In "Interpreting the *Variorum*" (1976), he argues that the "stability of interpretation among readers" is a function of shared "interpretive strategies." These strategies, which "exist prior to the act of reading and therefore determine the shape of what is read," are held in common by "interpretive communities" such as the one constituted by American college students reading a novel as a class assignment (*Text* 167, 171). In developing the model of interpretive communities, Fish truly has made the break with formalist or New Critical predecessors, becoming in the process something of a social, structuralist, reader-response critic. Recently, he has been engaged in studying reading communities and their interpretive conventions in order to understand the conditions that give rise to a work's intelligibility.

Fish's shift in focus is in many ways typical of changes that have taken place within the field of reader-response criticism—a field that, because of those changes, is increasingly being referred to as "reader-oriented" criticism. Less and less common are critical analyses examining the transactional interface between the text and its individual reader. Increasingly, reader-oriented critics are investigating reading communities, as the reader-oriented cultural critic Janice A. Radway has done in her study of female readers of romance paperbacks (*Reading the Romance*, 1984). They are also studying the changing reception of literary works across time; see, for example, Mailloux in his "pragmatic readings" of American literature in *Interpretive Conventions* (1982) and *Rhetorical Power* (1989).

An important catalyst of this gradual change was the work of Hans Robert Jauss, a colleague of Iser's whose historically oriented reception theory (unlike Iser's theory of the implied reader) was not available in English book form until the early 1980s. Rather than focusing on the implied, informed, or intended reader, Jauss examined actual past readers. In *Toward an Aesthetic of Reception* (1982), he argued that the reception of a work or author tends to depend upon the reading public's "horizons of expectations." He noted that, in the morally conservative climate of mid-nineteenth-century France, *Madame Bovary* was literally put on trial, its author Flaubert accused of glorifying adultery in passages representing the protagonist's fevered delirium via free indirect discourse, a mode of narration in which a third-person narrator tells us in an unfiltered way what a character is thinking and feeling.

As readers have become more sophisticated and tolerant, the popularity and reputation of *Madame Bovary* have soared. Sometimes, of course, changes in a reading public's horizons of expectations cause a work to be *less* well received over time. As American reception theorists influenced by Jauss have shown, Mark Twain's *Adventures of Huckleberry Finn* has elicited an increasingly ambivalent reaction from a reading public increasingly sensitive to demeaning racial stereotypes and racist language. The rise of feminism has prompted a downward revaluation of everything from Andrew Marvell's "To His Coy Mistress" to D. H. Lawrence's *Women in Love.*

Some reader-oriented feminists, such as Judith Fetterley, Patrocinio Schweickart, and Monique Wittig, have challenged the reader to become what Fetterley calls "the resisting reader." Arguing that literature written by men tends, in Schweickart's terms, to "immasculate" women, they have advocated strategies of reading that involve substituting masculine for feminine pronouns and male for female characters in order to expose the sexism inscribed in patriarchal texts. Other feminists, such as Nancy K. Miller in *Subject to Change* (1988), have suggested that there may be essential differences between the way women and men read and write.

That suggestion, however, has prompted considerable disagreement. A number of gender critics whose work is oriented toward readers and reading have admitted that there is such a thing as "reading like a woman" (or man), but they have also tended to agree with Peggy Kamuf that such forms of reading, like gender itself, are cultural rather than natural constructs. Gay and lesbian critics, arguing that sexualities have been similarly constructed within and by social discourse, have argued that there is a homosexual way of reading; Wayne Koestenbaum has defined "the (male twentieth-century first world) gay reader" as one who "reads resistantly for inscriptions of his condition, for texts that will confirm a social and private identity founded on a desire for other men. . . . Reading becomes a hunt for histories that deliberately foreknow or unwittingly trace a desire felt not by author but by reader, who is most acute when searching for signs of himself" (in Boone and Cadden, 176–77).

Given this kind of renewed interest in the reader and reading, some students of contemporary critical practice have been tempted to conclude that reader-oriented theory has been taken over by feminist, gender, gay, and lesbian theory. Others, like Elizabeth Freund, have suggested that it is deconstruction with which the reader-oriented approach has mixed and merged. Certainly, all of these approaches have informed and been informed by reader-response or reader-oriented theory. The case can be made, however, that there is in fact still a distinct reader-oriented approach to literature, one whose points of tangency are neither with deconstruction nor with feminist, gender, and so-called queer theory but, rather, with the new historicism and cultural criticism.

This relatively distinct form of reader theory is practiced by a number of critics, but is perhaps best exemplified by the work of scholars like Mailloux and Peter J. Rabinowitz. In *Before Reading: Narrative Conventions and the Politics of Interpretation* (1987), Rabinowitz sets forth four conventions or rules of reading, which he calls the rules of "notice," "signification," "configuration," and "coherence"—rules telling us which parts of a narrative are important, which details have a reliable secondary or special meaning, which fit into which familiar patterns, and how stories fit together as a whole. He then proceeds to analyze the misreadings and misjudgments of critics and to show that politics governs the way in which those rules are applied and broken. ("The strategies employed by critics when they read [Raymond Chandler's] *The Big Sleep*," Rabinowitz writes, "can teach us something about the structure of misogyny, not the misogyny of the novel itself, but the misogyny of the world outside it" [195].) In subsequent critical essays, Rabinowitz proceeds similarly, showing how a society's ideological assumptions about gender, race, and class determine the way in which artistic works are perceived and evaluated.

Mailloux, who calls his approach "rhetorical reception theory" or "rhetorical hermeneutics," takes a similar tack, insofar as he describes the political contexts of (mis)interpretation. In a recent essay on "Misreading as a Historical Act" (1993), he shows that a mid-nineteenth-century review of Frederick Douglass's *Narrative* by proto-feminist Margaret Fuller seems to be a misreading until we situate it "within the cultural conversation of the 'Bible politics' of 1845" (Machor 9). Woven through Mailloux's essay on Douglass and Fuller are philosophical pauses in which we are reminded, in various subtle ways, that all reading (including Mailloux's and our own) is culturally situated and likely to seem like *mis*reading someday. One such reflective pause, however, accomplishes more; in it, Mailloux reads the map of where reader-oriented criticism is today, affords a rationale for its being there, and plots its likely future direction. "However we have arrived at our present juncture," Mailloux writes,

> the current talk about historical acts of reading provides a welcome opportunity for more explicit consideration of how reading is historically contingent, politically situated, institutionally embedded, and materially conditioned; of how reading any text, literary or nonliterary, relates to a larger cultural politics that goes well beyond some hypothetical private interaction between an autonomous reader and an independent text; and of how our particular views of reading relate to the liberatory potential of literacy and the transformative power of education. (5)

In the essay that follows, "Patterns of Communication in Joyce's *Ulysses*," influential reader-response theorist Wolfgang Iser points out that, despite the novel's Homeric title and Dublin setting, "No Homeric figures actually appear in *Ulysses*, and yet the novel cannot be described as a realistic depiction of ordinary life in Dublin." Although *Ulysses* contains a wealth of detail concerning Dublin and people's lives there, the novel is hardly a realistic work of fiction; indeed, rather than creating "the illusion of reality," these details "become a sort of end in themselves, such as one finds in the art-form of the collage." Readers, realizing that these details "illustrate nothing," feel compelled to make something of the classical parallel implied by the novel's title; hence, they "try to create—through recourse to the *Odyssey*—some sort of frame of reference that will bring this chaos of detail under control and will endow everyday life with a pattern, with meaning, and with significance." But Homer's *Odyssey*, Iser argues, no more suffices to contain and explain all we experience in *Ulysses* than do the address books and newspaper cuttings from which Joyce drew the novel's details of everyday Dublin life.

Iser maintains that

> by giving his novel this structure—whether consciously or unconsciously—Joyce was complying with a basic disposition of the reader, described by Northrop Frye as follows: "Whenever we read anything, we find our attention moving in two directions at once. One direction is outward or centrifugal, in which we keep going outside our reading, from the individual words to the things they mean, or, in practice, to our memory of the conventional association between them. The other direction is inward or centripetal, in

which we try to develop from the words a sense of the larger verbal pattern they make."

In the case of *Ulysses*, we read in terms of possible "outward" Homeric parallels while, at the same time, looking for "internal" patterns like those we have observed in our personal lives and experiences. "Both approaches are, in themselves, rather flabby, and the task of stiffening them up, and indeed bringing them together, is what the novel sets its reader."

Iser develops his argument regarding the reader's dual-track task by discussing the way in which Joyce chose to present the material in *Ulysses:* through eighteen chapters, each written from its own distinct perspective. (One of these, "The Oxen of the Sun" chapter, shows the inadequacy of various linguistic styles associated with different historical periods.) Joyce thereby shows "the one-sidedness" of "characterizations" and "presentations"—that is, the degree to which they are idiosyncratic interpretations bound to leave us with a "surplus of non-integrated, unstructured material." To "moderate, if not actually neutralize, the interpretive nature of style," Iser goes on to argue, "Joyce called upon virtually every stylistic mode that the novel had evolved during its comparatively short history. These he enriched with the whole armory of allusions and with the recall of archetypes." As a result, style cannot be accused of controlling or limiting the novel's possible interpretations.

In a novel in which such things as allusion and style do not establish meaning by limiting interpretive possibility, Iser proposes, "readers themselves [must] reduce the amount of observable material to manageable proportions." This hardly means that all readers will reduce the material in the same way, or even that individual readers will reduce it the same way every time they read the novel. "Each reading," Iser maintains, "gives us a new chance to integrate the details in a different way," but also leaves us with surplus details unaccounted for by that reading—details calling out for yet other readings. *Ulysses*, in Iser's view, "offers only a potential presentation, the working out of which has to be done actively by the reader. Thus it is possible to discover many different 'pictures' of the everyday world, but they will never converge into a defined picture—and it is this very fact that compels the reader to continue his/her search."

In his several discussions of actual passages from the novel, Iser shows how readers of *Ulysses* become "involved personally" in the making of meaning. In reading a scene in which Stephen tries to teach

a history lesson, Iser argues that readers must choose between or synthesize "interior monologue, direct speech, and literary quotation"
and then ultimately bridge the gap between that sort of passage and
later ones, such as the passage in which Mr. Deasy makes "unequivocal
utterances." The text, Iser maintains,

> says nothing about any relationship between these two passages,
> but the reader will soon find a relatively straightforward way to
> bridge this gap. Viewed against the background of infinite possi-
> bilities, Mr. Deasy's self-confidence appears absurdly narrow-
> minded, and so the reader will most likely come to two conclu-
> sions: first, that Mr. Deasy is a pompous ass; second, and far more
> important, that any claim to knowledge is an automatic reduc-
> tion of the infinite and discounts above all the changeability of
> phenomena.

Such an interpretation, however, is the reader's and the reader's alone,
for, as Iser emphasizes, "there is no such statement in the text itself."

Even as Iser reads *Ulysses* anew, he advances and extends arguments he has made about the act of reading in *The Act of Reading* and
The Implied Reader. He remains interested in textual gaps, especially
as manifested in "the unconnected allusions and the abrupt alternation
of stylistic devices" in *Ulysses*. But these gaps, he insists, account for

> the stimulating quality of the text. On the one hand, the density
> of allusions and the continual segmentation of style involve an in-
> cessant changing of perspectives, which seem to go out of control
> whenever the reader tries to pin them down; on the other hand,
> the gaps resulting from cuts and abbreviations tempt the reader to
> fill them in. He / she will try to group things, because this is the
> only way in which he / she can recognize situations or understand
> characters in the novel.

Iser ultimately argues, however, that Joyce's gap-filled structure
and style inspire readers to do more than try to recognize situations
or understand characters. Rather, Joyce "makes us aware that the degree of indeterminacy is irreducible, thus indicating that all the semi-
consistent conceptions we have of everyday phenomena can only
become conceptions because they ignore the inexplicability of reality."

Ross C Murfin

READER-RESPONSE CRITICISM:
A SELECTED BIBLIOGRAPHY

Some Introductions to
Reader-Response Criticism

Beach, Richard. *A Teacher's Introduction to Reader-Response Theories.*
Urbana: NCTE, 1993.

Fish, Stanley E. "Literature in the Reader: Affective Stylistics." *New
Literary History* 2 (1970): 123–61. Rpt. in Fish, *Text* 21–67, and
in Primeau 154–79.

Freund, Elizabeth. *The Return of the Reader: Reader-Response Criticism.* London: Methuen, 1987.

Holub, Robert C. *Reception Theory: A Critical Introduction.* New
York: Methuen, 1984.

Leitch, Vincent B. *American Literary Criticism from the Thirties to the
Eighties.* New York: Columbia UP, 1988.

Mailloux, Steven. "Learning to Read: Interpretation and Reader-
Response Criticism." *Studies in the Literary Imagination* 12
(1979): 93–108.

———. "Reader-Response Criticism?" *Genre* 10 (1977): 413–31.

———. "The Turns of Reader-Response Criticism." *Conversations:
Contemporary Critical Theory and the Teaching of Literature.* Ed.
Charles Moran and Elizabeth F. Penfield. Urbana: NCTE, 1990.
38–54.

Rabinowitz, Peter J. "Whirl Without End: Audience-Oriented Criticism." *Contemporary Literary Theory.* Ed. G. Douglas Atkins and
Laura Morrow. Amherst: U of Massachusetts P, 1989. 81–100.

Rosenblatt, Louise M. "Towards a Transactional Theory of Reading."
Journal of Reading Behavior 1 (1969): 31–47. Rpt. in Primeau
121–46.

Suleiman, Susan R. "Introduction: Varieties of Audience-Oriented
Criticism." Suleiman and Crosman 3–45.

Tompkins, Jane P. "An Introduction to Reader-Response Criticism."
Tompkins ix–xxiv.

Reader-Response Criticism in
Anthologies and Collections

Flynn, Elizabeth A., and Patrocinio P. Schweickart, eds. *Gender and
Reading: Essays on Readers, Texts, and Contexts.* Baltimore: Johns
Hopkins UP, 1986.

Garvin, Harry R., ed. *Theories of Reading, Looking, and Listening.* Lewisburg: Bucknell UP, 1981. Essays by Cain and Rosenblatt.

Machor, James L., ed. *Readers in History: Nineteenth-Century American Literature and the Contexts of Response.* Baltimore: Johns Hopkins UP, 1993. Contains Mailloux essay "Misreading as a Historical Act: Cultural Rhetoric, Bible Politics, and Fuller's 1845 Review of Douglass's *Narrative.*"

Primeau, Ronald, ed. *Influx: Essays on Literary Influence.* Port Washington: Kennikat, 1977. Essays by Fish, Holland, and Rosenblatt.

Suleiman, Susan R., and Inge Crosman, eds. *The Reader in the Text: Essays on Audience and Interpretation.* Princeton: Princeton UP, 1980. See especially the essays by Culler, Iser, and Todorov.

Tompkins, Jane P., ed. *Reader-Response Criticism: From Formalism to Post-Structuralism.* Baltimore: Johns Hopkins UP, 1980. See especially the essays by Bleich, Fish, Holland, Prince, and Tompkins.

Reader-Response Criticism: Some Major Works

Bleich, David. *Subjective Criticism.* Baltimore: Johns Hopkins UP, 1978.

Booth, Stephen. *An Essay on Shakespeare's Sonnets.* New Haven: Yale UP, 1969.

Booth, Wayne C. *A Rhetoric of Irony.* Chicago: U of Chicago P, 1974.

Eco, Umberto. *The Role of the Reader: Explorations in the Semiotics of Texts.* Bloomington: Indiana UP, 1979.

Fish, Stanley Eugene. *Doing What Comes Naturally: Change, Rhetoric, and the Practice of Theory in Literary and Legal Studies.* Durham: Duke UP, 1989.

———. *Is There a Text in This Class? The Authority of Interpretive Communities.* Cambridge: Harvard UP, 1980. This volume contains most of Fish's most influential essays, including "Literature in the Reader: Affective Stylistics," "What It's Like to Read *L'Allegro* and *Il Penseroso,*" "Interpreting the *Variorum,*" "How to Recognize a Poem When You See One," "Is There a Text in This Class?" and "What Makes an Interpretation Acceptable?"

———. *Self-Consuming Artifact: The Experience of Seventeenth-Century Literature.* Berkeley: U of California P, 1972.

———. *Surprised by Sin: The Reader in "Paradise Lost."* 2nd ed. Berkeley: U of California P, 1971.

Holland, Norman N. *5 Readers Reading.* New Haven: Yale UP, 1975.

———. "UNITY IDENTITY TEXT SELF." *PMLA* 90 (1975): 813–22.

Iser, Wolfgang. *The Act of Reading: A Theory of Aesthetic Response.* Baltimore: Johns Hopkins UP, 1978.

———. *The Implied Reader: Patterns of Communication in Prose Fiction from Bunyan to Beckett.* Baltimore: Johns Hopkins UP, 1974.

Jauss, Hans Robert. *Toward an Aesthetic of Reception.* Trans. Timothy Bahti. Intro. Paul de Man. Brighton, Eng.: Harvester, 1982.

Mailloux, Steven. *Interpretive Conventions: The Reader in the Study of American Fiction.* Ithaca: Cornell UP, 1982.

———. *Rhetorical Power.* Ithaca: Cornell UP, 1989.

Messent, Peter. *New Readings of the American Novel: Narrative Theory and Its Application.* New York: Macmillan, 1991.

Prince, Gerald. *Narratology.* New York: Mouton, 1982.

Rabinowitz, Peter J. *Before Reading: Narrative Conventions and the Politics of Interpretation.* Ithaca: Cornell UP, 1987.

Radway, Janice A. *Reading the Romance: Women, Patriarchy, and Popular Literature.* Chapel Hill: U of North Carolina P, 1984.

Rosenblatt, Louise M. *Literature as Exploration.* 4th ed. New York: MLA, 1983.

———. *The Reader, the Text, the Poem: The Transactional Theory of the Literary Work.* Carbondale: Southern Illinois UP, 1978.

Slatoff, Walter J. *With Respect to Readers: Dimensions of Literary Response.* Ithaca: Cornell UP, 1970.

Steig, Michael. *Stories of Reading: Subjectivity and Literary Understanding.* Baltimore: Johns Hopkins UP, 1989.

Exemplary Short Readings of Major Texts

Anderson, Howard. "*Tristram Shandy* and the Reader's Imagination." *PMLA* 86 (1971): 966–73.

Berger, Carole. "The Rake and the Reader in Jane Austen's Novels." *Studies in English Literature, 1500–1900* 15 (1975): 531–44.

Booth, Stephen. "On the Value of *Hamlet.*" *Reinterpretations of English Drama: Selected Papers from the English Institute.* Ed. Norman Rabkin. New York: Columbia UP, 1969. 137–76.

Easson, Robert R. "William Blake and His Reader in *Jerusalem.*" *Blake's Sublime Allegory.* Ed. Stuart Curran and Joseph A. Wittreich. Madison: U of Wisconsin P, 1973. 309–28.

Kirk, Carey H. "*Moby-Dick:* The Challenge of Response." *Papers on Language and Literature* 13 (1977): 383–90.

Leverenz, David. "Mrs. Hawthorne's Headache: Reading *The Scarlet Letter*." *Nathaniel Hawthorne, "The Scarlet Letter."* Ed. Ross C Murfin. Case Studies in Contemporary Criticism. Boston: Bedford–St. Martin's, 1991. 263–74.

Lowe-Evans, Mary. "Reading with a 'Nicer Eye': Responding to *Frankenstein*." *Mary Shelley, "Frankenstein."* Ed. Johanna M. Smith. Case Studies in Contemporary Criticism. Boston: Bedford–St. Martin's, 1992. 215–29.

Rabinowitz, Peter J. "'A Symbol of Something': Interpretive Vertigo in 'The Dead.'" *James Joyce, "The Dead."* Ed. Daniel R. Schwarz. Case Studies in Contemporary Criticism. Boston: Bedford–St. Martin's, 1994. 137–49.

Treichler, Paula. "The Construction of Ambiguity in *The Awakening*." *Kate Chopin, "The Awakening."* Ed. Nancy A. Walker. Case Studies in Contemporary Criticism. Boston: Bedford–St. Martin's, 1993. 308–28.

Other Works Referred to in "What Is Reader-Response Criticism?"

Booth, Wayne C. *A Rhetoric of Irony*. Chicago: U of Chicago P, 1974.

Culler, Jonathan. *Structural Poetics: Structuralism, Linguistics, and the Study of Literature*. Ithaca: Cornell UP, 1975.

Koestenbaum, Wayne. "Wilde's Hard Labor and the Birth of Gay Reading." *Engendering Men: The Question of Male Feminist Criticism*. Ed. Joseph A. Boone and Michael Cadden. New York: Routledge, 1990.

Richards, I. A. *Practical Criticism*. New York: Harcourt, 1929. Rpt. in *Criticism: The Major Texts*. Ed. Walter Jackson Bate. Rev. ed. New York: Harcourt, 1970. 575.

Wimsatt, William K., and Monroe C. Beardsley. *The Verbal Icon*. Lexington: U of Kentucky P, 1954. See especially the discussion of "The Affective Fallacy," with which reader-response critics have so sharply disagreed.

Reader-Response Approaches to Joyce

Iser, Wolfgang. "Doing Things in Style: An Interpretation of 'The Oxen of the Sun' in James Joyce's *Ulysses*." *The Implied Reader: Patterns of Communication in Prose Fiction from Bunyan to Beckett*. Baltimore: Johns Hopkins UP, 1974.

James Joyce Quarterly 16 (Fall 1978 / Winter 1979). "Structuralist / Reader-Response" issue.

Lawrence, Karen. *The Odyssey of Style in "Ulysses."* Princeton: Princeton UP, 1981.

Riquelme, John Paul. *Teller and Tale in Joyce's Fiction: Oscillating Perspectives.* Baltimore: Johns Hopkins UP, 1983.

Senn, Fritz. *Joyce's Dislocutions: Essays on Reading as Translation.* Ed. John Paul Riquelme. Baltimore: Johns Hopkins UP, 1984.

Thomas, Brook. *James Joyce's "Ulysses": A Book of Many Happy Returns.* Baton Rouge: Louisiana State UP, 1982.

A READER-RESPONSE PERSPECTIVE

WOLFGANG ISER

Patterns of Communication in Joyce's *Ulysses*

No Homeric figures actually appear in *Ulysses*, and yet the novel cannot be described as a realistic depiction of ordinary life in Dublin, despite the vast number of verifiable details that run right through it. We have since learned that a great deal of this material was drawn from Dublin address books, topographical descriptions, and the daily press of that time, so that an astonishing wealth of names, addresses, local events, and even newspaper cuttings can actually be identified (Adams), though in the text they frequently form a montage that is stripped of its context. Sometimes the details vanish away into the impenetrable private sphere of Joyce himself, and sometimes they seem to lead the reader into a veritable labyrinth when he/she attempts to collate them. In searching for and visualizing connections, he/she often loses the organizing principle of the connections thought to have been discovered. And frequently it seems as though the many details are simply there for their own sake and, through sheer weight of numbers, more or less deliberately blur the outline of events in the narrative.

The effect of all this is somewhat paradoxical, for it runs completely contrary to the expectations that the realistic novel had established in its readers. There, too, one was confronted with a wealth of details which the reader could see reflected in his/her own world of experience. Their appearance in the novel served mainly to authenticate the view of life offered (Jauss 161 f., 241 f.). But in *Ulysses* they are, to a great extent, deprived of this function. When details no longer serve to reinforce probability or to stabilize the illusion of reality, they must become a sort of end in themselves, such as one finds in the art-form of the collage. The unstructured material of *Ulysses* is taken directly *from* life itself, but since it no longer testifies to the author's preconception of reality, it cannot be taken *for* life itself. Thus the details illustrate nothing; they simply present themselves, and since they bear witness to nothing beyond themselves, they revoke the normal assumption that a novel represents a given reality. It is not surprising, then, that one is constantly returning to the title in order to try to create—through recourse to the *Odyssey*—some sort of frame of reference that will bring this chaos of detail under control and will endow everyday life with a pattern, with meaning, and with significance.

We now have a double frustration of our expectations: not only do the Homeric figures fail to appear in *Ulysses* but also the many details are deprived of their usual function. As a result, our attention is drawn to the evocative nature of the novel. We realize that all these details constitute a surplus that projects far beyond any organizational schema that the novel may offer us. And so each reading gives us a new chance to integrate the details in a different way—with the result, however, that each form of integration brings about a sort of kaleidoscopic reshuffling of the material excluded.

By giving his novel this structure—whether consciously or unconsciously—Joyce was complying with a basic disposition of the reader, described by Northrop Frye as follows: "Whenever we read anything, we find our attention moving in two directions at once. One direction is outward or centrifugal, in which we keep going outside our reading, from the individual words to the things they mean, or, in practice, to our memory of the conventional association between them. The other direction is inward or centripetal, in which we try to develop from the words a sense of the larger verbal pattern they make" (Frye, *Anatomy* 73). These two tendencies seem to take the reader of *Ulysses* in completely different directions, which are divergent rather than convergent. As he/she reads, he/she finds that everyday life in Dublin is, so to speak, continually breaking its banks, and the resultant flood of detail induces the reader to try and build his/her own dams of meaning—though these in turn are inevitably broken down. Even the signal contained in the title seems to dispel rather than fulfill one's hopes of controlling the material, for the central frame of reference that one would so like to deduce from the *Odyssey* is never formulated anywhere in the text. According to whether one reads the novel from the Dublin viewpoint or from that of the *Odyssey*, one will get quite different 'images.' In the first case, the apparent lack of connection between the many details creates the impression of a thoroughly chaotic world; in the second, one wonders what the return of Ulysses in modern trappings is supposed to signify. Both approaches are, in themselves, relatively flabby, and the task of stiffening them up, and indeed bringing them together, is what the novel sets its reader.

The Homeric allusions in *Ulysses* open up an horizon which is certainly not identical with that of the modern "World-Weekday" (Broch 187), for between the present and the archetypes of the Homeric epic lies the whole of history, which could only be passed over if *Ulysses* were concerned with nothing but the return of archetypes. One should not forget, when considering the Homeric parallel, that Joyce permeated his novel with just as many Shakespearean allusions as Homeric. And even if one tries to equate Shakespeare's presence in *Ulysses* with the return of archetypes, nevertheless there is no denying the fact that Joyce was obviously more interested in the various manifestations of such archetypes than in merely establishing their return. This certainly indicates that for him the archetype was, at most, a vehicle, but not a subject. The history of its manifestations takes precedence over its mythical nature. But what is this history, and in what form is it reflected in the novel?

Our answer to this question can, perhaps, best proceed from the experiments in style. These in themselves are an innovation, insofar as the eighteen chapters of the novel present the narrative through eighteen differently structured perspectives. Normally, when reading a novel, we are asked only once to adopt the author's chosen standpoint in order to fulfill his intentions—but here the same demand is made of us no less than seventeen extra times, for each chapter is written in a different style. Style, according to John Middleton Murry, "is a quality of language which communicates . . . a system of emotions or thoughts, peculiar to the author" (Murry 65). We can talk of style when systematic viewpoints bring about a frame of reference that is to direct the reader's observations by selecting which facts are or are not to be presented.

This function of style is both its strength and its weakness, for inevitably it must restrict the field of observation. The meaning that it is to express can only take its shape through the process of selecting particular aspects of phenomena to be presented, and so phenomena are reproduced mainly for the sake of what they will communicate to the reader. As style imposes a specific meaning and edits reality to coincide with this meaning, it reveals itself to be a "mythical analogue" (Lugowski 12), which—as Clemens Lugowski has shown—not only implies a particular conception of reality but is also the agent that actually forms it. Although this "'mythical artifice' . . . is the result of a deeply unconscious and indirect act of interpretation" (Lugowski 206), for this very reason it will freeze the historical conditions under which such acts of interpretation came into being.

In *Ulysses* Joyce shows up these limitations by thematizing the capacity of style itself. In constantly changing the perspective through the eighteen chapters, he draws attention to the normative pressure caused by the modes of observation inherent in any one style, thus revealing the extreme one-sidedness of each individual "act of interpretation." While the change of styles shows up these limitations, the process is underlined in the individual chapters by the surplus of nonintegrated, unstructured material. This, too, makes one aware of the limitations of the style in question, so that it often seems more real than the view of reality being presented at the time.

Thus we have changes of style and nonintegrated material to show up the limitations of each style, and in addition to these two factors, there is even a kind of authorial commentary (Goldberg 288) which has these very limitations as its subject. This is the case in "The Oxen of the Sun," which Joyce critics have always approached with a kind of embarrassment (Iser 179–95). T. S. Eliot had the impression that this chapter showed the "futility of all the English styles" (Ellmann 490), and this must certainly have been at least one of the effects that Joyce was aiming at.

In this display of individual and period styles, we are made aware of the various assumptions that condition the different presentations of the theme. By parodying the styles, Joyce makes sure that we do not overlook the 'interpretive' nature of the forms of presentation. Leopold Bloom finds himself transformed into a variety of figures, in accordance with the particular style used: the medieval "traveller Leopold" changes into the Arthurian knight "Sir Leopold," who in turn leaps into a new context as "childe Leopold" (pp. 369–70). The reader cannot help being aware of the one-sidedness of all these characterizations, as he/she has already become familiar in the preceding chapters with the many-sidedness of Bloom's character. This same one-sidedness is equally evident in the central theme of the chapter. This does not deal with love, but only with the way in which Malory, Bunyan, Addison and the other writers conceived of love. The basically comic effect arises out of the impression one has that the views, expressed in such a variety of styles, exclude rather than supplement one another. With each author the main theme takes on a different shape, but as each style automatically and unquestioningly assumes that it has captured the reality of the phenomenon, the latent naiveté comes to the surface. The question arises as to which of these individual views comes closest to the truth, but even then we realize that the individual authors, precisely through their selection of a particular means of presentation, have in fact edited the subject to form a single meaning and a single evaluation. The very fact that these meanings and evaluations seem to assume a normative validity makes us aware of the extent to which they depend on the historical situation from which they have sprung. If "The Oxen of the Sun" is taken, then, as the author's own 'commentary' on his work, one can scarcely expect him to organize his novel as yet another "act of interpretation." It is the *presentation* of everyday life that concerns him, and not the evaluation.

However, such a presentation also requires a form, and inevitably any form that Joyce chose would automatically foreshorten the phenomenon to be presented. And so one might assume that the chapters of the novel were organized, each as a sort of rebuttal to the others, with their respective *principium stilisationis*. The consequences of this principle of construction are very far-reaching. Joyce could parody the different styles in order to show the limitations of their capacity, but if he applied this technique to the whole novel, it would mean that in trying to present the events, etc., of June 16, 1904, he would have to parody himself continually. There are certainly traces of this in the text, but a constant self-parody would ultimately distract the reader from coming to grips with the events of June 16, 1904. And would this not in turn—like all parodies—lead primarily to a negative evaluation, as limited in its own way as the evaluations of the authors parodied? Such a form would itself constitute an "act of interpretation."

Is it possible for anything to be presented, and yet at the same time for the "act of interpretation" to be suspended without the object of presentation becoming incomprehensible? *Ulysses* is the answer to this question. In order to moderate, if not actually neutralize, the interpretive nature of style, Joyce called upon virtually every stylistic mode that the novel had evolved during its comparatively short history. These he enriched with the whole armory of allusions and with the recall of archetypes. The multiplicity of these schemata, together with the complexity of their interrelationships, results in a form of presentation that in fact presents each incipient meaning simultaneously with its own diffusion. Thus the novel does not paint a picture of the "World-Weekday"—which means, ultimately, that it does not 'present' anything in the conventional sense—but, through the great variety of its perspectives, it offers possibilities for conceiving or imagining the "World-Weekday." These possibilities must be fulfilled by the readers themselves, if they want to make contact with the reality of the novel. One must therefore differentiate between 'presentation' (that is, by the author) and 'imagination' (on the part of the reader). Of course, even if the 'interpretive acts' of the novel are obvious, the readers still have to imagine things for themselves. But they will only conduct these 'interpretive acts' if the system of presentation leaves out the co-ordinating elements between observable phenomena and situations. In *Ulysses* this is brought about mainly through the overprecision of the system, which presents more conceivable material than the reader is capable of processing as he/she reads. And so it is not the style of the novel but the overtaxed readers themselves that reduce the amount of observable material to manageable proportions. In doing so, they can scarcely avoid equating this reduced amount with the meaning. If one considers reactions to *Ulysses* over the last forty years—insofar as these can be gauged by the different interpretations offered—one can see how historically conditioned such meanings are. At the same time, it cannot be denied that the many possible permutations of meaning in *Ulysses* act as a constant inducement to the reader to formulate a meaning—and in doing so, he/she is forced to enter into the action of the novel.

The individual chapters of *Ulysses* act, to a greater or lesser degree, as signposts that point the way through the "World-Weekday," rather than guidebooks that impose on the reader a specific interpretation of the regions they represent. If we want to get a proper understanding of the function of the patterns of presentation, the allusions, and also the archetypes, it might be as well first to examine one or two concrete examples.

The novel begins with the parody of a church ritual. Mulligan, the medical student, holds his shaving-bowl aloft at the top of the Martello tower, and intones: *Introibo ad altare Dei* (1). If this little curtain-raiser is a sign of what is to come, then we appear to be due for one long parody. At first this impression seems to be confirmed by the subsequent conversation between Mulligan and Stephen, for as he talks the former jumps around abruptly from one stylistic level to another, everyday slang alternating with scholarly allusions to Greece, Irish mythology, and even Zarathustra (5, 9, 20). Indeed individual allusions are sometimes broken up and even corrupted. Are we now to have a series of parodied stylistic levels? If so, there would be a danger of the tension soon flagging, for a parody of stylistic levels here might seem trivial after the initial 'exposing' of the mass. Moreover, it is scarcely possible to find a *tertium comparationis* for the various intersecting levels of Mulligan's speech.

It is also impossible to establish a purpose for such a parody, unless one wanted to conclude from the diffusion of stylistic levels that Joyce was advocating a purist use of language — an idea that is hardly worth considering. In fact, one gets the impression that what is stated is nothing but a stimulus to call forth its own reversal. Thus the profane distortions of the ritual of the mass take on a significance other than that of mere parody. Like the subsequent conversation, they point up the limitations of all clearly formulated statements that induce the reader to supply his/her own connections between the segmented stylistic levels. As the text offers no point of convergence for the phenomena it sets before him, the reader tends to load each detail with meaning, and since the meaning cannot be fully realized, there arises a latent tension between the unconnected phenomena. This basic pattern, with a few variations, runs right through the first chapter, which Joyce called "Telemachus" in his 'notesheets' (Litz 39). The most important type of variation is the abrupt switch of narrator. In the middle of a third-person narrative we are suddenly confronted with statements in the first person (7–8), which strike the reader so forcibly that he/she soon becomes more conscious of narrative patterns than of things narrated. And so here, as elsewhere in the novel, one gets the impression that one must constantly differentiate between the linguistic possibilities of style and the possible nature of the phenomena concerned.

The predominant pattern of reversal in this first chapter reduces all that is clear and concrete to a mere position in life, but life itself goes far beyond such positions. The next chapter, originally called "Nestor," reveals the implications of this fact, and naturally another collection of stylistic patterns is necessary to uncover these hidden consequences. Stephen's interior monologue is the dominant pattern in this chapter, but it is broken up by authorial passages, direct speech, and also quotations from Milton's *Lycidas* (22–23), all set against and arising out of the background of the morning lesson. They lead to reflections on history and man's possible place in history:

> For them too history was a tale like any other too often heard, their land a pawnshop.
> Had Pyrrhus not fallen by a beldam's hand in Argos or Julius Caesar not been knifed to death? They are not to be thought away. Time has branded them and fettered they are lodged in the room of the infinite possibilities they have ousted. But can those have been possible seeing that they never were? Or was that only possible which came to pass? Weave, weaver of the wind . . . It must be a movement then, an actuality of the possible as possible. (22–23)

It is not insignificant that this reflection on the possible is inspired specifically by historical processes in which everything appears to be so irrevocably fixed. Is this determinacy ultimately to be seen as one possibility among many? What about the existences of historical individuals? If, through their deeds and sufferings, they stepped outside the jurisdiction of infinite possibilities, why should they now fall back into it? It seems almost like a sophism when Stephen asks whether Pyrrhus and Caesar even considered the possibility, when they were alive, that one day they would not be there, or that they would end as they did. Although he himself considers such thoughts to be mere speculations, they do not stop him from concluding that real life can only be understood as an actuality of one possibility among many. But if what happened did not happen inevitably, then the real is nothing but a chance track left by the possible. And if reality is nothing but one chance track, then it pales to insignificance beside the vast number of unseen and unfulfilled possibilities; it shrinks to the dimensions of a mere curiosity. The tendency apparent in these reflections of Stephen's runs parallel to that at the beginning of the novel, where whatever was said pointed the way to its own reversal, and whatever possibilities were excluded by each utterance were brought out by another.

The children are bored by the history lesson, and want Stephen to tell them a story: "Tell us a story, sir.—Oh, do, sir. A ghoststory" (22). Stephen himself has just had the impression that, when one thinks

about it, history changes into a ghost story, albeit a different type from
the one the children would like to hear. Bored by the factual, they
are now asking for the fantastic, without realizing how much incom-
prehensibility lies in the factual. The text, of course, does not state
this, but the manner in which the different perspectives are thrust
against one another compels the reader to search for a link between
them. The text offers him/her no guide as to how the different standpoints might be evaluated, and at best he/she can only orient himself/
herself through the next perspective which, like that of the children,
is inserted into Stephen's monologue. There is no "ghoststory"; instead, the children begin to read verses from Milton's *Lycidas*—those
lines where the mourning shepherd is consoled with the assurance that
the dead do not perish. Evidently only poetry eternalizes; but poetry
is fiction.

   In this comparatively short section of the text, there are three
different intersecting patterns: interior monologue, direct speech, and
literary quotations—all focused upon a relatively uniform theme
which, however, takes on three different forms as it is presented to
the reader. For Stephen reality is so overshadowed by the possible that
it is deprived of its unique significance. The children are bored by what
has been and want the titillation of the unreal. The literary quotation
shows how clearly that eternalization only exists in the medium of
fiction. The text does not say how these three viewpoints are to be
joined together, but simply offers three different possibilities for relating the real to the unreal. As the individual stylistic patterns intersect
within the text, there is no hierarchic construction. The reflections
of the inner monologue point inevitably to the private nature of the
opinion expressed; the desires of the school children appear as something spontaneous and naive and the quotation as a kind of insurance
without any reality. Although this need not be regarded as the only
possible interpretation of the different patterns of the text, the conditions are certainly there for such an interpretation. Since these patterns
are without a point of convergence, their meaning arises out of their
interaction—a process which is set in motion by the readers themselves and which will therefore involve them personally in the text.

   Apart from the patterns we have mentioned, this process is encouraged above all by the end of the chapter, which deals with a conversation between Stephen and the headmaster, Mr. Deasy. The headmaster gives Stephen a letter which he wants published in the *Evening
Telegraph*, because it contains his (Deasy's) solution to an important

problem: foot-and-mouth disease. "I have put the matter into a nut-shell, Mr Deasy said. It's about the foot and mouth disease. Just look through it. There can be no two opinions on the matter" (30). For Mr. Deasy, there can be no two opinions about this or about a number of other political problems in Ireland. But now the segmented text pattern of Stephen's history lesson becomes the background to Mr. Deasy's unequivocal utterances, through which he seeks once and for all to set right existing realities. Again the text says nothing about any relationship between these two passages, but the reader will soon find a relatively straightforward way to bridge this gap. Viewed against the background of infinite possibilities, Mr. Deasy's self-confidence appears absurdly narrow-minded, and so the reader will most likely come to two conclusions: first, that Mr. Deasy is a pompous ass; second, and far more important, that any claim to knowledge is an automatic reduction of the infinite and discounts above all the changeability of phenomena. However, let it be empha-sized once again—this interpretation will be the reader's, for there is no such statement in the text itself.

As regards the original chapter heading—"Nestor"—this offers yet another perspective, insofar as the reader will try to link the wis-dom of Nestor with the pretension of Mr. Deasy. He/she will proba-bly find that not only does Mr. Deasy suffer from the comparison, but so, too, does Nestor. For if, in Mr. Deasy's case, claims to knowledge presuppose unawareness of the changeability of phenomena, then the mythical wisdom of Nestor is open to re-evaluation by the reader.

As it would be beyond the scope of this essay to deal with all the experiments of style in *Ulysses*, we shall confine ourselves to those that evince the most striking variations. One of these is undoubtedly the "Aeolus" chapter. Bloom's visit to the newspaper office provides the framework for a curiously patterned form of narration. Analysis reveals two separate levels of the text, which one might call, for the sake of convenience, the micro- and the macrostructure of the chapter. The microstructural level consists of a large number of allusions which basically can be divided into three different groups: (1) those dealing with the immediate situation, Bloom's effort to place an advertisement at the newspaper office and the events connected with it; (2) those referring to completely different episodes outside the chapter itself, sometimes relating to incidents already described and sometimes anticipating things; (3) those passages which seem to slide into obscurity when one tries to work out exactly where they might be heading. However, as these allusions are not only distinctly separated, but are in fact woven into an intricate pattern, each one of them tends to entice the reader to follow it. Thus the allusions themselves turn into microperspectives which, because of their very density, simply cannot be followed through to the end. They form abbreviated extracts from reality which inevitably compel the reader to a process of selection.

This is also true of the other stylistic pattern to be discerned within the microstructural stratum. Just as with the allusions, there is throughout an abrupt alternation between dialogue, direct and indirect speech, authorial report, first-person narrative, and interior monologue. Although such techniques do impose a certain order on the abundance of allusions, they also invest them with differing importance. An allusion by the author himself certainly has a function for the context different from one that is made in indirect speech by one of the characters. Thus extracts from reality and individual events are not contracted merely into allusions, but, through the different patterns of style, emerge in forms that endow them with a varied range of relevance. At the same time, the unconnected allusions and the abrupt alternation of stylistic devices disclose a large number of gaps.

All this gives rise to the stimulating quality of the text. On the one hand, the density of allusions and the continual segmentation of style involve an incessant changing of perspectives, which seem to go out of control whenever the reader tries to pin them down; on the other hand, the gaps resulting from cuts and abbreviations tempt the reader to fill them in. He/she will try to group things, because this is the only way in which he/she can recognize situations or understand characters in the novel.

The macrostructure of the chapter lends itself to this need for 'grouping,' though in a peculiar way. Heading and 'newspaper column' form the schema that incorporates the allusions and stylistic changes. The heading is an instruction as to what to expect. But the text which follows the caption reveals the composition described above, and so in most cases does not fulfill the expectation raised by the heading. As the newspaper headlines refer to various incidents in the city, the situation of Ireland, and so forth, they would seem to be concerned with everyday events, the reality of which is beyond question. But the column that follows frustrates this expectation, not only by leading commonplace realities off in unforeseeable directions, thus destroying the grouping effect of the headline, but also by fragmenting facts and occurrences in such a way that to comprehend the commonplace becomes a real effort. While the heading appears to gratify our basic need for grouping, this need is predominantly subverted by the text that follows.

In the "Aeolus" chapter, the reader not only learns something about events in Dublin on June 16, 1904, but he also experiences the difficulties inherent in the comprehension of the barest outline of events. It is precisely because the heading suggests a way of grouping from a particular viewpoint that the text itself seems so thoroughly to contradict our familiar notions of perception. The text appears to defy transcription of the circumstances indicated and instead offers the reader nothing but attitudes or possibilities of perception concerning these circumstances.

Sometimes it does, however, occur in this chapter that the expectations aroused by the headings are fulfilled. At such moments, the text seems banal, for when the reader has adjusted himself to the nonfulfillment of his expectations, he will view things differently when they *are* fulfilled. The reason for this is easy to grasp. If the text of the column does not connect up with the heading, the readers must supply the missing links. Their participation in the intention of the text is thus enhanced. If the text does fulfill the expectations aroused by the heading, no removing of gaps is required of the reader and he/she feels the 'letdown' of banality. In this way, the textual pattern in this chapter arouses continual conflicts with the reader's own modes of perception, and as the author has completely withdrawn from this montage of possibilities, the reader is given no guidance as to how to resolve the conflicts. But it is through these very conflicts, and the confrontation with the array of different possibilities, that the reader of such a text is given the impression that something does happen to him/her.

It is perhaps not by chance that in this chapter the Homeric parallel has shrunk to the barest recollection, for the basic schema of composition is determined not by the scattering of news to all winds, but by the manner in which this scattered news is received. Joyce makes his theme out of what did not concern Homer, and this also reveals something of the strategy of literary allusions that Joyce used in *Ulysses*.

Of a quite different sort is the stylistic experiment in the chapter originally called "Ithaca," which is of particular interest since it deals with the theme of homecoming. This archetypal situation is presented here as an uninterrupted sequence of questions and answers involving the main characters. To all appearances this interrogation is conducted by an anonymous narrator, who more or less asks himself what Bloom and Stephen think, do, feel, intend, communicate, mean, etc., and then proceeds himself to give answers that are as wide-ranging as they are detailed. But what exactly is the purpose of this inquiry, and why should the narrator be asking all the questions, since he appears to know all the answers anyway?

The effect of the mode of presentation in this chapter is that it seems constantly to place a barrier between the reader and the events of Bloom's nocturnal homecoming that are to be narrated; instead of describing these events, it appears to be continually interrupting them. In this way, the characters in the novel seem to fade into the distance—especially since each question is assigned an answer which is so loaded with precise detail that the reader's comprehension is in danger of being utterly swamped. This tends to divert the reader's attention away from the events and onto the curious nature of this question-and-answer process. For, obviously, the intention of the chapter must lie in this and not in the details of the nocturnal events. But if the mode of presentation sets aside rather than describes the events, and obtrudes on the reader instead of orienting him/her, then the only justification for this 'going against the grain' must be that it exposes something which generally would be obscured by the mode of presentation.

Let us consider an example. When Bloom comes home, he puts some water on the stove because he wants to have a shave. The question-and-answer process now concerns the boiling of the water:

> What concomitant phenomenon took place in the vessel of liquid by the agency of fire?
> The phenomenon of ebullition. Fanned by a constant updraught of ventilation between the kitchen and the chimney-flue, ignition was communicated from the faggots of precombustible fuel to polyhedral masses of bituminous coal, containing in compressed mineral form the foliated fossilised decidua of primeval forests which had in turn derived their vegetative existence from the sun, primal source of heat (radiant), transmitted through omnipresent luminiferous diathermanous ether. Heat (convected), a mode of motion developed by such combustion, was constantly and increasingly conveyed from the source of calorification to the liquid contained in the vessel, being radiated through the uneven unpolished dark surface of the metal iron, in

part reflected, in part absorbed, in part transmitted, gradually rais-
ing the temperature of the water from normal to boiling point, a
rise in temperature expressible as the result of an expenditure of
72 thermal units needed to raise 1 pound of water from 50° to
212° Fahrenheit. (634)

The amount of scientific data—in this chapter a typical feature which
becomes even more complicated elsewhere—shows how difficult it is
to give the required reason for the phenomenon in question.

An impression akin to fantasy is evoked by the chain of cause and
effect which, instead of going straight back to the primal cause, seems
only to bring out more and more dependent factors. The more precise
the description of these factors, the further into the distance recedes
the primal cause and the more aware we become of the unexplainabil-
ity of what is to be explained. As the narrator asks more and more
questions, the answers demonstrate not his knowledge so much as the
unobtainability of the right answers—and this is emphasized by the
very preciseness of what *is* known. Thus the tendency underlying this
question-and-answer process is one that aims at showing the degree of
indeterminability inherent in all phenomena. It is scarcely surprising
then that new questions are constantly thrown up which are meant to
limit the amount of indeterminacy, but instead—thanks to their very
precision—in fact increase it.

The question-and-answer process makes us aware that the degree of indeterminacy is irreducible, thus indicating that all the semi-
consistent conceptions we have of everyday phenomena can only become conceptions because they ignore the inexplicability of reality.
They are, in this sense, a fiction.

Now if indeterminacy is only to be removed by means of fiction,
the reader finds the ground cut away from beneath his/her feet whenever he/she realizes this. The "Ithaca" chapter keeps maneuvering
him/her into a position from which he/she can escape only by taking
up a definite attitude. He/she might decide that the chain of ironic
answers forms a parody of scientific pedantry. But, as Northrop Frye
states in another context, the ironic solution is: "the negative pole of
the allegorical one. Irony presents a human conflict which . . . is unsat-
isfactory and incomplete unless we see in it a significance beyond itself . . . What that significance is, irony does not say: it leaves that question up to the reader or audience" (Frye, "Road" 14). This is the sort of
irony we find in the "Ithaca" chapter, which uses its ironic elements to
give the reader responsibility for finding his/her own solution. This, of

course, involves interpreting, and in order to ensure that interpretation be kept in its proper perspective, certain warning signals are built into the text. To the question: "What qualifying considerations allayed his [that is, Bloom's] perturbations?" comes the answer: "The difficulties of interpretation since the significance of any event followed its occurrence as variably as the acoustic report followed the electrical discharge and of counterestimating against an actual loss by failure to interpret the total sum of possible losses proceeding originally from a successful interpretation" (637).

The main problem of interpretation, then, lies in the fact that the meaning of any one event is incalculably variable. The image of electrical discharge, which disperses its sound waves in all directions, shows that every event, as soon as it happens, sets up a whole spectrum of meanings. If we try to extract one of these meanings and pass it off as *the* meaning of the event, then automatically we are shutting out all other meanings.

Normally we understand by a successful interpretation one that conveys a specific meaning. But according to the answer given here, an interpretation can only be successful if it takes into account the "possible losses" caused by interpretation—in other words, if it succeeds in returning to the phenomenon interpreted its whole spectrum of possible meanings. And this, as the answer makes clear, is difficult.

Meanings have a heuristic character which, particularly in these scientifically couched answers, bring out the many-sidedness of the phenomena described. In such a description, the phenomena will appear all the richer in meaning if no one meaning dominates. In the "Ithaca" chapter, aspects are not static but seem to be moving, offering an infinitely wider range of perspectives than could be offered if the author were merely to present the readers with their own classified interpretation of the phenomenon. And however confused the readers may feel through this bewildering multiplicity, at least they now have the chance of experiencing for themselves something of the essential character of the phenomena. The heightened indeterminacy enables them to view so many different aspects from so many different standpoints, and from the interaction of these aspects and perspectives they themselves continually and dynamically formulate the meaning. In this way it is possible for the readers to experience the phenomenon more as itself than as the expression of something else.

Joyce called this chapter "Ithaca." But what sort of homecoming is this? For Ulysses it meant the end of his adventurous journey, with all its attendant dangers and sufferings, and also his reckoning with the suitors; but for Bloom the homecoming passes with innumerable trivial acts and a fantastic, if impotent, condemnation of all Molly's lovers. No one is excepted from this universal anathema; it applies ultimately to marriage as an institution and even to Bloom himself. "What then remains after this holocaust? Only himself with his desires—not as husband or householder but as Leopold Bloom, an Einziger with no Eigentum" (Budgen 261). Yet again, then, we have in the Homeric allusion a parallel which, if anything, runs in the opposite direction from the original, showing up the individuality of Bloom against the background of what the reader might expect from the archetypal homecoming.

The implication of a novel written in several different styles is that the view expressed by each style is to be taken only as one possible facet of everyday reality. The accumulation of facts has the effect of making these seem like a mere suggestion to the reader as to how he/she might observe reality. The perspectives provided by the various chapters of the novel abruptly join up, overlap, are segmented, even clash, and through their very density they begin to overtax the reader's vision. The density of the presentational screen, the confusing montage and its interplay of perspectives, the invitation to the reader to look at identical incidents from many conflicting points of view—all this makes it extremely difficult for the reader to find his/her way. The novel refuses to divulge any way of connecting up this interplay of perspectives, and so the reader is forced to provide his/her own liaison. This has the inevitable consequence that reading becomes a process of selection, with the reader's own imagination providing the criteria for the selection. For the text of *Ulysses* only offers the conditions that make it possible to conceive of this everyday world—conditions which each reader will exploit in his/her own way.

What does the achievement of the various modes of presentation consist of? First, one can say that they bring to bear a form of observation which underlies the very structure of perception. For we "have the experience of a world, not understood as a system of relations which wholly determine each event, but as an open totality the synthesis of which is inexhaustible . . . From the moment that experience—that is, the opening on to our *de facto* world—is recognized as the beginning of knowledge, there is no longer any way of distinguishing a level of *a priori* truths and one of factual ones, what the world must necessarily be and what it actually is" (Merleau-Ponty 219, 221). Through their countless offshoots, the different styles of *Ulysses* preclude any meaning directed toward integration, but they also fall into a pattern of observation that contains within itself the possibility of a continual extension. It is the very abundance of perspectives that conveys the abundance of the world under observation.

The effect of this continual change is dynamic, unbounded as it is by any recognizable teleology. From one chapter to the next the 'horizon' of everyday life is altered and constantly shifted from one area to another through the links which the reader tries to establish between the chapter styles. Each chapter prepares the 'horizon' for the next, and it is the process of reading that provides the continual overlapping and interweaving of the views presented by each of the chapters. The reader is stimulated into filling the 'empty spaces' between the chapters in order to group them as a coherent whole. This process, however, has the following results: The conceptions of everyday life which the reader forms undergo constant modifications in the reading process. Each chapter provides a certain amount of expectation concerning the next chapter. However, the gaps of indeterminacy which open up between the chapters tend to diminish the importance of these expectations as a means of orientating the reader. As the process continues, a 'feedback' effect is bound to develop, arising from the new chapter and reacting back upon the preceding, which under this new and somewhat unexpected impression is subjected to modifications in the reader's mind. The more frequently the reader experiences this effect, the more cautious and the more differentiated will be his/her expectations, as they arise through his/her realization of the text. Thus what has just been read modifies what had been read before, so that the readers themselves operate the 'fusion of horizons,' with the result that they produce an experience of reality which is real precisely because it happens, without being subjected to any representational function. Reality, then, is a process of realization necessitating the reader's involvement, because only the reader can bring it about. This is why the chapters are not arranged in any sequence of situations that might be complementary to one another; in fact, the unforeseen difference of style rather seems to make each chapter into a turning-point as opposed to a continuation. And as the whole novel consists of such turning-points the process of reading unfolds itself as a continual modification of all previous conceptions, thus inverting the traditional teleological structure of the novel.

Edmund Wilson has summed up both the reader's impression and the structure of the novel as follows: "I doubt whether any human memory is capable, on a first reading, of meeting the demands of 'Ulysses.' And when we reread it, we start in at any point, as if it were indeed something solid like a city which actually existed in space and which could be entered from any direction" (Wilson 210). The reader is virtually free to choose his/her own direction, but he/she will not be able to work his/her way through every possible perspective, for the number of these is far beyond the capacity of any one reader's naturally selective perception. If the novel sometimes gives the impression of unreality, this is not because it presents unreality, but simply because it swamps us with aspects of reality that overburden our limited powers of absorption. We are forced to make our own selections from the perspectives offered and, consequently, in accordance with our own personal disposition, to formulate ideas that have their roots in *some* of the signs and situations confronting us.

This form of reading is predetermined by the novel itself, with its network of superimposed patterns that evoke constantly changing 'pictures' of everyday life. Each reading is a starting-point for the composition of such 'pictures', and indeed the whole process of reading *Ulysses* is a kind of composition. (The same, it is true, can be said of all reading, but in the case of this novel, the demands made on the reader's creativity are far greater than normal.) No one picture is representative, and one cannot even say that any one pattern is in itself determinate or determinant, for the different sections of the text only go so far as to offer signs that can be grouped together to form a context. The patterns are, as it were, transitory units which are necessary if everyday life is to be experienced, but are in no way binding as to the nature of experience.

Each 'picture' composed out of each pattern represents one possible meaning of the text concerned, but the reader will not be content to accept each 'picture' as an end in itself. He/she will search for a 'complete picture' of everyday life, and this is precisely what the novel withholds from him/her. The patterns offer him/her nothing but the conditions for and variations of the presentability of everyday life. There is no overriding tendency, and the mass of details presents itself to the reader to organize in accordance with his/her own acts of comprehension. This, in turn, demands a heightened degree of participation on the reader's part. The novel thus places itself in the category of "cool media" (McLuhan 22–23), as McLuhan called those texts and other media which, through their indeterminacy, allow and even demand a high degree of participation.

Herein lies the main difference between *Ulysses* and the tradition of the novel. Instead of providing an illusory coherence of the reality it presents, this novel offers only a potential presentation, the working out of which has to be done actively by the reader. Thus it is possible to discover many different 'pictures' of the everyday world, but they will never converge into a defined picture—and it is this very fact that compels the reader to continue his/her search. Even though he/she will never find the object of his/her search, on his/her way he/she will meet with a vast array of possible conceptions, through which the reality of everyday life will come alive in a corresponding number of ways. As these conceptions are not joined together, every picture remains representative of no more than one aspect of reality. The reading process unfolds as a "categorical aspection" (Aldrich 21–24), in the sense that the aspects of reality that group together into a 'picture' are continually merging and diverging, so that the readers can experience that reality as they go along, but being thus entangled in it they can never hope to encompass it all.

The readers, however, will still be continually tempted to try to establish some consistency in all the signs, patterns, fragments, etc. But whenever we establish consistency, "illusion takes over" (Gombrich 278). "Illusion is whatever is fixed or definable, and reality is best understood as its negation: whatever reality is, it's not *that*" (Frye, *Anatomy* 169–70). The truth of this statement becomes apparent as one reads *Ulysses*. At first the inconsistency of the stylistic patterns and structures impels the reader to formulate illusions, because only by joining things can he/she comprehend an unfamiliar experience. But even while he/she is in the process of linking things up, he/she is bringing into being all the other possibilities of the text that defy integration; and these in turn proceed to overshadow the consistency he/she had begun to establish, so that in the process of illusion-forming the reader also creates the latent destruction of those very illusions. He/she will begin to distrust the convenient patterns he/she has been building and will eventually himself/herself perceive that they are nothing but the instruments he/she uses to grasp and pare down the mass of detail. Now the very fact that it is he/she who produces and destroys the illusions makes it impossible for him/her to stand aside and view 'reality' from a distance—the only reality for him/her to view is the one he/she is creating. He/she is involved in it, in precisely the same way that he/she gets involved in 'real life' situations. Thus for many Joyce readers, 'interpretation' is a form of refuge-seeking—an effort to reclaim the ground which has been cut from under their feet. Perhaps Bloom's attempts to instruct his wife contain the most succinct summary of Joyce's whole method:

> With what success had he attempted direct instruction? She followed not all, a part of the whole, gave attention with interest, comprehended with surprise, with care repeated, with greater difficulty remembered, forgot with ease, with misgiving rerememberd, rerepeated with error. What system had proved more effective? Indirect suggestion implicating selfinterest. (647–48)

WORKS CITED

Adams, Robert Martin. *Surface and Symbol: The Consistency of James Joyce's "Ulysses."* New York: Oxford UP, 1962.

Aldrich, Virgil C. *Philosophy of Art.* Englewood Cliffs: Prentice, 1963.

Broch, H. *Dichten und Erkennen.* Zurich: Rhein-Verlag, 1955.

Budgen, Frank. *James Joyce and the Making of "Ulysses."* Bloomington: Indiana UP, 1960.

Ellmann, Richard. *James Joyce.* Oxford: Oxford UP, 1966.

Frye, Northrop. *Anatomy of Criticism: Four Essays.* New York: Atheneum, 1967.

———. "The Road of Excess." *Myth and Symbol: Critical Approaches and Applications.* Ed. Bernice Slote. Lincoln: U of Nebraska P, 1964.

Goldberg, S. L. *The Classical Temper: A Study of James Joyce's "Ulysses."* London: Chatto, 1961.

Gombrich, E. H. *Art and Illusion: A Study in the Psychology of Pictorial Representation.* London: Phaidon, 1962.

Iser, Wolfgang. *The Implied Reader: Patterns of Communication from Bunyan to Beckett.* Baltimore: Johns Hopkins UP, 1974.

Jauss, Hans Robert. "Nachahmungsprinzip und Wirklichkeitsbegriff in der Theorie des Romans von Diderot bis Stendhal." *Nachahmung und Illusion: Poetik und Hermeneutik I.* Ed. Hans Robert Jauss. Munich: Fink, 1964.

Joyce, James. *Ulysses.* London: Bodley Head, 1937.

Litz, A. Walton. *The Art of James Joyce: Method and Design in "Ulysses" and "Finnegans Wake."* London: Oxford UP, 1961.

Lugowski, Clemens. *Die Form der Individualität im Roman.* Berlin: Dunker, 1932.

McLuhan, Marshall. *Understanding Media: The Extensions of Man.* New York: McGraw, 1966.

Merleau-Ponty, Maurice. *Phenomenology of Perception.* Trans. Colin Smith. New York: Humanitas, 1962.

Murry, John Middleton. *The Problem of Style.* London: Oxford UP, 1960.

Wilson, Edmund. *Axel's Castle: A Study in the Imaginative Literature of 1870–1930.* New York: Scribner's, 1969.

Feminist and Gender Criticism and *Ulysses*

WHAT ARE FEMINIST
AND GENDER CRITICISM?

Among the most exciting and influential developments in the field of literary studies, feminist and gender criticism participate in a broad philosophical discourse that extends far beyond literature, far beyond the arts in general. The critical *practices* of those who explore the representation of women and men in works by male or female, lesbian or gay writers inevitably grow out of and contribute to a larger and more generally applicable *theoretical* discussion of how gender and sexuality are constantly shaped by and shaping institutional structures and attitudes, artifacts and behaviors.

Feminist criticism was accorded academic legitimacy in American universities "around 1981," Jane Gallop claims in her book *Around 1981: Academic Feminist Literary Theory* (1992). With Gallop's title and approximation in mind, Naomi Schor has since estimated that "around 1985, feminism began to give way to what has come to be called gender studies" (275). Some would argue that feminist criticism became academically legitimate well before 1981. Others would take issue with the notion that feminist criticism and women's studies have been giving way to gender criticism and gender studies, and with the either/or distinction that such a claim implies. Taken together, however, Gallop and Schor provide us with a useful fact—that of feminist criticism's historical precedence—and a chronological focus on the early to mid-1980s, a period during which the feminist approach was unquestionably influential and during which new interests emerged, not all of which were woman centered.

During the early 1980s, three discrete strains of feminist theory and practice—commonly categorized as French, North American, and British—seemed to be developing. French feminists tended to focus their attention on language. Drawing on the ideas of the psychoanalytic philosopher Jacques Lacan, they argued that language as we commonly think of it—as public discourse—is decidedly phallocentric, privileging what is valued by the patriarchal culture. They also spoke of the possibility of an alternative, feminine language and of *l'écriture féminine:* women's writing. Julia Kristeva, who is generally seen as a pioneer of French feminist thought even though she dislikes the feminist label, suggested that feminine language is associated with the maternal and derived from the pre-oedipal fusion between mother and child. Like Kristeva, Hélène Cixous and Luce Irigaray associated feminine writing with the female body. Both drew an analogy between women's writing and women's sexual pleasure, Irigaray arguing that just as a woman's *"jouissance"* is more diffuse and complex than a man's unitary phallic pleasure ("woman has sex organs just about everywhere"), so "feminine" language is more diffuse and less obviously coherent than its "masculine" counterpart (*This Sex* 101–03).

Kristeva, who helped develop the concept of *l'écriture féminine,* nonetheless urged caution in its use and advocacy. Feminine or feminist writing that resists or refuses participation in "masculine" discourse, she warned, risks political marginalization, relegation to the outskirts (pun intended) of what is considered socially and politically significant. Kristeva's concerns were not unfounded: the concept of *l'écriture féminine* did prove controversial, eliciting different kinds of criticism from different kinds of feminist and gender critics. To some, the concept appears to give writing a biological basis, thereby suggesting that there is an *essential* femininity, and/or that women are *essentially* different from men. To others, it seems to suggest that men can write as women, so long as they abdicate authority, sense, and logic in favor of diffusiveness, playfulness, even nonsense.

While French feminists of the 1970s and early 1980s focused on language and writing from a psychoanalytic perspective, North American critics generally practiced a different sort of criticism. Characterized by close textual reading and historical scholarship, it generally took one of two forms. Critics like Kate Millett, Carolyn Heilbrun, and Judith Fetterley developed what Elaine Showalter called the "feminist critique" of "male constructed literary history" by closely examining canonical works by male writers, exposing the patriarchal ideology implicit in such works and arguing that traditions of systematic masculine dominance are indelibly inscribed in our literary tradition. Fetterley urged women to become "resisting readers"—to notice how biased most of the classic texts by male authors are in their language, subjects, and attitudes and to actively reject that bias as they read, thereby making reading a different, less "immasculating" experience. Meanwhile, another group of North American feminists, including Showalter, Sandra Gilbert, Susan Gubar, and Patricia Meyer Spacks, developed a different feminist critical model—one that Showalter referred to as "gynocriticism." These critics analyzed great books by women from a feminist perspective, discovered neglected or forgotten women writers, and attempted to recover women's culture and history, especially the history of women's communities that nurtured female creativity.

The North American endeavor to recover women's history—for example, by emphasizing that women developed their own strategies to gain power within their sphere—was seen by British feminists like Judith Newton and Deborah Rosenfelt as an endeavor that "mystifies" male oppression, disguising it as something that has created a special world of opportunities for women. More important from the British standpoint, the universalizing and "essentializing" tendencies of French theory and a great deal of North American practice disguised women's oppression by highlighting sexual difference, thereby seeming to suggest that the dominant system may be impervious to change. As for the North American critique of male stereotypes that denigrate women, British feminists maintained that it led to counterstereotypes of female virtue that ignore real differences of race, class, and culture among women.

By now, the French, North American, and British approaches have so thoroughly critiqued, influenced, and assimilated one another that the work of most Western practitioners is no longer easily identifiable along national boundary lines. Instead, it tends to be characterized according to whether the category of *woman* is the major focus in the exploration of gender and gender oppression or, alternatively, whether the interest in sexual difference encompasses an interest in other differences that also define identity. The latter paradigm encompasses the work of feminists of color, Third World (preferably called post-colonial) feminists, and lesbian feminists, many of whom have asked whether the universal category of woman constructed by certain French and North American predecessors is appropriate to describe women in minority groups or non-Western cultures.

These feminists stress that, while all women are female, they are something else as well (such as African American, lesbian, Muslim Pakistani). This "something else" is precisely what makes them—including their problems and their goals—different from other women. As Armit Wilson has pointed out, Asian women living in Great Britain are expected by their families and communities to preserve Asian cultural traditions; thus, the expression of personal identity through clothing involves a much more serious infraction of cultural rules than it does for a Western woman. Gloria Anzaldúa has spoken personally and eloquently about the experience of many women on the margins of Eurocentric North American culture. "I am a border woman," she writes in *Borderlands: La Frontera = The New Mestiza* (1987). "I grew up between two cultures, the Mexican (with a heavy Indian influence) and the Anglo. . . . Living on the borders and in margins, keeping intact one's shifting and multiple identity and integrity is like trying to swim in a new element, an 'alien' element" (i).

Instead of being divisive and isolating, this evolution of feminism into femin*isms* has fostered a more inclusive, global perspective. The era of recovering women's texts, especially texts by white Western women, has been succeeded by a new era in which the goal is to recover entire cultures of women. Two important figures of this new era are Trinh T. Minh-ha and Gayatri Spivak. Spivak, in works such as *In Other Worlds: Essays in Cultural Politics* (1987) and *Outside in the Teaching Machine* (1993), has shown how political independence (generally looked upon by metropolitan Westerners as a simple and beneficial historical and political reversal) has complex implications for "subaltern" or subproletarian women.

The understanding of woman not as a single, deterministic category but rather as the nexus of diverse experiences has led some white, Western, "majority" feminists like Jane Tompkins and Nancy K. Miller to advocate and practice "personal" or "autobiographical" criticism. Once reluctant to reveal themselves in their analyses for fear of being labeled idiosyncratic, impressionistic, and subjective by men, some feminists are now openly skeptical of the claims to reason, logic, and objectivity that male critics have made in the past. With the advent of more personal feminist critical styles has come a powerful new interest in women's autobiographical writings, manifested in essays such as "Authorizing the Autobiographical" by Shari Benstock, which first appeared in her influential collection *The Private Self: Theory and Practice of Women's Autobiographical Writings* (1988).

Traditional autobiography, some feminists have argued, is a gendered, "masculinist" genre; its established conventions call for a lifeplot that turns on action, triumph through conflict, intellectual selfdiscovery, and often public renown. The body, reproduction, children, and intimate interpersonal relationships are generally well in the background and often absent. Arguing that the lived experiences of women and men differ—women's lives, for instance, are often characterized by interruption and deferral—Leigh Gilmore has developed a theory of women's self-representation in her book *Autobiographics: A Feminist Theory of Self-Representation.*

Autobiographics was published in 1994, well after the chronological divide that, according to Schor, separates the heyday of feminist criticism and the rise of gender studies. Does that mean that Gilmore's book is a feminist throwback? Is she practicing gender criticism instead, the use of the word "feminist" in her book's subtitle notwithstanding? Or are both of these questions overly reductive? As implied earlier, many knowledgeable commentators on the contemporary critical scene are skeptical of the feminist/gender distinction, arguing that feminist criticism is by definition gender criticism and pointing out that one critic whose work *everyone* associates with feminism (Julia Kristeva) has problems with the feminist label while another critic whose name is continually linked with the gender approach (Teresa de Lauretis) continues to refer to herself and her work as feminist.

Certainly, feminist and gender criticism are not polar opposites but, rather, exist along a continuum of attitudes toward sex and sexism, sexuality and gender, language and the literary canon. There are, however, a few distinctions to be made between those critics whose writings are inevitably identified as being toward one end of the continuum or the other.

One distinction is based on focus: as the word implies, "feminists" have concentrated their efforts on the study of women and women's issues. Gender criticism, by contrast, has not been woman centered. It has tended to view the male and female sexes—and the masculine and feminine genders—in terms of a complicated continuum, much as we are viewing feminist and gender criticism. Critics like Diane K. Lewis have raised the possibility that black women may be more like white men in terms of familial and economic roles, like black men in terms of their relationships with whites, and like white women in terms of their relationships with men. Lesbian gender critics have asked whether lesbian women are really more like straight women than they are like gay (or for that matter straight) men. That we refer to gay and lesbian studies as gender studies has led some to suggest that gender studies is a misnomer; after all, homosexuality is not a gender. This objection may easily be answered once we realize that one purpose of gender criticism is to criticize gender as we commonly conceive of it, to expose its insufficiency and inadequacy as a category.

Another distinction between feminist and gender criticism is based on the terms "gender" and "sex." As de Lauretis suggests in *Technologies of Gender* (1987), feminists of the 1970s tended to equate gender with sex, gender difference with sexual difference. But that equation doesn't help us explain "the differences among women, . . . the differences *within women*." After positing that "we need a notion of gender that is not so bound up with sexual difference," de Lauretis provides just such a notion by arguing that "gender is not a property of bodies or something originally existent in human beings"; rather, it is "the product of various social technologies, such as cinema" (2). Gender is, in other words, a construct, an effect of language, culture, and its institutions. It is gender, not sex, that causes a weak old man to open a door for an athletic young woman. And it is gender, not sex, that may cause one young woman to expect old men to behave in this way, another to view this kind of behavior as chauvinistic and insulting, and still another to have mixed feelings (hence de Lauretis's phrase "differences *within women*") about "gentlemanly gallantry."

Still another related distinction between feminist and gender criticism is based on the *essentialist* views of many feminist critics and the *constructionist* views of many gender critics (both those who would call themselves feminists and those who would not). Stated simply and perhaps too reductively, the term "essentialist" refers to the view that women are essentially different from men. "Constructionist," by contrast, refers to the view that most of those differences are characteristics not of the male and female sex (nature) but, rather, of the masculine and feminine genders (nurture). Because of its essentialist tendencies, "radical feminism," according to the influential gender critic Eve Kosofsky Sedgwick, "tends to deny that the meaning of gender or sexuality has ever significantly changed; and more damagingly, it can make future change appear impossible" (*Between Men* 13).

Most obviously essentialist would be those feminists who emphasize the female body, its difference, and the manifold implications of that difference. The equation made by some avant-garde French feminists between the female body and the *maternal* body has proved especially troubling to some gender critics, who worry that it may paradoxically play into the hands of extreme conservatives and fundamentalists seeking to reestablish patriarchal family values. In her book *The Reproduction of Mothering* (1978), Nancy Chodorow, a sociologist of gender, admits that what we call "mothering"—not having or nursing babies but mothering more broadly conceived—is commonly associated not just with the feminine gender but also with the female sex, often considered nurturing by nature. But she critically interrogates the common assumption that it is in women's nature or biological destiny to "mother" in this broader sense, arguing that the separation of home and workplace brought about by the development of capitalism and the ensuing industrial revolution made mothering *appear* to be essentially a woman's job in modern Western society.

If sex turns out to be gender where mothering is concerned, what differences *are* grounded in sex—that is, nature? *Are* there *essential* differences between men and women—other than those that are purely anatomical and anatomically determined (for example, a man can exclusively take on the job of feeding an infant milk, but he may not do so from his own breast)? A growing number of gender critics would answer the question in the negative. Sometimes referred to as "extreme constructionists" and "postfeminists," these critics have adopted the viewpoint of philosopher Judith Butler, who in her book *Gender Trouble* (1990) predicts that "sex, by definition, will be shown to have been gender all along" (8). As Naomi Schor explains their position, "there is nothing outside or before culture, no nature that is not always and already enculturated" (278).

Whereas a number of feminists celebrate women's difference, postfeminist gender critics would agree with Chodorow's statement that men have an "investment in difference that women do not have" (Eisenstein and Jardine 14). They see difference as a symptom of oppression, not a cause for celebration, and would abolish it by dismantling gender categories and, ultimately, destroying gender itself. Since gender categories and distinctions are embedded in and perpetuated through language, gender critics like Monique Wittig have called for the wholesale transformation of language into a nonsexist, and nonheterosexist, medium.

Language has proved the site of important debates between feminist and gender critics, essentialists and constructionists. Gender critics have taken issue with those French feminists who have spoken of a feminine language and writing and who have grounded differences in language and writing in the female body.[1] For much the same reason, they have disagreed with those French-influenced Anglo-American critics who, like Toril Moi and Nancy K. Miller, have posited an essential relationship between sexuality and textuality. (In an essentialist sense, such critics have suggested that when women write, they tend to break the rules of plausibility and verisimilitude that men have created to evaluate fiction.) Gender critics like Peggy Kamuf posit a relationship only between *gender* and textuality, between what most men and women *become* after they are born and the way in which they write. They are therefore less interested in the author's sexual "signature"—in whether the author was a woman writing—than in whether the author was (to borrow from Kamuf) "Writing Like a Woman."

Feminists like Miller have suggested that no man could write the "female anger, desire, and selfhood" that Emily Brontë, for instance, inscribed in her poetry and in *Wuthering Heights* (*Subject* 72). In the view of gender critics, it is and has been possible for a man to write like a woman, a woman to write like a man. Shari Benstock, a noted feminist critic whose investigations into psychoanalytic and poststructuralist theory have led her increasingly to adopt the gender approach, poses the following question to herself in *Textualizing the Feminine* (1991): "Isn't it precisely 'the feminine' in Joyce's writings and Derrida's that carries me along?" (45). In an essay entitled "Unsexing Language: Pronominal Protest in Emily Dickinson's 'Lay this Laurel,'" Anna Shannon Elfenbein has argued that "like Walt Whitman, Emily Dickinson crossed the gender barrier in some remarkable poems," such as "We learned to like the Fire / By playing Glaciers—when a Boy—" (Berg 215).

It is also possible, in the view of most gender critics, for women to read as men, men as women. The view that women can, and indeed have been forced to, read as men has been fairly noncontroversial. Everyone agrees that the literary canon is largely "androcentric" and that writings by men have tended to "immasculate" women, forcing

---

[1]Because feminist/gender studies, not unlike sex/gender, should be thought of as existing along a continuum of attitudes and not in terms of simple opposition, attempts to highlight the difference between feminist and gender criticism are inevitably prone to reductive overgeneralization and occasional distortion. Here, for instance, French feminism is made out to be more monolithic than it actually is. Hélène Cixous has said that a few men (such as Jean Genet) have produced "feminine writing," although she suggests that these are exceptional men who have acknowledged their own bisexuality.

them to see the world from a masculine viewpoint. But the question of whether men can read as women has proved to be yet another issue dividing feminist and gender critics. Some feminists suggest that men and women have some essentially different reading strategies and outcomes, while gender critics maintain that such differences arise entirely out of social training and cultural norms. One interesting outcome of recent attention to gender and reading is Elizabeth A. Flynn's argument that women in fact make the best interpreters of imaginative literature. Based on a study of how male and female students read works of fiction, she concludes that women come up with more imaginative, open-ended readings of stories. Quite possibly the imputed hedging and tentativeness of women's speech, often seen by men as disadvantages, are transformed into useful interpretive strategies—receptivity combined with critical assessment of the text—in the act of reading (Flynn and Schweickart 286).

In singling out a catalyst of the gender approach, many historians of criticism have pointed to Michel Foucault. In his *History of Sexuality* (1976, tr. 1978), Foucault distinguished sexuality (that is, sexual behavior or practice) from sex, calling the former a "technology of sex." De Lauretis, who has deliberately developed her theory of gender "along the lines of . . . Foucault's theory of sexuality," explains his use of "technology" this way: "Sexuality, commonly thought to be a natural as well as a private matter, is in fact completely constructed in culture according to the political aims of the society's dominant class" (*Technologies* 2, 12). Foucault suggests that homosexuality as we now think of it was to a great extent an invention of the nineteenth century. In earlier periods there had been "acts of sodomy" and individuals who committed them, but the "sodomite" was, according to Foucault, "a temporary aberration," not the "species" he became with the advent of the modern concept of homosexuality (42–43). By historicizing sexuality, Foucault made it possible for his successors to consider the possibility that all of the categories and assumptions that currently come to mind when we think about sex, sexual difference, gender, and sexuality are social artifacts, the products of cultural discourses.

In explaining her reason for saying that feminism began to give way to gender studies "around 1985," Schor says that she chose that date "in part because it marks the publication of *Between Men*," a seminal book in which Eve Kosofsky Sedgwick "articulates the insights of feminist criticism onto those of gay-male studies, which had up to then pursued often parallel but separate courses (affirming the existence of a homosexual or female imagination, recovering lost traditions, decoding the cryptic discourse of works already in the canon by homosexual or feminist authors)" (276). Today, gay and lesbian criticism is so much a part of gender criticism that some people equate it with the gender approach, while others have begun to prefer the phrase "sexualities criticism" to "gender criticism."

Following Foucault's lead, some gay and lesbian gender critics have argued that the heterosexual/homosexual distinction is as much a cultural construct as is the masculine/feminine dichotomy. Arguing that sexuality is a continuum, not a fixed and static set of binary oppositions, a number of gay and lesbian critics have critiqued heterosexuality as a norm, arguing that it has been an enforced corollary and consequence of what Gayle Rubin has referred to as the "sex/gender system." (Those subscribing to this system assume that persons of the male sex should be masculine, that masculine men are attracted to women, and therefore that it is natural for masculine men to be attracted to women and unnatural for them to be attracted to men.) Lesbian gender critics have also taken issue with their feminist counterparts on the grounds that they proceed from fundamentally heterosexual and even heterosexist assumptions. Particularly offensive to lesbians like the poet-critic Adrienne Rich have been those feminists who, following Doris Lessing, have implied that to make the lesbian choice is to make a statement, to act out feminist hostility against men. Rich has called heterosexuality "a beachhead of male dominance" that, "like motherhood, needs to be recognized and studied as a political institution" ("Compulsory Heterosexuality" 143, 145).

If there is such a thing as reading like a woman and such a thing as reading like a man, how then do lesbians read? Are there gay and lesbian ways of reading? Many would say that there are. Rich, by reading Emily Dickinson's poetry as a lesbian—by not assuming that "heterosexual romance is the key to a woman's life and work"—has introduced us to a poet somewhat different from the one heterosexual critics have made familiar (*Lies* 158). As for gay reading, Wayne Koestenbaum has defined "the (male twentieth-century first world) gay reader" as one who "reads resistantly for inscriptions of his condition, for texts that will confirm a social and private identity founded on a desire for other men. . . . Reading becomes a hunt for histories that deliberately foreknow or unwittingly trace a desire felt not by author but by reader, who is most acute when searching for signs of himself" (Boone and Cadden 176–77).

Lesbian critics have produced a number of compelling reinterpretations, or in-scriptions, of works by authors as diverse as Emily Dickinson, Virginia Woolf, and Toni Morrison. As a result of these
provocative readings, significant disagreements have arisen between
straight and lesbian critics and among lesbian critics as well. Perhaps
the most famous and interesting example of this kind of interpretive
controversy involves the claim by Barbara Smith and Adrienne Rich
that Morrison's novel *Sula* can be read as a lesbian text—and author
Toni Morrison's counterclaim that it cannot.

Gay male critics have produced a body of readings no less revision-
ist and controversial, focusing on writers as staidly classic as Henry
James and Wallace Stevens. In Melville's *Billy Budd* and *Moby-Dick,*
Robert K. Martin suggests, a triangle of homosexual desire exists. In
the latter novel, the hero must choose between a captain who represents "the imposition of the male on the female" and a "Dark
Stranger" (Queequeg) who "offers the possibility of an alternate sexuality, one that is less dependent upon performance and conquest" (5).

Masculinity as a complex construct producing and reproducing a
constellation of behaviors and goals, many of them destructive (like
performance and conquest) and most of them injurious to women, has
become the object of an unprecedented number of gender studies. A
1983 issue of *Feminist Review* contained an essay entitled "Anti-Porn:
Soft Issue, Hard World," in which B. Ruby Rich suggested that the
"legions of feminist men" who examine and deplore the effects of
pornography on women might better "undertake the analysis that can
tell us why men like porn (not, piously, why this or that exceptional
man does *not*)" (Berg 185). The advent of gender criticism makes precisely that kind of analysis possible. Stephen H. Clark, who alludes to
Ruby Rich's challenge, reads T. S. Eliot "as a man." Responding to
"Eliot's implicit appeal to a specifically masculine audience—'"You!
hypocrite lecteur!—mon semblable,—mon *frère!*"'—Clark concludes
that poems like "Sweeney Among the Nightingales" and "Gerontion,"
rather than offering what they are usually said to offer—"a social critique into which a misogynistic language accidentally seeps"—instead
articulate a masculine "psychology of sexual fear and desired retaliation" (Berg 173).

Some gender critics focusing on masculinity have analyzed "the
anthropology of boyhood," a phrase coined by Mark Seltzer in an
article in which he comparatively reads, among other things, Stephen
Crane's *Red Badge of Courage,* Jack London's *White Fang,* and the
first *Boy Scouts of America* handbook (Boone and Cadden 150).

Others have examined the fear men have that artistry is unmasculine, a guilty worry that surfaces perhaps most obviously in "The Custom-House," Hawthorne's lengthy preface to *The Scarlet Letter*. Still others have studied the representation in literature of subtly erotic disciple-patron relationships, relationships like the ones between Nick Carraway and Jay Gatsby, Charlie Marlow and Lord Jim, Doctor Watson and Sherlock Holmes, and any number of characters in Henry James's stories. Not all of these studies have focused on literary texts. Because the movies have played a primary role in gender construction during our lifetimes, gender critics have analyzed the dynamics of masculinity (vis-à-vis femininity and androgyny) in films from *Rebel Without a Cause* to *Tootsie* to last year's Best Picture. One of the "social technologies" most influential in (re)constructing gender, film is one of the media in which today's sexual politics is most evident.

Necessary as it is, in an introduction such as this one, to define the difference between feminist and gender criticism, it is equally necessary to conclude by unmaking the distinction, at least partially. The two topics just discussed (film theory and so-called "queer theory") give us grounds for undertaking that necessary deconstruction. The alliance I have been creating between gay and lesbian criticism on one hand and gender criticism on the other is complicated greatly by the fact that not all gay and lesbian critics are constructionists. Indeed, a number of them (Robert K. Martin included) share with many feminists the *essentialist* point of view; that is to say, they believe homosexuals and heterosexuals to be essentially different, different by nature, just as a number of feminists believe men and women to be different.

In film theory and criticism, feminist and gender critics have so influenced one another that their differences would be difficult to define based on any available criteria, including the ones outlined above. Cinema has been of special interest to contemporary feminists like Minh-ha (herself a filmmaker) and Spivak (whose critical eye has focused on movies including *My Beautiful Laundrette* and *Sammie and Rosie Get Laid*). Teresa de Lauretis, whose *Technologies of Gender* (1987) has proved influential in the area of gender studies, continues to publish film criticism consistent with earlier, unambiguously feminist works in which she argued that "the representation of woman as spectacle—body to be looked at, place of sexuality, and object of desire—so pervasive in our culture, finds in narrative cinema its most complex expression and widest circulation" (*Alice* 4).

Feminist film theory has developed alongside a feminist performance theory grounded in Joan Riviere's recently rediscovered essay "Womanliness as a Masquerade" (1929), in which the author argues that there is no femininity that is *not* masquerade. Marjorie Garber, a contemporary cultural critic with an interest in gender, has analyzed the constructed nature of femininity by focusing on men who have apparently achieved it—through the transvestism, transsexualism, and other forms of "cross-dressing" evident in cultural productions from Shakespeare to Elvis, from "Little Red Riding Hood" to *La Cage aux Folles*. The future of feminist and gender criticism, it would seem, is not one of further bifurcation but one involving a refocusing on femininity, masculinity, and related sexualities, not only as represented in poems, novels, and films but also as manifested and developed in video, on television, and along the almost infinite number of way-stations rapidly being developed on the information highways running through an exponentially expanding cyberspace.

Vicki Mahaffey begins the following essay on *Ulysses* by discussing Joyce's belief that "sexuality as it has been socially and historically defined" underlies numerous and "different failures of communication." In Joyce's view, which he expressed as early as *Dubliners* (1914), "rigidly heterosexual imperatives" have impeded relationships not only between persons of the same sex but also between men and women—for instance, by making heterosexual Platonic friendship difficult if not impossible.

A writer, Joyce realized, cannot easily change a culture's "gender imperatives." If a writer's "intentions are revisionary, those intentions can be derailed by the reader's wishes, which may not cooperate to produce the intended meaning." A writer *can*, however, resist and begin to revise those imperatives. In writing *Ulysses*, "Joyce first identified what the socially conditioned reader is most likely to want and expect from male and female characters of different ages" and then created characters that "frustrate" and "challenge" those expectations. By "composing characters who violate popular preconceptions of what makes men and women admirable," he revealed "the gender system" to be "arbitrary and inadequate."

The socially conditioned or "acculturated" Western reader, Mahaffey asserts, expects an epic or mythic hero to be brave, strong, handsome, and well-born; "Joyce counters that expectation with Stephen Dedalus," a "scrawny intellectual who is poor, physically dirty, periodically infested with vermin, and a coward. . . . [I]nstead of being optimistic, confident, and determined, he is morose and riddled with guilt." Leopold Bloom is "the next model of male heroism that Joyce proceeds to display and partly dismantle." Bloom's "caution, his propensity to delay action, and his distrust of reprisal" make him more unlike than like Homer's Odysseus, who slaughtered his wife's suitors and reclaimed his wife (along with all his other possessions) when he returned home after a ten-year absence.

Joyce uses both Stephen and Bloom to challenge Western conceptions of the hero and the heroic. Through Stephen, Mahaffey argues, Joyce forces us to see that we have trouble viewing as heroes young men facing the negativity of need, degradation, humility, hopelessness, and deprivation. Through Bloom, she maintains, Joyce contests "the traditions of epic and romance" by redefining the older male hero as one who is "neither brave nor vengeful" but, rather, "cautious, realistic, and slowly willing to contemplate the possibility that his relation to those he loves has inadvertently been hurtful."

Joyce's most positive and admirable male characters, Mahaffey suggests, are men with the "moral courage to imagine freshly the perspectives of people they have wronged," including women and people of other races, places, and religions. Conversely, Joyce's most negative and least admirable male characters—Blazes Boylan and the Citizen, for example—approximate the image of the epic or mythic hero as it is inscribed in Western culture. Thus, "the reader's expectation clashes loudly with the actual experience of reading *Ulysses*, and the cacophony that results brings the currency of our cultural definition of gender categories comically into question."

Joyce's women, Mahaffey goes on to argue, challenge the reader's culture-coded expectations as fully as do Joyce's men. Readers expect female characters to be attractive, innocent, virginal, and weak— "beauties" in search of some rough male beast who, in turn, views winsome young women as commodities to be acquired. *Ulysses* is not without such conventional heroines but, as Mahaffey shows through an extended analysis of the Gerty MacDowell episode, Joyce uses them to demonstrate that the beauty associated with such characters is a mirage and that, indeed, women who ascribe to the culture's conventional definitions of femininity are "defenseless against the pressure of natural desires"—their own and those of exploitative men.

By way of contrast, Joyce creates a different, unconventional kind of woman character in Molly Bloom, termed by Mahaffey an "anti-Gerty" who projects herself in a way that the culture would define as "aggressive" and, therefore, "masculine." Comfortable with all aspects and functions of her body, Molly is as different from the traditional ideal of womanhood as Stephen (who lacks her physicality and strength) is from the traditional ideal of manhood. "But neither Stephen nor Molly," Mahaffey argues, "is presented as a counter-ideal," for Joyce's "attack is on the unreality and counterproductive-ness of ideals in general, as well as on specific, mutually exclusive ideals for men and women, in particular."

Although several statements Mahaffey makes (about female power and sexuality, for instance) are feminist in their attitude and outlook, "*Ulysses* and the End of Gender" is not best described as a work of feminist criticism. It neither represents Joyce as a feminist (indeed, it admits that he dissociated himself from the feminist cause) nor offers a feminist critique of Joyce or of *Ulysses*. Instead, Mahaffey's essay is best understood as a work of gender criticism, for it interrogates not only those traditional restrictions that make women less than fully human but also the debilitating limits placed on men, male characters, and de-finitions of masculine *character*.

Without going so far as to suggest that men can write like women, "*Ulysses* and the End of Gender" effectively demonstrates how one male writer with a critical sensibility and an interest in resisting and re-vising literary conventions simultaneously resisted and revised those cultural stereotypes that simplistically (over)determine gender and gender difference. Mahaffey herself describes gender difference—increasingly a focus of gender criticism—as a "mirage," one of those "borders designed to be surpassed—not lightly, but at the appropriate time, to initiate new stages of cognitive and emotional development."

Ross C Murfin

FEMINIST AND GENDER CRITICISM: A SELECTED BIBLIOGRAPHY

French Feminist Theory

Cixous, Hélène. "The Laugh of the Medusa." Trans. Keith Cohen and Paula Cohen. *Signs* 1 (1976): 875–93.

Cixous, Hélène, and Catherine Clément. *The Newly Born Woman.* Trans. Betsy Wing. Minneapolis: U of Minnesota P, 1986.

Irigaray, Luce. *An Ethics of Sexual Difference.* Trans. Carolyn Burke and Gillian C. Gill. Ithaca: Cornell UP, 1993.

———. *This Sex Which Is Not One.* Trans. Catherine Porter. Ithaca: Cornell UP, 1985.

Jones, Ann Rosalind. "Inscribing Femininity: French Theories of the Feminine." *Making a Difference: Feminist Literary Criticism.* Ed. Gayle Green and Coppélia Kahn. London: Methuen, 1985. 80–112.

———. "Writing the Body: Toward an Understanding of *L'Écriture féminine.*" Showalter, *The New Feminist Criticism* 361–77.

Kristeva, Julia. *Desire in Language: A Semiotic Approach to Literature and Art.* Ed. Leon S. Roudiez. Trans. Thomas Gora, Alice Jardine, and Roudiez. New York: Columbia UP, 1980.

Marks, Elaine, and Isabelle de Courtivron, eds. *New French Feminisms: An Anthology.* Amherst: U of Massachusetts P, 1980.

Moi, Toril, ed. *French Feminist Thought: A Reader.* Oxford: Basil Blackwell, 1987.

Feminist Theory: Classic Texts, General Approaches, Collections

Abel, Elizabeth, and Emily K. Abel, eds. *The "Signs" Reader: Women, Gender, and Scholarship.* Chicago: U of Chicago P, 1983.

Barrett, Michèle, and Anne Phillips. *Destabilizing Theory: Contemporary Feminist Debates.* Stanford: Stanford UP, 1992.

Beauvoir, Simone de. *The Second Sex.* 1953. Trans. and ed. H. M. Parshley. New York: Bantam, 1961.

Benstock, Shari. *Textualizing the Feminine: On the Limits of Genre.* Norman: U of Oklahoma P, 1991.

Butler, Judith. *Gender Trouble: Feminism and the Subversion of Identity.* New York: Routledge, 1990.

de Lauretis, Teresa, ed. *Feminist Studies/Critical Studies.* Bloomington: Indiana UP, 1986.

Felman, Shoshana. "Women and Madness: The Critical Phallacy." *Diacritics* 5 (1975): 2–10.

Fetterley, Judith. *The Resisting Reader: A Feminist Approach to American Fiction.* Bloomington: Indiana UP, 1978.

Fuss, Diana. *Essentially Speaking: Feminism, Nature and Difference.* New York: Routledge, 1989.

Gallop, Jane. *Around 1981: Academic Feminist Literary Theory.* New York: Routledge, 1992.

———. *The Daughter's Seduction: Feminism and Psychoanalysis.* Ithaca: Cornell UP, 1982.

hooks, bell. *Feminist Theory: From Margin to Center.* Boston: South End, 1984.

Kolodny, Annette. "Dancing Through the Minefield: Some Observations on the Theory, Practice, and Politics of a Feminist Literary Criticism." Showalter, *The New Feminist Criticism* 144–67.

———. "Some Notes on Defining a 'Feminist Literary Criticism.'" *Critical Inquiry* 2 (1975): 78.

Lovell, Terry, ed. *British Feminist Thought: A Reader.* Oxford: Basil Blackwell, 1990.

Meese, Elizabeth, and Alice Parker, eds. *The Difference Within: Feminism and Critical Theory.* Philadelphia: John Benjamins, 1989.

Miller, Nancy K., ed. *The Poetics of Gender.* New York: Columbia UP, 1986.

Millett, Kate. *Sexual Politics.* Garden City: Doubleday, 1970.

Rich, Adrienne. *On Lies, Secrets, and Silence: Selected Prose, 1966–1979.* New York: Norton, 1979.

Showalter, Elaine. "Toward a Feminist Poetics." Showalter, *The New Feminist Criticism* 125–43.

———, ed. *The New Feminist Criticism: Essays on Women, Literature, and Theory.* New York: Pantheon, 1985.

Stimpson, Catharine R. "Feminist Criticism." *Redrawing the Boundaries: The Transformation of English and American Literary Studies.* Ed. Stephen Greenblatt and Giles Gunn. New York: MLA, 1992. 251–70.

Warhol, Robyn, and Diane Price Herndl, eds. *Feminisms: An Anthology of Literary Theory and Criticism.* New Brunswick, NJ: Rutgers UP, 1991.

Weed, Elizabeth, ed. *Coming to Terms: Feminism, Theory, Politics.* New York: Routledge, 1989.

Woolf, Virginia. *A Room of One's Own.* New York: Harcourt, 1929.

Women's Writing and Creativity

Abel, Elizabeth, ed. *Writing and Sexual Difference.* Chicago: U of Chicago P, 1982.

Berg, Temma F., ed. *Engendering the Word: Feminist Essays in Psychosexual Poetics.* Co-ed. Anna Shannon Elfenbein, Jeanne Larsen, and Elisa Kay Sparks. Urbana: U of Illinois P, 1989.

DuPlessis, Rachel Blau. *The Pink Guitar: Writing as Feminist Practice.* New York: Routledge, 1990.

Finke, Laurie. *Feminist Theory, Women's Writing.* Ithaca: Cornell UP, 1992.

Gilbert, Sandra M., and Susan Gubar. *The Madwoman in the Attic: The Woman Writer and the Nineteenth-Century Literary Imagination.* New Haven: Yale UP, 1979.

Homans, Margaret. *Bearing the Word: Language and Female Experience in Nineteenth-Century Women's Writing.* Chicago: U of Chicago P, 1986.

Jacobus, Mary, ed. *Women Writing and Writing about Women.* New York: Barnes, 1979.

Miller, Nancy K. *Subject to Change: Reading Feminist Writing.* New York: Columbia UP, 1988.

Newton, Judith Lowder. *Women, Power and Subversion: Social Strategies in British Fiction, 1778–1860.* Athens: U of Georgia P, 1981.

Poovey, Mary. *The Proper Lady and the Woman Writer: Ideology as Style in the Works of Mary Wollstonecraft, Mary Shelley, and Jane Austen.* Chicago: U of Chicago P, 1984.

Showalter, Elaine. *A Literature of Their Own: British Women Novelists from Brontë to Lessing.* Princeton: Princeton UP, 1977.

Spacks, Patricia Meyer. *The Female Imagination.* New York: Knopf, 1975.

Feminism, Race, Class, and Nationality

Anzaldúa, Gloria. *Borderlands: La Frontera* = *The New Mestiza.* San Francisco: Spinsters/Aunt Lute, 1987.

Christian, Barbara. *Black Feminist Criticism: Perspectives on Black Women Writers.* New York: Pergamon, 1985.

hooks, bell. *Ain't I a Woman?: Black Women and Feminism.* Boston: South End, 1981.

———. *Black Looks: Race and Representation.* Boston: South End, 1992.

Kaplan, Cora. *Sea Changes: Essays on Culture and Feminism.* London: Verso, 1986.

Moraga, Cherríe, and Gloria Anzaldúa. *This Bridge Called My Back: Writings by Radical Women of Color.* New York: Kitchen Table, 1981.

Newton, Judith, and Deborah Rosenfelt, eds. *Feminist Criticism and Social Change: Sex, Class, and Race in Literature and Culture.* New York: Methuen, 1985.

Pryse, Marjorie, and Hortense Spillers, eds. *Conjuring: Black Women, Fiction, and Literary Tradition.* Bloomington: Indiana UP, 1985.

Robinson, Lillian S. *Sex, Class, and Culture.* 1978. New York: Methuen, 1986.

Smith, Barbara. "Towards a Black Feminist Criticism." Showalter, *The New Feminist Criticism* 168–85.

Feminism and Postcoloniality

Emberley, Julia. *Thresholds of Difference: Feminist Critique, Native Women's Writings, Postcolonial Theory.* Toronto: U of Toronto P, 1993.

Mohanty, Chandra Talpade, Ann Russo, and Lourdes Torres, eds. *Third World Women and the Politics of Feminism.* Bloomington: Indiana UP, 1991.

Schipper, Mineke, ed. *Unheard Words: Women and Literature in Africa, the Arab World, Asia, the Caribbean, and Latin America.* London: Allison, 1985.

Spivak, Gayatri Chakravorty. *In Other Worlds: Essays in Cultural Politics.* New York: Methuen, 1987.

———. *Outside in the Teaching Machine.* New York: Routledge, 1993.

Trinh T. Minh-ha. *Woman, Native, Other: Writing Postcoloniality and Feminism.* Bloomington: Indiana UP, 1989.

Wilson, Armit. *Finding a Voice: Asian Women in Britain.* 1979. London: Virago, 1980.

Women's Self-Representation and Personal Criticism

Benstock, Shari, ed. *The Private Self: Theory and Practice of Women's Autobiographical Writings.* Chapel Hill: U of North Carolina P, 1988.

Gilmore, Leigh. *Autobiographics: A Feminist Theory of Self-Representation.* Ithaca: Cornell UP, 1994.

Martin, Biddy, and Chandra Talpade Mohanty. "Feminist Politics: What's Home Got to Do with It?" *Life/Lines: Theorizing Women's Autobiography.* Ed. Bella Brodski and Celeste Schenck. Ithaca: Cornell UP, 1988.

Miller, Nancy K. *Getting Personal: Feminist Occasions and Other Autobiographical Acts.* New York: Routledge, 1991.

Smith, Sidonie. *A Poetics of Women's Autobiography: Marginality and the Fictions of Self-Representation.* Bloomington: Indiana UP, 1988.

Feminist Film Theory

de Lauretis, Teresa. *Alice Doesn't: Feminism, Semiotics, Cinema.* Bloomington: Indiana UP, 1986.

Doane, Mary Ann. *Re-vision: Essays in Feminist Film Criticism.* Frederick: U Publications of America, 1984.

Modleski, Tania. *Feminism without Women: Culture and Criticism in a "Postfeminist" Age.* New York: Routledge, 1991.

Mulvey, Laura. *Visual and Other Pleasures.* Bloomington: Indiana UP, 1989.

Penley, Constance, ed. *Feminism and Film Theory.* New York: Routledge, 1988.

Studies of Gender and Sexuality

Boone, Joseph A., and Michael Cadden, eds. *Engendering Men: The Question of Male Feminist Criticism.* New York: Routledge, 1990.

Butler, Judith. *Gender Trouble: Feminism and the Subversion of Identity.* New York: Routledge, 1990.

Chodorow, Nancy. *The Reproduction of Mothering: Psychoanalysis and the Sociology of Gender.* Berkeley: U of California P, 1978.

Claridge, Laura, and Elizabeth Langland, eds. *Out of Bounds: Male Writing and Gender(ed) Criticism.* Amherst: U of Massachusetts P, 1990.

de Lauretis, Teresa. *Technologies of Gender: Essays on Theory, Film, and Fiction.* Bloomington: Indiana UP, 1987.

Doane, Mary Ann. "Masquerade Reconsidered: Further Thoughts on the Female Spectator." *Discourse* 11 (1988–89): 42–54.

Eisenstein, Hester, and Alice Jardine, eds. *The Future of Difference.* Boston: G. K. Hall, 1980.

Flynn, Elizabeth A., and Patrocinio P. Schweickart, eds. *Gender and Reading: Essays on Readers, Texts, and Contexts.* Baltimore: Johns Hopkins UP, 1986.

Foucault, Michel. *The History of Sexuality: Volume I: An Introduction.* Trans. Robert Hurley. New York: Random, 1978.

Kamuf, Peggy. "Writing Like a Woman." *Women and Language in Literature and Society.* New York: Praeger, 1980. 284–99.

Laqueur, Thomas. *Making Sex: Body and Gender from the Greeks to Freud*. Cambridge: Harvard UP, 1990.

Riviere, Joan. "Womanliness as a Masquerade." 1929. Rpt. in *Formations of Fantasy*. Ed. Victor Burgin, James Donald, and Cora Kaplan. London: Methuen, 1986. 35–44.

Rubin, Gayle. "Thinking Sex: Notes for a Radical Theory of the Politics of Sexuality." Abelove et al., *The Lesbian and Gay Reader* 3–44.

———. "The Traffic in Women: Notes on the 'Political Economy' of Sex." *Toward an Anthropology of Women*. Ed. Rayna R. Reiter. New York: Monthly Review, 1975. 157–210.

Schor, Naomi. "Feminist and Gender Studies." *Introduction to Scholarship in Modern Languages and Literatures*. Ed. Joseph Gibaldi. New York: MLA, 1992. 262–87.

Sedgwick, Eve Kosofsky. *Between Men: English Literature and Male Homosocial Desire*. New York: Columbia UP, 1988.

———. "Gender Criticism." *Redrawing the Boundaries: The Transformation of English and American Literary Studies*. Ed. Stephen Greenblatt and Giles Gunn. New York: MLA, 1992. 271–302.

Lesbian and Gay Criticism

Abelove, Henry, Michèle Aina Barale, and David Halperin, eds. *The Lesbian and Gay Studies Reader*. New York: Routledge, 1993.

Butters, Ronald, John M. Clum, and Michael Moon, eds. *Displacing Homophobia: Gay Male Perspectives in Literature and Culture*. Durham: Duke UP, 1989.

Craft, Christopher. *Another Kind of Love: Male Homosexual Desire in English Discourse, 1850–1920*. Berkeley: U of California P, 1994.

de Lauretis, Teresa. *The Practice of Love: Lesbian Sexuality and Perverse Desire*. Bloomington: Indiana UP, 1994.

Dollimore, Jonathan. *Sexual Dissidence: Augustine to Wilde, Freud to Foucault*. Oxford: Clarendon, 1991.

Fuss, Diana, ed. *Inside/Out: Lesbian Theories, Gay Theories*. New York: Routledge, 1991.

Garber, Marjorie. *Vested Interests: Cross-Dressing and Cultural Anxiety*. New York: Routledge, 1992.

Halperin, David M. *One Hundred Years of Homosexuality and Other Essays on Greek Love*. New York: Routledge, 1990.

The Lesbian Issue. Special issue, *Signs* 9 (1984).

Martin, Robert K. *Hero, Captain, and Stranger: Male Friendship, Social Critique, and Literary Form in the Sea Novels of Herman Melville.* Chapel Hill: U of North Carolina P, 1986.

Munt, Sally, ed. *New Lesbian Criticism: Literary and Cultural Readings.* New York: Harvester Wheatsheaf, 1992.

Rich, Adrienne. "Compulsory Heterosexuality and Lesbian Existence." Elizabeth Abel and Emily K. Abel, *The "Signs" Reader,* 139–68.

Stimpson, Catherine R. "Zero Degree Deviancy: The Lesbian Novel in English." *Critical Inquiry* 8 (1981): 363–79.

Weeks, Jeffrey. *Sexuality and Its Discontents: Meanings, Myths, and Modern Sexualities.* London: Routledge, 1985.

Wittig, Monique. "The Mark of Gender." Miller, *The Poetics of Gender,* 63–73.

———. "One Is Not Born a Woman." *Feminist Issues* 1.2 (1981): 47–54.

———. *The Straight Mind and Other Essays.* Boston: Beacon, 1992.

Queer Theory

Butler, Judith. *Bodies That Matter: On the Discursive Limits of "Sex."* New York: Routledge, 1993.

Cohen, Ed. *Talk on the Wilde Side: Towards a Genealogy of Discourse on Male Sexualities.* New York: Routledge, 1993.

de Lauretis, Teresa, ed. Issue on Queer Theory, *differences* 3.2 (1991).

Sedgwick, Eve Kosofsky. *Epistemology of the Closet.* Berkeley: U of California P, 1991.

———. *Tendencies.* Durham: Duke UP, 1993.

Sinfield, Alan. *Cultural Politics—Queer Reading.* Philadelphia: U of Pennsylvania P, 1994.

———. *The Wilde Century: Effeminacy, Oscar Wilde, and the Queer Moment.* New York: Columbia UP, 1994.

Warner, Michael, ed. *Fear of a Queer Planet: Queer Politics and Social Theory.* Minneapolis: U of Minnesota P, 1993.

Feminist and Gender Approaches to Joyce

Boheemen, Christine van. *The Novel as Family Romance: Language, Gender, and Authority from Fielding to Joyce.* Ithaca: Cornell UP, 1987.

Brivic, Sheldon. *Joyce's Waking Women*. Madison: U of Wisconsin P, 1995.

Henke, Suzette A. *James Joyce and the Politics of Desire*. New York: Routledge, 1990.

Henke, Suzette, and Elaine Unkeless, eds. *Women in Joyce*. Urbana: U of Illinois P, 1982.

Jones, Ellen Carol, guest co-ed. *Modern Fiction Studies* 35 (Autumn 1989). "Feminist Readings of Joyce" issue.

Lawrence, Karen. "Joyce and Feminism." *The Cambridge Companion to James Joyce*. Ed. Derek Attridge. New York: Cambridge UP, 1990. 237–58.

Mahaffey, Vicki. *Reauthorizing Joyce*. New York: Cambridge UP, 1988.

Norris, Margot. *Joyce's Web: The Social Unraveling of Modernism*. Austin: U of Texas P, 1992.

Pearce, Richard, ed. *Molly Blooms: A Polylogue on "Penelope" and Cultural Studies*. Madison: U of Wisconsin P, 1994.

Scott, Bonnie Kime. *Joyce and Feminism*. Bloomington: Indiana UP, 1984.

Valente, Joseph. *James Joyce and the Problem of Justice: Negotiating Sexual and Colonial Difference*. Cambridge: Cambridge UP, 1995.

A GENDER PERSPECTIVE

VICKI MAHAFFEY

Ulysses and the End of Gender

It is easiest to begin a discussion of Joyce's gender politics in *Ulysses* by identifying the positions he does not adopt: his is not an activist stance, nor is he an advocate for disenfranchised groups— whether women or the Irish. Joyce disavows that he is a feminist; as he playfully employs the term in the "Circe" episode of *Ulysses*, feminism is concerned primarily with action (as opposed to thought) and with a desire to appropriate (rather than redistribute) male privilege. When Bloom is being hailed as the world's greatest reformer, a group of women whisper his praises in such a way as to highlight not his but their own attributes: a millionairess appreciates him "richly," a noblewoman lauds him "nobly," and a feminist commends his numerous accomplishments "masculinely" (*U* 15.1461–66). Joyce here presents feminism as a paradoxically masculine, action-oriented position, from which he implicitly differentiates his own practices.

To say, however, that Joyce dissociates himself from the feminist movements of his time does not mean that Joyce was unconcerned with the social construction of gender and its subtle ramifications. On the contrary, he repeatedly traces many apparently different failures of communication—between Irish and English, between men and men, between women and men, between women and women, between parents and children—to the fault line of sexuality as it has been socially and historically defined. His characters discover again and again that there is no sexual, textual, or parental relation;[1] that the call of desire evokes only fantasy and despair. As early as *Dubliners* Joyce links the paralysis of desire to society's insistence on the commodification of the beloved, which he associates with the sin of simony, and on the rigidly heterosexual imperatives that turn characters such as Father Flynn of "The Sisters" and the stranger in "An Encounter" into "gnomons," geometrical figures of spiritual and sexual incompleteness. As Mr. Duffy writes after breaking off his relation with Mrs. Sinico in "A Painful Case," "Love between man and man is impossible because there must not be sexual intercourse and friendship between man and woman is impossible because there must be sexual intercourse" (*D* 112).

If *Dubliners* records the longing of isolated individuals for meaningful connection, counterpointing their poignant but futile yearning against the rules of a social system that effectively (if not intentionally) prohibits relation in favor of idealized admiration, manipulation, and competition, *Ulysses* takes a lighter attitude towards the impossibility of communication. If *Dubliners* aims to expose the vision of human connection as a mirage, precluded by the very social mechanisms that promote it, *Ulysses* begins with the literally utopian conviction that there is no place (*u-topia*) where such connection can happen because there is no discursive or conceptual space free from the implied rules of gendered (non)relation. Writing is an address, a letter from writer to reader, and from one time and place to another; one writer alone cannot rewrite the play of social interaction and communication because he or she is always writing against a background of expectation and de-

---

[1]I am echoing Jacques Lacan's famous assertion that there is no sexual relation. He first makes this argument in Seminar XX, *Encore* (1972–1973); see *Feminine Sexuality: Jacques Lacan and the école freudienne*, ed. Juliet Mitchell and Jacqueline Rose (New York: Norton, 1982), 138. He then repeats the claim several times in his seminars.

sire that is socially programmed and often unconscious. Even if the writer's own intentions are revisionary, those intentions can be derailed by the reader's wishes, which may not cooperate to produce the intended meaning. In designing *Ulysses*, Joyce first identified what the socially conditioned reader is most likely to want and expect from male and female characters of different ages, and then he provides his readers with characters who frustrate and implicitly challenge that desire. The bewildering friction that results is designed to expose the gender system itself as an arbitrary and inadequate fiction, to measure its isolating mechanisms against the urgent complexity of personal desire. Joyce turns the threnody of nonrelation in *Dubliners* into the stuff of comedy in *Ulysses* by composing characters who violate popular preconceptions of what makes men and women admirable.[2]

Joyce begins his dialogue with the acculturated reader by offering an anti-portrait of the young male "hero." Even a cursory review of the epic tradition confirms that the young male hero is defined by courage and physical strength; Joyce counters that expectation with Stephen Dedalus, who fears dogs, thunderstorms, and drowning and is easily felled by a drunken British soldier. If the frame were mythological instead of epic, the hero would be a fearless, brawny, handsome prince, heir to a just and well-managed kingdom. Joyce evokes the dream of the charming prince through the twin shadows of

---

[2]Compare the project proposed by Lieutenant Puddock and Captain Devereux in Sheridan Le Fanu's *The House by the Churchyard*, which Joyce would later use as a point of reference in *Finnegans Wake*. Puddock suggests that he and Devereux devise an Irish variation upon the plays of Shakespeare:

> Seriously, by sometimes changing an old person to a young, sometimes a comical to a melancholy, or the reverse, sometimes a male for a female, or a female for a male—I assure you, you can so entirely disguise the piece, and yet produce situations so new and surprising—

Devereux responds by proposing a new version of *Othello*, in which

> [a] gay young Venetian nobleman, of singular beauty, charmed by her tales of "anthropophagites and men whose heads do grow beneath their shoulders," is seduced from his father's house and married by a middle-aged, somewhat hard-featured black woman, Juno, or Dido.

Sheridan Le Fanu, *The House by the Churchyard*, intro. by Thomas Kilroy (Belfast: Appletree, 1992), 135.

Joyce's project in *Ulysses*, although it is a variation on not one but two literary works (the *Odyssey* and *Hamlet*), resembles that of Puddock and Devereux in its comic design to expose the hero as a gendered construction, defined not only by sex but also by age, race, and class. The different roles in a Shakespeare play or in a Homeric epic are not reversible without dramatic alterations in meaning, for the simple reason that the meanings of sex, age, and class inhere in the culture; the text merely plays against them.

Telemachus and Hamlet, only to puncture it by presenting his readers with a scrawny intellectual who is poor, physically dirty, periodically infested with vermin, and a coward. Even Stephen's disposition violates generic expectations; instead of being optimistic, confident, and determined, he is morose and riddled with guilt. Unlike Telemachus in the *Odyssey*, who resolves to perform whatever feats are necessary to gain information about his father, confronting Nestor and appealing to Menelaus in his determined effort to gain control of his home, Stephen, depressed by the crass "wisdom" of Mr. Deasy, struggles blindly with the sea-changes of language and philosophy, only to drink himself into a stupor and go berserk in a whorehouse. As a troubled protagonist, Stephen is most temperamentally akin to Shakespeare's Hamlet, who *is* a prince, but a prince who disdains the corruption he is heir to. Joyce darkens the portrait of disaffected youth still further in his portrayal of Stephen, whose indulgence in obscure thought is more oblique than Hamlet's affected madness, and who—as a freethinking Irish Catholic youth in a poor, colonized country—occupies a dramatically reduced economic and social position.

The portrait of Stephen, offered as a replacement for that of the conventional young male hero, is not a narcissistic celebration of Joyce's own vulgarity, as some early readers charged. On the contrary, its function is to provoke a reappraisal of the criteria for heroism in Western culture. Why admire young men whose courage is due partly to the accident of age and health and partly to a rash refusal to assess danger realistically? Why privilege the accident of class and social position, which insulates young "heroes" from more lethal dangers that spring from need, hopelessness, and deprivation? Why is the avoidance of humiliation and degradation (through birth, appearance, and youth) valued more highly than the experience and survival of injustice? Joyce's depiction of Stephen against a grain of expectation makes him an ugly duckling from the perspective of what we were prepared to admire, but at the same time it exposes the hidden basis of our admiration. It becomes clear in retrospect that what makes a young male hero in the popular sense is not bravery, but luck. The hero does not *earn* admiration at all; he merely makes use of the blessings of strength and riches. Moreover, valuing luck gives us no way of differentiating between heroes and villains, since a successful—or lucky—villain is indistinguishable from a hero.[3] When Joyce presents

[3]In Le Fanu's *The House by the Churchyard*, the villain, whom everyone had taken for a powerful and successful man, declares his "heroic" faith when he is unmasked: "I believe in luck, Sir, and there's the sum of my creed." He argues, with coldly logical so-

us with "twin" heroes at the beginning of *Ulysses* in the characters of Stephen and Buck Mulligan, he uses them to make just such a point. Buck is the conventional hero—not only does he have the sunny disposition, good health, and financial solvency of the hero, but he is also clean, well-groomed, and has saved a man from drowning. Stephen uncertainly tries to determine whether he could do what Buck did:

> He saved men from drowning and you shake at a cur's yelping. But the courtiers who mocked Guido in Or san Michele were in their own house. House of . . . We don't want any of your medieval abstrusiosities. Would you do what he did? A boat would be near, a lifebuoy. *Natuerlich*, put there for you. Would you or would you not? . . . The truth, spit it out. I would want to. I would try. I am not a strong swimmer . . . If I had land under my feet. I want his life still to be his, mine to be mine. A drowning man. His human eyes scream to me out of horror of his death. I . . . With him together down. . . . I could not save her. Waters: bitter death: lost. (*U* 3.317–30).

Set against Buck's animal health, Stephen's honest interrogation of his strengths ("I am not a strong swimmer") and his memory of failure at saving others, especially his mother ("I could not save her"), emerge as thoughtful and realistic. His values are less competitive than egalitarian ("I want his life still to be his, mine to be mine"). Instead of idealizing the feat of salvation, Stephen tries to focus on the reality of support ("A boat would be near, a lifebuoy"). Very gradually, as Joyce explained to Frank Budgen, the reader should begin to appreciate the slow discipline of Stephen's ethics, contrasting it to the easier panache of Buck's.

The next model of male heroism that Joyce proceeds to display and partly dismantle is that of the mature man, epitomized by Ulysses. The heroism of an older man is more complex than that of a younger one, but ultimately it still depends on the exercise of ruthless physical strength. The *Odyssey* suggests that the mature male hero is cunning, patient, and adept at lying and disguise. He has the capacity to sustain hardships for a very long time, but ultimately he too gathers his resources for a violent, merciless confrontation in which he slaughters

---

cial criticism, that his actions were perpetrated in the name of the same principle that his accusers evoke in putting him to death, "justice, which means only the collective selfishness of my fellow-creatures" (412). The book builds to the climactic and significant revelation that the much-admired Paul Dangerfield and the villainous Charles Archer are the same man.

his opponents and reclaims his possessions (which include his wife). Joyce endows Bloom with Odysseus' more unconventional character-istics—his adaptability, his taste for disguise, and above all his capacity for survival—but he translates Odysseus' bloody slaughter of the suit-ors into Bloom's rational dismissal of his scruples in "Ithaca."[4] More-over, he stretches Odysseus' talent for deception to include a tendency toward self-deception.

In a powerful critique of the ethos of manly heroism (in *Finnegans Wake* Joyce renames the hero a "zero," or "belowes hero," *FW* 343.17), Joyce intimates that it is the powerful and subtle temptation to deceive oneself, to which everyone is susceptible, that renders self-righteous confrontation and retribution suspect rather than heroic. By building his complex verbal structure around a protagonist who tries to avoid the knowledge that his wife has a sexual assignation with an-other man on that very day, Joyce implicitly challenges two of the most common assumptions about heroism: that the hero is fully aware of his motives for acting, and that those motives are simple, uncon-flicted, and completely endorsed by the society he epitomizes. In con-trast to the stock hero, Bloom is as suspicious of himself as he is of others. Bloom's caution, his propensity to delay action, and his dis-trust of reprisal make him a different kind of hero, one who will never be guilty of violent abuse. Like Stephen, Bloom aims not to "be mas-ter of others or their slave" (*U* 3.295–96), a goal that prods him to question—half unconsciously—his own complicity in his wife's desire for other men. Bloom's bipartisan refusal of mastery and enslavement prevents him from becoming like Farrington in "Counterparts," driven to deny his sociopolitical impotence by ignobly beating a child. Moreover, Bloom's half-conscious preoccupation with the painful knowledge he is trying to disown also signals his refusal to detach him-self from Molly by employing the easy, self-congratulatory mechanisms of contempt. His rejection of detachment as a solution to the prob-lems of relation is what differentiates him from cold and haunted char-acters such as Mr. Duffy in "A Painful Case."

Defying the traditions of epic and romance, Joyce redefines a male hero as neither brave nor vengeful, but as cautious, realistic, and slowly willing to contemplate the possibility that his relation to those he loves

---

[4]In the schema he gave Stuart Gilbert, Joyce suggests that instead of violently slaughtering Molly's suitors, like Odysseus, Bloom uses reason to destroy his scruples. Under "Correspondences" for the "Ithaca" episode, Joyce identifies the suitors as "scruples" and the bow with which Ulysses slaughters them as "reason." See Don Gif-ford, with Robert J. Seidman, *"Ulysses" Annotated: Notes for James Joyce's "Ulysses,"* rev. ed. (Berkeley: U of California P, 1988), 566.

has inadvertently been hurtful. Joyce's most sympathetic male characters see themselves, painfully, as fallible; their heroism grows not out
of boundless confidence in the rightness of physical might, but out
of what might be called the moral courage to imagine freshly the
perspectives of people they have wronged. Although Stephen is unable
to change his relations with his dead mother and unwilling to show
gratitude to Bloom for Bloom's tactful solicitude, his appreciation of
Jewish merchants as patient and knowing (*U* 2.364–73), and his vision
of Muslim and Jewish intellectuals as "dark men in mien and
movement, flashing in their mocking mirrors the obscure soul of the
world, a darkness shining in brightness which brightness could not
comprehend (*U* 2.158–60)," suggest that he feels an empathy with
other races and other times that he is not yet capable of experiencing
in the present at the level of individual relations. Stephen's view of
woman is also sympathetic, if abstract. Stephen sees her as irresistible,
lonely, overburdened, and weary; he calls her the handmaid of the
moon, journeying ever westward, "followed by the sun's flaming
sword" (*U* 3.391–92), pulling the tide in her wake. Stephen also sees
tides within woman—blood, "a winedark sea"—a red flood that
attracts man, in his role of vampire, toward her (*U* 3.397–98). As the
moon, she wearily gathers and releases the waves in splendid isolation;
in her perpetual toil, she (like the harp in "Two Gallants") cares nothing for her lovers: "Weary too in sight of lovers, lascivious men, a
naked woman shining in her courts, she draws a toil of waters" (*U*
3.468–69).

Although Stephen romanticizes and denigrates woman by turns,[5]
he is also able to picture to himself her loneliness, toil, pain, and even
indifference. Bloom, too, is led by "ruth": "Woman's woe with wonder pondering" (*U* 14.186); "Ruth red him, love led on with will to
wander, loth to leave" (*U* 14.201). Bloom is sensitive not only to the
travail of woman in childbirth, but also to the deprivation and creep-
ing despair of Josie Breen, caring for a crazed husband: Bloom notes
with compassion her worn clothes, the lines around her mouth, the
cruel eye of a passing woman upon her (*U* 8.265–69). He is also quick
to sympathize with Gerty MacDowell when he realizes she is lame,
"Poor girl!" (*U* 13.772), and he even imagines how difficult rejection
must be for whores-in-training: "Aho! If you don't answer when they
solicit must be horrible for them till they harden" (*U* 13.869–70).
Most important, Bloom is able to sympathize with woman's hardships

---

[5]He expresses disgust at "woman's unclean loins, of man's flesh made not in God's
likeness, the serpent's prey" (*U* 1.421–22).

without sentimentalizing them; he stops short of condescending to woman as an innocent (and therefore childlike) victim of brutal male desire. He knows, for example, that Gerty solicits his gaze, that she is driven by powerful yearnings that she cannot identify to herself as sexual. Bloom is quick to adopt the woman's perspective in a variety of situations, but in his awareness of the manifold compromises of relation, he is wary of delivering definitive judgments. He imagines the feelings of a woman who is married to a drunk:

> Husband rolling in drunk, stink of pub off him like a polecat. Have that in your nose in the dark, whiff of stale boose. Then ask in the morning: was I drunk last night? Bad policy however to fault the husband. Chickens come home to roost. They stick by one another like glue. Maybe the women's fault also. (*U* 13.964–68)

Bloom sees woman as capable and possibly culpable, but his reluctance to judge never prevents him from imagining himself vividly in her place: "Have that in your nose in the dark, whiff of stale boose."

The image of male heroism embedded in Western culture is emphatically physical; as the male hero ages, his courage is supplemented by cunning, but the basis of his appeal is the power of brute force and a willingness to use that force to protect (and simultaneously to restrict) women in particular and the community in general. In *Ulysses*, Joyce constructs a verbal edifice that promises to house popular epic heroes, but what the reader finds within it instead are thinking, caring men who—like most people—are prone to self-deception and error. The only men in the novel who pride themselves on their physical prowess are an adulterer and a bigot: the exaggeratedly hot Blazes Boylan and the hypocritical Citizen. The reader's expectation clashes loudly with the actual experience of reading *Ulysses*, and the cacophony that results brings the currency of our cultural definition of gender categories comically into question.

Given the premium placed on physical strength in men, it is perhaps surprising that cultural prescriptions for women demand an erasure or concealment of the body and of sexual power. If male heroes should be strong and active, female heroes must be aesthetically pleasing and passive; moreover, they should be immature, the innocent cause and reward of man's desire. The ideal role of the female heroine is to serve as an inspirational icon who is also the prize in a patriarchal contest, as Joyce suggests in *Finnegans Wake* by rendering "beauty" as "booty" (*FW* 560.20). In a typically compressed fashion, Joyce suggests that romantic love, in the popular imagination, is epitomized by

the story of "booty with the bedst" (Beauty and the Beast), a tale of
rapine in which the brawny man—simultaneously identified as "best"
and "beast"—aims to land his "booty" in bed.[6]
Joyce's critique of popular culture's objectification of the young
"heroine"—who learns to see herself from the outside and to adver-
tise herself even in her thoughts as a desirable commodity on the marriage market—is perhaps his most trenchant exposé of the ludicrous
cultural prescriptions for women. (As Issy notes in *Finnegans Wake*, in
partial response to her name: "I sold/Isolde"—"One must sell it to
some one, the sacred name of love," *FW* 268 n. 1.) In "Nausicaa,"
Joyce introduces us to the thoughts of Gerty MacDowell, who is so
thoroughly indoctrinated by the image of the culturally desirable young
woman that she cannot own or realize her own desires, revealing them
by indirection, cloaking them with narrative fantasies, burying them in
the sand on which she sits. From Gerty we learn that a heroine should
be an inanimate *objet d'art*, "ivorylike . . . Greekly perfect . . . hands
were of finely veined alabaster" (*U* 13.88–89), and that she resembles
a fairytale heroine. Like Cinderella, she has small feet: "Edy Boardman
prided herself that she was very *petite* but she never had a foot like Gerty
MacDowell, a five, and never would ash, oak or elm" (*U* 13.165–67).[7]
Also like Cinderella, her inborn qualities reveal her as belonging to a
more privileged class from which an unkind fate has exiled her:

> There was an innate refinement, a languid queenly *hauteur* about
> Gerty which was unmistakably evidenced in her delicate hands
> and higharched instep. Had kind fate but willed her to be born a
> gentlewoman of high degree in her own right and had she only re-
> ceived the benefit of a good education Gerty MacDowell might
> easily have held her own beside any lady in the land. (*U* 13.96–102)

Most poignantly, we observe that although Gerty is careful to deck her
body for constant display, she herself is discouraged from inhabiting it:
she cannot refer to bodily functions or even the place where they
occur. She is uncomfortable both with eating ("she didn't like the
eating part when there were any people that made her shy and often

---

[6]"Booty" is also a boot, or a glass slipper, a fetish that represents the hero's desire
for her to contain his foot (or *foutre*), while remaining inert.
[7]In *Finnegans Wake*, Joyce stresses the relation between Cinderella and her ashes,
which signify the mortality her story denies, more emphatically than he does here by issuing a warning to Cinderella in language that echoes that of the Ash Wednesday service: "Remember, maid, thou dust art powder but Cinderella thou must return" (*FW*
440.26–27).

she wondered why you couldn't eat something poetical like violets or roses," *U* 13.228–30) and with elimination. When Cissy refers to a part of the body, "the beeoteetom," Gerty "bent down her head and crimsoned at the idea of Cissy saying an unladylike thing like that out loud she'd be ashamed of her life to say" (*U* 13.263–66). And when she goes to "that place where she never forgot every fortnight the chlorate of lime" (*U* 13.332–33), she distracts herself from what she is doing by gazing at a

> picture of halcyon days where a young gentleman in the costume they used to wear then with a threecornered hat was offering a bunch of flowers to his ladylove with oldtime chivalry . . . She often looked at them dreamily when she went there for a certain purpose and felt her own arms that were white and soft just like hers. (*U* 13.334–41)

Although Gerty is physically mature, she is unable to realize that maturity and accept the complexity of physical being because she must constantly identify herself in her own mind with beauty. Even in the outhouse she must block out her surroundings by staring at a picture of old-fashioned gallantry. Gerty relentlessly censors her thoughts and perceptions, vigilantly replacing them with sentimental pictures: of herself as a model in a fashion magazine decked out in "a neat blouse of electric blue . . . and a navy threequarter skirt cut to the stride" (*U* 13.150–55); of herself as rescued by "a manly man with a strong quiet face who had not found his ideal, perhaps his hair slightly flecked with grey, and who would understand, take her in his sheltering arms, strain her to him in all the strength of his deep passionate nature and comfort her with a long long kiss" (*U* 13.210–14). She paints a highly touched-up picture of marriage, complete with "a beautifully appointed drawingroom with pictures and engravings" and "that silver toastrack in Clery's summer jumble sales" (*U* 13.231–34), where her tall husband with broad shoulders and "glistening white teeth under his carefully trimmed sweeping moustache" (*U* 13.236–37) has "brekky" with her every morning, "simple but perfectly served." "[B]efore he went out to business he would give his dear little wifey a good hearty hug and gaze for a moment deep down into her eyes" (*U* 13.240–42).

In accordance with what Joyce identified as the meaning of this episode, "The Projected Mirage,"[8] Gerty has replaced herself with a

[8]According to the Linati schema, the "Sense (Meaning)" of the episode is "The Projected Mirage," and its Symbol is "Onanism: Female: Hypocrisy." See Gifford *Ulysses Annotated* 384.

series of aesthetically pleasing pictures, or mirages, that serve the function of advertisements (and that are in fact modeled on advertisements). Gerty has read the signs of popular culture accurately, and she has done as directed by turning herself into something to be seen, like a painting (the "Art" of the episode is "painting"). Gerty has fashioned herself quite literally into a heroine, "as fair a specimen of winsome Irish girlhood as one could wish to see" (*U* 13.80–81), and she seems to epitomize the most admirable aspects of her age and gender: virginity, innocence, a deep longing to minister to the needs of men, aesthetic appeal enhanced by the judicious and thrifty use of clothes and cosmetics, religious faith, and "sweet girlish shyness" (*U* 13.121). One of her favorite poems is called "*Art thou real, my ideal?*" by Louis J Walsh, Magherafelt (*U* 13.645–46), and she has constructed herself as an answer to that question. Gerty represents the Irish feminine ideal that Irish audiences so hotly defended in their protests against W. B. Yeats's *The Countess Cathleen* (1899) and J. M. Synge's *The Playboy of the Western World* (1907),[9] but Joyce examines the implications of this ideal more carefully than did the nationalist protesters; he exposes its pathetic limitations, reducing a real, potentially complex woman into a lonely caricature and common cliché, although one that is tremendously exciting to men at a distance.

Moreover, Joyce uses Gerty to show that an icon of purity carries within it the seeds of a necessary defilement; this is what Joyce somewhat imprecisely refers to in his schema as the hypocrisy equivalent to female onanism: "Onanism: Female: Hypocrisy." What is hypocritical is not women but the feminine ideal, which in "Circe" is represented by the immortal nymph (*U* 15.3232). The nymph advertises

---

[9]The *Playboy* riots erupted after Christy Mahon, the playboy, tells the Widow Quin, "It's Pegeen I'm seeking only, and what'd I care if you brought me a drift of chosen females, standing in their shifts itself, maybe, from this place to the Eastern World?" J. M. Synge, *The Playboy of the Western World*, act 3, *Modern Irish Drama*, ed. John P. Harrington (New York: Norton, 1991), 115. Joseph Holloway, in a theater journal entry for Thursday, January 31, 1907, refers to this as filth and libel of the Irish peasant girl on the stage. *Modern Irish Drama*, 459. In a letter to the *Freeman's Journal* on January 28, 1907, an Irishwoman writes,

in no part of Ireland are the women so wanting in modesty as to make advances to a total stranger, much less to a criminal.

Cited in James Kilroy, *The Playboy Riots* (Dublin: Dolmen, 1971), 10. Interestingly, *The Playboy of the Western World* takes as its subject the difference between the *image* of heroism and its ugly realities. The townspeople in Synge's play celebrate Christy's heroic pose as a man who killed his father but revile him when they see actual evidence of the attempt, much as a reader might expect Gerty to remain a picture but express shock when she is actually looked at with desire.

herself as "stonecold and pure" (*U* 15.3393) as she castigates Bloom
for his furtive indecencies, but then she begins to undergo a transformation. She first turns into an eyeless nun, intoning "No more desire . . . Only the ethereal" (*U* 15.3436–37), then she starts showing
stains, and finally "her plaster cast" cracks, emitting a cloud of stench
(*U* 15.3457, 3469–70). The ideal is itself corrupt, and it cannot hide
that corruption indefinitely.

Like the nymph-nun in "Circe," Gerty, by constructing herself as
pure and by censoring any indelicate thoughts, renders herself defenseless against the pressure of natural desires. As the ideal female, Gerty is
a "sleeping beauty," which Joyce translates in *Finnegans Wake* as a
"slipping beauty" (*FW* 477.23); Gerty's unawareness of her own desires is precisely what makes her vulnerable to the penetration of
Bloom's gaze.[10] What Joyce shows, by having Gerty swing her shoe
buckle and then her leg for Bloom, leaning far back until "he had a
full view high up above her knee where no-one ever not even on the
swing or wading and she wasn't ashamed and he wasn't either to look
in that immodest way" (*U* 13.728–30), is that her behavior is totally
consistent with her cultural definition as something to be looked at.
Although "from everything in the least indelicate her finebred nature
instinctively recoiled" (*U* 13.660–61), Gerty can picture her self-
display as a romantic dream-encounter:

> She had to go but they would meet again, there, and she would
> dream of that till then, tomorrow, of her dream of yester eve . . .
> Their souls met in a last lingering glance and the eyes that reached
> her heart, full of a strange shining, hung enraptured on her sweet
> flowerlike face. She half smiled at him wanly, a sweet forgiving
> smile, a smile that verged on tears, and then they parted. (*U*
> 13.760–65)

Even her image of physical perfection is unveiled as a mirage, when
she is revealed as lame.

The attitude that *Ulysses* takes toward female beauty is exuberantly
unconventional. Joyce depicts beauty as a sleight-of-hand, a trick of

---

[10]Joyce's insistence on the interdependence of "sleeping" and "slipping" is reinforced by different variants of the "Sleeping Beauty" tale that portray sleeping as an end
to innocence. In an Irish version, "The Queen of Tubber Tintye," or "The King of Erin
and the Queen of the Lonesome Island," the queen is not only impregnated but also
gives birth while sleeping (she awakens when her son is six years old). And in the version
from *The Pentamerone of Giambattista Basile*, "Sole, Luna, e Talia," Sleeping Beauty is
again raped while sleeping, whereupon she gives birth to two children, Sun and Moon.
See P. L. Travers, *About the Sleeping Beauty* (London: Collins, 1975), 96–123.

costume, an accident of lighting, a byproduct of style, designed to make women feel less ordinary and to provoke sexual desire in men. The language of beauty is rooted in the language of magic; as Gerty amply demonstrates, the desired transformation is risibly, poignantly transitory. However, those who counsel women in the deception of beauty do so, unethically, in the name of truth:

> Time was when those brows were not so silkily seductive. It was Madame Vera Verity [true truth], directress of the Woman Beautiful page of the Princess Novelette, who had first advised her to try eyebrowleine which gave that haunting expression to the eyes, so becoming in leaders of fashion. (U 13.108–12)

Beauty traffics in the illusion that a woman's body may transcend "those discharges she used to get and that tired feeling" (U 13.86–87), that she may be transformed into a spiritual, young, and virginal vision of unstained perfection, a lady whose "innate refinement" refutes the indignities of her present station (U 13.97).

By humorously dissecting the magic of cosmetic transformation and by exposing the purposes that the cult of beauty serves for men and women, Joyce derails the reader's desire for a beautiful, faithful heroine and spotlights its implied misogyny. If what we want is a heroine with a "waxen pallor . . . almost spiritual in its ivorylike purity" (U 13.87–88), then we are simultaneously expressing a distaste for real women, with the physical afflictions and imperfections that make them long for the magical transformations promised by cosmetics.

Joyce's exposure of the ideal that Gerty worships and imitates as both false and blind (her "little strangled cry" aligns her with the blind bat that flies out at dusk "with a tiny lost cry," U 13.735, 13.626–27) helps to contextualize his decision to design his mature female heroine along radically unpopular lines. Joyce rejects "beauty parlous" (beauty parlors, parlous beauty, FW 454.19–20) as the source of Molly Bloom's attractiveness. Molly is not beautiful in the cosmetic sense, although she is powerfully attractive in the gravitational sense. Moreover, part of what makes her attractive is precisely what prevents her from being conventionally beautiful in fairytale terms: her large mass. Attractive not beautiful, Molly exercises considerable sexual power instead of becoming "booty."

Molly was never designed to "represent" Joyce's idea of womanhood, which would indeed make her a problematic character;[11]

---

[11]See, for example, Karen Lawrence's discussion of Sandra Gilbert and Susan Gubar's attack on Joyce's "misogyny" in "Joyce and Feminism," *The Cambridge*

instead, her character is a supplement, an antiphonal answer to the popular (and risibly anemic) idea of a heroine. She is, in a sense, an anti-Gerty, if Gerty is understood to typify someone who, under strong cultural pressure, has replaced herself as she is in biological reality with a picture of what a young woman should be. If Gerty's introjected ideal image is feminine, Joyce has Molly project herself as aggressive and even masculine ("the missus is master," *U* 15.2759). If Gerty airbrushes her body out of consciousness, clothing her body parts in a conscientious effort to deny and replace them,[12] Molly takes pleasure in her ample flesh and consciously registers all aspects of her physical existence—from sexual arousal and climax to urination and menstruation ("wait O Jesus wait yes that thing has come on me yes now wouldnt that afflict you of course all the poking and rooting and ploughing he had up in me," *U* 18.1104–06). If Gerty is defined by the clothes she uses simultaneously to reveal and conceal herself, Molly is either minimally clothed or nude, like the picture of *The Bath of the Nymph* over the bed that reminds Bloom of her: "Not unlike her with her hair down: slimmer . . . Naked nymphs" (*U* 4.371–73). Instead of looking at her clothes, Bloom looks through Molly's clothes to appreciate her "ample bedwarmed flesh" (*U* 4.238–39): "He looked calmly down on her bulk and between her large soft bubs, sloping within her nightdress like a shegoat's udder" (*U* 4.304–05). All we see

---

Companion to James Joyce, ed. Derek Attridge (New York: Cambridge UP, 1990), 237–58. Gilbert and Gubar object that Joyce identifies woman too completely with "matter"; Lawrence lends some credence to this view by pointing out Joyce's expressions of guilt over his treatment of women in his fiction and his dreams, but then she goes on to argue that "a catalogue of misogynistic images or female stereotypes in Joyce's work fails to account for his undermining of the grounds of representation" (240). She suggests that "woman in writing is beyond [Joyce's] control and might stand for a play of language that always exceeds the writer's intention" (240), and that woman "becomes the figure for illegitimacy, errancy, and forgery rather than patriarchal signature" (241). My own emphasis is somewhat different, in that I see Molly less as a principle of excess than as an embodiment of physical realities that are conspicuously missing from what might be called the compound cultural self-image that all women are called on to measure themselves against.

[12]Interestingly, what Gerty "reveals" to Bloom is not her body but her underclothing, the fetishized substitute for her body that corresponds to the picture she has substituted for herself. To allow the reader a glimpse of what Gerty fears about the body, the narrator (speaking in Gerty's idiom) refers to underwear as "undies," thereby highlighting not only Gerty's taste for common diminutives but also underscoring the fact that clothes, unlike the body, don't die. "As for undies they were Gerty's chief care and who that knows the fluttering hopes and fears of sweet seventeen (though Gerty would never see seventeen again) can find it in his heart to blame her?" (*U* 13.171–73). Gerty is exceptionally conscious of the passing of time, since she has passed the most marriageable age. "Then they could talk about her till they went blue in the face, Bertha Supple too, and Edy, little spitfire, because she would be twentytwo in November" (*U* 13.220–22).

of Molly in "Wandering Rocks" is "a plump bare generous arm" shining "from a white petticoatbodice and taut shiftstraps" (*U* 10.251–52). Molly is presented in a shift, that item of clothing that it was controversial for actors even to name in *The Playboy of the Western World*; an Irishwoman in a letter to the *Freeman's Journal* declared that the word used to indicate this "essential item of female attire" was one that a "lady would probably never utter in ordinary circumstances, even to herself."[13]

Unlike Gerty, Molly is triumphantly, painfully presented as "a nature full and volatile in its free state" that is naturally the agent and reagent of attraction (*U* 17.2163–64). In sharp contrast to Gerty's self-advertising picture of feminine underwear, the last image we are given of Molly before she begins to speak is an unprecedentedly alluring image of her nude breasts and rump,

> adipose anterior and posterior female hemispheres, redolent of milk and honey and of excretory sanguine and seminal warmth, reminiscent of secular families of curves of amplitude, insusceptible of moods of impression or of contrarieties of expression, expressive of mute immutable mature animality. (*U* 17.2232–36)

Joyce refuses to reduce Molly to the fat tissue of her rump, but where else in literature or culture can we find a comparable instance of appreciation for female corporeality? To a culture that protested raucously against the use of the *word* shift as a libel upon womanhood, Joyce offers an image of Bloom kissing "the plump mellow yellow smellow melons of [a woman's] rump, on each plump melonous hemisphere, in their mellow yellow furrow" (*U* 17.2241–42). Which is the more misogynist stance, the one that celebrates the full experience of female flesh, or the one that censors even the mention of intimate articles of female clothing? In a culture in which thousands of anorectic young women are trying to melt the flesh off their bodies, amenorrheal from the attempt to eat nothing but "violets and roses," how can a representation of ample female flesh as something more beautiful than any work of art, something as vital as the earth itself, be considered misogynist? And when Molly starts to speak, the reader learns that she is far more than the "2 lumps of lard" to which she fears Bloom has reduced her (*U* 18.1404): she is full of memory and desire, sensation and longing, poetry and dross. Unlike so many women who think of themselves even in the third person, she speaks for herself—powerfully, lyrically, sometimes crudely, and without inhibition. Unlike

[13]Kilroy, *The Playboy Riots* 10.

Gerty, who has so pitifully suppressed hers, Molly has a voracious appetite for life, and as a result she sometimes cannot find "this mortal world enough."[14] But her famous affirmation with which the book ends expresses her willed acceptance of life *and* loss, her resistance to attenuation and despair, to being turned to stone by a realistic sight of the world as it is, and not in the romantic world of faery.

Even Nora, Joyce's wife, was not immune to the shock of being asked to read against the grain of glossy fashion images by seeing Molly as a female hero. When asked if she was a model for Molly Bloom, Nora denied it, claiming with some vanity that Molly was fatter than she was.[15] Although men have long appreciated the proportional relation of size and power (a relation that made small men like Napoleon famously anxious), women as a rule do not interrogate the possible correlation of a petite figure and powerlessness. Although Joyce certainly could have made Molly more intellectual (more like her namesake Molly Ivors in "The Dead"), the role of resistant intellectual had already been assigned to Stephen as a way of countering the expectation that heroes *must be* physical. The characters of Stephen and Molly were designed to violate cultural prescriptions insisting that men must be physical and women may not be physical, a prescription that seems to preclude any meaningful heterosexual connection. But neither Stephen nor Molly is presented as a counter-ideal; Joyce's attack is on the unreality and counterproductiveness of ideals in general, as well as on specific, mutually exclusive ideals for men and women, in particular.

Joyce sees woman as powerful; where he differs radically from the culture at large is that he does not brand female sexual power as evil.[16] *Ulysses* is shot through with references to powerful female figures: Ann Hathaway, Helen of Troy, Kitty O'Shea, "naked Eve": "She had no navel. Gaze. Belly without blemish, bulging big, a buckler of taut vellum, no, whiteheaped corn, orient and immortal, standing from ever-

---

[14]W. H. Auden, "Lullaby." *The Norton Anthology of English Literature*. 4th Edition. Vol. 2. (New York: W. W. Norton & Company, Inc., 1979), 2397.

[15]Brenda Maddox, *Nora: A Biography of Nora Joyce* (New York: Fawcett Columbine, 1988), 198.

[16]There are very few representations of mature female sexual power that are not demonized as evil. Shakespeare's portrait of Cleopatra in *Antony and Cleopatra* may be one, although Cleopatra is far from triumphant at the end; Queen Elizabeth consolidated her political power by refusing to allow it to be interpreted as sexual, billing herself as "The Virgin Queen." The notion of the femme fatale sums up the prevailing sense that female sexual power is dangerous, at best, and fatal, at worst, and there are almost no examples of good-intentioned, successful women who are physically strong and resistant to oppression (even Joan of Arc was martyred).

lasting to everlasting" (*U* 3.41–44). Although men like Garrett Deasy blame women for our "many errors and many sins" (*U* 2.389–90), Joyce dismisses such bigotry as an insidiously disguised personal complaint (Deasy's wife is an unpredictable alcoholic), focusing instead on women's loneliness, a loneliness enhanced by a legacy of shame. Although *Ulysses* is built around a single decisive event, Molly's adultery, Joyce refuses to categorize Molly as an evil or corrupt woman; like Thomas Hardy, who controversially described Tess of the d'Urbervilles as "A Pure Woman," Joyce levels his criticism not at the individual but at the institutions that ravage her, reminding the reader that "from outrage (matrimony) to outrage (adultery) there arose nought but outrage (copulation)" (*U* 17.2196–97). Joyce makes it clear that the "debility of the female" has been "fallaciously inferred" (*U* 17.2215–16) and, along with Bloom, he asserts "the futility of triumph or protest or vindication," spurning "the inanity of extolled virtue" (*U* 17.2224–25).

Ulysses is unusual in that it expresses neither fear nor denigration nor denial of the power of female sexuality. The burden of Stephen's theory of Shakespeare is that Shakespeare's productivity grew out of his encounter with a sexually powerful woman, a woman whose capacity for desire—like that of Queen Gertrude in *Hamlet*—is read by others as faithlessness.[17] Stephen tells his listeners that Ann Hathaway was no mere mistake of Shakespeare's youth; she was the portal of discovery through which he passed without ever really learning the significance of what his writing everywhere reveals, the central importance of his early receptivity to an older, assured woman: "he passes on towards eternity in undiminished personality, untaught by the wisdom he has written or by the laws he has revealed" (*U* 9.476–79). The "events which cast their shadow over the hell of time of *King Lear, Othello, Hamlet, Troilus and Cressida*," are the events that surrounded Shakespeare's seduction by Ann Hathaway, who tumbled "in a cornfield a lover younger than herself" (*U* 9.260). What his experience of a sexually powerful, physically alive woman produces in Shakespeare is—crucially—ambivalence, an ambivalence that makes him "Ravisher and ravished," pursuing "what he would but would not" (*U* 9.472–73); "Belief in himself has been untimely killed" (*U* 9.455–56), and his ego is splintered in painfully productive ways. He has lost the assured ease of judgmental condemnation but gained the capacity to find himself in

[17]Compare Virginia Woolf's famous imaginary account of Shakespeare's "sister" in *A Room of One's Own* (1929; New York and London: Harcourt, 1957).

all his characters, finding "in the world without as actual what was in his world within as possible" (*U* 9.1041–42). It is not Ann Hathaway's beauty that produces such a harvest (as "beautifulinsadness Best" says to "ugling Eglinton," "The sense of beauty leads us astray," *U* 9.735), but her vivid reality, the physical and erotic strength that society would debar to women.

Cultural stereotypes, ideals, even gender differences themselves (insofar as they prescribe differences in thought and behavior) are attempts to contain and sterilize the contaminating power of a reality that, like mortality itself, ultimately destroys all categories. Joyce's war with convention in *Ulysses* highlights the vitality of eschewing judgment and embracing the catalytic force of change. Perhaps Joyce is mistaken in his view that woman, having been sharply forbidden fleshly indulgence for at least a millennium, has a capacity to experience physical life exceeding that of men. Virginia Woolf certainly thought that Joyce underestimated the effects on women of centuries of repression. But what Joyce systematically attacks throughout *Ulysses* are those compound cultural images that crowd out individual apprehension, experimentation, and thought, the products and prescriptions of what Gerty calls "Society with a big ess" (*U* 13.666). Gender difference is one such debilitating mirage; boundaries, as Joyce describes them, are heuristic borders designed to be surpassed—not lightly, but at the appropriate time, to initiate new stages of cognitive and emotional development. *Ulysses* is designed to inculcate "heterodox resistance" to simplistic cultural constructions (*U* 17.23); it both protests and mourns the increasing "restriction of the . . . domain of interindividual relations" (*U* 17.64–65). Instead of feminine young women and masculine young men, it offers its readers the fuller, surer touch of a "firm full masculine feminine passive active hand" (*U* 17.289–90). Its categories are mixed, controversial, changing, and alive; its stance is a feminist one in the sense that it prefers "sins of excess" to "sins of denial."[18] Like Bloom, Joyce expresses in *Ulysses* a desire "to amend many social conditions, the product of inequality and avarice and international animosity" (*U* 17.990–92), and in *Ulysses*, he commits himself fully to the "convulsions of metamorphosis, from infancy through maturity to decay" (*U* 17.1005–06). *Ulysses* affirms "the fact of vital growth" (*U* 17.1005), not artificial categories such as gender, a word with an "end" in it.

---

[18]Jeanette Winterson, *Sexing the Cherry* (New York: Random-Vintage, 1989), 70.

Psychoanalytic Criticism
and
Ulysses

WHAT IS PSYCHOANALYTIC CRITICISM?

It seems natural to think about literature in terms of dreams. Like dreams, literary works are fictions, inventions of the mind that, although based on reality, are by definition not literally true. Like a literary work, a dream may have some truth to tell, but, like a literary work, it may need to be interpreted before that truth can be grasped. We can live vicariously through romantic fictions, much as we can through daydreams. Terrifying novels and nightmares affect us in much the same way, plunging us into an atmosphere that continues to cling, even after the last chapter has been read—or the alarm clock has sounded.

The notion that dreams allow such psychic explorations, of course, like the analogy between literary works and dreams, owes a great deal to the thinking of Sigmund Freud, the famous Austrian psychoanalyst who in 1900 published a seminal text, *The Interpretation of Dreams*. But is the reader who feels that Emily Brontë's *Wuthering Heights* is dreamlike—who feels that Mary Shelley's *Frankenstein* is nightmarish—necessarily a Freudian literary critic? To some extent the answer has to be yes. We are all Freudians, really, whether or not we have read a single work by Freud. At one time or another, most of us have referred to ego, libido, complexes, unconscious desires, and sexual repression. The premises of Freud's thought have changed the way the

Western world thinks about itself. Psychoanalytic criticism has influenced the teachers our teachers studied with, the works of scholarship and criticism they read, and the critical and creative writers *we* read as well. What Freud did was develop a language that described, a model that explained, a theory that encompassed human psychology. Many of the elements of psychology he sought to describe and explain are present in the literary works of various ages and cultures, from Sophocles' *Oedipus Rex* to Shakespeare's *Hamlet* to works being written in our own day. When the great novel of the twenty-first century is written, many of these same elements of psychology will probably inform its discourse as well. If, by understanding human psychology according to Freud, we can appreciate literature on a new level, then we should acquaint ourselves with his insights.

Freud's theories are either directly or indirectly concerned with the nature of the unconscious mind. Freud didn't invent the notion of the unconscious; others before him had suggested that even the supposedly "sane" human mind was conscious and rational only at times, and even then at possibly only one level. But Freud went further, suggesting that the powers motivating men and women are *mainly* and *normally* unconscious.

Freud, then, powerfully developed an old idea: that the human mind is essentially dual in nature. He called the predominantly passional, irrational, unknown, and unconscious part of the psyche the *id,* or "it." The *ego,* or "I," was his term for the predominantly rational, logical, orderly, conscious part. Another aspect of the psyche, which he called the *superego,* is really a projection of the ego. The superego almost seems to be outside of the self, making moral judgments, telling us to make sacrifices for good causes even though self-sacrifice may not be quite logical or rational. And, in a sense, the superego *is* "outside," since much of what it tells us to do or think we have learned from our parents, our schools, or our religious institutions.

What the ego and superego tell us *not* to do or think is repressed, forced into the unconscious mind. One of Freud's most important contributions to the study of the psyche, the theory of repression, goes something like this: much of what lies in the unconscious mind has been put there by consciousness, which acts as a censor, driving underground unconscious or conscious thoughts or instincts that it deems unacceptable. Censored materials often involve infantile sexual desires, Freud postulated. Repressed to an unconscious state, they emerge only in disguised forms: in dreams, in language (so-called Freudian slips), in creative activity that may produce art (including literature), and in neurotic behavior.

According to Freud, all of us have repressed wishes and fears; we all have dreams in which repressed feelings and memories emerge disguised, and thus we are all potential candidates for dream analysis. One of the unconscious desires most commonly repressed is the childhood wish to displace the parent of our own sex and take his or her place in the affections of the parent of the opposite sex. This desire really involves a number of different but related wishes and fears. (A boy—and it should be remarked in passing that Freud here concerns himself mainly with the male—may fear that his father will castrate him, and he may wish that his mother would return to nursing him.) Freud referred to the whole complex of feelings by the word *oedipal,* naming the complex after the Greek tragic hero Oedipus, who unwittingly killed his father and married his mother.

Why are oedipal wishes and fears repressed by the conscious side of the mind? And what happens to them after they have been censored? As Roy P. Basler puts it in *Sex, Symbolism, and Psychology in Literature* (1975), "from the beginning of recorded history such wishes have been restrained by the most powerful religious and social taboos, and as a result have come to be regarded as 'unnatural,'" even though "Freud found that such wishes are more or less characteristic of normal human development":

> In dreams, particularly, Freud found ample evidence that such wishes persisted. . . . Hence he conceived that natural urges, when identified as "wrong," may be repressed but not obliterated. . . .
> In the unconscious, these urges take on symbolic garb, regarded as nonsense by the waking mind that does not recognize their significance. (14)

Freud's belief in the significance of dreams, of course, was no more original than his belief that there is an unconscious side to the psyche. Again, it was the extent to which he developed a theory of how dreams work—and the extent to which that theory helped him, by analogy, to understand far more than just dreams—that made him unusual, important, and influential beyond the perimeters of medical schools and psychiatrists' offices.

The psychoanalytic approach to literature not only rests on the theories of Freud; it may even be said to have *begun* with Freud, who was interested in writers, especially those who relied heavily on symbols. Such writers regularly cloak or mystify ideas in figures that make sense only when interpreted, much as the unconscious mind of a neurotic disguises secret thoughts in dream stories or bizarre actions that need to be interpreted by an analyst. Freud's interest in literary artists led him to make some unfortunate generalizations about creativity; for example, in the twenty-third lecture in *Introductory Lectures on Psycho-Analysis* (1922), he defined the artist as "one urged on by instinctive needs that are too clamorous" (314). But it also led him to write creative literary criticism of his own, including an influential essay on "The Relation of a Poet to Daydreaming" (1908) and "The Uncanny" (1919), a provocative psychoanalytic reading of E. T. A. Hoffmann's supernatural tale "The Sandman."

Freud's application of psychoanalytic theory to literature quickly caught on. In 1909, only a year after Freud had published "The Relation of a Poet to Daydreaming," the psychoanalyst Otto Rank published *The Myth of the Birth of the Hero*. In that work, Rank subscribes to the notion that the artist turns a powerful, secret wish into a literary fantasy, and he uses Freud's notion about the "oedipal" complex to explain why the popular stories of so many heroes in literature are so similar. A year after Rank had published his psychoanalytic account of heroic texts, Ernest Jones, Freud's student and eventual biographer, turned his attention to a tragic text: Shakespeare's *Hamlet*. In an essay first published in the *American Journal of Psychology*, Jones, like Rank, makes use of the oedipal concept: he suggests that Hamlet is a victim of strong feelings toward his mother, the queen.

Between 1909 and 1949, numerous other critics decided that psychological and psychoanalytic theory could assist in the understanding of literature. I. A. Richards, Kenneth Burke, and Edmund Wilson were among the most influential to become interested in the new approach. Not all of the early critics were committed to the approach; neither were all of them Freudians. Some followed Alfred Adler, who believed that writers wrote out of inferiority complexes, and others applied the ideas of Carl Gustav Jung, who had broken with Freud over Freud's emphasis on sex and who had developed a theory of the *collective* unconscious. According to Jungian theory, a great work of literature is not a disguised expression of its author's personal, repressed wishes; rather, it is a manifestation of desires once held by the whole human race but now repressed because of the advent of civilization.

It is important to point out that among those who relied on Freud's models were a number of critics who were poets and novelists as well. Conrad Aiken wrote a Freudian study of American literature, and poets such as Robert Graves and W. H. Auden applied Freudian insights when writing critical prose. William Faulkner, Henry James, James Joyce, D. H. Lawrence, Marcel Proust, and Toni Morrison are only a few of the novelists who have either written criticism influenced by Freud or who have written novels that conceive of character, conflict, and creative writing itself in Freudian terms. The poet H.D. (Hilda Doolittle) was actually a patient of Freud's and provided an account of her analysis in her book *Tribute to Freud*. By giving Freudian theory credibility among students of literature that only they could bestow, such writers helped to endow earlier psychoanalytic criticism with a largely Freudian orientation that has begun to be challenged only in the last two decades.

The willingness, even eagerness, of writers to use Freudian models in producing literature and criticism of their own consummated a relationship that, to Freud and other pioneering psychoanalytic theorists, had seemed fated from the beginning; after all, therapy involves the close analysis of language. René Wellek and Austin Warren included "psychological" criticism as one of the five "extrinsic" approaches to literature described in their influential book *Theory of Literature* (1942). Psychological criticism, they suggest, typically attempts to do at least one of the following: provide a psychological study of an individual writer; explore the nature of the creative process; generalize about "types and laws present within works of literature"; or theorize about the psychological "effects of literature upon its readers" (81). Entire books on psychoanalytic criticism began to appear, such as Frederick J. Hoffman's *Freudianism and the Literary Mind* (1945).

Probably because of Freud's characterization of the creative mind as "clamorous" if not ill, psychoanalytic criticism written before 1950 tended to psychoanalyze the individual author. Poems were read as fantasies that allowed authors to indulge repressed wishes, to protect themselves from deep-seated anxieties, or both. A perfect example of author analysis would be Marie Bonaparte's 1933 study of Edgar Allan Poe. Bonaparte found Poe to be so fixated on his mother that his repressed longing emerges in his stories in images such as the white spot on a black cat's breast, said to represent mother's milk.

A later generation of psychoanalytic critics often paused to analyze the characters in novels and plays before proceeding to their authors. But not for long, since characters, both evil and good, tended to be seen by these critics as the author's potential selves or projections of various repressed aspects of his or her psyche. For instance, in *A Psychoanalytic Study of the Double in Literature* (1970), Robert Rogers begins with the view that human beings are double or multiple in

nature. Using this assumption, along with the psychoanalytic concept
of "dissociation" (best known by its result, the dual or multiple personality), Rogers concludes that writers reveal instinctual or repressed
selves in their books, often without realizing that they have done so.
In the view of critics attempting to arrive at more psychological insights into an author than biographical materials can provide, a work
of literature is a fantasy or a dream—or at least so analogous to day-
dream or dream that Freudian analysis can help explain the nature of
the mind that produced it. The author's purpose in writing is to gratify secretly some forbidden wish, in particular an infantile wish or desire that has been repressed into the unconscious mind. To discover
what the wish is, the psychoanalytic critic employs many of the terms
and procedures developed by Freud to analyze dreams.

The literal surface of a work is sometimes spoken of as its "manifest content" and treated as a "manifest dream" or "dream story"
would be treated by a Freudian analyst. Just as the analyst tries to figure out the "dream thought" behind the dream story—that is, the latent or hidden content of the manifest dream—so the psychoanalytic
literary critic tries to expose the latent, underlying content of a work.
Freud used the words *condensation* and *displacement* to explain two of
the mental processes whereby the mind disguises its wishes and fears in
dream stories. In condensation, several thoughts or persons may be
condensed into a single manifestation or image in a dream story; in
displacement, an anxiety, a wish, or a person may be displaced onto
the image of another, with which or whom it is loosely connected
through a string of associations that only an analyst can untangle. Psychoanalytic critics treat metaphors as if they were dream condensa-
tions; they treat metonyms—figures of speech based on extremely
loose, arbitrary associations—as if they were dream displacements.
Thus figurative literary language in general is treated as something that
evolves as the writer's conscious mind resists what the unconscious
tells it to picture or describe. A symbol is, in Daniel Weiss's words, "a
meaningful concealment of truth as the truth promises to emerge as
some frightening or forbidden idea" (20).

In a 1970 article entitled "The 'Unconscious' of Literature," Norman Holland, a literary critic trained in psychoanalysis, succinctly sums
up the attitudes held by critics who would psychoanalyze authors, but
without quite saying that it is the *author* that is being analyzed by the
psychoanalytic critic. "When one looks at a poem psychoanalytically,"
he writes, "one considers it as though it were a dream or as though some
ideal patient [were speaking] from the couch in iambic pentameter."

One "looks for the general level or levels of fantasy associated with the language. By level I mean the familiar stages of childhood development—oral [when desires for nourishment and infantile sexual desires overlap], anal [when infants receive their primary pleasure from defecation], urethral [when urinary functions are the locus of sexual pleasure], phallic [when the penis or, in girls, some penis substitute is of primary interest], oedipal." Holland continues by analyzing not Robert Frost but Frost's poem "Mending Wall" as a specifically oral fantasy that is not unique to its author. "Mending Wall" is "about breaking down the wall which marks the separated or individuated self so as to return to a state of closeness to some Other"—including and perhaps essentially the nursing mother ("'Unconscious'" 136, 139).

While not denying the idea that the unconscious plays a role in creativity, psychoanalytic critics such as Holland began to focus more on the ways in which authors create works that appeal to *our* repressed wishes and fantasies. Consequently, they shifted their focus away from the psyche of the author and toward the psychology of the reader and the text. Holland's theories, which have concerned themselves more with the reader than with the text, have helped to establish another school of critical theory: reader-response criticism. Elizabeth Wright explains Holland's brand of modern psychoanalytic criticism in this way: "What draws us as readers to a text is the secret expression of what we desire to hear, much as we protest we do not. The disguise must be good enough to fool the censor into thinking that the text is respectable, but bad enough to allow the unconscious to glimpse the unrespectable" (117).

Holland is one of dozens of critics who have revised Freud significantly in the process of revitalizing psychoanalytic criticism. Another such critic is R. D. Laing, whose controversial and often poetical writings about personality, repression, masks, and the double or "schizoid" self have (re)blurred the boundary between creative writing and psychoanalytic discourse. Yet another is D. W. Winnicott, an "object relations" theorist who has had a significant impact on literary criticism. Critics influenced by Winnicott and his school have questioned the tendency to see reader/text as an either/or construct; instead, they have seen reader and text (or audience and play) in terms of a *relationship* taking place in what Winnicott calls a "transitional" or "potential" space—space in which binary terms such as *real* and *illusory, objective* and *subjective,* have little or no meaning.

Psychoanalytic theorists influenced by Winnicott see the transitional or potential reader/text (or audience/play) space as being *like* the space entered into by psychoanalyst and patient. More important, they also see it as being similar to the space between mother and infant: a space characterized by trust in which categorizing terms such as *knowing* and *feeling* mix and merge and have little meaning apart from one another.

Whereas Freud saw the mother-son relationship in terms of the son and his repressed oedipal complex (and saw the analyst-patient relationship in terms of the patient and the repressed "truth" that the analyst could scientifically extract), object-relations analysts see both relationships as *dyadic*—that is, as being dynamic in both directions. Consequently, they don't depersonalize analysis or their analyses. It is hardly surprising, therefore, that contemporary literary critics who apply object-relations theory to the texts they discuss don't depersonalize critics or categorize their interpretations as "truthful," at least not in any objective or scientific sense. In the view of such critics, interpretations are made of language—itself a transitional object—and are themselves the mediating terms or transitional objects of a relationship.

Like critics of the Winnicottian school, the French structuralist theorist Jacques Lacan focused on language and language-related issues. He treated the unconscious *as* a language and, consequently, viewed the dream not as Freud did (that is, as a form and symptom of repression) but rather as a form of discourse. Thus we may study dreams psychoanalytically to learn about literature, even as we may study literature to learn more about the unconscious. In Lacan's seminar on Poe's "The Purloined Letter," a pattern of repetition like that used by psychoanalysts in their analyses is used to arrive at a reading of the story. According to Wright, "the new psychoanalytic structural approach to literature" employs "analogies from psychoanalysis . . . to explain the workings of the text as distinct from the workings of a particular author's, character's, or even reader's mind" (125).

Lacan, however, did far more than extend Freud's theory of dreams, literature, and the interpretation of both. More significantly, he took Freud's whole theory of psyche and gender and added to it a crucial third term—that of language. In the process, he both used and significantly developed Freud's ideas about the oedipal stage and complex.

Lacan pointed out that the pre-oedipal stage, in which the child at first does not even recognize its independence from its mother, is also a pre*verbal* stage, one in which the child communicates without the medium of language, or—if we insist on calling the child's communications a language—in a language that can only be called *literal.* ("Coos," certainly, cannot be said to be figurative or symbolic.) Then, while still in the pre-oedipal stage, the child enters the *mirror* stage.

During the mirror period, the child comes to view itself and its mother, later other people as well, *as* independent selves. This is the stage in which the child is first able to fear the aggressions of another, to desire what is recognizably beyond the self (initially the mother), and, finally, to want to compete with another for the same desired object. This is also the stage at which the child first becomes able to feel sympathy with another being who is being hurt by a third, to cry when another cries. All of these developments, of course, involve projecting beyond the self and, by extension, constructing one's own self (or "ego" or "I") as others view one—that is, as *another.* Such constructions, according to Lacan, are just that: constructs, products, artifacts—fictions of coherence that in fact hide what Lacan called the "absence" or "lack" of being.

The mirror stage, which Lacan also referred to as the *imaginary* stage, is fairly quickly succeeded by the oedipal stage. As in Freud, this stage begins when the child, having come to view itself as self and the father and mother as separate selves, perceives gender and gender differences between its parents and between itself and one of its parents. For boys, gender awareness involves another, more powerful recognition, for the recognition of the father's phallus as the mark of his difference from the mother involves, at the same time, the recognition that his older and more powerful father is also his rival. That, in turn, leads to the understanding that what once seemed wholly his and even indistinguishable from himself is in fact someone else's: something properly desired only at a distance and in the form of socially acceptable *substitutes.*

The fact that the oedipal stage roughly coincides with the entry of the child into language is extremely important for Lacan. For the linguistic order is essentially a figurative or "Symbolic" order; words are not the things they stand for but are, rather, stand-ins or substitutes for those things. Hence boys, who in the most critical period of their development have had to submit to what Lacan called the "Law of the Father"—a law that prohibits direct desire for and communicative intimacy with what has been the boy's whole world—enter more easily into the realm of language and the Symbolic order than do girls, who have never really had to renounce that which once seemed continuous with the self: the mother. The gap that has been opened up for boys, which includes the gap between signs and what they substitute—the gap marked by the phallus and encoded with the boy's sense of his maleness—has not opened up for girls, or has not opened up in the same way, to the same degree. For Lacan, the father need not be present to trigger the oedipal stage; nor does his phallus have to be seen to catalyze the boy's (easier) transition into the Symbolic order. Rather, Lacan argued, a child's recognition of its gender is intricately tied up with a growing recognition of the system of names and naming, part of the larger system of substitutions we call language. A child has little doubt about who its mother is, but who is its father, and how would one know? The father's claim rests on the mother's *word* that he is in fact the father; the father's relationship to the child is thus established through language and a system of marriage and kinship—names—that in turn is basic to rules of everything from property to law. The name of the father (*nom du père,* which in French sounds like *non du père*) involves, in a sense, nothing of the father—nothing, that is, except his word or name.

Lacan's development of Freud has had several important results. First, his sexist-seeming association of maleness with the Symbolic order, together with his claim that women cannot therefore enter easily into the order, has prompted feminists not to reject his theory out of hand but, rather, to look more closely at the relation between language and gender, language and women's inequality. Some feminists have gone so far as to suggest that the social and political relationships between male and female will not be fundamentally altered until language itself has been radically changed. (That change might begin dialectically, with the development of some kind of "feminine language" grounded in the presymbolic, literal-to-imaginary communication between mother and child.)

Second, Lacan's theory has proved of interest to deconstructors and other poststructuralists, in part because it holds that the ego (which in Freud's view is as necessary as it is natural) is a product or construct. The ego-artifact, produced during the mirror stage, *seems* at once unified, consistent, and organized around a determinate center. But the unified self, or ego, is a fiction, according to Lacan. The yoking together of fragments and destructively dissimilar elements takes its psychic toll, and it is the job of the Lacanian psychoanalyst to "deconstruct," as it were, the ego, to show its continuities to be contradictions as well.

Kimberly J. Devlin's psychoanalytic approach to *Ulysses* begins with an epigraph from Freud's *The Ego and the Id* (1923). Freud, after defining a "word" as "the mnemic residue" (memory trace) of "a word that has been heard," speaks of an "optical" mnemic residue, that is, the memory trace of a thing that has been seen. He then contends that this sort of visual as opposed to verbal thinking, this sort of "thinking in pictures . . . , stands nearer to unconscious processes than does thinking in words." As a result, he maintains, it is possible to bring previously unconscious thought processes to consciousness "through a reversion to visual residues." In Devlin's words, "pictorial thought" can be "a mediating aid . . . in enabling unconscious thoughts to return."

In an earlier case history of his so-called Wolf Man patient, an essay entitled "From the History of an Infantile Neurosis" (1918), Freud asserted even more strongly the claims that visual thought mediates between what can and cannot be verbally expressed. His analysis of the Wolf Man suggests that optic images (for example, dream images of wolves) can simultaneously represent not only unconscious thoughts and wishes but also "the regulatory agencies that attempt to overpower unconscious thoughts" (for example, the "vigilant gaze" of the mind's "dream censor"). Using Freud's insight as a starting point, Devlin proceeds to analyze *Ulysses* and, more particularly, the psyche of Leopold Bloom. What she demonstrates is that Bloom's pictorial thought reveals an unconscious desire for optical surveillance and subsequent control, what Devlin calls "scopic power."

Like "Freud's analysand," the Wolf Man, Bloom "emerges as an individual with a highly sensitive visual psyche." He is pleased by particular sights and displeased by others; for instance, he notices that a woman's "stockings are loose over her ankles" and thinks: "I detest that: so tasteless." Bloom, however, is also a man of words, words that lead him from thought to (subtly related) thought. A critically important feature of what Devlin calls "opticality" in *Ulysses* is "the way Joyce interweaves a strand of Bloom's pictorial thinking" with a specific and "richly symptomatic" verbal signifier, namely, "the common feminine forename of 'Mary.'" This name interwoven with a strand of images, this verbal thinking embedded in visual thinking, enables Devlin to consider auditory *and* optical mnemic residues—words *and* things, signifiers in general—and their relation to unconscious thought in the world of Joyce's novel.

In the first part of her essay, Devlin discusses "the contexts in which 'Mary' surfaces in Bloom's psyche." It first enters Bloom's consciousness in "Lotus-Eaters," where a pin that Martha Clifford has used to attach a flower to a letter reminds Bloom of a song he once heard some "sluts" singing about a "Mairy" who "lost the pin of her drawers." At this point, Devlin points out, Bloom "produces what will turn out to be a visual symptom—a recollection of a specific painting of Jesus with the sisters of Lazarus," Mary and Martha. ("Martha, Mary. I saw that picture somewhere I forget now old master or faked for money.") He then associates the two women in the picture with "the two sluts in the Coombe" because, as Devlin points out, Mary the sister of Lazarus "is sometimes confused with Mary Magdalene," the prostitute who became one of Jesus' followers and friends.

The signifier "Mary" recurs in "Lotus-Eaters" as Bloom associates Martha Clifford with a fantasy woman named Mary, whom he pictures confessing her sins to a priest. "Bloom's fantasy here," Devlin maintains, "symptomatizes an unconscious phobia inherent in his relationship with Martha," the fear "that she has confessed her epistolary affair to the counterpart of the clergy, the local police force." In Devlin's view, the optical image of the confessional as a soundbooth enabling "spousal eavesdropping" also reflects Bloom's desire to scrutinize his wife Molly's "flirtations," his desire for "surveillance" that would lead to "a masterful sense" of scopic "power-knowledge."

Devlin analyzes a number of other scenes, such as the one in "Lestrygonians" in which Bloom, on seeing some constables, remembers an unpleasant encounter he once had with the police, speculates about police spies, and has a fantasy— "both visual and auditory"—in which a servant girl named Mary is asked about the clothes she is ironing by a "hotblooded young student" who pretends to be courting her. Devlin suggests that the student is connected in Bloom's mind with plainclothed policemen who might pry out of household servants, or "slaveys," information about the families employing them. Thus, the female servant in possession of family secrets is also subject to surveillance by officials who would have her "confess" all she knows.

The Mary of this fantasy, Devlin asserts, is connected in Bloom's psyche to a servant girl named Mary Driscoll, whom he employed and toward whom he once made sexual advances. (In "Circe," Devlin suggests, the fantasy of Mary Driscoll testifying that Bloom entered her quarters while Molly was out shopping on the pretense of needing a safety pin "retrospectively explains why the pin in Martha's letter unconsciously evokes a ditty about a 'Mairy.'") Devlin also views Mary Driscoll as the "latent subtext" of Bloom's reaction to the sweet, high voice of the acolyte singing at Paddy Dignam's funeral service. Hearing the Latin word "*tentationem*" (temptation) sung by a "soprano and hence feminized voice," Bloom's mind turns to images of domestic servants. It does so "symptomatically," in Devlin's view, because of Bloom's "association of the signifier 'Mary' with personal temptation." The scenes in *Ulysses* analyzed by Devlin show how "the scopic powers" Bloom exercises over the bodies of young women associated with the signifier "Mary" reveal "unconscious thoughts" about "personal temptation of a sexual nature." Ultimately, however, the threat posed to Bloom's psyche by the "two types of exploited women in *Ulysses*—the slavey and the prostitute, merged under the signifier of 'Mary'"—is not merely or perhaps even predominantly sexual. Such women also have a "definite power in Bloom's psyche, on account of their access to taboo secrets." Devlin speculates that "Molly's dismissal of Mary from live-in maid service is motivated not only by the slavey's unwanted status as sexual rival, but also by her equally unwanted status as domestic countergaze, as inevitable witness to marital rifts and disharmonies (and finally, of course, their fallguy)."

In concluding her essay, Devlin summarizes but also extends her argument by suggesting that images called forth by and associated with the signifier "Mary" in *Ulysses* signify one character's but also a patriarchal culture's "desire for control over particular female *bodies*." Beyond that, they signify an even deeper wish to "regulate" not only those bodies but also the "*speech* of a specific subculture of exploited women. . . . Submerged beneath its masochistic surface, this fantasy scenario bespeaks a phobic need to control the discourse of those perversely privileged female subjectivities who constitute a countergaze, a countergaze that knows the dirty secrets hidden in many a male Dubliner's bottom drawer."

Ross C Murfin

PSYCHOANALYTIC CRITICISM: A SELECTED BIBLIOGRAPHY

Some Short Introductions to Psychological and Psychoanalytic Criticism

Holland, Norman. "The 'Unconscious' of Literature: The Psychoanalytic Approach." *Contemporary Criticism*. Ed. Malcolm Bradbury and David Palmer. Stratford-upon-Avon Studies 12. New York: St. Martin's, 1971. 131–53.

Natoli, Joseph, and Frederik L. Rusch, comps. *Psychocriticism: An Annotated Bibliography*. Westport: Greenwood, 1984.

Scott, Wilbur. *Five Approaches to Literary Criticism*. London: Collier-Macmillan, 1962. See the essays by Burke and Gorer as well as Scott's introduction to the section "The Psychological Approach: Literature in the Light of Psychological Theory."

Wellek, René, and Austin Warren. *Theory of Literature*. New York: Harcourt, 1942. See the chapter "Literature and Psychology" in pt. 3, "The Extrinsic Approach to the Study of Literature."

Wright, Elizabeth. "Modern Psychoanalytic Criticism." *Modern Literary Theory: A Comparative Introduction*. Ed. Ann Jefferson and David Robey. Totowa: Barnes, 1982. 113–33.

Freud, Lacan, and Their Influence

Basler, Roy P. *Sex, Symbolism, and Psychology in Literature*. New York: Octagon, 1975. See especially 13–19.

Bowie, Malcolm. *Lacan*. Cambridge: Harvard UP, 1991.

Clément, Catherine. *The Lives and Legends of Jacques Lacan*. Trans. Arthur Goldhammer. New York: Columbia UP, 1983.

Freud, Sigmund. *Introductory Lectures on Psycho-Analysis*. Trans. Joan Riviere. London: Allen, 1922.

Gallop, Jane. *Reading Lacan*. Ithaca: Cornell UP, 1985.

Hoffman, Frederick J. *Freudianism and the Literary Mind*. Baton Rouge: Louisiana State UP, 1945.

Hogan, Patrick Colm, and Lalita Pandit, eds. *Lacan and Criticism: Essays and Dialogue on Language, Structure, and the Unconscious*. Athens: U of Georgia P, 1990.

Kazin, Alfred. "Freud and His Consequences." *Contemporaries*. Boston: Little, 1962. 351–93.

Lacan, Jacques. *Écrits: A Selection*. Trans. Alan Sheridan. New York: Norton, 1977.

———. *Feminine Sexuality: Lacan and the École Freudienne*. Ed. Juliet Mitchell and Jacqueline Rose. Trans. Rose. New York: Norton, 1985.

———. *The Four Fundamental Concepts of Psychoanalysis*. Trans. Alan Sheridan. London: Penguin, 1980.

Macey, David. *Lacan in Contexts*. New York: Verso, 1988.

Meisel, Perry, ed. *Freud: A Collection of Critical Essays*. Englewood Cliffs: Prentice, 1981.

Muller, John P., and William J. Richardson. *Lacan and Language: A Reader's Guide to "Écrits."* New York: International UP, 1982.

Porter, Laurence M. *"The Interpretation of Dreams": Freud's Theories Revisited.* Twayne's Masterwork Studies Ser. Boston: G. K. Hall, 1986.

Reppen, Joseph, and Maurice Charney. *The Psychoanalytic Study of Literature.* Hillsdale: Analytic, 1985.

Schneiderman, Stuart. *Jacques Lacan: The Death of an Intellectual Hero.* Cambridge: Harvard UP, 1983.

———. *Returning to Freud: Clinical Psychoanalysis in the School of Lacan.* New Haven: Yale UP, 1980.

Selden, Raman. *A Reader's Guide to Contemporary Literary Theory.* 2nd ed. Lexington: U of Kentucky P, 1989. See "Jacques Lacan: Language and the Unconscious."

Sullivan, Ellie Ragland. *Jacques Lacan and the Philosophy of Psychoanalysis.* Champaign: U of Illinois P, 1986.

Sullivan, Ellie Ragland, and Mark Bracher, eds. *Lacan and the Subject of Language.* New York: Routledge, 1991.

Trilling, Lionel. "Art and Neurosis." *The Liberal Imagination.* New York: Scribner's, 1950. 160–80.

Wilden, Anthony. "Lacan and the Discourse of the Other." In Lacan, *Speech and Language in Psychoanalysis.* Trans. Wilden. Baltimore: Johns Hopkins UP, 1981. (Published as *The Language of the Self* in 1968.) 159–311.

Žižek, Slavoj. *Looking Awry: An Introduction to Jacques Lacan through Popular Culture.* Cambridge: MIT P, 1991.

Psychoanalysis, Feminism, and Literature

Chodorow, Nancy. *The Reproduction of Mothering: Psychoanalysis and the Sociology of Gender.* Berkeley: U of California P, 1978.

Gallop, Jane. *The Daughter's Seduction: Feminism and Psychoanalysis.* Ithaca: Cornell UP, 1982.

Garner, Shirley Nelson, Claire Kahane, and Madelon Sprengnether. *The (M)other Tongue: Essays in Feminist Psychoanalytic Interpretation.* Ithaca: Cornell UP, 1985.

Grosz, Elizabeth. *Jacques Lacan: A Feminist Introduction.* New York: Routledge, 1990.

Irigaray, Luce. *The Speculum of the Other Woman.* Trans. Gillian C. Gill. Ithaca: Cornell UP, 1985.

———. *This Sex Which Is Not One.* Trans. Catherine Porter. Ithaca: Cornell UP, 1985.

Jacobus, Mary. "Is There a Woman in This Text?" *New Literary History* 14 (1982): 117–41.

Kristeva, Julia. *The Kristeva Reader.* Ed. Toril Moi. New York: Columbia UP, 1986. See especially the selection from *Revolution in Poetic Language,* 89–136.

Mitchell, Juliet. *Psychoanalysis and Feminism.* New York: Random, 1974.

Mitchell, Juliet, and Jacqueline Rose. "Introduction I" and "Introduction II." Lacan, *Feminine Sexuality: Jacques Lacan and the École Freudienne.* New York: Norton, 1985. 1–26, 27–57.

Sprengnether, Madelon. *The Spectral Mother: Freud, Feminism, and Psychoanalysis.* Ithaca: Cornell UP, 1990.

Psychological and Psychoanalytic Studies of Literature

Bettelheim, Bruno. *The Uses of Enchantment: The Meaning and Importance of Fairy Tales.* New York: Knopf, 1976. Although this book is about fairy tales instead of literary works written for publication, it offers model Freudian readings of well-known stories.

Crews, Frederick C. *Out of My System: Psychoanalysis, Ideology, and Critical Method.* New York: Oxford UP, 1975.

———. *Relations of Literary Study.* New York: MLA, 1967. See the chapter "Literature and Psychology."

Diehl, Joanne Feit. "Re-Reading *The Letter:* Hawthorne, the Fetish, and the (Family) Romance." *Nathaniel Hawthorne, The Scarlet Letter.* Ed. Ross C Murfin. Case Studies in Contemporary Criticism Ser. Ed. Ross C Murfin. Boston: Bedford–St. Martin's, 1991. 235–51.

Hallman, Ralph. *Psychology of Literature: A Study of Alienation and Tragedy.* New York: Philosophical Library, 1961.

Hartman, Geoffrey, ed. *Psychoanalysis and the Question of the Text.* Baltimore: Johns Hopkins UP, 1978. See especially the essays by Hartman, Johnson, Nelson, and Schwartz.

Hertz, Neil. *The End of the Line: Essays on Psychoanalysis and the Sublime.* New York: Columbia UP, 1985.

Holland, Norman N. *Dynamics of Literary Response.* New York: Oxford UP, 1968.

———. *Poems in Persons: An Introduction to the Psychoanalysis of Literature.* New York: Norton, 1973.

Kris, Ernest. *Psychoanalytic Explorations in Art.* New York: International, 1952.

Lucas, F. L. *Literature and Psychology.* London: Cassell, 1951.

Natoli, Joseph, ed. *Psychological Perspectives on Literature: Freudian Dissidents and Non-Freudians: A Casebook.* Hamden: Archon Books–Shoe String, 1984.

Phillips, William, ed. *Art and Psychoanalysis.* New York: Columbia UP, 1977.

Rogers, Robert. *A Psychoanalytic Study of the Double in Literature.* Detroit: Wayne State UP, 1970.

Skura, Meredith. *The Literary Use of the Psychoanalytic Process.* New Haven: Yale UP, 1981.

Strelka, Joseph P. *Literary Criticism and Psychology.* University Park: Pennsylvania State UP, 1976. See especially the essays by Lerner and Peckham.

Weiss, Daniel. *The Critic Agonistes: Psychology, Myth, and the Art of Fiction.* Ed. Eric Solomon and Stephen Arkin. Seattle: U of Washington P, 1985.

Lacanian Psychoanalytic Studies of Literature

Collings, David. "The Monster and the Imaginary Mother: A Lacanian Reading of *Frankenstein*." *Mary Shelley, Frankenstein.* Ed. Johanna M. Smith. Case Studies in Contemporary Criticism. Ser. Ed. Ross C Murfin. Boston: Bedford–St. Martin's, 1992. 245–58.

Davis, Robert Con, ed. *The Fictional Father: Lacanian Readings of the Text.* Amherst: U of Massachusetts P, 1981.

———. "Lacan and Narration." *Modern Language Notes* 5 (1983): 848–59.

Felman, Shoshana, ed. *Jacques Lacan and the Adventure of Insight: Psychoanalysis in Contemporary Culture.* Cambridge: Harvard UP, 1987.

———. *Literature and Psychoanalysis: The Question of Reading: Otherwise.* Baltimore: Johns Hopkins UP, 1982.

Froula, Christine. "When Eve Reads Milton: Undoing the Canonical Economy." *Canons.* Ed. Robert von Hallberg. Chicago: U of Chicago P, 1984. 149–75.

Homans, Margaret. *Bearing the Word: Language and Female Experience in Nineteenth-Century Women's Writing.* Chicago: U of Chicago P, 1986.

Mellard, James. *Using Lacan, Reading Fiction*. Urbana: U of Illinois P, 1991.

Muller, John P., and William J. Richardson, eds. *The Purloined Poe: Lacan, Derrida, and Psychoanalytic Reading*. Baltimore: Johns Hopkins UP, 1988. Includes Lacan's seminar on Poe's "The Purloined Letter."

Psychoanalytic Approaches to Joyce

Brivic, Sheldon. *The Veil of Signs: Joyce, Lacan, and Perception*. Urbana: U of Illinois P, 1985.

Brivic, Sheldon, with Ellie Ragland-Sullivan, guest co-eds. *James Joyce Quarterly* 29 (Fall 1991). "Joyce Between Genders: Lacanian Views" issue.

Devlin, Kimberly J. *Wandering and Return in "Finnegans Wake": An Integrative Approach to Joyce's Fictions*. Princeton: Princeton UP, 1991.

Ferrer, Daniel. "Circe, Regret and Regression." *Post-structuralist Joyce*. Ed. Derek Attridge and Daniel Ferrer. Cambridge: Cambridge UP, 1984.

Friedman, Susan Stanford, ed. *Joyce: The Return of the Repressed*. Ithaca: Cornell UP, 1993.

Kimball, Jean. "Freud, Leonardo, and Joyce: The Dimensions of a Childhood Memory." *James Joyce Quarterly* 17:2 (Winter 1980): 165–82.

Leonard, Garry M. *Reading "Dubliners" Again: A Lacanian Perspective*. Syracuse: Syracuse UP, 1993.

Restuccia, Frances L. *Joyce and the Law of the Father*. New Haven: Yale UP, 1989.

Shechner, Mark. *Joyce in Nighttown: A Psychoanalytic Inquiry into "Ulysses."* Berkeley: U of California P, 1974.

A PSYCHOANALYTIC PERSPECTIVE

KIMBERLY J. DEVLIN

"I saw that picture somewhere": Tracking the Symptom of the Sisters of Lazarus

Verbal residues are derived primarily from auditory perceptions, so that the system *Pcs.* [preconscious] has, as it were, a special sensory source. The visual components of word-presentations are secondary, acquired through reading. . . . In essence a word is after all the mnemic residue of a word that has been heard.

We must not be led, in the interests of simplification perhaps, to forget the importance of optical mnemic residues, when they are of *things*, or to deny that it is possible for thought-processes to become conscious through a reversion to visual residues, and that in many people this seems to be the favoured method. The study of dreams and of preconscious phantasies as shown in Varendonck's observations can give us an idea of the special character of this visual thinking. We learn that what becomes conscious in it is as a rule only the concrete subject-matter of the thought, and that the relations between the various elements of this subject-matter, which is what specially characterizes thoughts, cannot be given visual expression. Thinking in pictures is, therefore, only a very incomplete form of becoming conscious. In some way, too, it stands nearer to unconscious processes than does thinking in words, and it is unquestionably older than the latter both ontogenetically and phylogenetically. (Freud 10–11)

This comment from *The Ego and Id*, published in 1923, is excerpted from Freud's theorization of how unconscious thoughts become preconscious or latent by attaching themselves to mnemic residues to emerge—potentially—into consciousness. The passage contains a slight ambivalence about visual thinking. On the one hand, it acknowledges the limitations of "thinking in pictures," hinting that such ideation eliminates crucial details, specifically "the relations between the various elements" in the subject-matter of the repressed thought being retrieved through memory traces. But on the other hand, it simultaneously insists at the outset that "the importance of optical mnemic residues" must not be forgotten and concludes by noting that "thinking in pictures" is the primal mode of ideation for both individuals and species. Pictorial thought becomes a potential crux of psychic development, as well as a mediating aid—albeit a limited one —in enabling unconscious thoughts to return, in allowing them to outwit the regulatory psychic agencies of repression.

A case history Freud published five years earlier, "From the History of an Infantile Neurosis" (1918), is much less equivocal about the pivotal role of visuality in translating unconscious thoughts into conscious ones. To be sure, as in all of Freud's works, "verbal residues . . . derived primarily from auditory perceptions" play a crucial part in this particular record of a psychoanalytic treatment and recovery. In Freud's analysis of the Wolf Man's symptoms,[1] for instance, the concrete sounds of names recurrently provide associative clues in unraveling the logic of the neurosis. When his sister rejects his sexual advances, the Wolf Man "at once turned away from her to a little peasant girl who was a servant in the house and had the same name as his sister" (178). Later a recollection of a pear and the Russian word for it, *grusha*, lead the analysand to a repressed memory of his nursery maid, whose forename occupied the exact same signifier. An auditory parapraxis—the Wolf Man's mispronunciation of *Wespe* (German for *wasp*) as *Espe*—reveals his own initials (S. P.) and emerges as his unconscious figuration of himself as a castrated being, as a signifier lacking a certain part, symbolized in its missing letter. This verbal play runs throughout the case history to reveal the acoustic ingenuity of the unconscious in its moving of ideas into latency; but this auditory dimension is overshadowed by a visual one that Freud, curiously, never explicitly comments on. The strong visual matrix of the analysis may lie behind Freud's later concession in 1923 of "the importance of optical mnemic residues."

The Wolf Man's castration complex originates from a phantasmic visual disturbance, an imagined visual absence, and expresses itself in mediating symptoms that have marked visual keys—memories of a chopped up snake, for instance, or a phallicized woman ("[the governess] had said to the people coming behind her: 'Do look at my little tail!'" [175]). The analysand also exhibits what Stephen Dedalus would characterize as "kinetic" responses to various sights: a desirous compulsion to kiss the holy pictures in his room or a phobic flight from a butterfly opening and shutting its wings, a flight motivated by its mnemic visual residue of a woman opening and shutting her legs. The laborious construction of the unconscious primal scene hinges on

---

[1]The patient in the case is often informally referred to as the Wolf Man because of his intense phobia of wolves.

many clues and details, but two visual images are foregrounded as central: a recalled illustration of an upright wolf from a childhood book, the sight of which produced extreme anxiety in the analysand when he was young, and a contrasting optical configuration of a being on all fours, the animal-like position that, when assumed by women, aroused in him sudden feelings of inexplicable desire. The major breakthrough of the analysis, of course, follows the remembered mediating dream of the wolves and its translation into its numerous unconscious referents: the dream involves a scenario about watching and being watched and is so vividly pictorial that the patient draws it for Freud. The dreamtext becomes oddly self-reflexive insofar as the staring wolves, screen images of the father and his law, figure forth the regulatory agencies that attempt to overpower unconscious thoughts; but in their over-determined encoded messages, the wolves operate on behalf of the unconscious, outwitting the dream censor and slipping by its vigilant gaze. The strong visual axis of the case history has its origins in the neurosis's own origins in the Wolf Man's infancy: the primal scene occurs during his preverbal state where thinking in pictures predominates. Significantly, however, the hegemonic visual symptomology perdures long after the analysand's entry into orality. Freud's study of the Wolf Man illustrates that the forces of repression are subverted by optical as well as auditory clues. The regulatory regimes of the psyche loose their control over the patient's secrets through the insistence of visual symptoms, of latent optical images and impulses that facilitate the entrance of unconscious ideas into consciousness.

Like Freud's analysand, Joyce's protagonist in *Ulysses* emerges as an individual with a highly sensitive visual psyche. Leopold Bloom is attuned to particular optical pleasures ("To catch up and walk behind her if she went slowly, behind her moving hams. Pleasant to see first thing in the morning" [*U* 4.171–73]) as well as to decided optical distastes ("Her stockings are loose over her ankles. I detest that: so tasteless" [*U* 8.542]). The sight of a blind young man causes Bloom to ponder how one survives without recourse to optic perception, and his meditation concludes on a note of restrained anguish that betrays an assumptional equation of the visual with reality itself: "Poor fellow! Quite a boy. Terrible. Really terrible. What dreams would he have, not seeing? Life a dream for him. Where is the justice being born that way?" (*U* 8.1144–46).

What interests me in this essay about opticality in *Ulysses* is the way Joyce interweaves a strand of Bloom's pictorial thinking with a specific signifier that emerges—retrospectively in the "Circe" episode—as richly symptomatic. The specific signifier is the common feminine forename of "Mary"—perhaps *the* most common feminine forename in a mariolatrous culture. But psychoanalytic inquiry is precisely interested in the ways in which an individual psyche appropriates ordinary signifiers (a name, a fairytale, an illustration) and cathects them with unique meanings. It explores the ways in which the unconscious charges everyday discourse with personal connotations that work to overturn the regulatory forces of repression. The initial part of this essay will discuss the contexts in which "Mary" surfaces in Bloom's psyche to speculate, ultimately, about what exactly this symptomatic signifier betrays. I hope also to delineate in the process a paradox about visuality when used within a psychoanalytic framework. On the one hand, vision—particularly scrutinizing or surveillant vision—is often aligned with regulatory agencies (such as the superego, the law of the father, the police, the clergy, omniscient deity, and what Jacques Lacan calls "the gaze"); but on the other hand, visions—optical memories and necessarily interpretive ways of seeing—work against regulatory agencies in that they often record latent thoughts, pressing for articulation against psychic resistances.

The signifier "Mary" enters Bloom's consciousness in "Lotus-Eaters," where it is triggered by the pin Martha Clifford has used to attach the flower to her letter. The pin reminds him of a street ditty he heard sung by "two sluts that night in the Coombe" about a woman who finds herself by accident in an exhibitionist pose: "*O, Mairy lost the pin of her drawers. / She didn't know what to do / To keep it up, / To keep it up*" (*U* 5.279–84). Bloom then produces what will turn out to be a visual symptom—a recollection of a specific painting of Jesus with the sisters of Lazarus:

> Martha, Mary. I saw that picture somewhere I forget now old master or faked for money. He is sitting in their house, talking. Mysterious. Also the two sluts in the Coombe would listen.
> *To keep it up.*
> Nice kind of evening feeling. No more wandering about. Just loll there: quiet dusk: let everything rip. Forget. Tell about the places you have been, strange customs. The other one, jar on her head, was getting the supper: fruit, olives, lovely cool water out of a well, stonecold like the hole in the wall at Ashtown. Must carry a paper goblet next time I go to the trottingmatches. She listens with big dark soft eyes. Tell her: more and more: all. Then a sigh: silence. Long long long rest. (*U* 5.289–99)

The two women in the picture are associated with "the two sluts in the Coombe," in part because Mary, the sister of Lazarus, is sometimes confused with Mary Magdalene (Gifford 90). This dyad of women, in other words, is ambivalently coded, as Bloom's psyche traverses a range of moral markings: the two fallen women ("the two sluts") are conflated with the virtuous ones (the sisters of Lazarus) through the hybrid combination created by the misrecognition of one of the figures as the former prostitute among Christ's followers. After recalling this particular pictorial text, Bloom unconsciously enters it by identifying with the figure of Jesus. He can feel the temperature of the water one of the women draws from the well, for example, and he imagines himself producing a narrative for the other female figure ("Tell about the places you have been, strange customs") that turns into a confession ("She listens with big dark soft eyes. Tell her: more and more: all")—a fantasy based in Martha Clifford's epistolary request ("Please write me a long letter and tell me more" [*U* 5.251]). It is also worth noting, for later associative purposes, that in the recalled picture one of the sisters is in a position of servitude ("The other one, jar on her head, was getting the supper"); in its biblical pretext, which Bloom may have heard in the course of his piecemeal exposure to Catholicism, this sister complains that she "was cumbered about such serving" and is called "careful and troubled about many things" (Luke 10: 38–42). The Bible story also clarifies which woman is Mary and which one is Martha, but Bloom's recollective vision fails to identify either woman with a specific name, marking them instead in terms of two roles: the female server, preparing food, and the female confessor, hearing the wanderings of a weary Christ.

The signifier "Mary" resurfaces again later in "Lotus-Eaters" when Bloom envisions a female confessant, thus inverting one of the sister's roles in the recalled picture. The recurrence of a phrase from Martha's letter ("Then I will tell you all" [*U* 5.254]) within the scenario suggests that Bloom is recalling her promise to share her secrets with him in their mutually confessional correspondence. It also hints that he subliminally identifies her with the fantasy woman spilling her sins to her priest:

Glorious and immaculate virgin. Joseph, her spouse. Peter and Paul. More interesting if you understood what it was all about. Wonderful organisation certainly, goes like clockwork. Confession. Everyone wants to. Then I will tell you all. Penance. Punish me, please. Great weapon in their hands. More than doctor or solicitor. Woman dying to. And I schschschschsch. And did you chachachachacha? And why did you? Look down at her ring to

find an excuse. Whispering gallery walls have ears. Husband learn
to his surprise. God's little joke. Then out she comes. Repentance
skindeep. Lovely shame. Pray at an altar. Hail Mary and Holy
Mary. Flowers, incense, candles melting. Hide her blushes. Salvation army blatant imitation. Reformed prostitute will address the
meeting. How I found the Lord. (U 5.423–34)

Bloom characterizes Catholicism as a well-regulated organization,
catering perfectly in its rituals to common psychic needs. But within
the supposedly hermetic regime of confession, he envisions potential
leaks: first a priest who could use his knowledge of various sins for
blackmail ("Great weapon in their hands") and then a confession
booth strategically placed to produce a whispering gallery, allowing
the husband of the confessant (and, of course, others) to hear the
details of the woman's transgressive dalliances. Bloom's fantasy here
symptomatizes an unconscious phobia inherent in his relationship with
Martha, a phobia made transparent in "Circe": namely, that she has
confessed her epistolary affair to the counterpart of the clergy, the
local police force.[2] The whimsical image of the confessional as a devi-
ous sound trap that facilitates spousal eavesdropping simultaneously
records an ongoing desire that inflects his relationship with his wife: a
desire for surveillance over her flirtations that aims to produce a masterful sense of power-knowledge. The associative logic of Bloom's
thinking, moving from Catholic ritual to the Salvation Army, is motivated by the shared confessional outlets of the two institutions; but his
vision earlier in the hour of the ambiguous biblical "Mary" (Mary,
sister of Lazarus, conflated with Mary Magdalene) operates as a secondary impetus for the psychic juxtaposition of the Blessed Virgin
Mary and the reformed prostitute.

Bloom's next explicitly visual symptom featuring the signifier
"Mary" appears toward the beginning of "Aeolus" and is structured
around a tripled textual mediation of William Brayden, the editor of
the *Freeman's Journal*. After noting this figure ascending the staircase,
"steered by an umbrella, a solemn beardframed face" (U 7.45–46),

---

[2]Joyce doubles these two regulatory forces explicitly in Stephen's retort to the nationalist Madden in *Stephen Hero:*

—We remain true to the Church because it is our national Church, the
Church our people have suffered for and would suffer for again. The police are different. We look upon them as aliens, traitors, oppressors of the people.

—The old peasant down the country doesn't seem to be of your opinion
when he counts over his greasy notes and says "I'll put the priest on Tom an' I'll
put the polisman on Mickey." (64)

Bloom hears Red Murray's question, "—Don't you think his face is like Our Saviour?," and responds to reveal his own visual associations:

> Our Saviour: beardframed oval face: talking in the dusk. Mary, Martha. Steered by an umbrella sword to the footlights: Mario the tenor.
> —Or like Mario, Mr Bloom said.
> —Yes, Red Murray agreed. But Mario was said to be the picture of Our Saviour.
> Jesusmario with rougy cheeks, doublet and spindle legs. Hand on his heart. In *Martha*.
> *Co-ome thou lost one,*
> *Co-ome thou dear one!* (*U* 7.52–60)

The allusion to an image of Christ reminds Bloom of the picture he visualized after reading Martha's letter, as the fragment "talking in the dusk" reveals: it refers back to the atmosphere of "quiet dusk" (*U* 5.294) he envisions earlier. The picture in turn reminds him of *Mario* the tenor, through the verbal associative link of *Mary* and *Mar*tha. This link is reinforced, of course, by Mario's performance of the role of Lionel in the light opera entitled *Martha* and by Mario's uncanny resemblance to a traditional image in the visual iconography of Christ. Because Mario gave his last stage appearance in 1871 when Bloom was only five years old, Bloom is probably remembering a picture of the tenor, just as surely as Red Murray is remembering a picture of "Our Saviour."[3] In this passage, Brayden's appearance is filtered through three textual screens (Christ, Mario, and Lionel), but by the end of it, Bloom once again unconsciously positions himself within the overdetermined representational image by silently singing Mario/Lionel's song ("*Co-ome thou lost one, / Co-ome thou dear one!*"). His earlier subliminal fantasy of himself as the pictorialized Christ facilitates the identification here. The "Mary, Martha" in Bloom's associative train refers back not only to the picture of the sisters of Lazarus, with its ambivalent moral inflections of the two female figures, but also to the light opera itself. *Martha* centers around two women who are hired at a fair as servant girls by well-to-do farmers. The ambivalent code in this operatic pretext is tied to class identity: the two female servants are in fact a queen and her maid of honor, who assume lower-class disguises out of boredom with court life (Gifford 129).

---

[3]This speculation about what Bloom is recalling in the above passage appeared in a recent issue of the *James Joyce Broadsheet*. The issue also features on its cover an illustrative portrait of Mario the tenor that makes patent his visual similarities to certain representations of Christ (see Bekker and Brown 4).

Yet another symptomatic "Mary" in Bloom's psychic meanderings emerges in "Lestrygonians," in the context of the most visible regulatory regime at work in Dublin. Seeing a squad of constables returning to their beats after their lunch, Bloom recalls a frightening encounter he had with the Dublin Metropolitan Police during a pro-Boer demonstration and its perduring unsettling affects: "Police whistle in my ears still" (*U* 8.431), he thinks to himself. This memory leads to speculations about the network of police spies that aids the workings of this particular disciplinary regime and, subsequently, a fantasy—both visual and auditory—that centers on a servant girl named "Mary":

> Never know who you're talking to. Corny Kelleher he has Harvey Duff in his eye. Like that Peter or Denis or James Carey that blew the gaff on the invincibles. Member of the corporation too. Egging raw youths on to get in the know all the time drawing secret service pay from the castle. Drop him like a hot potato. Why those plainclothes men are always courting slaveys. Easily twig a man used to uniform. Squarepushing up against a backdoor. Maul her a bit. Then the next thing on the menu. And who is the gentleman does be visiting there? Was the young master saying anything? Peeping Tom through the keyhole. Decoy duck. Hotblooded young student fooling round her fat arms ironing.
>
> —Are those yours, Mary?
>
> —I don't wear such things. . . . Stop or I'll tell the missus on you. Out half the night.
>
> —There are great times coming, Mary. Wait till you see.
>
> —Ah, gelong with your great times coming. (*U* 8.441–55)

Although the politics of this imagined scenario are not unambiguous, its context suggests that the "young student" flirting with "Mary" may be an example of one of the "plainclothes men" employed by the police and the castle to milk unsuspecting slaveys for information about the households where they work. The "great times coming" may refer to the improved economic situation the young man anticipates as a consequence of his unofficial new job. The servant girl "Mary" in this fantasy is represented as a resistant but potential leak within a domestic enclosure. She is familiar not only with the family undergarments, which she is ironing, but also with the family's politics, its visitors, and—by inference—its internal dynamics. She is psychically connected to the other female maid Bloom imagines at the outset of "Lestrygonians" and codes as the repository of compromising knowledge, as the potential witness to her priestly employer's excesses and lapses:

> I'd like to see them do the black fast Yom Kippur. Crossbuns. One meal and a collation for fear he'd collapse on the altar. A housekeeper of one of those fellows if you could pick it out of her. Never pick it out of her. Like getting L. s. d. out of him. Does himself well. No guests. All for number one. Watching his water. Bring your own bread and butter. His reverence: mum's the word. (*U* 8.35–40)

In both these fantasies, the confined space of the domicile remains inviolate, but only precariously so, much like the confession box in "Lotus-Eaters." The plainclothes deputy puts pressure on "Mary" to talk, and the hypothetical priest takes pains to swear his domestic to secrecy. Within the regulated unit known as the house*hold* (with its implicit suggestion of containment), the female servant may function as a barely visible countergaze and epistemological pore, potentially exploitable by larger regulatory structures.

In the stylistic parody in "Cyclops" that opens with "Love loves to love love," we find within the listed affairs of the heart, "Constable 14A loves Mary Kelly" (*U* 12.1493–94). This comic clue, read in conjunction with Bloom's fantasy about the servant "Mary" fondled by a secret agent of the police force, leads me to speculate that the first but unnamed "Mary" figure is actually "the nextdoor girl" Bloom ogles at the porkbutcher's in "Calypso," for he phantasmically pairs this servant with a policeman as well:

> The porkbutcher snapped two sheets from the pile, wrapped up her prime sausages and made a red grimace.
> —Now, my miss, he said.
> She tendered a coin, smiling boldly, holding her thick wrist out.
> —Thank you, my miss. And one shilling threepence change. For you, please?
> Mr Bloom pointed quickly. To catch up and walk behind her if she went slowly, behind her moving hams. Pleasant to see first thing in the morning. Hurry up, damn it. Make hay while the sun shines. She stood outside the shop in sunlight and sauntered lazily to the right. He sighed down his nose: they never understand. Sodachapped hands. Crusted toenails too. Brown scapulars in tatters, defending her both ways. The sting of disregard glowed to

weak pleasure within his breast. For another: a constable off duty cuddling her in Eccles lane. They like them sizeable. Prime sausage. O please, Mr Policeman, I'm lost in the wood. (*U* 4.165–79)

A visual symptom can be located in the psychic appearance of the police force—the regulatory gaze of the metropolis—after an instance of actual and then fantasized voyeurism. The scopic powers that Bloom exercises over the young woman's body are checked by a more powerful source of visual surveillance: "*They* like them sizeable" refers to the Dublin Metropolitan Police, who had a minimum height requirement for jobs on the force (Gifford 73). The servant girl's fantasized lament to the enforcer of law—"O please, Mr Policeman, I'm lost in the *wood*"—contains a parapraxis, for shortly before Bloom thinks, "*Woods* his name is. Wonder what he does. Wife is oldish. New blood. No followers allowed" (*U* 4.148–50, my emphasis).[4] Bloom imagines a relationship between the older male employer and his female domestic, and one can residually hear in her complaint of helplessness to the policeman her protest against her sexual exploitation. In "Sirens" Bloom psychically pairs this young woman (linked to the phantasmic "Mary" of "Lestrygonians") with his penpal Martha, by calling up a memory of her in Woods's backyard while he writes to his mystery correspondent: "P. S. The rum tum tum. How will you pun? You punish me? Crooked skirt swinging, whack by. Tell me I want to. Know" (*U* 11.890–92). In "Nausicaa" the female dyad resurfaces in its original form as the sisters of Lazarus, recalled by Bloom for the timelessness of their apparel and revealingly contextualized in ruminations about women-on-the-market: "Dressed up to the nines for somebody. Fashion part of their charm. Just changes except when you're on the track of the secret. Except the east: Mary, Martha: now as then. No reasonable offer refused" (*U* 13.804–06).

The "Circe" episode reveals many of the unconscious thoughts that lie behind Bloom's latent visions and associations. It exposes the repressed referent behind the anonymous signifier "Mary," for instance, as a specific and real young woman, Mary Driscoll, the Blooms' former slavey and victim of the husband's unwanted sexual advances. Bloom allows this psychically troubling figure from his past to enter his consciousness very obliquely in "Hades" in a suggestive

---

[4]This parapraxis was pointed out to me by James Mitchell, a student of mine in an undergraduate course on *Ulysses* at the University of California, Riverside, in Spring 1995.

but significantly truncated thought. Mary Driscoll is more than likely the latent subtext of his response to the high voice of the acolyte at Paddy Dignam's funeral service: "*Et ne nos inducas in tentationem.* / The server piped the answer in the treble. I often thought it would be better to have boy servants. Up to fifteen or so. After that, of course . . ." (*U* 6.618–20, Joyce's ellipsis). Recognizing the word *temptation* in the Latinate phrase ("And lead us not into temptation") and hearing the soprano and hence feminized voice of the priest's server, Bloom's mind symptomatically turns to domestic servants. His tendency to sexualize the Blessed Virgin Mary ("By Bassi's blessed virgins Bloom's dark eyes went by. Bluerobed, white under, come to me. . . . That brings those rakes of fellows in: her white" [*U* 11.151–55]) may not be merely an example of desublimated mariolatry but also a function of his association of the signifier "Mary" with personal temptation. In the hint in "Hades" that mature male servants might offer a temptation to Molly and be vulnerable to her lustful overtures, the Blooms' household offers perverse equal opportunities for sexual harassment.

It is not difficult to trace the signifiers in Bloom's Circean fantasies that trigger Mary Driscoll's appearance, which allow the repressed referent of the waking visual symptoms to surface. The first mnemonic triggers are the two police agents (the First and Second Watch) whom Bloom earlier suspects of using female slaveys for inside information. The second is Signor Maffei's announced introduction of "Mademoiselle Ruby, the pride of the ring" (*U* 15.716), the abused indentured servant of circus reform fiction. The third is the accusation of "unlawfully watching and besetting" (*U* 15.733–34), Bloom's crime against his former employee. The fourth is the witness Martha, recurrently paired with Mary in Bloom's thoughts on account of the recalled picture of Lazarus's sisters. The fifth is a voice that recalls Bloom's participation in the pro-Boer demonstration ("Turncoat! Up the Boers! Who booed Joe Chamberlain?" [*U* 15.791]), the political event that generates the fantasy of the Mary pressured to reveal household secrets. The resisting domestic leak of Bloom's imagined scenario in "Lestrygonians" becomes in "Circe" the all too willing witness for the prosecution. Mary's testimony about Bloom's pathetic pretense for his sexual advances—"He surprised me in the rere of the premises, Your honour, when the missus was out shopping one morning with a request for a safety pin" (*U* 15.885–86)—retrospectively explains why the pin in Martha's letter unconsciously evokes a ditty about "Mairy." The two working-class female witnesses are succeeded by accusatory upper-class women: this transformation may be motivated in part by Bloom's earlier association of Martha and Mary with the two servant women in the light opera *Martha*, who are in fact a queen and her maid of honor in disguise.

The regional specificity of Mary's accusation ("He surprised me in the rere of the premises") hints that Bloom assaulted her in a domestic zone he was supposed to steer clear of while she worked; the charge also resonates unmistakably of attempted anal rape. Indeed, the Circean context in which Mary Driscoll appears suggests that Bloom understands his attempted sexual exploits as a territorial violation. The fantasy sequence containing Mary includes as well Sir Philip Beaufoy, accusing Bloom of appropriating his works ("A plagiarist. A soapy sneak masquerading as a *littérateur*" [*U* 15.822–23]); Bloom himself, pretending to be pro-colonialist ("I'm as staunch a Britisher as you are, sir. I fought with the colours for king and country in the absentminded war" [*U* 15.794–95])—as if "legitimized" military boundary assaults are an adequate defense against unauthorized private ones; and the society ladies, claiming Bloom has overstepped class lines ("This plebeian Don Juan observed me from behind a hackney car and sent me in double envelopes an obscene photograph, such as are sold after dark on Paris boulevards, insulting to any lady. I have it still" [*U* 15.1064–67]). Bloom allegedly responds to Mary's remonstrations with the command "keep it quiet" (*U* 15.893); according to her testimony, he has defensively requested either that she not report his territorial advances to Molly or that she keep her voice down, perhaps for fear that the neighbors—or, more specifically, that the neighbors' servant—will hear. Earlier in the day when he walks out to the jakes, he is warily self-conscious of the potential presence of the Woods's slavey: "He went out through the backdoor into the garden: stood to listen towards the next garden. No sound. Perhaps hanging clothes out to dry. The maid was in the garden" (*U* 4.472–74); he may be checking for her again when "before sitting down he peered through a chink up at the nextdoor windows. The king was in his countinghouse. Nobody" (*U* 4.497–99). Mary Driscoll's allegations against Bloom add a new psychological dimension to his conscious thoughts about garters and oysters. The former are his figurative attempted bribe for her sexual compliance, while the latter provide the trumped-up charges a jealous Molly uses as a pretext for firing the girl. In his waking thoughts, Bloom associates oysters with Boylan and his own imminent cuckolding ("Fizz and Red bank oysters. Effect on the sexual. Aphrodis. He was in the Red Bank this morning. Was he oysters old fish at table perhaps he young flesh in bed no June has no ar no oysters" [*U* 8.865–68]); in the unconscious phantasmagoria of "Circe," he betrays that they also have a referent to a sexual scenario in which he is not the victim but rather the victimizer. Perhaps the most disturbing and revealing element of Mary's testimony resides in the policeman's opening question to her: "Are you of the unfortunate class?" (*U* 15.865). Mary indignantly assures him that she is not, but the very possibility raised in the inquiry suggests that psychically Bloom fears that his former slavey has had to turn to prostitution for alternative employment. The victim of Bloom's failure to regulate his lusts becomes the victim of Molly's corrective ousting and, in the nightmarish question of one of his psychic watchmen, the possible victim, in turn, of the Dublin sex trade.

The policeman's imagined inquiry may explain why Bloom, out of the forty-four responses to his ad, chooses to establish a confessionary sado-masochistic correspondence with a woman named Martha. Having potentially ruined Mary, he seeks punishment—through a patent transference—from her figurative sister and *Doppelgänger* in his psychic economy. He moves, in other words, from the female server to the female confessor, substituting one figure in the pictorial text for the other. Bloom's unconscious fears about Mary's plight may motivate the vicarious and distanced forms his sexual pleasures take: his one direct extramarital dalliance backfired surely beyond his expectations in its victimizing fallout, perhaps explaining why in the present he opts for the relative safety of fantasy, voyeurism, scripted "dirty talk" from prostitutes, or the controlled erotic correspondence. Significantly, the ditty of " *O, Mairy lost the pin of her drawers*" enters Bloom's thoughts in "Lotus-Eaters" immediately after he dismisses the possibility of Martha's requested meeting ("Could meet one Sunday after the rosary. Thank you: not having any. Usual love scrimmage" [*U* 5.270–71]): the rejection of personal contact with his penpal reminds him in a latent image of the young woman whom he did indeed risk touching. The policeman's disturbing question to Mary Driscoll also hints at why the dual female figures of Mary and Martha are coded ambiguously in his mind—as virgins, as prostitutes, as a virgin and a prostitute. When one reads his early visual symptom—the recalled painting of the biblical sisters—retrospectively from the vantage point of "Circe," one can speculate that he unconsciously enters the image as a thoroughly unholy and inverse Christ-figure: as a man who turns respectable women into prostitutes, rather than the other way around. This is Bloom's dreaded counter-conversionary power.

He symptomatically enacts this perverse role in the sexgame he plays with his weary wife: "who is in your mind now tell me who are you thinking of who is it tell me his name who tell me who the german Emperor is it yes imagine Im him think of him can you feel him trying to make a whore of me what he never will" (*U* 18.94–97).

The wording of the police constable's question—"Are you of the unfortunate *class?*" (my emphasis)—implies that Bloom's sense of guilt stems primarily from the economic consequences of his lapse. Indeed, the sexual dimension of the scenario (as in most couplings in Joyce's fictions, be they successful or merely attempted) borders on the ludicrous, the comical—in the very mundanity of the setting, in the clumsiness of the encounter, and in the shabbiness of the would-be seducer's attire (*"housejacket of ripplecloth, flannel trousers, heelless slippers, unshaven, his hair rumpled"* [*U* 15.875–76]). But the economic implications of the Circean fantasy cannot be included within the comedy of the scene, simply because we know from Bloom's waking thoughts that he takes economic issues seriously and that potential impoverishment is never a laughing matter for him. After all, Bloom's main critique of Irish nationalism, as it manifested itself in 1904, is that the movement does not place preeminent emphasis on pragmatic economic concerns ("That the language question should take precedence of the economic question" [*U* 8.466–67], he thinks with exasperation in "Lestrygonians," a chapter that addresses Dublin's economic plight through contrasting images of dietary abundance and scarcity, gluttony and starvation). The phantasm of Mary Driscoll suggests that he fears he has committed what is ultimately a class-based crime: an implicit coercion of a laborer from a lower-class position that is nonetheless respectable and relatively secure to an even "lower" means of employment that is disreputed, physically hazardous, and economically unreliable. Joyce hints at the potential psychological tolls of prostitution through the sad figure of "the whore of the lane" (*U* 11.1250–51), who appears to be suffering from dementia.

These two types of exploited women in *Ulysses*—the slavey and the prostitute, merged under the signifier of "Mary"—have a definite power in Bloom's psyche, on account of their access to taboo secrets. One can speculate that Molly's dismissal of Mary from live-in maid service is motivated not only by the slavey's unwanted status as sexual rival, but also by her equally unwanted status as domestic counter-gaze, as inevitable witness to marital rifts and disharmonies (and finally, of course, their fallguy). The Blooms' one remaining domestic assistant—Mrs. Fleming, the cleaning woman—works for the couple only part-time ("Mrs Fleming is in to clean," Bloom thinks in "Hades" [U 6.237]) and, from Molly's account of her, sounds conveniently short-sighted ("that old Mrs Fleming you have to be walking round after her putting the things into her hands" [U 18.1081–83]). In retaliation for his flirtation with their nubile maid, Molly fantasizes about pairing her husband off with this older employee ("a picnic suppose we all gave 5/- each and or let him [Boylan] pay it and invite some other woman for him [Bloom] who Mrs Fleming" [U 18.946–47]).

Like the full-time domestic, the prostitute, too, becomes a sort of countergaze by default, a figure whose very economic disempowerment forces her into positions of epistemic power. Suggestively, the "whore of the lane" wearing the black straw sailor hat—whose appearances in both "Sirens" and "Eumaeus" make Bloom noticeably uneasy because she knows who his wife is—earns her income not only through sex but also laundering, another trade that necessarily implicates the worker in potentially compromising knowledge of others' intimate affairs. At the close of "Sirens," Bloom notes of this unnamed woman, "Off her beat here" (U 11.1255), turning her into a sort of policeman with a demarcated part of the city to patrol. And the "Circe" episode indeed hints—both in Bella's threat to call the police and in the provocative appearance of Corny Kelleher, the police tout—that the police and the prostitutes, at least in some circumstances, have a collaborative rather than an adversarial relationship. Bloom desires a more conventional antagonistic positioning of the police station and the brothel, as is made clear in his professed belief that the bodies of prostitutes should be subjected to a regime of mandatory inspections, regulated by an intrusive governmental gaze. This desire for control over particular female *bodies* may mask a deeper wish and express it only in displaced form. This deeper wish is disguised and symptomatized in one of Bloom's remnant sexual pleasures, in his interaction with Martha's other *Doppelgänger*, the young prostitute he pays to speak his particular language of desire (as he does his penpal, through his pecuniary gifts): "Girl in Meath street that night. All the dirty things I made her say. All wrong of course. My arks she called it. . . . And kissed my hand when I gave her the extra two shillings. Parrots. Press the button and the bird will squeak. Wish she hadn't called me sir" (U 13.867–72). On the surface, of course, Bloom's pleasure may appear masochistic, insofar as the girl's mispronunciation of "arse" hints that she speaks to him (or at least tries to speak to him) in a punitive discourse of flagellation. But if we read the structure of this attempted enactment of fantasy as opposed to its content, an alternate wish emerges, a wish in which Bloom is not the abject penitent, but rather the domineering master. As his insistence on the prostitute's verbal mimicry implies, Bloom secretly desires to regulate not merely the *bodies,* but also the *speech* of a specific subculture of exploited women. In his psyche, the young prostitute is not only the orally mimetic parrot but also a mechanical toy, encodings that doubly desubjectify and silence her point of view. Bloom is clearly irritated when she departs from his script—"Wish she hadn't called me sir"— in such a way that emphasizes his real position of power beneath his fantasized role of abjection. Submerged beneath its masochistic surface, this fantasy scenario bespeaks a phobic need to control the discourse of those perversely privileged female subjectivities who constitute a countergaze, a countergaze that knows the dirty secrets hidden in many a male Dubliner's bottom drawer.

WORKS CITED

Bekker, Pieter, and Richard Brown, eds. *James Joyce Broadsheet* 19 (Feb. 1986): 1–4.

Freud, Sigmund. *The Ego and the Id.* Trans. Joan Riviere. Ed. James Strachey. New York: Norton, 1962.

———. "From the History of an Infantile Neurosis." *Three Case Histories.* Ed. Philip Rieff. New York: Collier, 1993. 161–280.

Gifford, Don, with Robert J. Seidman. *"Ulysses" Annotated: Notes for James Joyce's "Ulysses."* Rev. ed. Berkeley: U of California P, 1988.

Joyce, James. *Stephen Hero.* New York: New Directions, 1963.

Lacan, Jacques. "Of the Gaze as *Objet Petit a.*" *The Four Fundamental Concepts of Psycho-Analysis.* Ed. Jacques-Alain Miller. Trans. Alan Sheridan. New York: Norton, 1981.

Marxist Criticism
and
Ulysses

WHAT IS MARXIST CRITICISM?

To the question "What is Marxist criticism?" it may be tempting to respond with another question: "What does it matter?" In light of the rapid and largely unanticipated demise of Soviet-style communism in the former USSR and throughout Eastern Europe, it is understandable to suppose that Marxist literary analysis would disappear too, quickly becoming an anachronism in a world enamored with full-market capitalism.

In fact, however, there is no reason why Marxist criticism should weaken, let alone disappear. It is, after all, a phenomenon distinct from Soviet and Eastern European communism, having had its beginnings nearly eighty years before the Bolshevik revolution and having thrived, since the 1940s, mainly in the West—not as a form of communist propaganda but rather as a form of critique, a discourse for interrogating *all* societies and their texts in terms of certain specific issues. Those issues—including race, class, and the attitudes shared within a given culture—are as much with us as ever, not only in contemporary Russia but also in the United States.

The argument could even be made that Marxist criticism has been strengthened by the collapse of Soviet-style communism. There was a time, after all, when few self-respecting Anglo-American journals would use Marxist terms or models, however illuminating, to analyze Western issues or problems. It smacked of sleeping with the enemy. With the collapse of the Kremlin, however, old taboos began to give way. Even the staid *Wall Street Journal* now seems comfortable using phrases like "worker alienation" to discuss the problems plaguing the American business world.

The assumption that Marxist criticism will die on the vine of a moribund political system rests in part on another mistaken assumption, namely, that Marxist literary analysis is practiced only by people who would like to see society transformed into a Marxist-communist state, one created through land reform, the redistribution of wealth, a tightly and centrally managed economy, the abolition of institutionalized religion, and so on. In fact, it has never been necessary to be a communist political revolutionary to be classified as a Marxist literary critic. (Many of the critics discussed in this introduction actually *fled* communist societies to live in the West.) Nor is it necessary to like only those literary works with a radical social vision or to dislike books that represent or even reinforce a middle-class, capitalist world-view. It is necessary, however, to adopt what most students of literature would consider a radical definition of the purpose and function of literary criticism.

More traditional forms of criticism, according to the Marxist critic Pierre Macherey, "set . . . out to deliver the text from its own silences by coaxing it into giving up its true, latent, or hidden meaning." Inevitably, however, non-Marxist criticism "intrude[s] its own discourse between the reader and the text" (qtd. in Bennett 107). Marxist critics, by contrast, do not attempt to discover hidden meanings in texts. Or if they do, they do so only after seeing the text, first and foremost, as a material product to be understood in broadly historical terms. That is to say, a literary work is first viewed as a product *of* work (and hence of the realm of production and consumption we call economics). Second, it may be looked upon as a work that *does* identifiable work of its own. At one level, that work is usually to enforce and reinforce the prevailing ideology, that is, the network of conventions, values, and opinions to which the majority of people uncritically subscribe.

This does not mean that Marxist critics merely describe the obvious. Quite the contrary: the relationship that the Marxist critic Terry Eagleton outlines in *Criticism and Ideology* (1978) among the soaring cost of books in the nineteenth century, the growth of lending libraries, the practice of publishing "three-decker" novels (so that three borrowers could be reading the same book at the same time), and the changing *content* of those novels is highly complex in its own way. But the complexity Eagleton finds is not that of the deeply buried meaning of the text. Rather, it is that of the complex web of social and economic relationships that were prerequisite to the work's production. Marxist criticism does not seek to be, in Eagleton's words, "a passage from text to reader." Indeed, "its task is to show the text as it cannot know itself, to manifest those conditions of its making (inscribed in its very letter) about which it is necessarily silent" (43).

As everyone knows, Marxism began with Karl Marx, the nineteenth-century German philosopher best known for writing *Das Kapital,* the seminal work of the communist movement. What everyone doesn't know is that Marx was also the first Marxist literary critic (much as Sigmund Freud, who psychoanalyzed E. T. A. Hoffmann's supernatural tale "The Sandman," was the first Freudian literary critic). During the 1830s Marx wrote critical essays on writers such as Goethe and Shakespeare (whose tragic vision of Elizabethan disintegration he praised).

The fact that Marxist literary criticism began with Marx himself is hardly surprising, given Marx's education and early interests. Trained in the classics at the University of Bonn, Marx wrote literary imitations, his own poetry, a failed novel, and a fragment of a tragic drama (*Oulanem*) before turning to contemplative and political philosophy. Even after he met Friedrich Engels in 1843 and began collaborating on works such as *The German Ideology* and *The Communist Manifesto,* Marx maintained a keen interest in literary writers and their works. He and Engels argued about the poetry of Heinrich Heine, admired Hermann Freiligrath (a poet critical of the German aristocracy), and faulted the playwright Ferdinand Lassalle for writing about a reactionary knight in the Peasants' War rather than about more progressive aspects of German history.

As these examples suggest, Marx and Engels would not—indeed, could not—think of aesthetic matters as being distinct and independent from such things as politics, economics, and history. Not surprisingly, they viewed the alienation of the worker in industrialized, capitalist societies as having grave consequences for the arts. How can people mechanically stamping out things that bear no mark of their producer's individuality (people thereby "reified," turned into things themselves) be expected to recognize, produce, or even consume things of beauty? And if there is no one to consume something, there will soon be no one to produce it, especially in an age in which production (even of something like literature) has come to mean *mass* (and therefore profitable) production.

In *The German Ideology* (1846), Marx and Engels expressed their sense of the relationship between the arts, politics, and basic economic reality in terms of a general social theory. Economics, they argued, provides the "base" or "infrastructure" of society, but from that base emerges a "superstructure" consisting of law, politics, philosophy, religion, and art.

Marx later admitted that the relationship between base and superstructure may be indirect and fluid: every change in economics may not be reflected by an immediate change in ethics or literature. In *The Eighteenth Brumaire of Louis Bonaparte* (1852), he came up with the word *homology* to describe the sometimes unbalanced, often delayed, and almost always loose correspondence between base and superstructure. And later in that same decade, while working on an introduction to his *Political Economy*, Marx further relaxed the base–superstructure relationship. Writing on the excellence of ancient Greek art (versus the primitive nature of ancient Greek economics), he conceded that a gap sometimes opens up between base and superstructure—between economic forms and those produced by the creative mind.

Nonetheless, *at* base the old formula was maintained. Economics remained basic and the connection between economics and superstructural elements of society was reaffirmed. Central to Marxism and Marxist literary criticism was and is the following "materialist" insight: consciousness, without which such things as art cannot be produced, is not the source of social forms and economic conditions. It is, rather, their most important product.

Marx and Engels, drawing upon the philosopher G. W. F. Hegel's theories about the dialectical synthesis of ideas out of theses and antitheses, believed that a revolutionary class war (pitting the capitalist class against a proletarian, antithetical class) would lead eventually to the synthesis of a new social and economic order. Placing their faith not in the idealist Hegelian dialectic but, rather, in what they called "dialectical materialism," they looked for a secular and material salvation of humanity—one in, not beyond, history—via revolution and not via divine intervention. And they believed that the communist society eventually established would be one capable of producing new forms of consciousness and belief and therefore, ultimately, great art.

The revolution anticipated by Marx and Engels did not occur in their century, let alone lifetime. When it finally did take place, it didn't happen in places where Marx and Engels had thought it might be successful: the United States, Great Britain, and Germany. It happened, rather, in 1917 Russia, a country long ruled by despotic czars but also enlightened by the works of powerful novelists and playwrights, including Chekhov, Pushkin, Tolstoy, and Dostoyevsky.

Perhaps because of its significant literary tradition, Russia produced revolutionaries like V.I. Lenin, who shared not only Marx's interest in literature but also his belief in literature's ultimate importance. But it was not without some hesitation that Lenin endorsed the significance of texts written during the reign of the czars. Well before 1917 he had questioned what the relationship should be between a society undergoing a revolution and the great old literature of its bourgeois past.

Lenin attempted to answer that question in a series of essays on Tolstoy that he wrote between 1908 and 1911. Tolstoy—the author of *War and Peace* and *Anna Karenina*—was an important nineteenth-century Russian writer whose views did not accord with all of those of young Marxist revolutionaries. Continuing interest in a writer like Tolstoy may be justified, Lenin reasoned, given the primitive and unenlightened economic order of the society that produced him. Since superstructure usually lags behind base (and is therefore usually *more* primitive), the attitudes of a Tolstoy were relatively progressive when viewed in light of the monarchical and precapitalist society out of which they arose.

Moreover, Lenin also reasoned, the writings of the great Russian realists would *have* to suffice, at least in the short run. Lenin looked forward, in essays like "Party Organization and Party Literature," to the day in which new artistic forms would be produced by progressive writers with revolutionary political views and agendas. But he also knew that a great proletarian literature was unlikely to evolve until a thoroughly literate proletariat had been produced by the educational system.

Lenin was hardly the only revolutionary leader involved in setting up the new Soviet state who took a strong interest in literary matters. In 1924 Leon Trotsky published a book called *Literature and Revolution*, which is still acknowledged as a classic of Marxist literary criticism.

Trotsky worried about the direction in which Marxist aesthetic theory seemed to be going. He responded skeptically to groups like Proletkult, which opposed tolerance toward pre- and nonrevolutionary writers, and which called for the establishment of a new, proletarian culture.

Trotsky warned of the danger of cultural sterility and risked unpopularity by pointing out that there is no necessary connection between the quality of a literary work and the quality of its author's politics.

In 1927 Trotsky lost a power struggle with Josef Stalin, a man who believed, among other things, that writers should be "engineers" of "human souls." After Trotsky's expulsion from the Soviet Union, views held by groups like Proletkult and the Left Front of Art (LEF), and by theorists such as Nikolai Bukharin and A. A. Zhdanov, became more prevalent. Speaking at the First Congress of the Union of Soviet Writers in 1934, the Soviet author Maxim Gorky called for writing that would "make labor the principal hero of our books." It was at the same writers' congress that "socialist realism," an art form glorifying workers and the revolutionary State, was made Communist party policy and the official literary form of the USSR.

Of those critics active in the USSR after the expulsion of Trotsky and the unfortunate triumph of Stalin, two critics stand out. One, Mikhail Bakhtin, was a Russian, later a Soviet, critic who spent much of his life in a kind of internal exile. Many of his essays were written in the 1930s and not published in the West or translated until the late 1960s. His work comes out of an engagement with the Marxist intellectual tradition as well as out of an indirect, even hidden, resistance to the Soviet government. It has been important to Marxist critics writing in the West because his theories provide a means to decode submerged social critique, especially in early modern texts. He viewed language—especially literary texts—in terms of discourses and dialogues. Within a novel written in a society in flux, for instance, the narrative may include an official, legitimate discourse, plus another infiltrated by challenging comments and even retorts. In a 1929 book on Dostoyevsky and a 1940 study titled *Rabelais and His World*, Bakhtin examined what he calls "polyphonic" novels, each characterized by a multiplicity of voices or discourses. In Dostoyevsky the independent status of a given character is marked by the difference of his or her language from that of the narrator. (The narrator's voice, too, can in fact be a dialogue.) In works by Rabelais, Bakhtin finds that the (profane) language of the carnival and of other popular festivals plays against and parodies the more official discourses, that is, of the king, church, or even socially powerful intellectuals. Bakhtin influenced modern cultural criticism by showing, in a sense, that the conflict between "high" and "low" culture takes place not only between classic and popular texts but also between the "dialogic" voices that exist within many books—whether "high" or "low."

The other subtle Marxist critic who managed to survive Stalin's dictatorship and his repressive policies was Georg Lukács. A Hungarian who had begun his career as an "idealist" critic, Lukács had converted to Marxism in 1919; renounced his earlier, Hegelian work shortly thereafter; visited Moscow in 1930–31; and finally emigrated to the USSR in 1933, just one year before the First Congress of the Union of Soviet Writers met. Lukács was far less narrow in his views than the most strident Stalinist Soviet critics of the 1930s and 1940s. He disliked much socialist realism and appreciated prerevolutionary, realistic novels that broadly reflected cultural "totalities"—and were populated with characters representing human "types" of the author's place and time. (Lukács was particularly fond of the historical canvases painted by the early nineteenth-century novelist Sir Walter Scott.) But like his more rigid and censorious contemporaries, he drew the line at accepting nonrevolutionary, modernist works like James Joyce's *Ulysses*. He condemned movements like expressionism and symbolism, preferring works with "content" over more decadent, experimental works characterized mainly by "form."

With Lukács its most liberal and tolerant critic from the early 1930s until well into the 1960s, the Soviet literary scene degenerated to the point that the works of great writers like Franz Kafka were no longer read, either because they were viewed as decadent, formal experiments or because they "engineered souls" in "nonprogressive" directions. Officially sanctioned works were generally ones in which artistry lagged far behind the politics (no matter how bad the politics were).

Fortunately for the Marxist critical movement, politically radical critics *outside* the Soviet Union were free of its narrow, constricting policies and, consequently, able fruitfully to develop the thinking of Marx, Engels, and Trotsky. It was these non-Soviet Marxists who kept Marxist critical theory alive and useful in discussing all *kinds* of literature, written across the entire historical spectrum.

Perhaps because Lukács was the best of the Soviet communists writing Marxist criticism in the 1930s and 1940s, non-Soviet Marxists tended to develop their ideas by publicly opposing those of Lukács. German dramatist and critic Bertolt Brecht countered Lukács by arguing that art ought to be viewed as a field of production, not as a container of "content." Brecht also criticized Lukács for his attempt to enshrine realism at the expense not only of other "isms" but also of poetry and drama, both of which had been largely ignored by Lukács.

Even more outspoken was Brecht's critical champion Walter Benjamin, a German Marxist who, in the 1930s, attacked those conventional and traditional literary forms conveying a stultifying "aura" of culture. Benjamin praised dadaism and, more important, new forms of art ushered in by the age of mechanical reproduction. Those forms—including radio and film—offered hope, he felt, for liberation from capitalist culture, for they were too new to be part of its stultifyingly ritualistic traditions.

But of all the anti-Lukácsians outside the USSR who made a contribution to the development of Marxist literary criticism, the most important was probably Theodor Adorno. Leader since the early 1950s of the Frankfurt school of Marxist criticism, Adorno attacked Lukács for his dogmatic rejection of nonrealist modern literature and for his belief in the primacy of content over form. Art does not equal science, Adorno insisted. He went on to argue for art's autonomy from empirical forms of knowledge and to suggest that the interior monologues of modernist works (by Beckett and Proust) reflect the fact of modern alienation in a way that Marxist criticism ought to find compelling.

In addition to turning against Lukács and his overly constrictive canon, Marxists outside the Soviet Union were able to take advantage of insights generated by non-Marxist critical theories being developed in post–World War II Europe. One of the movements that came to be of interest to non-Soviet Marxists was structuralism, a scientific approach to the study of humankind whose proponents believed that all elements of culture, including literature, could be understood as parts of a system of signs. Using modern linguistics as a model, structuralists like Claude Lévi-Strauss broke down the myths of various cultures into "mythemes" in an attempt to show that there are structural correspondences, or homologies, between the mythical elements produced by various human communities across time.

Of the European structuralist Marxists, one of the most influential was Lucien Goldmann, a Rumanian critic living in Paris. Goldmann combined structuralist principles with Marx's base–superstructure model in order to show how economics determines the mental structures of social groups, which are reflected in literary texts. Goldmann rejected the idea of individual human genius, choosing to see works, instead, as the "collective" products of "trans-individual" mental structures. In early studies, such as *The Hidden God* (1955), he related seventeenth-century French texts (such as Racine's *Phèdre*) to the ideology of Jansenism. In later works, he applied Marx's base–superstructure model even more strictly, describing a relationship between economic conditions and texts unmediated by an intervening, collective consciousness.

In spite of his rigidity and perhaps because of his affinities with structuralism, Goldmann came to be seen in the 1960s as the proponent of a kind of watered-down, "humanist" Marxism. He was certainly viewed that way by the French Marxist Louis Althusser, a disciple not of Lévi-Strauss and structuralism but rather of the psychoanalytic theorist Jacques Lacan and of the Italian communist Antonio Gramsci, famous for his writings about ideology and "hegemony." (Gramsci used the latter word to refer to the pervasive, web-like system of assumptions and values that shapes the way things look, what they mean, and therefore what reality *is* for the majority of people within a culture.)

Like Gramsci, Althusser viewed literary works primarily in terms of their relationship to ideology, the function of which, he argued, is to (re)produce the existing relations of production in a given society. Dave Laing, in *The Marxist Theory of Art* (1978), has attempted to explain this particular insight of Althusser by saying that ideologies, through the "ensemble of habits, moralities, and opinions" that can be found in any literary text, "ensure that the work-force (and those responsible for re-producing them in the family, school, etc.) are maintained in their position of subordination to the dominant class" (91). This is not to say that Althusser thought of the masses as a brainless multitude following only the dictates of the prevailing ideology: Althusser followed Gramsci in suggesting that even working-class people have some freedom to struggle against ideology and to change history. Nor is it to say that Althusser saw ideology as being a coherent, consistent force. In fact, he saw it as being riven with contradictions that works of literature sometimes expose and even widen. Thus Althusser followed Marx and Gramsci in believing that although literature must be seen in *relation* to ideology, it—like all social forms—has some degree of autonomy.

Althusser's followers included Pierre Macherey, who in *A Theory of Literary Production* (1978) developed Althusser's concept of the relationship between literature and ideology. A realistic novelist, he argued, attempts to produce a unified, coherent text, but instead ends up producing a work containing lapses, omissions, gaps. This happens because within ideology there are subjects that cannot be covered, things that cannot be said, contradictory views that aren't recognized as contradictory. (The critic's challenge, in this case, is to supply what the text cannot say, thereby making sense of gaps and contradictions.)

But there is another reason why gaps open up and contradictions become evident in texts. Works don't just reflect ideology (which Goldmann had referred to as "myth" and which Macherey refers to as a system of "illusory social beliefs"); they are also "fictions," works of art, *products* of ideology that have what Goldmann would call a "world-view" to offer. What kind of product, Macherey implicitly asks, is identical to the thing that produced it? It is hardly surprising, then, that Balzac's fiction shows French peasants in two different lights, only one of which is critical and judgmental, only one of which is baldly ideological. Writing approvingly on Macherey and Macherey's mentor Althusser in *Marxism and Literary Criticism* (1976), Terry Eagleton says: "It is by giving ideology a determinate form, fixing it within certain fictional limits, that art is able to distance itself from [ideology], thus revealing . . . [its] limits" (19).

A follower of Althusser, Macherey is sometimes referred to as a "post-Althusserian Marxist." Eagleton, too, is often described that way, as is his American contemporary Fredric Jameson. Jameson and Eagleton, as well as being post-Althusserians, are also among the few Anglo-American critics who have closely followed and significantly developed Marxist thought.

Before them, Marxist interpretation in English was limited to the work of a handful of critics: Christopher Caudwell, Christopher Hill, Arnold Kettle, E. P. Thompson, and Raymond Williams. Of these, Williams was perhaps least Marxist in orientation: he felt that Marxist critics, ironically, tended too much to isolate economics from culture; that they overlooked the individualism of people, opting instead to see them as "masses"; and that even more ironically, they had become an elitist group. But if the least Marxist of the British Marxists, Williams was also by far the most influential. Preferring to talk about "culture" instead of ideology, Williams argued in works such as *Culture and Society 1780–1950* (1958) that culture is "lived experience" and, as such, an interconnected set of social properties, each and all grounded in and influencing history.

Terry Eagleton's *Criticism and Ideology* (1978) is in many ways a response to the work of Williams. Responding to Williams's statement in *Culture and Society* that "there are in fact no masses; there are only ways of seeing people as masses" (289), Eagleton writes:

> That men and women really are now unique individuals was
> Williams's (unexceptionable) insistence; but it was a proposition
> bought at the expense of perceiving the fact that they must mass

and fight to achieve their full individual humanity. One has only to adapt Williams's statement to "There are in fact no classes; there are only ways of seeing people as classes" to expose its theoretical paucity. (*Criticism* 29)

Eagleton goes on, in *Criticism and Ideology*, to propose an elaborate theory about how history—in the form of "general," "authorial," and "aesthetic" ideology—enters texts, which in turn may revivify, open up, or critique those same ideologies, thereby setting in motion a process that may alter history. He shows how texts by Jane Austen, Matthew Arnold, Charles Dickens, George Eliot, Joseph Conrad, and T. S. Eliot deal with and transmute conflicts at the heart of the general and authorial ideologies behind them: conflicts between morality and individualism, and between individualism and social organicism and utilitarianism.

As all this emphasis on ideology and conflict suggests, a modern British Marxist like Eagleton, even while acknowledging the work of a British Marxist predecessor like Williams, is more nearly developing the ideas of Continental Marxists like Althusser and Macherey. That holds, as well, for modern American Marxists like Fredric Jameson. For although he makes occasional, sympathetic references to the works of Williams, Thompson, and Hill, Jameson makes far more *use* of Lukács, Adorno, and Althusser as well as non-Marxist structuralist, psychoanalytic, and poststructuralist critics.

In the first of several influential works, *Marxism and Form* (1971), Jameson takes up the question of form and content, arguing that the former is "but the working out" of the latter "in the realm of superstructure" (329). (In making such a statement Jameson opposes not only the tenets of Russian formalists, for whom content had merely been the fleshing out of form, but also those of so-called vulgar Marxists, who tended to define form as mere ornamentation or windowdressing.) In his later work *The Political Unconscious* (1981), Jameson uses what in *Marxism and Form* he had called "dialectical criticism" to synthesize out of structuralism and poststructuralism, Freud and Lacan, Althusser and Adorno, a set of complex arguments that can only be summarized reductively.

The fractured state of societies and the isolated condition of individuals, he argues, may be seen as indications that there originally existed an unfallen state of something that may be called "primitive communism." History—which records the subsequent divisions and alienations—limits awareness of its own contradictions and of that lost,

Better State, via ideologies and their manifestation in texts whose strategies essentially contain and repress desire, especially revolutionary desire, into the collective unconscious. (In Conrad's *Lord Jim*, Jameson shows, the knowledge that governing classes don't *deserve* their power is contained and repressed by an ending that metaphysically blames Nature for the tragedy and that melodramatically blames wicked Gentleman Brown.)

As demonstrated by Jameson in analyses like the one mentioned above, textual strategies of containment and concealment may be discovered by the critic, but only by the critic practicing dialectical criticism, that is to say, a criticism aware, among other things, of its *own* status as ideology. All thought, Jameson concludes, is ideological; only through ideological thought that knows itself as such can ideologies be seen through and eventually transcended.

Patrick McGee begins the following essay, " 'Heavenly Bodies': *Ulysses* and the Ethics of Marxism," in a somewhat unusual, autobiographical mode, recounting his involvement in a radical Marxist group, the Spartacists, during the early 1970s. He also recalls the close questioning he endured from the group when he read *Ulysses*; in fact, his fellow revolutionaries questioned him not only about the appropriateness and value of Joyce's work but also of other books and movies they perceived as "bourgeois." McGee, a self-described housepainter's son, dropped out of the Spartacist League shortly thereafter and commenced the study of literary and cinematic art. He admits that, in so doing, he abandoned one world of illusion for another, but he also points out the difference between the consciously intended illusions of art and the unwitting ones embraced and perpetuated by political dogma.

McGee proceeds by quoting German Marxist Walter Benjamin's claim that "discretion concerning one's own existence, once an aristocratic virtue, has become more and more an affair of petty-bourgeois parvenus." Benjamin, McGee maintains, "saw a link between a Marxist vision of the world and certain monumental acts of indiscretion," that is, artistic works that "collapse the boundary between the personal and the social, the private and the public, the individual and the collective." McGee argues that Joyce produced just such a monumental act in *Ulysses*, "disclos[ing] with shocking indifference" everything from family secrets to bodily functions. In doing so, Joyce, though not a Maxist himself, placed art in the context of social and economic reality; to use broader and, more specifically, Marxist terminology, Joyce presented superstructure in terms of the economic base and prevailing means of production. Joyce also accomplished, in a radically creative way, what McGee hopes to accomplish critically by beginning and ending his reading of *Ulysses* with details of his own personal political history. McGee's "Heavenly Bodies" may not be the "monumental act of indiscretion" that *Ulysses* is, but its author does seek to be indiscreet in the Benjaminian sense of avoiding the "petty-bourgeois parvenus" of supposedly impersonal and objective political discourse.

McGee uses the Marxist notion that art mediates between the material and social world on one hand and the realm of the ideal on the other to explain that Joyce's *Ulysses* mediates "between bodily social existence and aesthetic form" by disclosing the relationship between the two. The body is explored or even rediscovered through linguistic mediation; conversely, language is shown to be invested with the imaginary value of bodily sensation. For instance, orgasmic delight pervades Gerty MacDowell's statement: "O so lovely, O, soft, sweet, soft!" And Stephen, McGee asserts, "speaks and writes in an effort to rediscover the body as a thing-in-itself, a thing that would be the ground of social change and that he identifies with the mother's womb as its point of origin."

McGee contrasts Stephen, who seeks to know the body through language, with Leopold Bloom, who "takes [the body] for granted and is much more interested in experiencing its different pleasures than in knowing its essence." For the "melancholic Stephen, art centers on the ego and makes the body—in this case, Stephen's body—into a symptom, the signifier of what it lacks in order to be whole." Bloom, by contrast, "subordinates his symbolic demand for love to his own physical needs and to the needs of those around him." The contrast McGee draws between the two characters is *not* meant to imply that "Bloom's relation to the body is natural, while Stephen's is unnatural or ideological." Rather, McGee seeks to show how "every character in *Ulysses* represents a limited vision of the social totality, whether it takes the form of Bloom's utopian fantasies in 'Circe' or Stephen's elitist disavowal of his sister's poverty in 'Wandering Rocks.'"

McGee's discussion of ideology is indebted not only to Terry Eagleton but, more significantly, to Louis Althusser's definition of ideology as "the imaginary relation of . . . individuals to the real relations in which they live" (165). In subsequently discussing the relation of the "imaginary" to the "real," McGee turns to the thought of French psychoanalytic theorist Jacques Lacan, who defined the imaginary and the real as two of the three "orders of subjectivity" (the third being the "symbolic"). Later, McGee applies Antonio Gramsci's concept of hegemony and, still later, Theodor Adorno's thought. He argues that "*Ulysses* is structured" by "a contradiction between the ideology of the aesthetic and the ideology of the body." Although "formally" the novel "is a pure expression of aesthetic ideology in so far as it posits itself as an autonomous work of art, what Adorno calls the 'windowless monad,'" it is "precisely as an autonomous whole, as an aesthetic body, that *Ulysses* manifests its materiality and reveals its commodity form as the form of its historical existence. *Ulysses* is what Adorno would call an absolute commodity, a social product which 'rids itself of the ideology inherent in the commodity form.'"

Unlike those Marxists who view Joyce ultimately as a traditionalist whose main interest is in literary forms and styles, McGee argues for the radical nature of Joyce's accomplishment. "There is no contradiction," he writes, "between Joyce's 'naturalism,' if you will, and his experiments with style. Joyce always insists on representing the unrepresentable, including the body's processes that have been disavowed by the norms of traditional literature and conventional culture." What makes Joyce's representations so revolutionary, McGee maintains, is the way they celebrate the pleasure Bloom takes in his bowel movement or that Gerty's language manifests rather than simply describing naturalistically "the process that would find its ideal version in a biology textbook." ("Joyce," McGee writes, "does not try to efface the gap between language and Gerty's 'real' orgasm (whatever that would be) in the manner of [D. H.] Lawrence. It isn't the orgasm that is Joyce's object of representation but the language that becomes charged with pleasure as its imaginary value.") Thus, "the styles of *Ulysses* and all of its technical innovations articulate the body not as something outside but immanent to representation," indeed, as the very "material basis of representation."

McGee concludes "Heavenly Bodies" by saying, "I don't know if it is appropriate for me to call myself a Marxist critic." He goes on to say, however, that he has "tried to model" his form of criticism on "the work of . . . Benjamin and Adorno"—not on their critical styles but, rather, on the "concept of constellation" that lies behind their work. According to that concept, the critic's job is to dismantle and reconfigure the components of a given text, thereby representing— and, in Eagleton's words, "redeeming"—the work's meaning and value.

But the appropriateness of referring to McGee as a Marxist critic is perhaps best belied by another statement, namely, that "Marxist or any other form of political criticism is not a substitute for political action:

it is a form of political action. . . . Critical practice occupies a position in a historical constellation of forces that must involve many other political and social positions. Within that constellation, there are many forms of action in which decisions have to be made—political decisions with implications for the lives of 'real' human beings. Even criticism requires a decision, and it is never simply an act of inconsequential free play."

Ross C Murfin

MARXIST CRITICISM: A SELECTED BIBLIOGRAPHY

Marx, Engels, Lenin, and Trotsky

Engels, Friedrich. *The Condition of the Working Class in England*. Ed. and trans. W. O. Henderson and W. H. Chaloner. Stanford: Stanford UP, 1968.

Lenin, V. I. *On Literature and Art*. Moscow: Progress, 1967.

Marx, Karl. *Selected Writings*. Ed. David McLellan. Oxford: Oxford UP, 1977.

Trotsky, Leon. *Literature and Revolution*. New York: Russell, 1967.

General Introductions to and Reflections on Marxist Criticism

Bennett, Tony. *Formalism and Marxism*. London: Methuen, 1979.

Demetz, Peter. *Marx, Engels, and the Poets*. Chicago: U of Chicago P, 1967.

Eagleton, Terry. *Literary Theory: An Introduction*. Minneapolis: U of Minnesota P, 1983.

———. *Marxism and Literary Criticism*. Berkeley: U of California P, 1976.

Elster, Jon. *An Introduction to Karl Marx*. Cambridge: Cambridge UP, 1985.

———. *Nuts and Bolts for the Social Sciences*. Cambridge: Cambridge UP, 1989.

Fokkema, D. W., and Elrud Kunne-Ibsch. *Theories of Literature in the Twentieth Century: Structuralism, Marxism, Aesthetics of Reception, Semiotics*. New York: St. Martin's, 1977. See ch. 4, "Marxist Theories of Literature."

Frow, John. *Marxism and Literary History.* Cambridge: Harvard UP, 1986.

Jefferson, Ann, and David Robey. *Modern Literary Theory: A Critical Introduction.* Totowa: Barnes, 1982. See the essay "Marxist Literary Theories," by David Forgacs.

Laing, Dave. *The Marxist Theory of Art.* Brighton, Eng.: Harvester, 1978.

Selden, Raman. *A Readers' Guide to Contemporary Literary Theory.* Lexington: U of Kentucky P, 1985. See ch. 2, "Marxist Theories."

Slaughter, Cliff. *Marxism, Ideology, and Literature.* Atlantic Highlands: Humanities, 1980.

Some Classic Marxist Studies and Statements

Adorno, Théodor. *Prisms: Cultural Criticism and Society.* Trans. Samuel Weber and Sherry Weber. Cambridge: MIT P, 1982.

Althusser, Louis. *For Marx.* Trans. Ben Brewster. New York: Pantheon, 1969.

Althusser, Louis, and Étienne Balibar. *Reading Capital.* Trans. Ben Brewster. New York: Pantheon, 1971.

Bakhtin, Mikhail. *The Dialogic Imagination: Four Essays.* Ed. Michael Holquist. Trans. Caryl Emerson. Austin: U of Texas P, 1981.

———. *Rabelais and His World.* Trans. Hélène Iswolsky. Cambridge: MIT P, 1968.

Benjamin, Walter. *Illuminations.* Ed. with introd. by Hannah Arendt. Trans. H. Zohn. New York: Harcourt, 1968.

Caudwell, Christopher. *Illusion and Reality.* 1935. New York: Russell, 1955.

———. *Studies in a Dying Culture.* London: Lawrence, 1938.

Goldmann, Lucien. *The Hidden God.* New York: Humanities, 1964.

———. *Towards a Sociology of the Novel.* London: Tavistock, 1975.

Gramsci, Antonio. *Selections from the Prison Notebooks.* Ed. Quintin Hoare and Geoffrey Nowell Smith. New York: International UP, 1971.

Kettle, Arnold. *An Introduction to the English Novel.* New York: Harper, 1960.

Lukács, Georg. *The Historical Novel.* Trans. H. Mitchell and S. Mitchell. Boston: Beacon, 1963.

———. *Studies in European Realism.* New York: Grosset, 1964.

———. *The Theory of the Novel.* Cambridge: MIT P, 1971.

Marcuse, Herbert. *One-Dimensional Man.* Boston: Beacon, 1964.

Thompson, E. P. *The Making of the English Working Class.* New York: Pantheon, 1964.

———. *William Morris: Romantic to Revolutionary.* New York: Pantheon, 1977.

Williams, Raymond. *Culture and Society 1780–1950.* New York: Harper, 1958.

———. *The Long Revolution.* New York: Columbia UP, 1961.

———. *Marxism and Literature.* Oxford: Oxford UP, 1977.

Wilson, Edmund. *To the Finland Station.* Garden City: Doubleday, 1953.

Studies by and of Post-Althusserian Marxists

Dowling, William C. *Jameson, Althusser, Marx: An Introduction to "The Political Unconscious."* Ithaca: Cornell UP, 1984.

Eagleton, Terry. *Criticism and Ideology: A Study in Marxist Literary Theory.* London: Verso, 1978.

———. *Exiles and Émigrés.* New York: Schocken, 1970.

Goux, Jean-Joseph. *Symbolic Economies after Marx and Freud.* Trans. Jennifer Gage. Ithaca: Cornell UP, 1990.

Jameson, Fredric. *Marxism and Form: Twentieth-Century Dialectical Theories of Literature.* Princeton: Princeton UP, 1971.

———. *The Political Unconscious: Narrative as a Socially Symbolic Act.* Ithaca: Cornell UP, 1981.

Macherey, Pierre. *A Theory of Literary Production.* Trans. G. Wall. London: Routledge, 1978.

Marxist Approaches to Joyce

Cheng, Vincent. *Joyce, Race, and Empire.* Cambridge: Cambridge UP, 1995.

Deane, Seamus. *Celtic Revivals: Essays in Modern Irish Literature, 1880–1980.* London: Faber, 1985.

Duffy, Enda. *The Subaltern "Ulysses."* Minneapolis: U of Minnesota P, 1994.

Eagleton, Terry, Fredric Jameson, and Edward W. Said. *Nationalism, Colonialism, and Literature.* Minneapolis: U of Minnesota P, 1990.

Herr, Cheryl. *Joyce's Anatomy of Culture.* Urbana: U of Illinois P, 1986.

Manganiello, Dominic. *Joyce's Politics.* London: Routledge, 1980.

McCormack, W. J., and Alistair Stead, eds. *James Joyce and Modern Literature*. London: Routledge, 1982.

McGee, Patrick. *Paperspace: Style as Ideology in Joyce's "Ulysses."* Lincoln: U of Nebraska P, 1988.

Moretti, Franco. *Signs Taken for Wonders: Essays in the Sociology of Literary Forms*. Trans. Susan Fisher, David Forgacs, and David Miller. London: Verso, 1983.

Segall, Jeffrey. *Joyce in America: Cultural Politics and the Trials of "Ulysses."* Berkeley: U of California P, 1993.

A MARXIST PERSPECTIVE

PATRICK McGEE

"Heavenly Bodies": *Ulysses* and the Ethics of Marxism

In the spring of 1970, right after the Kent State debacle, I went to New York City as a member of a left-wing organization known as the Spartacist League. I thought I was a dedicated Marxist, a Trotskyite, and an almost fanatical believer in the injustice of the capitalist system. On a personal level, I blamed everything negative in my life—the violence I associated with my working-class background—on the system that I had every desire to change "by any means necessary." Once in New York, I did odd jobs, painted apartments, and eventually took a position at a post office in lower Manhattan that had just recently been the scene of a wildcat strike. I gave half of my salary to "the organization," as we called it, and I can't recall a moment's hesitation on that account. After some months, however, I began to have other doubts. Why was it that the daughter of a Fifth Avenue millionaire was the one member of our group entitled to earn a degree in comparative literature at New York University? Why was I, the son of a housepainter, discouraged from seeking more education and expected to become a foot soldier for the revolution? I must admit that I had no in-depth analysis of the gender relations in that organization, except for an utterly superficial commitment to women's liberation (as long as it did not conflict with the class struggle). When I finally left, I did so for many reasons, most of them having to do with my desire for an education. But one incident in particular has stuck in my memory.

From the late summer to the early fall of 1970, I read *Ulysses* for the first time. I could not possibly say what I got out of that book with the help of a Webster's dictionary, but my reading created an incident within the organization that certainly made me suspicious of my comrades' intentions with respect to my future. In a casual way, my roommate mentioned to the organization's head that I was reading Joyce; and the next thing you know I was called into the office for discussions of socialism and art, gentle admonitions about reading books that might be over my head, and not so subtle queries about whatever it was that might have leaked into my head from Joyce's writing. The word "bourgeois" was prominent in these discussions. Before long, one member of the group, the one I had already picked out as the future Stalin, wanted a list of every book I had read and every film I had seen for the last six months. Fortunately, shortly after this request was made, I started working the night shift at the post office and virtually dropped out of sight. A few months later, weary of dogmatism and illusions that did not know themselves as such, I left New York.

Many literary critics would probably question the purpose of the last two paragraphs. In my defense, I will quote this remark from the writing of Walter Benjamin: "Discretion concerning one's own existence, once an aristocratic virtue, has become more and more an affair of petty-bourgeois parvenus" (228). Benjamin probably would have thought twice about this statement in the age of Oprah and Donahue; but he nonetheless saw a link between a Marxist vision of the world and certain monumental acts of indiscretion, which he identified with the works of the surrealists. This view refers, I believe, to the tendency of such art to collapse the boundary between the personal and the social, the private and the public, the individual and the collective. In a sense, Marxism anticipated the feminist claim that the personal is political, though in this case the personal means the ideology of the bourgeois subject. Today indiscretions about class, race, gender, and sexual orientation threaten the stability of social institutions that thrive on the denial that such differences have any consequences for the quality of life and demand for social justice. Though "race," "gender," and "sexual orientation" have become key signifiers in the discourse of cultural difference (and the first two have entered into demands for economic justice under the rubric of affirmative action), wealth inequity as a system, which determines the specific attributes of these categories in any particular context, tends to undergo a "disavowal" as to its effects; it has even found a new source of legitimacy in the general distribution of tokens, who would seem to prove the overall justice of the claim that there is equal opportunity.

Still, I don't want to create the impression that my departure from New York was a simple move from illusion to truth. When I left behind one form of illusion in 1970, I knew perfectly well that I was probably going to dedicate my life to another form, to the study of those literary works and films that were also illusions, but with this difference: they knew it. I did not have any theory about that knowledge at the time, but I think I arrived at some elementary understanding of materialist art through Joyce. For me, *Ulysses* was the most monumental act of indiscretion I had ever come across. It was only later that I came to know how recklessly but ingeniously Joyce used the most minute details of his own life in *Ulysses* and in every other work that he wrote. He disclosed with shocking indifference the intimate secrets of his father and mother, his brothers and sisters, his wife and even (in *Finnegans Wake*) his children. He did not spare schoolmasters, friends, casual acquaintances, possible lovers, former students, and every conceivable representative of state authority. In a sense, everything in Joyce's books happened to Joyce.

But long before I knew enough about Joyce's life and historical context to appreciate his complete lack of discretion in the above respect, I was stunned by another indiscretion in his work. Leopold Bloom defecates in private and manages to masturbate in public without being completely visible (though I think at least one person sees what he is doing); Molly Bloom menstruates after recreating in her mind the intimate details of sexual intercourse with Blazes Boylan; Stephen Dedalus may masturbate while leaning against a rock on the beach (as some have argued, though I did not see that in 1970 and don't see it now) and certainly urinates on the beach and then picks his nose while looking around to see who has seen. In other words, Joyce's first indiscretion was the admission of the human body into literature—not the idealized body we get in the work of D. H. Lawrence but the "real" human body that is usually reduced to so many biological processes. Only the Marquis de Sade can be said to have fully anticipated Joyce, though Joyce evades the moral law that is the ironic condition of Sadean pleasure in cruelty. Joyce accepts the body as a thing that resists even as it shapes value and representation, and even morality.

When I later appreciated the extent of Joyce's indiscretions, I also realized that the body was the key to all of them. In *A Portrait of the Artist as a Young Man*, Stephen Dedalus picks lice off the back of his neck as a prelude to a long disquisition on art. The relation between Stephen's material poverty and his aesthetic idealizations lies in the Marxist term *mediation*, which sometimes carries some of the same value as the psychoanalytic term *sublimation*. If *Portrait* presents Stephen's theory as a distorted expression or disavowal of his material conditions, *Ulysses* could be said to demonstrate a more positive view of mediation as a process that does not hide but discloses the relationship between bodily social existence and aesthetic form. In the "Proteus" episode, Stephen's body is present by virtue of its absence from the language that articulates it. The body is like Proteus, the sea god who constantly changes his form, because its material reality can only reach us through the mediations of language and other forms of symbolic representation. Whatever the body may be as a thing-in-itself, as a construction of history it reaches Stephen as a linguistic representation (as opposed to Bloom's more visual imagination); and he can contact and possibly change it only through the same means: "His lips lipped and mouthed fleshless lips of air: mouth to her moomb. Oomb, allwombing tomb. His mouth moulded issuing breath, unspeeched: ooeeehah: roar of cataractic planets, globed, blazing, roaring wayaway-awayawayaway. Paper" (*U* 3.401–04). Stephen speaks and writes in an effort to rediscover the body as a thing-in-itself, a thing that would be the ground of social change and that he identifies with the mother's womb as its point of origin.

The reader should note that for Stephen speech, writing, and perception itself, though they are distinguishable, share a common structure, which he identifies with the curiously materialist idealism of the philosopher Berkeley: "The good bishop of Cloyne took the veil of the temple out of his shovel hat: veil of space with coloured emblems hatched on its field" (*U* 3.416–18). Though Berkeley was an idealist who saw nothing beyond the veil except the presence of God, for Joyce the veil is more like the trace of the body, its cultural form. Later Stephen fantasizes about the body of a man who drowned in Dublin Bay: "Bag of corpsegas sopping in foul brine. A quiver of minnows, fat of a spongy titbit, flash through the slits of his buttoned trouserfly. God becomes man becomes fish becomes barnacle goose becomes featherbed mountain" (*U* 3.476–79). Death is the most critical signifier of bodily existence because only in the destruction of the body do we become aware of something beyond our representations, something beyond death itself as a signifier that cannot be subjected to any cultural norm or value. Stephen's God, or the "Chewer of corpses" (*U* 1.278), is not so much death as the material process that concludes

life but the thing that lies beyond process, the thing to which we give
the name "matter" or "God" though it is really nothing in itself except the condition that we infer from its symbolic mediations in the
process of becoming or history. The body as thing is neither human
nor divine but the fundamental emptiness onto which those values can
be projected.

Joyce's exploration of the body through its symbolic mediations in
a particular historical location is the remarkable indiscretion that saves
him from being just another one of those "petty-bourgeois parvenus"
Benjamin refers to. It is not only Stephen's body that interests Joyce;
neither is it only the other prominent bodies in *Ulysses*. Leopold and
Molly Bloom, of course, and scores of minor characters, whose bodies
we come to know almost intimately. Blazes Boylan's genitals, Lydia
Douce's thigh, Simon Dedalus's thumbnail, Father Cowley's earlobes,
Gerty MacDowell's hair, Nosey Flynn's nose, and so forth: at every
turn in *Ulysses* the reader is confronted by the body and its processes,
including its pains and its pleasures. But underlying all these individual
bodies is the suggestion of the larger bodily formation that Joyce
hinted at in the schema he put together for Stuart Gilbert. Joyce suggested an organ or body part for each episode of *Ulysses* after "Proteus," which suggests that Stephen is in some sense absent from his
own body as the signifier of this larger social body, though he desperately seeks it somewhere in the vast network of symbolic forms that
constitute his social identity. Leopold Bloom, on the other hand,
though his body is no less mediated, takes it for granted and is much
more interested in experiencing its different pleasures than in knowing
its essence. One could argue, after Michel Foucault, that Stephen is
the prisoner of sex as a discursive formation. He is captured by

> this desirability of sex that attaches each one of us to the injunc-
> tion to know it, to reveal its law and its power; it is this desirability
> that makes us think we are affirming the rights of our sex against
> all power, when in fact we are fastened to the deployment of sexu-
> ality that has lifted up from deep within us a sort of mirage in
> which we think we see ourselves reflected—the dark shimmer of
> sex. (156–57)

Stephen stands in the tradition of D. H. Lawrence and the romantic
dream of sexual experience as a form of spiritual transfiguration.
Bloom, by contrast, anticipates Foucault's critique of the whole modern discourse of sex / desire (though later I will question this use of
the term *desire*): "The rallying point for the counterattack against the

deployment of sexuality ought not to be sex-desire, but bodies and pleasures" (157). Bloom does not seek so much to *know* the body in the manner of Stephen and Lawrence as to *experience* it through its multiple pleasures. He eats, defecates, masturbates, and voyeuristically devours the world with his eye (and, in this context, it is no accident that Stephen has broken his glasses and cannot see [*U* 15.3628–29]). Perhaps more important, though, Bloom never understands his body as something detached from the bodies that surround him; he never isolates his needs from the needs of the community of bodies through which he circulates like a blood cell through the human circulatory system (a metaphor made flesh in "Wandering Rocks"). *Ulysses* begins with a mock mass in which Buck Mulligan parodies the transubstantiation of "body and soul and blood and ouns," though he has a "little trouble about those white corpuscles" (*U* 1.21–23). Bloom repeats this gesture at the end of "Lotus-Eaters" with the simple phrase, "This is my body." Neither transubstantiation nor transfiguration is the issue in this case but the anticipation of bodily pleasure in bathing: "He foresaw his pale body reclined in it at full, naked, in a womb of warmth, oiled by scented melting soap, softly laved" (*U* 5.567–68).

I don't mean to imply, of course, that Bloom's relation to the body is natural, while Stephen's is unnatural or ideological. As literary constructions, both characters are deeply implicated in and determined by ideological structures or discourses. As Terry Eagleton demonstrates, however, the term *ideology* is notoriously difficult to get a handle on and cannot be pinned down to one meaning. He cites at least six possible definitions derived from the history of Western Marxism, and they all could have a bearing on our reading of *Ulysses*. First, ideology is the "general material process of production of ideas, beliefs and values in social life"; and as a character it is Bloom who most thoroughly foregrounds this process as the very condition of what we call his endless and indiscriminate "stream of consciousness." Second, it is the system of ideas and beliefs of "a specific, socially significant group or class." From this perspective, every character in *Ulysses* represents a limited vision of the social totality, whether it takes the form of Bloom's utopian fantasies in "Circe" or Stephen's elitist disavowal of his sister's poverty in "Wandering Rocks." A third definition of ideology refers to "the *promotion* and *legitimation* of the interests of such social groups in the face of opposing interests," which includes a fourth meaning referring exclusively to "the activities of a dominant social power." Practically every page of *Ulysses* contains some symbol of the dominance of Britain over Ireland, including "His Majesty's

vermilion mailcars" at the opening of "Aeolus" (*U* 7.16). These symbols, along with the many signifiers of class distinction and power, reinforce forms of social dominance by virtue of their insertion into an
everyday reality that becomes a sort of second nature. The fifth definition involves the legitimation of such dominant interests explicitly by
"distortion and dissimulation." Sixth and finally, such "false or decep-
tive beliefs" can be defined as "arising . . . from the material structure
of society as a whole" (*Ideology: An Introduction* 28–30). *Ulysses* is almost an encyclopedia of the social distortions (of women, Jews, the
Irish, blacks, vagrants, revolutionaries, and so forth) that facilitate the
system of exclusions by which most societies tend to operate. Nevertheless, I believe that all of these meanings can be derived from a
broad interpretation of Louis Althusser's definition of ideology as "the
imaginary relation of . . . individuals to the real relations in which they
live" (*For Marx* 231). The use of this definition need not force one to
accept a rigid distinction between ideology and science, with which
many have faulted Althusser's structural Marxism, if one understands
the term "imaginary" in its psychoanalytic sense as one of three critical
registers: imaginary, real, and symbolic. The symbolic is the cultural
system with its storehouse of representations; the imaginary is how we
construct meanings out of those representations; and the real is what
every representation leaves behind as the remainder of its meaning, as
the impossibility of the absolute closure of the system.

   In the work of Lacan, from which Althusser takes the term, the
imaginary is not the simple antithesis of the real but rather the realm
of meaning itself, which always requires the arbitrary closure of the
process of signification. At the risk of oversimplifying, one could think
of the symbolic as the material structure of language and everything
that can signify like a language, a structure that belies the term "structure" since it is in a state of constant flux or process. It is the material
condition of meaning, the potential for signification in the finite,
though always expanding, storehouse of sounds, graphic marks, and
visual images that are the traces of historical process itself. The imaginary is the arbitrary closure of that process, the means by which one
signifier is subordinated to another in the effort to pin down or
capture a piece of the real. If the symbolic is the historical chain of
signifiers, then the imaginary is the act of meaning–production that in-
terrupts or momentarily breaks that chain. Though the imaginary
closes in on the real as the object of its signification, it never reaches it
because the signifier never escapes its own historicity as a moment or
discrete unit in an open process. One could say that the signifier can

never make contact with the real as the absolute object of signification, that is, its absolute other, because it is also a piece of the real, a thing-in-itself. The real can only be known as that which the imaginary misses, as that which cannot be symbolized, as the historical limit of any possible meaning.

From these observations, it should be clear why the Joycean body is curiously present by virtue of its absence. There is no contradiction between Joyce's "naturalism," if you will, and his experiments with style. Joyce always insists on representing the unrepresentable, including the body's processes that have been disavowed by the norms of traditional literature and conventional culture. The reader can only approach the body as a thing-in-itself by deconstructing the signifiers that invest the body with meanings in a cultural context. In representing Bloom's act of defecation at the end of "Calypso," Joyce does not produce a naturalistic description of the process that would find its ideal version in a biology textbook. Rather, he represents the pleasure Bloom takes from the act, a pleasure that can never be fully anchored in the thing itself because it derives from the organization of signifiers into imaginary meanings and values. Of his bowel movement, Bloom thinks, "Life might be so. It did not move or touch him but it was something quick and neat" (U 4.511–12). Similarly, in "Nausicaa," Joyce does not try to efface the gap between language and Gerty's "real" orgasm (whatever that would be) in the manner of Lawrence. It isn't the orgasm that is Joyce's object of representation but the language that becomes charged with pleasure as its imaginary value. It is Gerty's (or this cultural symptom's) investment of imaginary value in the system of language that she inherits from her social context and that points toward something real, a thing in excess of meaning: "O so lovely, O, soft, sweet, soft!" (U 13.740).

None of the three terms I have discussed—imaginary, symbolic, real—is privileged over the others; rather, they are implicated in one another in the form of a knot. Consequently, the imaginary should be thought of as a "lived relation" to the real, as a historically determined construction of reality through a specific organization of the symbolic. It may be that Althusser understands by the term "real relations" the classical Marxist concept of the base as the relations of production that constitute "the economic structure of society, the real foundation," and by the term "imaginary relations" the concept of the superstructure, or the "social, political and intellectual life process in general" (Marx and Engels, 182). Still, he gives to the superstructure its own relative autonomy, which means that his concept of the social totality tends to slide over into a formation resembling what the Italian Marxist, Antonio Gramsci, calls "hegemony." Raymond Williams has defined hegemony, in its broadest terms, as "a whole body of practices and expectations" and "a lived system of meanings and values" that, taken as a whole, constitute "a sense of reality for most people in the society." It is "a 'culture,' but a culture which has also to be seen as the lived dominance and subordination of particular classes." From this perspective, concludes Williams, cultural practices and ideological systems are no longer a superstructure but "are among the basic processes of the formation itself and, further, related to a much wider area of reality than the abstractions of 'social' and 'economic' experience" (110-11).

The concept of hegemony enables one to grasp the relation between base and superstructure as a whole process. Though the economy is crucial to the understanding of any society, it is not possible to explain all forms of consciousness as expressions of economic interests. Still, since Marx's critique of capitalism is historical, it necessarily works on the assumption that capitalist hegemony identifies a particular economic structure as the privileged expression of human nature and uses that claim to explain and justify capitalist social relations and cultural values. For this reason, Althusser quite properly identifies the economic mode of production as the "*determination in the last instance*" of an overdetermined capitalist culture (*For Marx* 111). But the capitalist economy itself would not have been able to become the hegemonic norm that it is without producing and colonizing ideologies and other forms of social practice. It follows that the real relations of a society that in some sense exceed the imaginary or "lived" relations cannot be reduced to the economic structure but are the whole material basis of culture. They are the body of culture that would include the real "bodies" of human beings and all the things that make up culture but that we can only know by virtue of their absence, by the failure of our representations to capture the real as a thing-in-itself. This body is the open-ended and irreducible structure of capitalist society and of history itself as a "process without a subject or a *telos*" (Althusser, *Lenin and Philosophy* 162). One can say that the real relations are the body of capitalist culture only if the "body" is understood as the thing that resists symbolization, that exceeds every meaning or interpretation—in other words, as what Fredric Jameson calls, in an interpretation of Althusser's concept of structural causality, the "absent cause" (Jameson, "On Interpretation"). This cause is absent, however, only in the sense that it is irreducible. It is the absolute material limit of any interpretation or construction of value. It is the limit that can be known only as a structural absence, as the historical finitude of any fixed meaning or lived relation to the world. In my view, this irreducible body is the object of Joyce's creation in *Ulysses* and the reason behind his insistence on the autonomy of the signifier, the privileging of style as ideology over any reductive view of the real as a simple given.

From this perspective, one can distinguish between Stephen's and Bloom's relations to the body without presuming that the difference in question is between a real and an ideological relation. Both viewpoints are ideological or imaginary relations to the real, but they nevertheless articulate a difference in the lived relation to the body that makes a difference. Bloom may represent the "petty-bourgeois" side of Joyce, but his relation to his own body figures a relation to the social body that presupposes the intersubjective ground of bodily existence. According to Eagleton, Marx believed "human powers and human society are an absolute end in themselves. To live well is to live in the free, many-sided realization of one's capacities, in reciprocal interaction with the similar self-expression of others" (*Ideology of the Aesthetic* 226). Still, the last part of this statement lays a restriction on human self-realization, which Eagleton identifies as the "foundation of a communist ethics": "The discriminatory norm in question is that we should foster only those particular powers which allow an individual to realize herself through and in terms of the similar free self-realization of others" (224). In Eagleton's view, this utopian vision is what Marxism owes to the aesthetic tradition going back to the eighteenth century and to Hegel in particular.

Joyce self-consciously participates in that tradition, though the difference between Stephen and Bloom points to a change in his own relation to the aesthetic between *Portrait* and *Ulysses*. For the melancholic Stephen, art centers on the ego and makes the body—in this case, Stephen's body—into a symptom, the signifier of what it lacks in order to be whole. The symptom articulates the demand for absolute meaning through the process of a compromise formation. In other words, the body as symptom is a compromise formation because it substitutes for the real an image of the body derived from ideology. As Lacan notes, "A symptom is the return by means of signifying substitution of that which is at the end of the drive in the form of an aim" (110). In *Ulysses*, the aim of Stephen's drive, the aim he will not surrender, is death; and the image of the body that dominates his consciousness, culminating in the image of his mother, is the body in death. Language as the material of art is the means by which he keeps this aim alive, though the aesthetic pleasure he takes from it depends on his ignorance, since, as Slavoj Žižek notes, "the subject can 'enjoy his symptom' only in so far as its logic escapes him" (21). In other words, the disinterested pleasure of the Kantian aesthetic, with which we can associate Stephen's aesthetic theory in *Portrait*, is simply the repression of the knowledge of desire. Though the image of Stephen's dead mother has become the articulation of his symptom, he projects onto her imaginary existence the repulsion that covers over and makes it possible for him to enjoy the real aim of his drive.

Bloom's mode of being in *Ulysses* suggests a relation to the aesthetic as a form of sublimation. For Lacan, sublimation is not, as it may have been for Freud, simply another kind of compromise formation. It refers to the "paradoxical fact that the drive is able to find its aim elsewhere than in that which is its aim—without its being a question of the signifying substitution that constitutes the overdetermined structure, the ambiguity, and the double causality, of the symptom as compromise formation" (110). Bloom may seem naive in his obsession with physical pleasure and in the utopian desires that emerge from his unconscious in the dream world of "Circe": "New worlds for old. Union of all, jew, moslem and gentile. . . . Free money, free rent, free love and a free lay church in a free lay state" (*U* 15.1685–93). In his more sober or conscious state of mind, he seems less optimistic about the future but no less concerned with the body of the other. Death may have its own attractions for Bloom, and the Circean unconscious spews out his fantasies of public immolation and private suicide (*U* 15.1930–37, 15.1964–68). In the context of a culture that is still dominated by Judeo-Christian values, death should be thought of as the aim of a collective drive; but the act of sublimation makes possible the ethical gesture of changing that aim, of surrendering the impossible demand for what calls itself love but secretly harbors the wish for the finality of death. In Lacanian terminology, demand is a symbolic articulation aimed at satisfying a need such as nourishment or sex, though we should not be led by this distinction into imagining that the need is transparent or self-evident. We can only infer the existence of needs through the representations of demands. As the demand is symbolic, something in it always exceeds the immediate necessities of the real and calls for the experience of absolute satisfaction. The only way to escape this absolute demand and satisfy an immediate need is to call up desire, which is a relation to the other, a compromise with reality that enables one to focus on a limited object that can never produce an absolute experience of satisfaction. Throughout *Ulysses*, Bloom subordinates his symbolic demand for love to his own physical needs and to the needs of those around him. Whether he feeds Molly or Stephen, the family cat or the stray dog; whether he contributes to the support of Paddy Dignam's widow or to the mental health of Mrs. Breen; whether he identifies with Mina Purefoy in labor or just helps the blind stripling across the street—in one way or another, Bloom is always thinking of the other's body and of the body as the other. Of course, Bloom also uses the other's body for his own pleasures; and, ideologically speaking, he is very much a creature of the world he lives in. Though he sees Dublin as the body of the other, it is a gendered body, "the womancity, nude, white, still, cool, in luxury"; and his utopia, or the "new Bloomusalem," takes the form of an animal body part with which he likes to satisfy his physical appetite, "a colossal edifice with crystal roof, built in the shape of a huge pork kidney" (*U* 15.1327–28, 1548–49). Even as he cares for the other, Bloom takes pleasure and pain from the other's body as from his own. It is as if these bodies were indistinguishable.

"Art," writes Eagleton, "is a form of creative surplus, a radical exceeding of necessity; in Lacanian terminology, it is what remains when need is subtracted from demand" (*Ideology of the Aesthetic* 204). In other words, art is the articulation of desire as the force that releases need from the tyranny of demand. Desire is something in excess of the body's needs, but it also protects the body from the destructive effects of the drive that translates physical need into symbolic demand. The drive is an absolute excess that could bring about total devastation since it seeks the final satisfaction of needs in their total extinction. The capitalist can never make too much profit, the consumer can never own too many goods, the politician can never have enough power, the philanderer can never have too many lovers, and so forth. The Lacanian terminology that Eagleton employs may not be transhistorical or universal, but it does seem to describe accurately enough the historical context from which it has emerged. It describes a capitalist system that has unleashed what Horkheimer and Adorno called instrumental reason as, if I may extrapolate, a form of reason fully in the service of an absolute demand for the domination of the physical world, even to the point of death. The only force that interferes with this process, that inhibits all the final solutions from the death camps to the nuclear arsenals, is desire as the absolute condition that can be laid upon unconditional demand. Demand destroys the other—including the body as an/other—because the other bars access to the experience of absolute satisfaction; desire, by contrast, gives ground to the other as the source of a compromise. Desire is never simply *my* desire but always the desire of the other. Unlike demand, which seeks an unmediated and absolute experience, desire is always mediated and substitutes for such an experience a socially determined goal. It comes from the other to the other; and one name for the other, in my view, is the body itself, not in its individuality but as a collective process. Thus, I would change Foucault's formulation of the "deployment of sexuality" as sex/desire in this way. It is not desire that fails to oppose the deployment of sexuality, for it is only desire that enables the body to experience pleasures that do not kill it. It is, rather, sex/demand, that is, sexual knowledge as the answer to the impossible demand of the drive. In *Ulysses*, Stephen makes a sexual demand that destroys the possibility of any relationship, sexual or otherwise, with a real person and drives him toward the place of his mother, the place of death. Bloom, on the other hand, evades demand by pursuing a series of objects and bodily pleasures that finally lead him back to his place with Molly. This is not the place of final satisfaction but, if you will, the place of the postponement of satisfaction, the suspension of demand in the vagaries of desire.

As a work of art, *Ulysses* is structured by the contradiction between the demand for absolute meaning and the desire that exceeds meaning as its material condition. It is a contradiction between the symptom as a compromise formation that keeps returning to the aim of the drive and the sublime object of desire that represents a change of aim as the possibility of ethical action. It is a contradiction between the ideology of the aesthetic and the ideology of the body. Formally, *Ulysses* is a pure expression of aesthetic ideology insofar as it posits itself as an autonomous work of art, what Adorno calls the "windowless monad." Its formal structure and the freedom of its stylistic play produces the illusion of historical transcendence, most profoundly registered in the systematic referencing of Homer's epic. The result, as Eagleton argues, is that "reality is coded to its roots, as the ephemeral working through of some deeper logic invisible to the naked eye, and randomness is accordingly banished" (*Ideology of the Aesthetic* 317). As such a reworking of the real, a process that reduces it to a totalized and universal meaning, *Ulysses* effectively becomes an aesthetic commodity, one that has erased the history of its production in a field of socially determined interests. It is a compromise formation or symptom of the real insofar as it posits itself as the imaginary resolution of the contradictions of real history. An Ireland colonized and dominated by an external power is transformed into a timeless present that transcends every historical specificity, including the language in which it is written. English is no longer the language of the colonizer but the neutral medium of a universal vision. Joyce proves that he can do anything with language as he proceeds to divorce the signifier from any necessary connection to the real. From this perspective, the work of art is what Bloom and Stephen become in "Ithaca": in Joyce's own words, they are "heavenly bodies, wanderers like the stars at which they gaze" (*Selected Letters* 278). *Ulysses* is such a heavenly or aesthetic body; and its language, like the stars, is "a mobility of illusory forms immobilised in space" (*U* 17.1143).

Yet, on this very note, the contradiction asserts itself. For it is precisely as an autonomous whole, as an aesthetic body, that *Ulysses* manifests its materiality and reveals its commodity form as the form of its historical existence. *Ulysses* is what Adorno would call an absolute commodity, a social product which "rids itself of the ideology inherent in the commodity form. The latter pretends that it is a being-for-other whereas in truth it is only for itself—that is, for the ruling interests of society" (336). In other words, as an absolute commodity, a work of art is always to some extent anti-art and subversive of its own relation to the order of aesthetic values. If I may rephrase Adorno's formulation, such art rids itself of the illusion that it expresses universal interests that lie beyond the particular interests of a social configuration of power. It discloses the institutional nature of art and its affirmative relation to hegemony, which would include "the lived dominance and subordination of particular classes" (Williams 110). Art can do this, ironically, because it never completely rids itself of ideology. As Adorno qualifies his own theory, "alas, even as an absolute commodity art has retained its commercial value, becoming a 'natural monopoly.' . . . It is possible that completely non-ideological art is entirely unfeasible" (336). Art never fully transcends its status as a commodity and a symptom of commodity culture. Yet, for that very reason, it is able to disclose the truth of the aesthetic commodity, its illusory form and the irreducible social body it reveals as the absent cause of its representations. Art rids itself of ideology by giving us a view of ideology that, in Althusser's words, "presupposes a *retreat*, an *internal distantiation*" (*Lenin and Philosophy* 204). Adorno takes one step beyond Althusser to recognize that this internal distance is art's self-contradiction.

"The collective," writes Benjamin, "is a body, too" (239). *Ulysses* posits that body as the absent cause of its exploration of style as ideology, as a mediation or lived relation to the real. But this body is absent not in the sense that it is somewhere else, an object external to language that language somehow represents. If understood in this way, such a sublime object of ideology, according to Žižek, would be "an embodiment of Nothing" (206). The real body—or rather the real itself—is not absent because it is elsewhere but because it is immanent to the thing itself. In other words, the styles of *Ulysses* and all of its technical innovations articulate the body not as something outside but immanent to representation. It is the material basis of representation, the fact that language and all other forms of representation are made up of something real, something in them more than them. Žižek describes "that strange body in my interior which is 'in me more than me,' which is radically interior and [at] the same time already exterior" (181). That strange body lies at the heart of Joyce's linguistic rearrangement of the world. It is the material force that connects the body of Joyce's text with the body of the world; and though it is nothing in itself, it is this collective body that must be liberated from the mode of production and all the ideological practices that enable the mode of production to become a cultural norm. It must be liberated from the tyranny of any single interpretation whether that interpretation takes the form of moral law, social convention, or human nature. It must be liberated not because in itself it embodies human freedom but because it is the condition of human freedom. It is the condition of those ideological practices that may be thought of as the practice of freedom. As Benjamin speculates about the collective body, "the *physis* that is being organized for it in technology can, through all its political and factual reality, only be produced in the image sphere to which profane illumination initiates us" (239). The image sphere is the realm of ideology, and only in ideology can the collective body, conditioned by technology, come to fruition as a new social reality. Joyce's *Ulysses* refuses to answer our demand for that new social reality even as it makes it possible to desire it. It does not substitute an imaginary for a historical reality, as some have argued, but insists that we confront the imaginary relation to the world, our interpretation of it, as a limit on the possibilities of human freedom, as a limit on our relation to the real.

As I argued earlier, for Stephen language as the material of art is the symptom of the body he misses. For Bloom, though he only has "a touch of the artist" (*U* 10.582), language is a function of the body itself. Stephen seeks an answer to his absolute demand for love from that mysterious feminine figure to whom he addresses this question in "Proteus": "What is that word known to all men?" (*U* 3.435). The answer to that question, though it may be "love," as some have argued, really signifies death. Stephen may begin to realize and resist this meaning in "Circe" when his mother becomes a green crab and "*sticks deep its grinning claws in Stephen's heart*" (*U* 15.4220–21). Stephen runs away from the image of his mother but cannot escape the death drive that brings him back to the place she occupies when he is knocked to the ground by a British soldier. To the imperialist system that the soldier represents, Stephen can only make the demand that the death drive compels him to make. In effect, Stephen imagines the object of love as a plenitude, a total fulfillment, and the absolute extinction of need and desire. It is as if Stephen did not know, first, that he is a body and, second, that a body can never know fulfillment before death except through an identification with the desire of the other. This identification is the key to Bloom and the ground of his ethical being. Though he knows that his wife has been unfaithful to him (however much he may exaggerate the degree of that infidelity), he does not act. He subordinates his own demand for love (which is always determined within the framework of culture by ideology) to the desire of the other as the structure of his own desire. As Eagleton summarizes the lessons of Freud for Marxist ethics:

> The one I love may not be able to give me the imaginary plenitude I seek, but she can at least give me the most real thing she has, namely her own desire for the same plenitude. We give each other our desire, which is to say exactly that which neither of us can fulfill in the other. To say "I love you" thus becomes equivalent to saying "It's *you* who can't satisfy me!" How privileged and unique I must be, to remind you that it isn't me you want . . .
> (*Ideology of the Aesthetic* 279)

I can think of nothing in literature that so powerfully exemplifies this economy of desire than the relationship between Leopold and Molly Bloom. They have not had complete carnal intercourse for "10 years, 5 months and 18 days" or complete mental intercourse since their daughter's "consummation of puberty" (*U* 17.2282–88). Their relationship is hardly ideal in the romantic sense or reciprocal in socioeconomic terms. Still, it could be taken as a model for a Marxist ethics of the body, not in the sense that it celebrates some sort of full self-realization of human powers but in the sense that it allows for the possibility of human freedom under the rule of desire as the absolute condition of unconditional demand. Such a freedom, of course, is relative to the desire of the other, which means that it is restricted by and limited to the necessity of compromise and negotiation as an ongoing political practice. It avoids the bad utopianism that, in Eagleton's view, "grabs instantly for a future, projecting itself by an act of will or imagination beyond the compromised political structures of the present." Without attending to these structures and what I would call the "real" body of the present, including the aesthetic bodies of works like *Ulysses*, such a bad utopianism "is in danger of persuading us to desire uselessly rather than feasibly, and so, like the neurotic, to fall ill with longing." Such utopianism answers to unconditional demand without the mediation of sublimated desire; and the same is true of that brand of social determinism that offers a future that is "inevitable but not necessarily desirable." Against both naive desire and political dogmatism, Eagleton suggests that "'value' must be somehow extrapolable from 'fact,' the outline of a future worth struggling for discerned within the practices of the degraded present" (*Ideology of the Aesthetic* 229). In my view, *Ulysses* aims at just this sort of "profane illumination" of the collective human body; it is what Stephen calls in the "Nestor" episode "an actuality of the possible as possible" (*U* 2.67).

It has been twenty-five years since I first read *Ulysses*, and I have become what no one in the political organization I referred to earlier either imagined or desired that I should become: a literary critic. I don't know if it is appropriate for me to call myself a Marxist critic, but I have tried to model my style of criticism on the work of two very problematic Marxists: Benjamin and Adorno. I don't mean that I emulate their styles (which I could not do), but I have tried to grasp within my own work the concept of constellation that governs their critical practices. That concept, according to Eagleton, posits

> a form of criticism so tenaciously immanent that it would remain entirely immersed in its object. The truth of that object would be disclosed not by referring it in rationalist style to a governing general idea, but by dismantling its component elements through the power of minutely particular concepts, then reconfigurating them in a pattern which redeemed the thing's meaning and value without ceasing to adhere to it. (*Ideology of the Aesthetic* 328)

This technique is not one that I can simply apply to Joyce, since I believe that the concept of constellation accurately describes Joyce's own approach to literary construction in *Ulysses* and *Finnegans Wake*. Joyce articulates the reality of colonial Ireland and the possibility of a postcolonial Ireland through the configuration of minute particulars, including those particulars that constitute the desires of the people. As a critic, I have never seen any *necessary* contradiction between this approach and the technique of deconstruction as it is practiced in the work of Jacques Derrida. As I suggested in my early work on Joyce, deconstruction and psychoanalysis should be considered advanced forms of ideology-critique, and I have always tried to incorporate them into that sort of analysis.

Marxist or any other form of political criticism is not a substitute for political action: *it is a form of political action*. But once this fact is recognized, it should become clear that no single form of political action is ever enough. Critical practice occupies a position in a historical constellation of forces that must involve many other political and social positions. Within that constellation, there are many forms of action in which decisions have to be made—political decisions with implications for the lives of "real" human beings. Even criticism requires a decision, and it is never simply an act of inconsequential free play. In every political act, there is a moment of commitment in which the political decision must be made; but there is also a responsibility that lies beyond commitment, an ethical responsibility to the desire of the other. This responsibility entails the refusal of dogmatism in every context, no matter how seductive, no matter how justified it may appear to be. In my view, it requires the refusal of a Manichean division of the world into the absolutely good and the absolutely evil. Today, after twenty-five years, I am as critical of the injustices of the capitalist system as I was in 1970. But I don't think the resolution of that injustice can be reduced to a simple formula. It will require, at the very least, the creation of a new socialist ethic as the foundation of a new collective social body that cannot be legislated or dynamited into existence. As Eagleton paraphrases the thought of Benjamin, in the production of this ethic and this body, "the function of the critic is to fashion those images by which humanity can assume this unfamiliar flesh" (336). For me, that "unfamiliar flesh" first made itself visible in the pages of *Ulysses*.

WORKS CITED

Adorno, Theodor. *Aesthetic Theory.* Trans. C. Lenhardt. Ed. Gretel Adorno and Rolf Tiedemann. London: Routledge, 1984.

Althusser, Louis. *For Marx.* Trans. Ben Brewster. New York: Pantheon, 1969.

————. *Lenin and Philosophy.* Trans. Ben Brewster. London: NLB, 1974.

Benjamin, Walter. "Surrealism: The Last Snapshot of the European Intelligentsia." *One-Way Street and Other Writings.* Trans. Edmund Jephcott and Kingsley Shorter. London: NLB, 1979. 225–239.

Eagleton, Terry. *The Ideology of the Aesthetic.* Oxford: Basil Blackwell, 1990.

————. *Ideology: An Introduction.* London: Verso, 1991.

Foucault, Michel. *The History of Sexuality.* Trans. Robert Hurley. Vol. 1. *An Introduction.* New York: Vintage, 1980.

Horkheimer, Max, and Theodor W. Adorno. *Dialectic of Enlightenment.* Trans. John Cumming. New York: Continuum, 1987.

Jameson, Fredric. "On Interpretation." *The Political Unconscious: Narrative as a Socially Symbolic Act.* Ithaca: Cornell UP, 1981.

Joyce, James. *Selected Letters.* Ed. Richard Ellmann. New York: Viking, 1975.

Lacan, Jacques. *The Ethics of Psychoanalysis 1959–1960.* Trans. Dennis Porter. New York: Norton, 1992. Book 7 of *The Seminar.*

Marx, Karl, and Frederick Engels. *Selected Works.* New York: International, 1968.

Williams, Raymond. *Marxism and Literature.* Oxford: Oxford UP, 1977.

Žižek, Slavoj. *The Sublime Object of Ideology.* London: Verso, 1989.

Glossary of Critical
and Theoretical Terms

Most terms have been glossed parenthetically where they first appear in the text. Mainly, the glossary lists terms that are too complex to define in a phrase or a sentence or two. A few of the terms listed are discussed at greater length elsewhere (*feminist criticism,* for instance); these terms are defined succinctly and a page reference to the longer discussion is provided.

AFFECTIVE FALLACY First used by William K. Wimsatt and Monroe C. Beardsley to refer to what they regarded as the erroneous practice of interpreting texts according to the psychological responses of readers. "The Affective Fallacy," they wrote in a 1946 essay later republished in *The Verbal Icon* (1954), "is a confusion between the poem and its *results* (what it *is* and what it *does*). . . . It begins by trying to derive the standards of criticism from the psychological effects of a poem and ends in impressionism and relativism." The affective fallacy, like the intentional fallacy (confusing the meaning of a work with the author's expressly intended meaning), was one of the main tenets of the New Criticism, or formalism. The affective fallacy has recently been contested by reader-response critics, who have deliberately dedicated their efforts to describing the way individual readers and "interpretive communities" go about "making sense" of texts.

See also: Authorial Intention, Formalism, Reader-Response Criticism.

AUTHORIAL INTENTION Defined narrowly, an author's intention in writing a work, as expressed in letters, diaries, interviews, and conversations. Defined more broadly, "intentionality" involves unexpressed motivations, designs, and purposes, some of which may have remained unconscious.

The debate over whether critics should try to discern an author's intentions (conscious or otherwise) is an old one. William K. Wimsatt and Monroe C. Beardsley, in an essay first published in the 1940s, coined the term "intentional fallacy" to refer to the practice of basing interpretations on the expressed or implied intentions of authors, a practice they judged to be erroneous. As proponents of the New Criticism, or formalism, they argued that a work of literature is an object in itself and should be studied as such. They believed that it is sometimes helpful to learn what an author intended, but the critic's real purpose is to show what is actually in the text, not what an author intended to put there.

See also: Affective Fallacy, Formalism.

BASE   *See* Marxist Criticism.

BINARY OPPOSITIONS   *See* Oppositions.

BLANKS   *See* Gaps.

CANON   Since the fourth century, used to refer to those books of the Bible that the Christian church accepts as being Holy Scripture. The term has come to be applied more generally to those literary works given special status, or "privileged," by a culture. Works we tend to think of as "classics" or the "Great Books" produced by Western culture—texts that are found in every anthology of American, British, and world literature—would be among those that constitute the canon.

Recently, Marxist, feminist, minority, and postcolonial critics have argued that, for political reasons, many excellent works never enter the canon. Canonized works, they claim, are those that reflect—and respect—the culture's dominant ideology and/or perform some socially acceptable or even necessary form of "cultural work." Attempts have been made to broaden or redefine the canon by discovering valuable texts, or versions of texts, that were repressed or ignored for political reasons. These have been published both in traditional and in nontraditional anthologies. The most outspoken critics of the canon, especially radical critics practicing cultural criticism, have called into question the whole concept of canon or "canonicity." Privileging no form of artistic expression that reflects and revises the culture, these critics treat cartoons, comics, and soap operas with the same cogency and respect they accord novels, poems, and plays.

See also: Cultural Criticism, Feminist Criticism, Ideology, Marxist Criticism.

CONFLICTS, CONTRADICTIONS   *See* Gaps.

CULTURAL CRITICISM   A critical approach that is sometimes referred to as "cultural studies" or "cultural critique." Practitioners of cultural criticism oppose "high" definitions of culture and take seriously popular cultural forms. Grounded in a variety of continental European influences, cultural criticism nonetheless gained institutional force in England, in 1964, with the founding of the Centre for Contemporary Cultural Studies at Birmingham University. Broadly interdisciplinary in its scope and approach, cultural criticism views the text as the locus and catalyst of a complex network of political and economic discourses. Cultural critics share with Marxist critics an interest in the ideological contexts of cultural forms.

DECONSTRUCTION A poststructuralist approach to literature that is strongly influenced by the writings of the French philosopher Jacques Derrida. Deconstruction, partly in response to structuralism and formalism, posits the undecidability of meaning for all texts. In fact, as the deconstructionist critic J. Hillis Miller points out, "deconstruction is not a dismantling of the structure of a text but a demonstration that it has already dismantled itself." *See* "What Is Deconstruction?" pp. 47–64.

DIALECTIC Originally developed by Greek philosophers, mainly Socrates and Plato, as a form and method of logical argumentation; the term later came to denote a philosophical notion of evolution. The German philosopher G. W. F. Hegel described dialectic as a process whereby a thesis, when countered by an antithesis, leads to the synthesis of a new idea. Karl Marx and Friedrich Engels, adapting Hegel's idealist theory, used the phrase "dialectical materialism" to discuss the way in which a revolutionary class war might lead to the synthesis of a new social economic order. The American Marxist critic Fredric Jameson has coined the phrase "dialectical criticism" to refer to a Marxist critical approach that synthesizes structuralist and poststructuralist methodologies. *See also:* Marxist Criticism, Poststructuralism, Structuralism.

DIALOGIC *See* Discourse.

DISCOURSE Used specifically, can refer to (1) spoken or written discussion of a subject or area of knowledge; (2) the words in, or text of, a narrative as opposed to its story line; or (3) a "strand" within a given narrative that argues a certain point or defends a given value system.

More generally, "discourse" refers to the language in which a subject or area of knowledge is discussed or a certain kind of business is transacted. Human knowledge is collected and structured in discourses. Theology and medicine are defined by their discourses, as are politics, sexuality, and literary criticism.

A society is generally made up of a number of different discourses or "discourse communities," one or more of which may be dominant or serve the dominant ideology. Each discourse has its own vocabulary, concepts, and rules, knowledge of which constitutes power. The psychoanalyst and psychoanalytic critic Jacques Lacan has treated the unconscious as a form of discourse, the patterns of which are repeated in literature. Cultural critics, following Mikhail Bakhtin, use the word "dialogic" to discuss the dialogue *between* discourses that takes place within language or, more specifically, a literary text. *See also:* Cultural Criticism, Ideology, Narrative, Psychoanalytic Criticism.

FEMINIST CRITICISM An aspect of the feminist movement whose primary goals include critiquing masculine-dominated language and literature by showing how they reflect a masculine ideology; writing the history of unknown or undervalued women writers, thereby earning them their rightful place in the literary canon; and helping create a climate in which women's creativity may be fully realized and appreciated. *See* "What Are Feminist and Gender Criticism?" pp. 129–43.

FIGURE *See* Metaphor, Metonymy, Symbol.

FORMALISM Also referred to as the New Criticism, formalism reached its height during the 1940s and 1950s, but it is still practiced today.

Formalists treat a work of literary art as if it were a self-contained, self-referential object. Rather than basing their interpretations of a text on the reader's response, the author's stated intentions, or parallels between the text and historical contexts (such as the author's life), formalists concentrate on the relationships *within* the text that give it its own distinctive character or form. Special attention is paid to repetition, particularly of images or symbols, but also of sound effects and rhythms in poetry.

Because of the importance placed on close analysis and the stress on the text as a carefully crafted, orderly object containing observable formal patterns, formalism has often been seen as an attack on Romanticism and impressionism, particularly impressionistic criticism. It has sometimes even been called an "objective" approach to literature. Formalists are more likely than certain other critics to believe and say that the meaning of a text can be known objectively. For instance, reader-response critics see meaning as a function either of each reader's experience or of the norms that govern a particular "interpretive community," and deconstructors argue that texts mean opposite things at the same time.

Formalism was originally based on essays written during the 1920s and 1930s by T. S. Eliot, I. A. Richards, and William Empson. It was significantly developed later by a group of American poets and critics, including R. P. Blackmur, Cleanth Brooks, John Crowe Ransom, Allen Tate, Robert Penn Warren, and William K. Wimsatt. Although we associate formalism with certain principles and terms (such as the "Affective Fallacy" and the "Intentional Fallacy" as defined by Wimsatt and Monroe C. Beardsley), formalists were trying to make a cultural statement rather than establish a critical dogma. Generally southern, religious, and culturally conservative, they advocated the inherent value of literary works (particularly of literary works regarded as beautiful art objects) because they were sick of the growing ugliness of modern life and contemporary events. Some recent theorists even suggest that the rising popularity of formalism after World War II was a feature of American isolationism, the formalist tendency to isolate literature from biography and history being a manifestation of the American fatigue with wider involvements.

See also: Affective Fallacy, Authorial Intention, Deconstruction, Reader-Response Criticism, Symbol.

GAPS   When used by reader-response critics familiar with the theories of Wolfgang Iser, refers to "blanks" in texts that must be filled in by readers. A gap may be said to exist whenever and wherever a reader perceives something to be missing between words, sentences, paragraphs, stanzas, or chapters. Readers respond to gaps actively and creatively, explaining apparent inconsistencies in point of view, accounting for jumps in chronology, speculatively supplying information missing from plots, and resolving problems or issues left ambiguous or "indeterminate" in the text.

Reader-response critics sometimes speak as if a gap actually exists in a text; a gap is, of course, to some extent a product of readers' perceptions. Different readers may find gaps in different texts, and different gaps in the same text. Furthermore, they may fill these gaps in different ways, which is why, a reader-response critic might argue, works are interpreted in different ways.

Although the concept of the gap has been used mainly by reader-response critics, it has also been used by critics taking other theoretical approaches.

Practitioners of deconstruction might use "gap" when speaking of the radical contradictoriness of a text. Marxists have used the term to speak of everything from the gap that opens up between economic base and cultural superstructure to the two kinds of conflicts or contradictions to be found in literary texts. The first of these, they would argue, results from the fact that texts reflect ideology, within which certain subjects cannot be covered, things cannot be said, contradictory views cannot be recognized as contradictory. The second kind of conflict, contradiction, or gap within a text results from the fact that works don't just reflect ideology; they are also fictions that, consciously or unconsciously, distance themselves from the same ideology.

See also: Deconstruction, Ideology, Marxist Criticism, Reader-Response Criticism.

GENDER CRITICISM Developing out of feminist criticism in the mid-1980s, this fluid and inclusive movement by its nature defies neat definition. Its practitioners include, but are not limited to, self-identified feminists, gay and lesbian critics, queer and performance theorists, and poststructuralists interested in deconstructing oppositions such as masculine/feminine, heterosexual/homosexual. This diverse group of critics shares an interest in interrogating categories of gender and sexuality and exploring the relationships between them, though it does not necessarily share any central assumptions about the nature of these categories. For example, some gender critics insist that all gender identities are cultural constructions, but others have maintained a belief in essential gender identity. Often gender critics are more interested in examining gender issues through a literary text than a literary text through gender issues. See "What Are Feminist and Gender Criticism?" pp. 129–43.

GENRE A French word referring to a kind or type of literature. Individual works within a genre may exhibit a distinctive form, be governed by certain conventions, and/or represent characteristic subjects. Tragedy, epic, and romance are all genres.

Perhaps inevitably, the term *genre* is used loosely. Lyric poetry is a genre, but so are characteristic *types* of the lyric, such as the sonnet, the ode, and the elegy. Fiction is a genre, as are detective fiction and science fiction. The list of genres grows constantly as critics establish new lines of connection between individual works and discern new categories of works with common characteristics. Moreover, some writers form hybrid genres by combining the characteristics of several in a single work. Knowledge of genres helps critics to understand and explain what is conventional and unconventional, borrowed and original, in a work.

HEGEMONY Given intellectual currency by the Italian communist Antonio Gramsci, the word (a translation of *egemonia*) refers to the pervasive system of assumptions, meanings, and values—the web of ideologies, in other words—that shapes the way things look, what they mean, and therefore what reality *is* for the majority of people within a given culture.

See also: Ideology, Marxist Criticism.

IDEOLOGY A set of beliefs underlying the customs, habits, and/or practices common to a given social group. To members of that group, the beliefs seem obviously true, natural, and even universally applicable. They may seem just as obviously arbitrary, idiosyncratic, and even false to outsiders or members of another group who adhere to another ideology. Within a society, several ideologies may coexist, or one or more may be dominant.

Ideologies may be forcefully imposed or willingly subscribed to. Their component beliefs may be held consciously or unconsciously. In either case, they come to form what Johanna M. Smith has called "the unexamined ground of our experience." Ideology governs our perceptions, judgments, and prejudices—our sense of what is acceptable, normal, and deviant. Ideology may cause a revolution; it may also allow discrimination and even exploitation.

Ideologies are of special interest to sociologically oriented critics of literature because of the way in which authors reflect or resist prevailing views in their texts. Some Marxist critics have argued that literary texts reflect and reproduce the ideologies that produced them; most, however, have shown how ideologies are riven with contradictions that works of literature manage to expose and widen. Still other Marxists have focused on the way in which texts themselves are characterized by gaps, conflicts, and contradictions between their ideological and anti-ideological functions.

Feminist critics have addressed the question of ideology by seeking to expose (and thereby call into question) the patriarchal ideology mirrored or inscribed in works written by men—even men who have sought to counter sexism and break down sexual stereotypes. New historicists have been interested in demonstrating the ideological underpinnings not only of literary representations but also of our interpretations of them. Fredric Jameson, an American Marxist critic, argues that all thought is ideological, but that ideological thought that knows itself as such stands the chance of seeing through and transcending ideology.

See also: Cultural Criticism, Feminist Criticism, Marxist Criticism, New Historicism.

IMAGINARY ORDER One of the three essential orders of the psychoanalytic field (*see* Real and Symbolic Order), it is most closely associated with the senses (sight, sound, touch, taste, and smell). The infant, who by comparison to other animals is born premature and thus is wholly dependent on others for a prolonged period, enters the Imaginary order when it begins to experience a unity of body parts and motor control that is empowering. This usually occurs between six and eighteen months, and is called by Lacan the "mirror stage" or "mirror phase," in which the child anticipates mastery of its body. It does so by identifying with the *image* of wholeness (that is, seeing its own image in the mirror, experiencing its mother as a whole body, and so on). This sense of oneness, and also difference from others (especially the mother or primary caretaker), is established through an image or a vision of harmony that is both a mirroring and a "mirage of maturation" or false sense of individuality and independence. The Imaginary is a metaphor for unity, is related to the visual order, and is always part of human subjectivity. Because the subject is fundamentally separate from others and also internally divided (conscious/unconscious), the apparent coherence of the Imaginary, its fullness and grandiosity, is always false, a *mis*recognition that the ego (or "me") tries to deny by imagining itself as coherent and empowered. The Imaginary operates in conjunction with the Real and Symbolic and is not a "stage" of development equivalent to Freud's "pre-oedipal stage," nor is it prelinguistic.

See also: Psychoanalytic Criticism, Real, Symbolic Order.

IMPLIED READER   A phrase used by some reader-response critics in place of the phrase "the reader." Whereas "the reader" could refer to any idiosyncratic individual who happens to have read or to be reading the text, "the implied reader" is *the* reader intended, even created, by the text. Other reader-response critics seeking to describe this more generally conceived reader have spoken of the "informed reader" or the "narratee," who is "the necessary counterpart of a given narrator."

See also: Reader-Response Criticism.

INTENTIONAL FALLACY   *See* Authorial Intention.

INTENTIONALITY   *See* Authorial Intention.

INTERTEXTUALITY   The condition of interconnectedness among texts. Every author has been influenced by others, and every work contains explicit and implicit references to other works. Writers may consciously or unconsciously echo a predecessor or precursor; they may also consciously or unconsciously disguise their indebtedness, making intertextual relationships difficult for the critic to trace.

Reacting against the formalist tendency to view each work as a freestanding object, some poststructuralist critics suggested that the meaning of a work emerges only intertextually, that is, within the context provided by other works. But there has been a reaction, too, against this type of intertextual criticism. Some new historicist critics suggest that literary history is itself too narrow a context and that works should be interpreted in light of a larger set of cultural contexts.

There is, however, a broader definition of intertextuality, one that refers to the relationship between works of literature and a wide range of narratives and discourses that we don't usually consider literary. Thus defined, intertextuality could be used by a new historicist to refer to the significant interconnectedness between a literary text and nonliterary discussions of or discourses about contemporary culture. Or it could be used by a poststructuralist to suggest that a work can be recognized and read only within a vast field of signs and tropes that is *like* a text and that makes any single text self-contradictory and "undecidable."

See also: Discourse, Formalism, Narrative, New Historicism, Poststructuralism, Trope.

MARXIST CRITICISM   An approach that treats literary texts as material products, describing them in broadly historical terms. In Marxist criticism, the text is viewed in terms of its production and consumption, as a product *of* work that does identifiable cultural work of its own. Following Karl Marx, the founder of communism, Marxist critics have used the terms *base* to refer to economic reality and *superstructure* to refer to the corresponding or "homologous" infrastructure consisting of politics, law, philosophy, religion, and the arts. Also following Marx, they have used the word *ideology* to refer to that set of cultural beliefs that literary works at once reproduce, resist, and revise.

See also: "What Is Marxist Criticism?" pp. 203–17.

METAPHOR   The representation of one thing by another related or similar thing. The image (or activity or concept) used to represent or "figure" something else is known as the "vehicle" of the metaphor; the thing represented is called the "tenor." In other words, the vehicle is what we substitute for the tenor. The relationship between vehicle and tenor can provide much additional meaning. Thus, instead of saying, "Last night I read a book," we might say, "Last night I plowed through a book." "Plowed through" (or the activity of plowing) is the vehicle of our metaphor; "read" (or the act of reading) is the tenor, the thing being figured. The increment in meaning through metaphor is fairly obvious. Our audience knows not only *that* we read but also *how* we read, because to read a book in the way that a plow rips through earth is surely to read in a relentless, unreflective way. Note that in the sentence above, a new metaphor—"rips through"—has been used to explain an old one. This serves (which is a metaphor) as an example of just how thick (another metaphor) language is with metaphors!

Metaphor is a kind of "trope" (literally, a "turning," that is, a figure of speech that alters or "turns" the meaning of a word or phrase). Other tropes include allegory, conceit, metonymy, personification, simile, symbol, and synecdoche. Traditionally, metaphor and symbol have been viewed as the principal tropes; minor tropes have been categorized as *types* of these two major ones. Similes, for instance, are usually defined as simple metaphors that usually employ *like* or *as* and state the tenor outright, as in "My love is like a red, red rose." Synecdoche involves a vehicle that is a *part* of the tenor, as in "I see a sail" meaning "I see a boat." Metonymy is viewed as a metaphor involving two terms commonly if arbitrarily associated with (but not fundamentally or intrinsically related to) each other. Recently, however, deconstructors such as Paul de Man and J. Hillis Miller have questioned the "privilege" granted to metaphor and the metaphor/metonymy distinction or "opposition." They have suggested that all metaphors are really metonyms and that all figuration is arbitrary.

See also: Deconstruction, Metonymy, Oppositions, Symbol.

METONYMY   The representation of one thing by another that is commonly and often physically associated with it. To refer to a writer's handwriting as his or her "hand" is to use a metonymic "figure" or "trope." The image or thing used to represent something else is known as the "vehicle" of the metonym; the thing represented is called the "tenor."

Like other tropes (such as metaphor), metonymy involves the replacement of one word or phrase by another. Liquor may be referred to as "the bottle," a monarch as "the crown." Narrowly defined, the vehicle of a metonym is arbitrarily, not intrinsically, associated with the tenor. In other words, the bottle just happens to be what liquor is stored in and poured from in our culture. The hand may be involved in the production of handwriting, but so are the brain and the pen. There is no special, intrinsic likeness between a crown and a monarch; it's just that crowns traditionally sit on monarchs' heads and not on the heads of university professors. More broadly, *metonym* and *metonymy* have been used by recent critics to refer to a wide range of figures and tropes. Deconstructors have questioned the distinction between metaphor and metonymy.

See also: Deconstruction, Metaphor, Trope.

NARRATIVE   A story or a telling of a story, or an account of a situation or of events. A novel and a biography of a novelist are both narratives, as are Freud's case histories.

Some critics use the word *narrative* even more generally; Brook Thomas, a new historicist, has critiqued "narratives of human history that neglect the role human labor has played."

NEW CRITICISM *See* Formalism.

NEW HISTORICISM First practiced and articulated in the late 1970s and early 1980s in the work of critics such as Stephen Greenblatt— who named this movement in contemporary critical theory—and Louis Montrose, its practitioners share certain convictions, primarily that literary critics need to develop a high degree of historical consciousness and that literature should not be viewed apart from other human creations, artistic or otherwise. They share a belief in referentiality—a belief that literature refers to and is referred to by things outside itself—that is fainter in the works of formalist, poststructuralist, and even reader-response critics. Discarding old distinctions between literature, history, and the social sciences, new historicists agree with Greenblatt that the "central concerns" of criticism "should prevent it from permanently sealing off one type of discourse from another, or decisively separating works of art from the minds and lives of their creators and their audiences."

See also: Authorial Intention, Deconstruction, Formalism, Ideology, Poststructuralism, Psychoanalytic Criticism.

OPPOSITIONS A concept highly relevant to linguistics, inasmuch as linguists maintain that words (such as *black* and *death*) have meaning not in themselves but in relation to other words (*white* and *life*). Jacques Derrida, a poststructuralist philosopher of language, has suggested that in the West we think in terms of these "binary oppositions" or dichotomies, which on examination turn out to be evaluative hierarchies. In other words, each opposition— beginning/end, presence/absence, or consciousness/unconsciousness—contains one term that our culture views as superior and one term that we view as negative or inferior.

Derrida has "deconstructed" a number of these binary oppositions, including two—speech/writing and signifier/signified—that he believes to be central to linguistics in particular and Western culture in general. He has concurrently critiqued the "law" of noncontradiction, which is fundamental to Western logic. He and other deconstructors have argued that a text can contain opposed strands of discourse and, therefore, can mean opposite things: reason *and* passion, life *and* death, hope *and* despair, black *and* white. Traditionally, criticism has involved choosing between opposed or contradictory meanings and arguing that one is present in the text and the other absent.

French feminists have adopted the ideas of Derrida and other deconstructors, showing not only that we think in terms of such binary oppositions as male/female, reason/emotion, and active/passive, but that we also associate reason and activity with masculinity and emotion and passivity with femininity. Because of this, they have concluded that language is "phallocentric," or masculine-dominated.

See also: Deconstruction, Discourse, Feminist Criticism, Poststructuralism.

PHALLUS The symbolic value of the penis that organizes libidinal development and which Freud saw as a stage in the process of human subjectivity. Lacan viewed the Phallus as the representative of a fraudulent power (male over female) whose "Law" is a principle of psychic division (conscious/unconscious) and sexual difference (masculine/feminine). The Symbolic order (*see* Symbolic Order) is ruled by the Phallus, which of itself has no inherent meaning *apart from* the power and meaning given to it by individual cultures and societies, and represented by the name of the father as lawgiver and namer.

POSTSTRUCTURALISM   The general attempt to contest and subvert structuralism initiated by deconstructors and certain other critics associated with psychoanalytic, Marxist, and feminist theory. Structuralists, using linguistics as a model and employing semiotic (sign) theory, posit the possibility of knowing a text systematically and revealing the "grammar" behind its form and meaning. Poststructuralists argue against the possibility of such knowledge and description. They counter that texts can be shown to contradict not only structuralist accounts of them but also themselves. In making their adversarial claims, they rely on close readings of texts and on the work of theorists such as Jacques Derrida and Jacques Lacan.

Poststructuralists have suggested that structuralism rests on distinctions between "signifier" and "signified" (signs and the things they point toward), "self" and "language" (or "text"), texts and other texts, and text and world that are overly simplistic, if not patently inaccurate. Poststructuralists have shown how all signifieds are also signifiers, and they have treated texts as "intertexts." They have viewed the world as if it *were* a text (we desire a certain car because it *symbolizes* achievement) and the self as the subject, as well as the user, of language; for example, we may shape and speak through language, but it also shapes and speaks through us.

See also: Deconstruction, Feminist Criticism, Intertextuality, Psychoanalytic Criticism, Semiotics, Structuralism.

PSYCHOANALYTIC CRITICISM   Grounded in the psychoanalytic theories of Sigmund Freud, it is one of the oldest critical methodologies still in use. Freud's view that works of literature, like dreams, express secret, unconscious desires led to criticism and interpreted literary works as manifestations of the authors' neuroses. More recently, psychoanalytic critics have come to see literary works as skillfully crafted artifacts that may appeal to *our* neuroses by tapping into our repressed wishes and fantasies. Other forms of psychological criticism that diverge from Freud, although they ultimately derive from his insights, include those based on the theories of Carl Jung and Jacques Lacan. *See* "What Is Psychoanalytic Criticism?" pp. 169–81.

READER-RESPONSE CRITICISM   An approach to literature that, as its name implies, considers the way readers respond to texts as they read. Stanley Fish describes the method by saying that it substitutes for one question, "What does this sentence mean?" a more operational question, "What does this sentence do?" Reader-response criticism shares with deconstruction a strong textual orientation and a reluctance to define a single meaning for a work. Along with psychoanalytic criticism, it shares an interest in the dynamics of mental response to textual cues. *See* "What Is Reader-Response Criticism?" pp. 91–103.

REAL   One of the three orders of subjectivity (*see* Imaginary Order and Symbolic Order), the Real is the intractable and substantial world that resists and exceeds interpretation. The Real cannot be imagined, symbolized, or known directly. It constantly eludes our efforts to name it (death, gravity, the physicality of objects are examples of the Real), and thus challenges both the Imaginary and the Symbolic orders. The Real is fundamentally "Other," the mark of the divide between conscious and unconscious, and is signaled in language by gaps, slips, speechlessness, and the sense of the uncanny. The Real is not what we call "reality." It is the stumbling block of the Imaginary (which thinks it can "imagine" anything, including the Real) and of the Symbolic, which tries to bring the Real under its laws (the Real exposes the "phallacy" of the Law of the Phallus). The Real is frightening; we try to tame it with laws and language and call it "reality."

See also: Imaginary Order, Psychoanalytic Criticism, Symbolic Order.

SEMIOLOGY, SEMIOTIC   See Semiotics.

SEMIOTICS   The study of signs and sign systems and the way meaning is derived from them. Structuralist anthropologists, psychoanalysts, and literary critics developed semiotics during the decades following 1950, but much of the pioneering work had been done at the turn of the century by the founder of modern linguistics, Ferdinand de Saussure, and the American philosopher Charles Sanders Peirce.

Semiotics is based on several important distinctions, including the distinction between "signifier" and "signified" (the sign and what it points toward) and the distinction between "langue" and "parole." *Langue* (French for "tongue," as in "native tongue," meaning language) refers to the entire system within which individual utterances or usages of language have meaning; *parole* (French for "word") refers to the particular utterances or usages. A principal tenet of semiotics is that signs, like words, are not significant in themselves, but instead have meaning only in relation to other signs and the entire system of signs, or langue.

The affinity between semiotics and structuralist literary criticism derives from this emphasis placed on langue, or system. Structuralist critics, after all, were reacting against formalists and their procedure of focusing on individual words as if meanings didn't depend on anything external to the text.

Poststructuralists have used semiotics but questioned some of its underlying assumptions, including the opposition between signifier and signified. The feminist poststructuralist Julia Kristeva, for instance, has used the word *semiotic* to describe feminine language, a highly figurative, fluid form of discourse that she sets in opposition to rigid, symbolic masculine language.

See also: Deconstruction, Feminist Criticism, Formalism, Oppositions, Poststructuralism, Structuralism, Symbol.

SIMILE   See Metaphor.

SOCIOHISTORICAL CRITICISM   See New Historicism.

STRUCTURALISM   A science of humankind whose proponents attempted to show that all elements of human culture, including literature, may be understood as parts of a system of signs. Structuralism, according to Robert Scholes, was a reaction to "'modernist' alienation and despair."

Using Ferdinand de Saussure's linguistic theory, European structuralists such as Roman Jakobson, Claude Lévi-Strauss, and Roland Barthes (before his shift toward poststructuralism) attempted to develop a "semiology" or "semiotics" (science of signs). Barthes, among others, sought to recover literature and even language from the isolation in which they had been studied and to show that the laws that govern them govern all signs, from road signs to articles of clothing.

Particularly useful to structuralists were two of Saussure's concepts: the idea of "phoneme" in language and the idea that phonemes exist in two kinds of relationships: "synchronic" and "diachronic." A phoneme is the smallest consistently significant unit in language; thus, both "a" and "an" are phonemes, but "n" is not. A diachronic relationship is that which a phoneme has with those that have preceded it in time and those that will follow it. These "horizontal" relationships produce what we might call discourse or narrative and what Saussure called "parole." The synchronic relationship is the "vertical" one that a word has in a given instant with the entire system of language ("langue") in which it may generate meaning. "An" means what it means in English because those of us who speak the language are using it in the same way at a given time.

Following Saussure, Lévi-Strauss studied hundreds of myths, breaking them into their smallest meaningful units, which he called "mythemes." Removing each from its diachronic relations with other mythemes in a single myth (such as the myth of Oedipus and his mother), he vertically aligned those mythemes that he found to be homologous (structurally correspondent). He then studied the relationships within as well as between vertically aligned columns, in an attempt to understand scientifically, through ratios and proportions, those thoughts and processes that humankind has shared, both at one particular time and across time. One could say, then, that structuralists followed Saussure in preferring to think about the overriding langue or language of myth, in which each mytheme and mytheme-constituted myth fits meaningfully, rather than about isolated individual paroles or narratives. Structuralists followed Saussure's lead in believing what the poststructuralist Jacques Derrida later decided he could not subscribe to—that sign systems must be understood in terms of binary oppositions. In analyzing myths and texts to find basic structures, structuralists tended to find that opposite terms modulate until they are finally resolved or reconciled by some intermediary third term. Thus, a structuralist reading of *Paradise Lost* would show that the war between God and the bad angels becomes a rift between God and sinful, fallen man, the rift then being healed by the Son of God, the mediating third term.

See also: Deconstruction, Discourse, Narrative, Poststructuralism, Semiotics.

SUPERSTRUCTURE   *See* Marxist Criticism.

SYMBOL   A thing, image, or action that, although it is of interest in its own right, stands for or suggests something larger and more complex—often an idea or a range of interrelated ideas, attitudes, and practices.

Within a given culture, some things are understood to be symbols: the flag of the United States is an obvious example. More subtle cultural symbols might be the river as a symbol of time and the journey as a symbol of life and its manifold experiences.

Instead of appropriating symbols generally used and understood within their culture, writers often create symbols by setting up, in their works, a complex but identifiable web of associations. As a result, one object, image, or action suggests others, and often, ultimately, a range of ideas.

A symbol may thus be defined as a metaphor in which the "vehicle," the thing, image, or action used to represent something else, represents many related things (or "tenors") or is broadly suggestive. The urn in Keats's "Ode on a Grecian Urn" suggests many interrelated concepts, including art, truth, beauty, and timelessness.

Symbols have been of particular interest to formalists, who study how meanings emerge from the complex, patterned relationships between images in a work, and psychoanalytic critics, who are interested in how individual authors and the larger culture both disguise and reveal unconscious fears and desires through symbols. Recently, French feminists have also focused on the symbolic. They have suggested that, as wide-ranging as it seems, symbolic language is ultimately rigid and restrictive. They favor semiotic language and writing, which, they contend, is at once more rhythmic, unifying, and feminine.

See also: Feminist Criticism, Metaphor, Psychoanalytic Criticism, Trope.

SYMBOLIC ORDER   One of the three orders of subjectivity (*see* Imaginary Order and Real), it is the realm of law, language, and society; it is the repository of generally held cultural beliefs. Its symbolic system is language, whose agent is the father or lawgiver, the one who has the power of naming. The human subject is commanded into this preestablished order by language (a process that begins long before a child can speak) and must submit to its orders of communication (grammar, syntax, and so on). Entrance into the Symbolic order determines subjectivity according to a primary law of referentiality that takes the male sign (phallus; *see* Phallus) as its ordering principle. Lacan states that both sexes submit to the Law of the Phallus (the law of order, language, and differentiation) but their individual relation to the law determines whether they see themselves as—and are seen by others to be—either "masculine" or "feminine." The Symbolic institutes repression (of the Imaginary), thus creating the unconscious, which itself is structured like the language of the symbolic. The unconscious, a timeless realm, cannot be known directly, but it can be understood by a kind of translation that takes place in language—psychoanalysis is the "talking cure." The Symbolic is not a "stage" of development (as is Freud's "oedipal stage"), nor is it set in place once and for all in human life. We constantly negotiate its threshold (in sleep, in drunkenness) and can "fall out" of it altogether in psychosis.

See also: Imaginary Order, Psychoanalytic Criticism, Real.

SYNECDOCHE   *See* Metaphor, Metonymy.

TENOR   *See* Metaphor, Metonymy, Symbol.

TROPE   A figure, as in "figure of speech." Literally a "turning," that is, a turning or twisting of a word or phrase to make it mean something else. Principal tropes include metaphor, metonymy, personification, simile, and synecdoche.

See also: Metaphor, Metonymy.

VEHICLE   *See* Metaphor, Metonymy, Symbol.

About the Contributors

THE VOLUME EDITOR

Margot Norris is professor of English and Comparative Literature at the University of California, Irvine. She is author of two books on Joyce, *The Decentered Universe of "Finnegans Wake"* (1976) and *Joyce's Web: The Social Unraveling of Modernism* (1992), and a book on modern intellectual history, *Beasts of the Modern Imagination: Darwin, Nietzsche, Kafka, Ernst, and Lawrence* (1985). Together with Vincent Cheng and Kimberly J. Devlin, she has edited a collection of essays called *Joycean Cultures: Culturing Joyces*, scheduled for publication in 1998. Margot Norris is currently working on two new book projects: one examining modern mass warfare and the second on Joyce's *Dubliners*.

THE CRITICS

Jacques Derrida is professor at the École des Hautes Études en Sciences Sociales, Paris, and since 1987, holds a visiting professorship at the University of California, Irvine. He is the author of over thirty books that have been translated into numerous languages, including landmark studies in philosophy and theory such as *Writing and Difference, Of Grammatology, Dissemination, Glas, Margins of Philosophy,*

Limited Inc, Positions, The Ear of the Other, The Truth in Painting,
Spurs: Nietzsche's Styles, and *Shibboleth: Pour Paul Celan.* His influential study *The Post Card: From Socrates to Freud and Beyond,* which appeared in a translation by Alan Bass in 1987, has particular relevance
for his essay on *Ulysses* in this volume. Books about Jacques Derrida
include studies by Christopher Norris (1987) and volumes of "Derrida-
Readers" by Peggy Kamuf (1992) and David Wood (1992).

Kimberly J. Devlin is associate professor of English at the University of California, Riverside. She is author of *Wandering and Return
in "Finnegans Wake"* (1991). With Marilyn Reizbaum, she has
coedited a forthcoming volume of new essays on the eighteen episodes
of *Ulysses* called *"Ulysses": (En)gendered Perspectives.* Devlin has published several articles on Joyce and, more recently, a Lacanian interpretation of Conrad's *Heart of Darkness.* She is presently at work on a
book entitled *Joycean Fraudstuff.*

Wolfgang Iser is professor emeritus in the Department of Literature of the University of Constance, Germany, and since 1978, holds
appointment at the University of California, Irvine. He has published
books on Edmund Spenser, William Shakespeare, Henry Fielding,
Laurence Sterne, Walter Pater, and Samuel Beckett but is best known
for his theoretical studies on reader-response, *The Implied Reader:
Patterns of Communication in Prose Fiction from Bunyan to Beckett*
(1974) and *The Act of Reading: A Theory of Aesthetic Response* (1978).
More recently he has published *Prospecting: From Reader Response to
Literary Anthropology* (1989) and *The Fictive and the Imaginary:
Charting Literary Anthropology* (1993).

Vicki Mahaffey is associate professor of English at the University
of Pennsylvania, where she teaches modernism, Irish literature, and
women's studies. She is author of *Reauthorizing Joyce* (1988) and a
book on experimentation and desire in the works of Oscar Wilde,
W. B. Yeats, and James Joyce that will be published in 1997. She is
currently working on a feminist introduction to modernist literature.

Patrick McGee teaches at Louisiana State University. He has published articles on Joyce, Faulkner, Woolf, postcolonial African fiction,
pedagogy, and cultural theory. He is the author of *Paperspace: Style as
Ideology in Joyce's "Ulysses"* (1988) and *Telling the Other: The Question
of Value in Modern and Postcolonial Writing* (1992). He has two

works forthcoming: *Cinema, Theory, and Political Responsibility in Contemporary Culture* and *Ishmael Reed and the Ends of Race.*

THE SERIES EDITOR

Ross C Murfin, general editor of Case Studies in Contemporary Criticism, and volume editor of Conrad's *Heart of Darkness* and Hawthorne's *The Scarlet Letter* in the series, is provost and vice president for Academic Affairs at Southern Methodist University. He has taught at the University of Miami, Yale University, and the University of Virginia and has published scholarly studies on Joseph Conrad, Thomas Hardy, and D. H. Lawrence.

DATE DUE

			PRINTED IN U.S.A.

RAY PRITCHARD

The

HEALING
POWER
OF
FORGIVENESS

HARVEST HOUSE PUBLISHERS

EUGENE, OREGON

THE HEALING POWER OF FORGIVENESS
Copyright © 2005 by Ray Pritchard
Published by Harvest House Publishers
Eugene, Oregon 97402

Library of Congress Cataloging-in-Publication Data
Pritchard, Ray, 1952–
     The healing power of forgiveness / Ray Pritchard.
        p. cm.
     ISBN 10: 0-7369-1567-2 (pbk.)
     ISBN 13: 978-0-7369-1527-0 (pbk.)
     1. Forgiveness of sin. I. Title.
     BT795.P75 2005
     234'.5—dc22   2005001903

Printed in the United States of America

08   09   10   11   12   / VP-CF /   10   9   8   7   6   5   4

To George and Joan Theis
with love and affection

Acknowledgments

I am grateful to Steve Miller, Bob Hawkins, Carolyn McCready, and Terry Glaspey of Harvest House Publishers. Thanks for sharing the vision for this book. I am grateful to the elders, staff, and congregation of Calvary Memorial Church for their continued encouragement. I especially thank my wife, Marlene, who never doubted this book would finally be written. Most of what I know that really matters I learned from her and from our three sons—Josh, Mark, and Nick.

Contents

A Prayer for You

$\mathscr{I}$'d like to begin this book by praying for you before you read it.

That may seem unusual to you, but I hope you won't mind if I say a prayer on your behalf. This book is about forgiveness. The only reason most people will read it is because they have some forgiving to do, and they don't know how to do it, or whether they should do it, or where they should begin.

Staying angry is easy. Forgiving is difficult. Alexander Pope, the English poet and essayist, famously remarked, "To err is human, to forgive divine." The first part is definitely true. We humans get straight As in messing things up. We're all on the honor roll of stupid statements, cutting remarks, unkind comments, and broken promises. And all of us have been on the receiving end of cruel mistreatment. We've hurt and been hurt. To use biblical terminology, we've sinned and been sinned against.

Sinning comes naturally. Forgiving is another story. After writing this book, I am more convinced than ever that the key to forgiveness lies in the middle syllable. Forgiveness is something we give to those who don't deserve it. It is grace pure and simple. If people deserved forgiveness, they wouldn't need it. Therein lies the fundamental problem that this book will not completely solve. Why in the world should we forgive people who do horrible things to us? What possible motive could we have to forgive people who hurt us deliberately and repeatedly? For instance, what about the woman who told of being abused by a family member as a child? The abuse continued from her childhood years into her late teens. The person who did it does not admit it. Why should she forgive him? And what exactly does forgiveness look like in that situation?

Some people would argue that forgiveness is impossible or inappropriate in such a situation. I reply that forgiveness—properly understood—is both possible and necessary. But that doesn't make it easy. Having written this book and wrestled long and hard with a long series of real-life situations, I conclude that forgiveness is not so much an event as it is an ongoing condition of the heart. It's a journey, not a destination. No one makes that journey easily or quickly.

And no one makes that journey without God. That may be the most important truth you take away from this book. True forgiveness is impossible without God. Since the heart of forgiveness is a gift we give to others who don't deserve it, no one will have the grace or strength or courage to give that gift unless God gives them the ability. Here we confront a familiar paradox of the Bible. We are commanded to do that which only God can do for us. If God does not do it for us, we will never do it on our own. Yet we are commanded to forgive as Christ forgave us (Ephesians 4:32).

Alexander Pope was right. Forgiveness is divine. That means you'll never give it to others unless God gives it to you first.

Forgiveness isn't about you.

And it's not about the person who hurt you so deeply.

Forgiveness is about God.

We forgive because God has forgiven us.

We forgive because God has commanded us to forgive.

We forgive because God has given us the strength to forgive.

We forgive because God will take care of judging the other person.

We forgive because God means more to us than staying angry.

We forgive because God matters more than the pain we feel.

We forgive because God can be trusted to do right.

We forgive because God is God and we are not.

So we need God's help desperately if we are going to forgive. Without God, this book will not help you at all. With God, this book could change your life. It's that radical and that simple.

I make no promises about this book except that it is biblical and it comes out of real life. I write as a pastor, not a professor or psychologist. Almost every day I talk with someone who struggles with hurts from the past and wonders what to do about them. In pointing people back to the Bible, I am pointing them back to God, the only real source of deliverance. With that in mind, here is my prayer for you:

> *Father, I thank You for every person who picks up this book and reads it. I know my words have no power in themselves to change anyone. You alone know the thoughts and intents of every heart. You alone can change the heart. You alone can lift the clouds of darkness and despair. But You*

can do it! I pray You will open the eyes of the heart so that Your truth will be received with gladness. I especially ask on behalf of those who have been cruelly mistreated by others and who may doubt that lasting forgiveness is possible. Set them free, O Lord! Give them hearts to believe in You. Show them Your power to deliver from anger, bitterness, revenge, and a critical spirit.

Lord, I pray that those who read my words will be driven back to Your Word. Help them to search out the Holy Scriptures so they will be convinced of what You have said. May they be protected from the attacks of the evil one, who wants to keep them in bondage through an unforgiving spirit. May doubt, distortion, deception, and discouragement be replaced with freedom, deliverance, certainty, and deep inner peace. May Your Spirit grant courage to those who right now feel they can never forgive. Show them a better way. May You pour out so much grace that they will be overwhelmed by Your grace and overcome by Your goodness. And now I pray for myself and for all who read this book...that we together might become great forgivers. We can't do this without You, Lord; but with You, all things are possible. Be glorified in us by the grace we extend to those who have hurt us. This is a great miracle we ask. Do it, O Lord. This is our prayer. In Jesus' name, amen.

One

Healing the Hurt
We Never Deserved

———————— ✿ ————————

When I learned to forgive,
it was like a million pounds were lifted from me.

REBA MCENTIRE

AY, HAVE YOU THOUGHT ABOUT PREACHING on forgiveness?"
The question came from George Theis. My answer was immediate. No, I hadn't given any thought to preaching on forgiveness.
Over the years, I had touched on our need to forgive others in various sermons, but never as the theme of a sermon series. "You
need to read a book by R. T. Kendall called *Total Forgiveness*, and
then you need to preach on forgiveness to your congregation."
George Theis is the former executive director of Word of Life, an
international youth ministry. Our conversation took place while
I was preaching at Word of Life Florida for a week. People often
recommend books to me, and most of the time I don't ever get
around to reading them. But George Theis is not the sort of man
who would recommend a book lightly. He told me that he had
been recommending the book to others, and had been preaching
its message himself with great impact in various churches.

11

So I said I would read it, which I eventually did. I found the book powerful and convicting. In the first chapter Pastor Kendall tells of a time when someone very near and dear to him hurt him greatly. He doesn't say who it was or exactly what he did—only that the pain was deep and the hurt profound because he had looked to this person as a surrogate father figure. The anger that he felt overwhelmed him. At length he talked it over with Josif Tson of Romania. After he poured out all the sordid details of what his so-called friend had done to him, he paused, waiting for Pastor Tson to say, "R. T., you are right to feel so angry. What happened to you was awful." But he didn't. After listening to all the details, Josif Tson said simply, "You must totally forgive him." Pastor Kendall was dumbfounded. So he started to tell the story all over again, this time adding more details. Josif Tson interrupted with words that would change R. T. Kendall's life: "You must totally forgive him. Release him, and you will be set free."[1]

I read through the book and immediately decided to preach on forgiveness to my congregation. The response overwhelmed me. In the 26 years I have been a pastor, no sermon series I have ever preached anywhere at any time has generated the sort of response I received to my sermons on forgiveness. Later I preached those messages at Bible conferences around the country, and the response was the same. God's people are so hungry to hear about forgiveness that it is as if they have never heard about it before.

Many Christians live in great pain because they have never discovered the liberating power of forgiveness. Here are a few examples:

A man called me on the phone and said, "Pastor Ray, could I come see you?" Then he told me his story. "My wife left me for another man, and when she got tired of him, she decided to come back to me. Everything seemed fine for a few weeks, then she left me again for the same man and stayed with him for a while. Then she came back a second time and I thought everything was fine. Then she left me again and she's been with him for a while. She just called me up and said, 'I want to come back.' Pastor, I'm not sure I want her back. I can trust someone who wrongs me once or even twice, but I'm not sure I can trust that person the third time."

A woman sat in my office and said, "I think I'm going to kill myself." "Why?" "I don't have any reason to live anymore," she replied. All her friends had deserted her. She couldn't get a job. She didn't have any money. Everything that she valued in the world was gone. She told me about her children—how they had deserted her, how they couldn't care less what happened to her. "When I told my son I was thinking about killing myself, he said, 'Mom, why don't you just go ahead and do it and get out of our hair.' "

A man in my church looked at me and said, "Pastor, you wouldn't believe what I have been through." Then he told me a story I found hard to believe. It involved a brutal divorce after many years of marriage, a financial collapse, the loss of his job, the end of his career, and lies told about him behind his back that have ruined his reputation. He told of people he had once trusted who had stabbed him in the back. He looked at me and said, "Pastor, do you want to know the worst of it? The people who have done this to me are Christians."

Sometimes I wish I could invite people to come into my office for a week just to sit in the corner and listen to the individuals who share their hearts with me. And listen to all the phone calls and read the letters I get and the e-mails that arrive day and night. Each week brings an unending series of heartbreaking problems. Divorce. Broken homes. Broken marriages. Broken promises. Children estranged from their parents. Parents estranged from their children. Longtime friends who don't speak to each other anymore. People who have lost their jobs because someone cheated them. People who have lost their fortunes because someone did them wrong. Families that don't even speak at Christmastime because they hate each other so much.

For all these heartaches, there are many answers and there is only one answer. There are many solutions you can carry out and one solution you must carry out: *Release them, and you will be set free.* The very moment we hear or read those words, however, the mind begins to argue:

> "But you don't know what he did to me."

> "They lied about me over and over again."

> "She intended to destroy my career—and she did."

> "You can't imagine the hell I've been through."

> "If you knew what this has done to my family, you would be angry, too."

> "They deserve to suffer like they've made me suffer."

> "I'm going to make them pay."

> "My daughter was raped. How do you forgive that?"

> "I was sexually abused by a priest. How do you forgive that?"

> "I will never forgive those people. Never!"

C. S. Lewis made this telling remark: "Everyone says forgiveness is a lovely idea until they have something to forgive." He's right, and in order for us to understand the message of forgiveness, we need to answer a few preliminary questions.

Questions About Forgiveness
1. *Why do we need forgiveness?*

If you know a bit about church history, you know that before Martin Luther became the father of the Protestant Reformation, he was a Catholic priest. As part of his training, he spent years studying Greek, Hebrew, Latin, the church fathers, and the doctrines of the Roman Catholic Church. By all accounts, he was brilliant, devout, and very devoted to his studies. But his soul was deeply troubled. Burdened with the haunting sense that his sins were not forgiven, he felt that God's judgment hung over him like a heavy weight he could not lift. Being a priest only made matters worse. No matter what he did, he never felt the assurance that his sins were forgiven. In desperation, he went to Rome, hoping to find answers, but he came away even deeper in despair.

Several years later, while studying the book of Romans, he encountered the phrase, "The just shall live by faith" (Romans 1:17 KJV). Slowly his eyes were opened and he saw clearly that God forgives us not because of anything we do, but solely on the basis of what Jesus did for us when He died on the cross and rose from the dead. He called that truth "the gate to heaven." So it is not surprising that Luther said that the phrase "I believe in the forgiveness of sins" was the most important article in the Apostles' Creed. He wrote, "If that is not true, what does it matter whether God is almighty or Jesus Christ was born and died and rose again? It is because these things have a bearing upon my forgiveness that they are important to me."

Psalm 130 points us in the right direction. This psalm has a long history in the Christian tradition. It's called *De Profundis*—a Latin phrase that means "out of the depths," taken from verse 1, which says, "Out of the depths I cry to you, O LORD." The whole psalm teaches us that we will never fix ourselves because we lack the inner resources to solve our own problems. That flies in the face of Oprah and Dr. Phil and a host of other self-help gurus who say that the answer is within us. The Bible says the opposite is true: *The problem is within us. The answer lies outside of us.* As long as you think you can solve your own problems, you can only get worse. When you finally say, "Lord, please help me. I can't do it on my own," you're a good candidate for salvation. Verse 3 of Psalm 130 goes on to say, "If you, O LORD, kept a record of sins, O LORD, who could stand?" Novelist Franz Kafka wrote in his diary that the problem with modern people is that we feel like sinners, yet independent of guilt. We sense that *something* is amiss in our lives, *something* is wrong. We live in a society that tells us to get rid of guilt by getting rid of the rules that make us feel guilty. So we do our best to ignore pesky things like the Ten Commandments. All those "Thou shalt nots" make us nervous. And why not? Guilt comes when you break the rules, and you know it. So the best way to get rid of guilt is to get rid of the rules—or so we think. We do away with the rules, but the rules won't go away because they weren't written by man in the first place. *It's as if they are written in indelible ink.* Even when you try to erase them, the image keeps coming back. So we cheat and steal and lust and sleep around. We lose our temper and then make excuses. We whisper about the sins of others and wonder why we can't sleep at night. We blame everyone else for our problems, but we won't take a good look at the person in the mirror.

> *We need forgiveness and cannot live without it.*

So why don't we confess our sins and find the forgiveness we need? We fear punishment. *We're afraid that if we own up to our own stupidity, the Lord will punish us.* So we lie about our lies and we cover up our cover-ups. We pretend that we didn't do what we know we did. No wonder we're so messed up. We think guilt is a bad thing so we avoid guilt at all costs. Our children learn to make excuses by watching us make excuses. We blame everyone except ourselves. But Psalm 130 liberates us from that self-destructive cycle. Verse 3 says that God doesn't keep a record of our sins. In the original Hebrew text, the verse literally says God doesn't keep an eye on our sins. That is, He's not looking for a reason to send us to hell. Many people picture God as a cranky old man with a long white beard who hopes to catch us messing up so He can send us to hell. But that's not the God of the Bible. He is willing to forgive those who repent of their sin and cry out for mercy.

We need forgiveness because we are sinners who try to change the rules so we can dodge the guilt question. And because the rules can't be changed, we end up extremely messed up on the inside. Here is the bottom line: *We need forgiveness and cannot live without it.* Without forgiveness, we are hollow men and women, empty and conflicted on the inside. The one piece of good news is that God doesn't keep an eye on our sins. If He did, we'd all be in hell already.[2]

2. *What hope do we have of forgiveness?*

By that I mean this: What are the chances that we can be forgiven? Is it just a distant dream, some kind of long shot? If the Vegas bookies laid odds on our forgiveness, what would the number be? Fifty thousand to 1? One hundred thousand to 1? One million to 1? Look in the mirror and consider your own soul. If you do, the outlook will not be hopeful. The first part of Psalm 130:4 brings us some very good news: "But with you there is forgiveness." Or to say it another way, God makes a habit of forgiving sin. He does not delight in punishing our sin. He looks for chances to forgive us because forgiveness is in His nature.

That's a significant insight because it affects how you see God.

> He is eager to forgive.
> He is ready to forgive.
> He wants to forgive you.

Exodus 34:6-7 calls Him "the compassionate and gracious God, slow to anger, abounding in love and faithfulness, maintaining love to thousands, and forgiving wickedness, rebellion and sin."

If you are in the pit, you need to know that sin is real. You can't break the rules and get away with it forever. But whenever you are ready to come clean, the Lord is right there waiting for you. It's never easy to confess your sins, but listen to the invitation given in Isaiah 55:7: "Let the wicked forsake his way and the evil man his thoughts. Let him turn to the LORD, and he will have mercy on him, and to our God, for he will freely pardon." Okay, so maybe you don't like that word "wicked" or the word "evil." Maybe that sounds harsh to you. But that's God's description of the whole human race. That's what you and I are apart from God's grace. We are wicked and evil. Get used to it, because that's the plain truth about all of us. Don't get hung up on the negative words and miss the invitation. Turn to the Lord, and you will find mercy and pardon.

Picture two doors, each with two words emblazoned across the top:

Door #1	Door #2
Evil	Mercy
Wicked	Pardon

Now which door do you like better? Answer: We all like mercy and pardon better. God says you have to go through the door marked Evil and Wicked to get to the door marked Mercy and Pardon. You have to go through the first door to get to the second. But someone says, "I'm going to skip Door #1 and go directly to Door #2." It doesn't work that way. You can't skip Door #1. And you can't climb through a window, either. The only way to reach Door #2 is to go through Door #1 first.

When you go through Door #2, you discover that "he will freely pardon." Freely means without cost. No charge. You want mercy? You've got it. You want a pardon for all your sins? You've got it. You can go in evil and wicked, and you can come out with mercy and a full pardon from the Lord. That's the best deal in the world.

3. *What happens when we are forgiven?*

The last part of Psalm 130:4 has the answer: "Therefore you are feared." Another way to say this is, "Therefore we worship you." Once we are forgiven, that vague feeling of unease is removed. Our slate is wiped clean. The prison cell door swings open and we walk out. We're free at last. Sometimes that's the hardest part to accept. Recently I received a letter from a prisoner who had read one of my books. Because of the heinous crime he had committed, he is afraid to go to church because he worries that people will find out what he did and thus shun him. That kind of shame works in all of us to keep us in bondage. The devil whispers to us, "You're no good. If people knew what you were really like, they'd have nothing to do with you. How can you call yourself a Christian and treat your wife that way? Your children that way? Your husband that way? You hypocrite."

The only way to deal with Satan's accusations is go back to the character of God: "With You there is forgiveness." Have you ever worried about the day when you stand before the Lord? Some Christians fear that God is going to push a button and project all their sins—even the sins of the mind—on some huge screen for the entire universe to see. We fear that all our ugly words and deeds, all our secret sins that no one else knows about, and every dark thought filled with anger, lust, pride, hatred, rage, and greed will be displayed for the millions to see. How could we endure such a moment? And how could God ever welcome us into His kingdom after putting our depravity on public display?

There are four different words for *forgiveness* in the Bible—three Hebrew words and one Greek. The first Hebrew word means "to cover"—like using a rug to cover the dirt on your floor. The second word means "to lift and take away"—which happens when you remove a stain from a carpet. The third word means "to pardon" or "to wipe the record clean." The fourth word means "to let go" or "to send away," as when you release a prisoner from jail.[3] When you put these words together, you get a graphic picture of forgiveness. God covers our sin, He removes the inner stain, He wipes our personal record clean, and then He releases us from our guilt so that we are set free.

If You, O Lord, kept a record of sins—if You gazed on our sins—who could stand? No one. We'd all be doomed and damned. That's the whole point of Psalm 130. We cry from the depths of shame and guilt, and God says, "Good news. With Me there is forgiveness." The Bible uses a number of images to describe how God deals with our sins:

• God blots out our sins as a thick cloud (Isaiah 44:22).

- God forgets our sins and remembers them no more (Jeremiah 31:34).
- God puts our sins behind His back (Isaiah 38:17).
- God buries our sins in the depths of the sea (Micah 7:19).
- God removes our sins as far as the east is from the west (Psalm 103:12).

When God forgives, He forgets our sins, clears the record, and erases the tape so that when He pushes the button, nothing shows up on the big screen in heaven. Our sins are forgiven, forgotten, removed, buried, and blotted out. They can never condemn us again. Let that thought grip your soul, and you will never be the same. But how could it be this way? How could God forgive us? Why doesn't He look at our sins? Here's the answer: A long time ago, God fixed His gaze on the cross of His Son, the Lord Jesus Christ. When we are honest enough to admit that we are wicked and evil, a stream of mercy flows out from the cross of Christ and our sins are covered by His blood. We discover, in one shining moment, that with God there is forgiveness.

4. *Why should we forgive others?*

Consider these words from the lips of our Lord:

> Do not judge, and you will not be judged. Do not condemn, and you will not be condemned. Forgive, and you will be forgiven (Luke 6:37).

In the Sermon on the Mount, Jesus said it very plainly:

> If you forgive men when they sin against you, your heavenly Father will also forgive you. But if you do not forgive men their sins, your Father will not forgive your sins (Matthew 6:14-15).

The apostle Paul put forgiveness into a slightly different framework in Ephesians 4:32:

> Be kind and compassionate to one another, forgiving each other, just as in Christ God forgave you.

He made a similar statement in Colossians 3:13:

> Bear with each other and forgive whatever grievances you may have against one another. Forgive as the Lord forgave you.

When Peter (a man who knew from experience the value of forgiveness) wrote his first epistle, he summed up forgiveness this way: "Above all, love each other deeply, because love covers over a multitude of sins" (1 Peter 4:8).

There is another way to express that truth, and it's found in the "Love Chapter"—1 Corinthians 13. While describing the greatest virtue, Paul declared that "love...keeps no record of wrongs" (1 Corinthians 13:5). That little phrase deserves a closer examination. Eugene Peterson in *The Message,* says it this way: "Love...doesn't keep score of the sins of others." Love doesn't keep score because love has a bad memory. It finds a way to forget the sins of others.

Finally, the greatest, most profound statement on this topic in the entire Bible—the finest, purest, highest example of forgiveness—came from Jesus Himself. When He hung on the cross dying, condemned to death by evil men who plotted to murder Him and produced lying witnesses to convict Him, as He surveyed the howling mob assembled to cheer His suffering, Jesus the Son of God, the One who knew no sin, the only truly innocent man who ever walked this sin-cursed planet, uttered some words that still ring across the centuries: "Father, forgive them, for they do not know what they are doing" (Luke 23:34). Those 12 tortured words sweep away all our shabby excuses. They reveal the barrenness of our heart; they rip the cover off our unrighteous anger and show it for what it is. Many of us say, "If only the people who hurt me would show some remorse, some sorrow, then maybe I would forgive them." But that rarely happens, and we use other people's inaction as an excuse to continue in our bitterness, our anger, and our desire to get even.

Consider Jesus on the cross. No one seemed very sorry. Even as He said those words, the crowd laughed, mocked, cheered, jeered. Those who passed by hurled insults at Him. They taunted Him. "If you are the king of Israel, come down from the cross and save Yourself." Let us be clear on this point: When He died, the people who put Him to death were quite pleased with themselves. Pilate washed his hands of the whole sordid affair. The Jewish religious leaders hated Him with a fierce, irrational hatred. They were happy to see Him suffer and die. Evil was in the air that day. The forces of darkness had done their work and the Son of God would soon be in the tomb. No one said, "I was wrong. This is a mistake. We were such fools." And yet He said, "Father, forgive them, for they do not know what they are doing."

That is precisely what we must say if we are going to follow Jesus. We must say it to people who hurt us deliberately and repeatedly. We must say it to those who intentionally attack us. We must say it to those who casually and thoughtlessly wound us. We must say it to those closest to us, to our husband or wife, to our children, to our parents, to our friends, to our neighbors, to our brothers and sisters, to our fellow Christians.

5. *What does it mean to forgive someone?*

At this point it is necessary to clear up some misconceptions about forgiveness. In some ways it is easier to say what forgiveness is not than what it is. These misconceptions matter because sometimes when we say we can't or won't forgive, we are actually talking about something other than biblical forgiveness. Let me list a few things forgiveness does *not* mean:

> It does not mean approving of what someone else did.
>
> It does not mean pretending that evil never took place.
>
> It does not mean making excuses for other people's bad behavior.

It does not mean justifying evil so that sin somehow becomes less sinful.

It does not mean overlooking abuse.

It does not mean denying that others tried to hurt you repeatedly.

It does not mean letting others walk all over you.

It does not mean refusing to press charges when a crime has been committed.

It does not mean forgetting the wrong that was done.

It does not mean pretending you were never hurt.

It does not mean you must restore the relationship to what it was before.

It does not mean you must become friends again.

It does not mean there must be a total reconciliation as if nothing ever happened.

It does not mean that you must tell the person you have forgiven them.

It does not mean that all negative consequences of sin are canceled.

A Matter of the Heart

I received an e-mail from someone who lives in a distant state. Recently he has come to grips with the fact that a neighbor abused him when he was a child. That trauma plus the fact that he was raised in a family where his parents could not express love to their children played havoc in his adult life. This is part of what he wrote:

> But just this year, through prayer and a Christian coun-
> selor, I am beginning to "let go" of the past. It is still very
> difficult to overcome the anger and maybe even the
> hatred I felt toward my father. It took me going to the

cemetery to visit my father's and mother's graves and having about a two-hour conversation with them that began to let the anger go that had kept me in a state of sadness most of my adult life.

He went on to say that for many years he focused on helping others because he knew how to "fix" people and "fix" problems. "Until the facts of my childhood awoke and slapped me in the face and I couldn't 'fix' it. If it were to be 'fixed,' then God would have to do it."

And the first step was learning to forgive.

> *Forgiveness allows you to let go and move on.*

That story is very helpful because it demonstrates that forgiveness is essentially a matter of the heart. This is a hugely important point because most of us think forgiveness is primarily about what we do or say. But it is quite possible to mouth kind words of forgiveness while harboring anger and bitterness within. Forgiveness begins in the heart and eventually works its way outward. There is a profound sense in which all forgiveness, even forgiving someone who hurt you deeply, is between you and God. Other people may or may not understand it, or recognize it, or own up to their need to receive it.

Forgiveness, in its essence, is a decision made on the inside to refuse to live in the past. It's a conscious choice to release others from their sins against you so that you can be set free. It doesn't deny the pain or change the past, but it does break the cycle of bitterness that binds you to the wounds of yesterday. Forgiveness allows you to let go and move on. And this story illustrates that you can forgive even when other people make no confession. You can forgive without a restoration of the relationship. You can forgive when the other person has done nothing to earn forgiveness because forgiveness is like salvation—it is a gift that is freely given, it cannot be earned. You can forgive and the other person may never even know about it. You can forgive without saying, "I forgive you" because forgiveness is a matter of the heart.

That brings me back to the statement by C. S. Lewis: "Everyone says forgiveness is a lovely idea until they have something to forgive." Then it becomes difficult.

Three Levels of Forgiveness

The late Lewis Smedes said there are three levels of forgiveness. *First, we rediscover the humanity of the person who hurt us.* That simply means that without diminishing their sin, we admit they are sinners just like we are sinners. *Second, we surrender our right to get even.* This is hard because it is natural to want someone else to pay for all the pain they caused us. But in the end, we must leave all judgment in the hands of our just and merciful God. *Third, we revise our feelings toward the other person.* This means giving up our hatred and letting go of our bitterness. Ultimately, it means taking Jesus seriously when He said, "Love your enemies, bless those who curse you, do good to those who hate you, and pray for those who spitefully use you and persecute you" (Matthew 5:44 NKJV). You'll know you have reached the final level of forgiveness when you are able to ask God to bless those who have hurt you so deeply. This is indeed a high standard—so high, that without God it is impossible. That's why Smedes calls forgiveness a miracle. He's right. Forgiveness is nothing less than a miracle of God.[4]

And it is the miracle we desperately need.

Two Final Thoughts

This is only the first chapter. There is much more to be said and much more we can learn together about the miracle of forgiveness. For the moment let's wrap things up with two final thoughts:

1. *Forgiveness is not an optional part of the Christian life.* It is a necessary part of what it means to be a Christian. If we are going to follow Jesus, we must forgive. We have no other choice. And we must forgive as God has forgiven us—freely, completely, graciously, totally. The miracle we have received is a miracle we pass on to others.

2. *We will forgive to the extent we appreciate how much we have been forgiven.* The best incentive to forgiveness is to remember how much God has already forgiven you. Think of how many sins He has covered for you. Think of the punishment you deserved that did not happen to you because of God's grace. Jesus said, "He who has been forgiven little loves little" (Luke 7:47). Your willingness to forgive is in direct proportion to your remembrance of how much you have been forgiven.

In order to experience the healing power of forgiveness, we need two things: soft hearts and courage. Some of us have been deeply hurt by what others have done to us. People have attacked us, maligned us, mistreated us, abused us, sexually assaulted us, ridiculed us, belittled us, publicly humiliated us, physically beaten us, and they have done it deliberately, repeatedly, viciously. In response we chose to become hard on the inside to protect ourselves from any further pain. But that hardness has made it difficult for us to hear the gentle call of the Holy Spirit. We need soft hearts to hear His voice. And then we need courage. The timid will never forgive. Only the brave will forgive. Only the strong will have the courage to let go of the past.

Two

Father,
Forgive Them

———— ❧ ————

Sins cannot be undone, only forgiven.

Igor Stravinsky

*L*ast words matter.

When loved ones die, we want to know if they had any final words. It's true that a dying person often doesn't know that their last words are really their last words, so the last statement they make may seem trivial. But there are times when a person's last words linger in our minds long after they die. That's especially true if their last words summarize who they were and what they lived for.

Just before he died, P. T. Barnum asked, "How were the circus receipts in Madison Square Gardens?"

A few seconds before Pat Garrett gunned down Billy the Kid in a dark room at Fort Sumner, he heard Billy the Kid ask, "Who is it?" The outlaw never knew who killed him.

After being shot by a soldier who fired into a burning barn where he was hiding, John Wilkes Booth cried out, "Tell mother, tell mother, I died for my country… useless…useless…"

Elizabeth I, Queen of England (1533-1603), declared, "All my possessions for a moment of time."

Author and poet Edgar Allan Poe said, "Lord, help my poor soul."

Union general John Sedgwick died at the Battle of the Wilderness in May 1864. While looking over a parapet, his men urged him to take cover because there were Confederate sharpshooters in the area. His final words were, "They couldn't hit an elephant at this dist—."

When actor and comedian Charlie Chaplin lay dying, a priest said to him, "May the Lord have mercy on your soul." Chaplin quickly replied, "Why not? After all, it belongs to Him."

When his housekeeper asked if he had any last words, Karl Marx brusquely replied, "Go on, get out! Last words are for fools who haven't said enough!"

But he was wrong about that. Sometimes last words tell us a great deal about the person who is dying. That is certainly true of Jesus Christ. As He hung on the cross, knowing that death was near, He spoke to the crowd that had gathered to watch Him die. Amidst that howling, restless, angry mob, He had very few friends. Some had come out of morbid curiosity. Others had come to cheer the death of this Galilean rabble-rouser. And some came because they hated Him and wanted to be there to make sure He suffered before He died.

Killing Time

It's Friday morning, a few minutes before 9:00 AM. Killing time. Outside the Damascus Gate is a road, and on the other side of the road is a flat area near the spot where the prophet Jeremiah is buried. Up above is a rocky outcropping that, if studied at a certain angle, looks like a skull. You can see eroded into the limestone two sockets for the eyes, a place for the nose, and maybe a place for the mouth. Skull Hill, they called it. Golgotha. It was the place where the Romans did their killing. And Friday was the day and nine o'clock was the time. The soldiers were ready to do their dirty work. They were Roman soldiers. This place called Judea was foreign territory to them. They weren't from Israel. They weren't followers of the law. They were simply soldiers who had a job to do. And it happened to be that they were on the death squad. They were in charge of crucifixions.

On this particular Friday morning, their workload was a little light. Only three this week. They usually didn't know the names, and it didn't matter. They were just the executioners. From their point of view, it didn't pay to stop and think about what they did. That was for someone up the ladder. Guilt or innocence wasn't their business. They'd go crazy if they started worrying about things like that. They just had a job to do. And to do their job, they needed two things. They needed toughness and they needed good technique. If they did a sloppy job, they were certain to hear about it later.

Mob Psychology

So it's 9:00 AM and up the road comes a group of people. The soldiers know that two of the men being crucified are just average, ordinary criminals—the kind you find in any big city anywhere in the world. They are no big deal. But the third man—the one from up north, the preacher from Nazareth—His case is different. They don't really know who He is. They know He's important because they sense the buzz in the crowd. There are more people than usual. By the way, this was one of the fringe benefits (if you want to call it that) for being on the crucifixion squad. You never worked alone. There's something morbidly fascinating about watching someone else die. The people of Jerusalem, at least some of them, loved to come out and watch the crucifixions. Well, maybe they didn't love it, but they couldn't stay away. Some strange magnetic force drew them back to Skull Hill again and again. And today there were more people than usual—a bigger crowd, noisier, rowdier, milling to and fro, waiting for the action to begin.

As the parade of people draws closer, the soldiers see it's led by a brawny foreigner carrying a cross. *That can't be the one we're going to crucify,* they thought. Sure enough, it turns out he was a man by the name of Simon—Simon of Cyrene. The crowd swirls around him and behind him is a stooped figure, a man not quite six feet tall. Now walking, now crawling, each step an agony to behold. Half a man, half a creature from the worst nightmare imaginable. He had been beaten within an inch of His life. His back was in shreds. His front was covered with the markings of the whip. His face was disfigured and swollen where they had ripped out the beard by the roots. And on His head was a crown of thorns six inches long and piercing His skin. A shell of a man. A man already more dead than alive. The soldiers weren't unhappy, because sometimes people got a little feisty when you tried to nail them to the cross. No, they didn't mind getting a person who was almost dead because it meant their work would be easier.

They set the cross on the ground and placed the body of Jesus on the cross. He moved, He moaned, He didn't do much. One hand over here, one hand over there. Wrapping rope around this arm and around that arm. Rope around the legs, probably bent and partially resting on a small platform. They drove the spikes on the forearm side of the wrist so that when the cross was propped up and the weight of the victim pulled downward, the spike wouldn't rip all the way through the hand. A spike in both wrists and then a spike through the legs. With the ropes in place, they begin to pull the cross up. Jesus' blood spurts from the raw wounds. Steady now, boys, steady. Don't drop it. It was a terrible thing to drop a cross before they got it in the hole. When the cross stood vertical, they then dropped it into the hole and it fell with a thud. And there was Jesus, naked and exposed before the world, beaten, bruised, and bloody. The soldiers stood back, satisfied. A job well done.

"Get the dice," someone said. "Let's roll dice for His clothes."

What Did Jesus Mean?

What happened that day at Skull Hill was unforgivable. That's the definition of what unforgivable is. When you crucify the Son of God, you have done that which is beyond forgiveness. It is truly unforgivable. And yet Jesus said, in His first words from the cross, "Father, forgive them, for they do not know what they are doing" (Luke 23:34). No one standing near the cross expected Him to say that. A dying man might scream or curse or utter threats, but you never heard a word of forgiveness when a man was being crucified. Yet that is precisely what Jesus offered to the men who were murdering Him. He offered them forgiveness. He prayed that they might be forgiven. He asked His righteous and holy Father in heaven, the Lord of all the universe, to forgive His murderers while they were murdering Him.

Before we consider what these words say to us today, perhaps it will help to consider what these words do *not* mean:

1. *They don't mean that God grants forgiveness apart from repentance.* That would contradict the rest of the Bible. God does not forgive our sins without true repentance (Luke 24:47; Acts 5:31). The word *repentance* literally means "to change the mind." It has to do with the way you think about something. You've been thinking one way, but now you think otherwise. That's repentance—a changing of the mind. Without that "change of mind" about your sin, there can be no forgiveness.

2. *They don't mean that the people who put Jesus to death were not guilty of a horrible crime.* Remember, you don't forgive innocent people. You only forgive guilty people. By the way, this sufficiently answers those who talk about "forgiving" God. You can't "forgive" God because He has done nothing wrong. But the Jewish and Gentile leaders who conspired together to put Jesus on the cross were definitely guilty. As Peter said in Acts 2:23 (KJV), with "wicked hands" they put Jesus to death.

3. *They don't mean that all the people who put Jesus to death would automatically be forgiven and go to heaven.* From later accounts in the book of Acts, we know that some of the people who joined in the death of Christ later came to trust Him as Lord and Savior. But not all did. Many continued in their unbelief and never came to saving faith. Whatever else Jesus' words in Luke 23:34 mean, they can't be taken as a blanket granting of forgiveness and salvation to everyone involved in His death.

4. *They don't mean that ignorance of what we have done somehow excuses our sin or lessens its impact.* Even in a human court, "ignorance of the law is no excuse." You can't say, "I didn't know it was wrong to steal that car," and expect the judge to say, "That's okay. I'm going to let you off because you didn't know it was wrong." You will still go to jail because you should have known what the law said.

It's also helpful to consider how Jesus responds to His own crucifixion:

• He doesn't offer a word in His own defense.
• He doesn't condemn Herod or Pilate or the Jewish leaders.
• He doesn't proclaim His innocence.
• He doesn't turn against God.
• He doesn't attack His attackers.
• He doesn't attempt to save Himself.
• He doesn't blame anyone—though many were to blame.

Instead, He prays. The last phrase of Isaiah 53:12 explains the significance of Jesus' cry from the cross: "For he bore the sin of many, and made intercession for the transgressors." No longer can His hands minister to the sick, for they are nailed to the tree. No longer can His feet take Him on errands of mercy. No longer can He take little children in His arms. No longer can He reach out to touch the lame and cause them to walk again. There is no time left for Him to instruct His disciples. Soon He will be dead. As His life ebbs from His beaten and bruised body, as the blood drips to the ground, He does the one thing He can do. He prays.

> *If we have any concept of grace at all, we understand that grace extends to the worst of sinners.*

His prayer is very brief and very specific. He prays that God would forgive His murderers, "for they do not know what they are doing." Among the many lessons we may glean here, none is more important than this: *No one is beyond the reach of God's grace.* I suppose most of us would agree with that statement in an abstract sense. If we have any concept of grace at all, we understand that grace extends to the worst of sinners. But that concept becomes very difficult when we have to forgive those who have sinned greatly against us.

- How does a wife forgive her husband for repeated adultery?
- How does a father forgive the man who raped his daughter?
- How does anyone forgive Hitler or Stalin or Saddam Hussein?

Exactly what does it mean to forgive the unforgivable? That's the problem posed by Jesus' first cry from the cross. It's hard enough to fully understand what He meant; it's even harder to know what those words should mean for us. And yet we know, if we know anything about God, that forgiveness lies at the heart of

God. "The LORD, the LORD, the compassionate and gracious God, slow to anger, abounding in love and faithfulness, maintaining love to thousands, and forgiving wickedness, rebellion and sin" (Exodus 34:6-7). Consider that word "abounding." Other translations use the words "abundant" or "rich" to describe the extent of God's forgiving love, conveying the idea that His love is both deep and broad. His love goes to the depth of our sin and it covers the full extent of our sin.

He forgives because that's the kind of God he is.

There is another way to say it. He forgives people we wouldn't forgive if we were God. And He saves people we would immediately send to hell. We know that His ways are not our ways, and no place can we see this more clearly than in His willingness to forgive even the worst sinners. That leads me to a question that is not just theological or historical, but a question that many of us wrestle with every day: How do you forgive the unforgivable? How do you forgive someone who has done something so terrible that it defies any attempt at human forgiveness?

Forgiving the Unforgivable

As we consider the account of Jesus' crucifixion, and especially Jesus' remarkable words regarding forgiveness, two observations come to mind that will help us understand how to forgive the unforgivable.

1. *You must give up trying to force people to understand how much they hurt you.*

This may be the greatest barrier to forgiveness. Many people who have been deeply hurt say, "I would be willing to forgive if only the one who hurt me knew how badly he hurt me." But this is an impossible standard, and as long as you hold to it, you will never forgive. And you will have a rock-solid excuse to live in bitterness for years. You can always blame it on "those people." If only *they* would come to their senses (but they won't). If only *they* would see the light (but they don't). If only *they* would understand how many nights you stayed awake because bad memories wouldn't let you go to sleep. If only *they* knew about your tears. You would forgive if *they* knew, if *they* understood, if *they* had some concept about what *they* did.

But if you are going to forgive, you must give all that up. Until you do, forgiveness will remain a distant dream, and you will remain chained to the past. You cannot set yourself free until you release others from the burden of understanding all that they did to you.

Here is the simple truth: They don't know what they did to you.

Some people, when I make that statement, immediately offer an objection: "You don't understand. They knew exactly what they were doing. They knew what they were doing before they were doing it. They knew they were going to hurt me and they went ahead and did it anyway." When she told that lie she knew what she was doing. When he double-crossed me he knew what he was doing. When he stepped out on me he knew what he was doing. When he broke the marriage vows he knew what he was doing. She knew what she was doing. They knew exactly what they were doing. How can you even bring up that subject? They knew they would hurt me and they did it on purpose. How can you say they didn't know what they were doing?

Consider Jesus. Who was He talking about when He said, "For they do not know what they are doing"? Who does the word "they" refer to? Perhaps the Roman soldiers. Did they know what they were doing or not? Well, yes, they knew they were crucifying a man. Did they know who He was? No, they didn't really know who He was. If anybody really didn't know what they were doing, it was the Roman soldiers. It was just a job to them, just the next grisly item on the Friday agenda. To them, crucifixion was what their commander ordered them to do. "Hand me the nails. Crucify this guy and get him out of here." This was just a job to them. Surely they didn't really know what they were doing.

Who else could "they" refer to? What about Pontius Pilate, the Roman governor? Did Pilate know what he was doing? Or to use a modern phrase, What did he know, and when did he know it? Pilate knew Jesus was called the King of the Jews. He knew Jesus claimed to have authority from heaven. He knew Jesus was unlike anyone else who had ever come before him. That's what Pilate knew. And what he knew scared him to death, and he tried to wash his hands of it. But he didn't know the whole story.

What about Caiaphas, the high priest? Caiaphas knew that Jesus was called the Son of God, the Messiah. What did Caiaphas do? He said, "He has spoken blasphemy!" (Matthew 27:65), and agreed with the other priests that Jesus was "worthy of death" (verse 66). What about Annas, also a high priest? The same. What about Judas? Didn't Judas know what he was doing? He was with Jesus for three-and-a-half years. But it's clear that Judas was totally confused about who Jesus was. He knew Jesus was supposed to be the Messiah, but it appears Judas thought Jesus was going to roll into Jerusalem, take over the place, and set Himself up as King. Judas was baffled because Jesus didn't fit his preconceptions about what the Messiah was going to do. That's one of the reasons Judas betrayed Him—because he was confused and disillusioned and disappointed at the end. And so it goes with everyone connected with the crucifixion of Jesus. Each person knew a little bit of the story, but none of them really had the big picture. We can certainly say the Jewish leaders *thought* they understood Jesus, but they didn't.

Does that mean these men (and their followers) are not guilty? Not at all. Each person involved in the death of Jesus is morally culpable. There is plenty of guilt to go round. Judas was guilty. Pilate was guilty. Caiaphas was guilty. Annas was guilty. The Roman soldiers were guilty and so were the Jewish leaders, the Pharisees, and the scribes who conspired to put Jesus to death. And what about the mob? Yes, they were guilty. And what about the spectators who came to cheer and laugh and to mock? Yes, they were guilty, too.

But still, we can't escape those haunting words: "Father, forgive them, for they do not know *what* they are doing." The word "what" is the key to understanding Christ's statment. The key is not *the fact* they do not know. The key is *what*. They do not know *what* they are doing. They know what they are doing, but they do not know what it really means. They know what they are doing, but they don't know who the man on the cross really is. They know what they are doing, but they don't grasp the ramifications. That is, they are guilty of killing a man, but they are guilty of much worse than they know. They are guilty of killing the Son of God Himself. When Jesus cried out, "Father, forgive them, for they do not know what they are doing," He was really saying, "Father, forgive them, because they need forgiveness more than they know. Forgive them, because they are in desperate need of forgiveness and they don't even know it."

The same is true about the people who hurt you. They need forgiveness more than they know. It's true they knew what they were doing when they made that telephone call, wrote that letter, or said words that tore into your heart. They knew exactly what they were doing, but they didn't know the enormity of it. They didn't know how bad and terrible it was. They can never know down deep how badly they hurt you. And yet they need your forgiveness more than they need anything else in the world. They need it more than they know, and they will probably never change until they get it. And some of them won't change even after they get it. But still, you have to forgive them.

Sometimes we refuse to forgive because we want the other person to feel what we felt when they hurt us so badly. That does not work, and will never work. If you wait until people truly understand what they did to you, in most cases you will wait forever. Even when they confess and seek forgiveness, you may feel that they still don't truly understand. But withholding forgiveness will not help them understand. They cannot crawl into your skin and feel as you felt. They can never enter into your pain. Your sorrows are yours alone. So if you make your pain the price of forgiveness, you will never forgive because no one else can ever pay that price.

- You do not forgive because they understand what they did.
- You do not forgive because they have suffered as much as you suffered.
- You do not forgive because they "deserve" forgiveness.
- You do not forgive to gain some personal advantage over them.
- You forgive in spite of what they've done.
- You forgive because of God's grace.
- You forgive because that's what Jesus did on the cross.
- You forgive because that's what Jesus did for you.

You can forgive the unforgivable if you remember that the people who have hurt you so deeply don't, at the deepest level, know what they have really done to you. Forgiveness is what they need, and you are the only one who can give it to them.

I have discovered that I need to apply this truth myself. Not long ago some dear friends were very upset with me. They were friends I had known for years. We had been through a lot together, and now they were unhappy with me. Both the husband and the wife sent me very hard e-mails. One was so harsh I simply could not answer it. The conflict had to do with disagreements and misunderstandings and things wrongly said or done. It had to do with perception and expectations and promises made or not made, and deep wounds and bruised feelings. And I was not the only one in the middle of that mess. My dear friends were unhappy with me and I with them, but there were others involved also, and the feelings ran deep. So I had my share of sleepless nights and anxious moments.

As with most relational conflicts, there weren't just two sides. There were many sides, and there was plenty of fault to go around. In hindsight, I can see that I made the situation worse at several points because of what I said or did. And I was unhappy about what others had said and done. As time went on, one great truth floated to the surface: *In order for healing to take place, everyone involved must be willing to forgive and be forgiven even while knowing they have not been fully understood.*

It's easy to fall into the trap of thinking that if we just keep talking, we'll eventually solve all our problems. But that's not true. Sometimes talking only makes matters worse, especially when we say, "But I just want you to understand where I'm coming from," which, being translated, means, "I want you to see what a fool you've been and how wrong you are because when you see that, you'll see things my way and you'll admit I was right all along." Sound familiar? We have thoughts like that all the time. But as long as we insist on always being right, we will never be set free.

> *As long as you demand that you be right all the time, you will never get well.*

In one of his books, Bruce Larson mentions visiting a halfway house in Western Ontario in Canada. It was a place where people with severe emotional struggles could come and find healing. The main meeting room was the living room of an old farmhouse. A beautiful sign above the fireplace caught his attention. It read, "Do you want to be right or well?" What a great question. Each one of us faces that same choice. As long as you demand that you be right all the time, you will never get well.[5]

Would you like to be healed?

Would you like to get better?

Would you like to see the power of the Holy Spirit released in your life?

Would you like to see God do something miraculous in the relationships that matter most to you?

If so, then here is a place to begin. If you willing to give up your right to always be right, the healing can start now.

Conflicts cannot be resolved until we realize that we have some forgiving to do and we need to be forgiven. Grace cannot be extended as long as we demand to be fully (or even mostly) understood. At some point we must release those who have hurt us, even though we know they don't know or understand all that they have done. And we must confess our sins even though we know our explanation will not be accepted or fully understood. And perhaps we won't even be believed. But that doesn't matter. There are some things we must do regardless of what others do. And we need God's help if we are ever to have the courage to do what is right.

If we probe a bit deeper in Luke 23:34, we discover another truth that flows from these amazing words of Jesus. The first truth we examined touches on how we view others; this one touches on how we view ourselves.

2. *God forgave you when you were unforgivable.*

This is where the words of Jesus become very personal. We're included in His prayer. When He said, "Father, forgive them, for they do not know what they are doing," who was included in "them"? The soldiers, the mob, the women, the disciples, Pilate, Caiaphas, Annas, Judas, Peter, and all the Jewish leaders. But that's not all. You were included in the "them," and so was I. He was praying for you, and He was praying for me. "No. No. You don't understand. I'm not like those people. I'm different. I'm not that bad. I'm not the kind of person who could crucify anyone. I'd never do anything like that." Oh, yes you are, and yes you would, and yes you have many times, and yes you will again. You're not as good as you look. If you had been there, you would have been holding the nails. If you had been there, you would have been clapping and cheering. If you had been there, you would have been saying, "Crucify Him. Crucify Him. Stick it to Him again.

Another nail. Let Him have it." We're not that much different. We're not that much better.

At this point we discover a hard reality that keeps us from forgiving the people who hurt us. At the root it is this: We think we're better than they are. We think we would never hurt anyone the way they have hurt us. "I'm just not as bad as that. I'd never treat anyone the way they treated me." We get angry because we think that we would never do to another person what they have done to us. How foolish. How false. How deluded we are when we think that way. It is our false pride that keeps us from the hard step of forgiving others.

Not So Good, Not So Nice

Consider for a moment the deeds of Jeffrey Dahmer, the notorious serial murderer. After he was arrested and imprisoned, he professed faith in Jesus Christ. That is, he claimed to have seen the error of his ways, confessed his sins, and cried out to Jesus for forgiveness. We'll never know the full story of what happened because he was beaten to death in prison not long after that.

When we think about Jeffrey Dahmer and the possibility that he might truly have become saved after committing such heinous crimes, our first response may be to say, "There is grace even for people like Jeffrey Dahmer." That statement, true as it is, reveals at least as much about us as it does about him. All of us would like to think (and in fact do think) that we are "better" than he was. Or we're not as "bad" as he was. I make no bones about the fact that I think I am "better" than Jeffrey Dahmer. I've never done the things he did. I've never even thought or dreamed or imagined any of them. So when I say there is grace "even" for the likes of Jeffrey Dahmer, while I'm willing to include him in the circle of those God might save, I'm not putting myself on his level. I truly believe I'm better than he was.

But it's not enough to say there is grace even for the likes of Jeffrey Dahmer. In truth, there is grace *only* for the Jeffrey Dahmers of this world. They alone can be saved. Right now you might be thinking, "This sounds crazy." Something deep inside the human heart resists this conclusion. How can it be true? Does it mean God somehow "favors" the perverse, that grace is a reward for truly terrible sin, that the greater your sin the more likely you are to find God's grace? That can't be right, can it? Read on, and you'll see what I'm getting at.

No Hope for "Semi-Sinners"

Too many religious people are like the Pharisee who prayed, "God, I thank you that I am not like other men—robbers, evil-doers, adulterers—or even like this tax collector" (Luke 18:11). He might as well have said, "I thank God I'm not like Jeffrey Dahmer." Well, it's true—he wasn't like Jeffrey Dahmer. And he didn't experience God's grace either. He went home still in his sins while the hated tax collector ended up justified by God. As long as you think you are better than other people, you are not ready to be saved from your sin because you have not yet considered how great your sin really is. Jesus did not come to save "semi" sinners or "partial" sinners or "not-so-bad" sinners. As long as you feel the need to put some kind of qualifying adjective before the word *sinner,* you aren't ready to come to Jesus. You won't see your need for the grace of God.

To put the matter this way is not to deny the real moral differences among people. Is there no difference between Jeffrey Dahmer and Mother Teresa? Of course there is. One was a sadistic killer, the other an instrument of God's mercy to multitudes of hurting people. But our perspective is all-important. Let's suppose we throw Jeffrey Dahmer into the deepest pit on earth. Then let's travel to the top of the Sears Tower in downtown Chicago. There we will look over the railing and jeer at Jeffrey Dahmer and congratulate ourselves for being so far above him.

Now consider what God sees. From heaven, as He looks down, it is as if earth is a trillion miles away. What happens to the distance between us and Jeffrey Dahmer? It vanishes from God's point of view. That's why Romans 3:22-23 says, "There is no

difference, for all have sinned and fall short of the glory of God."
We're all in the same boat—like it or not.

Wanted: A Righteous Man

During a sermon one Sunday, I said that there are no righteous
people in Oak Park, Chicago (where our church is located), nor
are there any righteous people anywhere else. None at all. The next
Sunday a woman shook my hand and said she wanted to ask me
a question. She began, "Last week you said there was no one righteous in all of Oak Park." Her statement was correct. I had said
that because apart from God's grace, there is no righteousness to
be found anywhere. With a face marked with intense concern,
she asked, "But Pastor Ray, if you aren't a righteous man, where
can we find one?" Her question was honest and sincere. I didn't
say what I could have said: "If you only knew me like my family
knows me, you wouldn't ask that question." Instead, I told her to
listen to my sermon and she would find the answer. I recounted
the story to the congregation and said I would show them the only
righteous person in Oak Park—or anywhere else, for that matter.
Pointing to the cross on the wall behind the pulpit, I declared
that Jesus is the only righteous man who ever lived.

And compared to Jesus, I am just as guilty as Jeffrey Dahmer.

> *Out of the worst evil
> God brought forth
> the greatest good.*

Jesus Christ was pure, holy, and perfect in every way. He never
sinned, not even one time. Though He was severely tempted, He
never gave in. All the rest of us fall so far short that we cannot
begin to be compared to Him. He is the only righteous man ever
to walk this earth. And we crucified Him. His reward for doing

God's will was death on a bloody Roman cross. Here is the wonder of grace at work. From the murder of a perfect man came God's plan to rescue the human race. "We all, like sheep, have gone astray, each of us has turned to his own way; *and the LORD has laid on him the iniquity of us all*" (Isaiah 53:6). Out of the worst evil God brought forth the greatest good. And only God could have done it. "But God demonstrates his own love for us in this: While we were still sinners, Christ died for us" (Romans 5:8). When I preached this sermon, I paused in the middle of quoting Romans 5:8 and had the concregation repeat the word "sinners" several times. That's what we were when Christ died for us. Note the little word "still." We were "still" sinners when Christ died for us. He didn't die for us while we were still "church members" or "good people" or "law-abiding citizens" or "nice neighbors" or "high achievers," but He died for us while we were still lost in our sin and far away from God. That's the truth about all of us. Christ died for sinners because it is only sinners who can be saved.

It's not as if we are all good and the people who hurt us are all bad. It's not as if we are all pure and they're all evil. It's not as if we've got all of life wired together and they're just a bunch of fools. It's not as if we're totally in the right and they're totally in the wrong. That's not the way the world really works. It's not as if we know all the answers. We're not as good and righteous as we think we are. Eventually the searing truth hits home even though we would rather avoid it. We get mad just like they do. We lose our temper just like they do. We write stinging letters just like they do. We say stupid things at Christmastime just like they do. We slap our friends just like they do. We hurt our children just like they do. We crucify our enemies just like they do. We break our promises just like they do.

If the truth be told and told fairly, we're just like them. But even that's not quite right. We are them and they are us, and if we don't see that, we've missed the real point of Jesus' first cry from the cross. If we think we're so much better than the people who have hurt us so deeply, we are self-deceived. If only we could see that we're all in the same boat together. We're all truly sinners in one way or another. We all fail in many ways. They fail in one way and we fail in another.

When Chuck Colson received the 1993 Templeton Prize for Progress in Religion, he spoke to an audience at the University of Chicago on "The Enduring Revolution." In describing the plight of modern society, he mentioned four myths that define our time—"the four horsemen of the present apocalypse." The first myth has to do with the goodness of man.

> This myth deludes people into thinking that they are always victims, never villains; always deprived, never depraved. It dismisses responsibility as the teaching of a darker age. It can excuse any crime, because it can always blame something else—a sickness of our society or a sickness of the mind.[6]

Holocaust survivor Yehiel Dinur was a witness during the trial of Adolph Eichmann, the architect of the Nazi's "final solution" during World War II. Eichmann presided over the slaughter of millions. "The court was hushed as a victim confronted a butcher." Suddenly Dinur broke into uncontrollable sobs and collapsed to the floor. When asked later to explain his actions, he said, "I was afraid about myself. I saw that I am capable to do this.... Exactly like he." The reporter who interviewed Dinur concluded that the most chilling fact about Adolph Eichmann was that he was normal. "Eichmann is in all of us."[7]

An Oasis of Forgiveness

It would keep us from being so angry if we could see ourselves the way we really are.

We aren't as good as we think we are.

We don't know as much as we think we do.

We don't really have it all together.

If we would ever admit the truth, we would find it easier to forgive the people who have hurt us in an unforgivable way.

The secret of forgiveness is to understand that in the ultimate sense, between you and the person who hurt you, there's really no difference at all. None whatsoever. It is possible to forgive the unforgivable, but you've got to realize before you do it, that Jesus forgave you when you were unforgivable. When He prayed that prayer, He wasn't just praying for the people back then, He was also praying for all of us 2,000 years later.

I believe it is enormously significant that the first word from the cross is a word of forgiveness. That teaches us Jesus came to establish a church marked by forgiveness. He is, at heart, a man of forgiveness. He came into this world to establish a church that would be an oasis of forgiveness, and to bring to the world a race of forgiving men and women.

One final word must be mentioned about Jesus' words in Luke 23:34. "Not only was this a prayer for forgiveness and a great forgiveness at that—it was also a forgiveness prayed for at an enormous cost."[8] Forgiveness does not come cheap. It will cost you greatly to forgive those who have hurt you greatly. Jesus paid the price in blood. Forgiveness is a gift we *give* to others. Even if they repent and ask for forgiveness, their repentance does not "earn" our forgiveness. Forgiveness is free, but it is never cheap. Perhaps the greatest irony is that when we pay the cost of forgiveness, we are the ones who are set free.

Forgiven...Forgiven...Forgiven

Would you like to become more like Jesus? I suggest you start where Jesus started—by forgiving the people who have hurt you deeply. I do not for a moment mean to suggest that this is easy. To forgive us cost Jesus His life. To forgive others will cost us greatly, too. We will have to give up our anger, turn away from our bitterness, and decide by a conscious choice that we will forgive those who have sinned against us. And very often we will have to perform that act of forgiveness over and over again until we learn the grace of continual forgiveness. I am sure that I am writing to someone who has reserved in the temple of his heart a room that is not open to the Holy Spirit. It is a private place, a citadel locked from the inside, a hidden storehouse of hatred and revenge. It is a dark room filled with pain and anger and you keep it locked because you don't want anyone else to know the room is there. And maybe you even pretend to yourself that the room doesn't exist. It is a room that God will not enter without your permission.

It's very possible you are nursing hatred and bitterness and a desire to get even with someone who hurt you terribly. And you may say, "But I'm justified in it. They did me wrong." And you may be entirely right about that. But I ask you: How can God's Holy Spirit do His work and bestow His blessing in a life filled with anger? If God is ever going to use you in powerful ways, and if your life is ever going to change, that door must be opened by you because it is locked from the inside. I can't open it for you, and God won't. He is the perfect gentleman. He waits to be invited inside.

No one is more miserable than the person who harbors secret hatred and wishes for revenge. And no one is happier than the person who finally opens the door to the Holy Spirit and says, "Come in and do Your work in me." In the moment when you say that, healing begins on the inside. Instead of hatred there is love. Instead of bitterness, kindness. Instead of revenge, forgiveness. If I am describing your life, then God's word to you is, "Open the hidden door and let My Spirit come in."

Every year in January we talk about turning over a new leaf. For many people that means taking all the leaves from last year and raking them over into this year. We don't turn anything over; we just carry our burdens and hurts from one year to the next— haunting memories, injured feelings, and thoughts about the past that we can't get out of our minds. Some people live for years under a terrible burden of pain from the past. At some point, we need to let go.

Here's a simple exercise that may help. Take a sheet of paper and write Jesus' words at the top: "Father, forgive them, for they do not know what they are doing." On the left side of the paper, write a list of the people and memories from the past that have hurt you so badly. Make it brief and simple; no one ever needs to see this list. When you are finished, add one word, in large letters, to the right of each item on your list: Forgiven…Forgiven…Forgiven.

And when you're finished, take that paper and rip it up. Don't keep it. Rip it into a dozen pieces, then flush the pieces down the toilet. Forgiven…Forgiven…Forgiven…Forgiven…Forgiven… Forgiven. Let go of those awful memories once and for all.

This isn't a magical exercise that can suddenly take away your pain, but it is a practical way of coming to grips with the first words from the cross. Do you want to be set free? Would you like to come closer to Jesus Christ than you've ever come before? Then start where Jesus began on the cross—by becoming a great forgiver.

All of us know that it is easier to talk about forgiveness than it is to do it. Yet if we are honest, we all know how much we suffer when we forget to do what Jesus did on the cross. We need courage to take the giant step of forgiveness. And however painful forgiveness may be, it is infinitely better than refusing to forgive. Besides, Jesus forgave us when we were unforgivable.

Three

Breaking the
Cycle of Bitterness

———————— ✿ ————————

Only the brave know how to forgive.

LAURENCE STERNE

On Thursday morning, November 21, 2002, as the sun rose over the horizon in the port city of Sidon in southern Lebanon, Bonnie Penner Witherall was up early. On this day she was going to work at the prenatal clinic that offers medical services to the Muslim women from a nearby refugee camp. Tensions were running high because of events elsewhere in the Middle East, and Americans in general and missionaries in particular had been warned of potential danger. Bonnie and her husband, Gary, both had come to Lebanon with a burden to share Christ in the Muslim world. For several years they had studied Arabic so they could communicate with the people they hoped to reach with the gospel.

At approximately 8:00 AM, Bonnie answered a knock at the clinic door. Authorities can only surmise what happened next. Evidently a man hit her in the face and chest, and then shot her three times in the head, killing her instantly. When Gary heard the news, he ran to the clinic. By this time the police had come and the gunman was nowhere to be found. Gary tried to fight his way into the room where his wife lay in a pool of blood, but the police wouldn't let him enter. In one of the cruel ironies of our modern world, someone took a picture of Bonnie after she died, and that gruesome picture somehow ended up on the Internet.

The next day, the *London Times* carried a report on the murder of Bonnie Penner Witherall. It quoted Gary Witherall as saying he had forgiven his wife's killers: "God led us to Lebanon and we knew that we might die.... It's a costly forgiveness.... It cost my wife." On the long flight home while accompanying his wife's body to America, Gary came to a simple conclusion: "God said there's a seed that's been planted in your heart. You either hate and be angry, or you forgive. I said I have to forgive."[9]

Whenever tragedy strikes, two enormous questions loom before us: Why did this happen? and Where is God in all this? Many times the second question is harder than the first. Most of us instinctively know we'll never have a final answer to the "Why?" question this side of heaven. We rarely fully know why things happen the way they do. The answer to that question remains in the heart and mind of God. But we can get some help with the second question: Where is God in all this? I am convinced many of us go wrong at this point because of bad theology. Let me say that another way: I am convinced good theology is the answer to the deepest questions of life. Not that good theology can tell us all we would like to know—it can't. But understanding who God is, who we are, and how God works in the world (which is what good theology is all about) gives us a framework for responding to life's darkest moments.

New Help from an Old Sermon

Back in the early 1830s, a man named Charles Simeon of Cambridge, England, published a sermon on Genesis 45 that provides some unique insights into how God works through evildoers to accomplish His purposes. He gave his sermon the unwieldy title, "God Viewed in Joseph's Advancement."[10] Though the title sounds odd to our ears, the truth it contains speaks to our twenty-first-century questions. Much of what I'm going to share in this chapter comes from Charles Simeon.

> *God gets involved even when we think nothing is happening.*

Simeon begins by speaking of the "hidden secrets of divine providence," which sounds like a phrase that would come from a television special on mysterious phenomena. What Simeon meant was that there is far more going on in the universe than we ever dreamed possible. If the total knowledge of reality were to equal a line that stretches for 100 yards, then we perhaps see an inch or two at most. No matter how much we think we understand, there is much more we don't understand because our vision is so limited.

With that in mind, how does God accomplish His own designs for us? Sometimes He uses adversity and mistreatment. When we are going through the ordeal of being unfairly attacked, when we are being lied about, when our reputation is being publicly smeared, when our friends betray us, when a husband or wife abandons us, it may appear impossible that such things could accomplish anything good, but they do. The key is the word *appear*. What we see is far less than what God sees. And the good that may come from the treachery of others is not planned by the hand of man, is not seen in advance, and is not seen at all except by faith.

Simeon used a fascinating word to describe how God brings good out of the evil of others. He says that God "interposes" Himself in the midst of the circumstances of life. That is, God gets involved even when we think nothing is happening. The end result (sometimes seen many years later) is easily and naturally seen to promote our good and God's glory. And we look back and say, "It had to happen that way."

Exhibit A: Joseph

In the entire Bible, there is no better example of this principle than the story of Joseph in the book of Genesis. It all begins when Joseph has a dream that someday he will be exalted above his brothers and even above his parents. Naturally his brothers aren't thrilled to hear this news, and soon their hearts burn with envy, jealousy, and malice against Joseph. When an opportunity presents itself, they throw Joseph into a pit, intending to leave him for dead. They end up selling him into slavery to a caravan of Midianite traders. Then they go back home, tell their father Jacob that Joseph is dead, and forget all about him. Meanwhile, Joseph is purchased by Potiphar (who was the Pharaoh's head of security). Potiphar makes Joseph head over his household, where Joseph rises to prominence and is the victim of an attempted seduction by Potiphar's wife—who later falsely accuses Joseph of rape. After being thrown in jail, Joseph meets a baker and a cupbearer and correctly predicts that the former will die but the latter will be released. He asks the cupbearer to remember him upon his release, but the cupbearer forgets—until Pharaoh has a dream he can't interpret. The cupbearer remembers Joseph, who is released, correctly interprets the dream, and is elevated by Pharaoh to the number-two position in Egypt. When a terrible famine strikes the Middle East, Jacob sends his sons to Egypt looking for food. They meet Joseph, but don't know it's their brother. Joseph implements a series of tests so he can determine their sincerity. Eventually the moment comes when Joseph decides to reveal his identity.

Joseph sends the Egyptians away, and in privacy, alone with his brothers, tells them who he is. They are understandably terrified to meet the brother they sold into slavery 22 years earlier. Now he has them firmly in his grasp. He can order them killed, and it will be done. Or tortured. Or thrown into jail. Or fined. Or anything else he desires to have done to them.

If anyone had a "right" to be bitter, it was Joseph. He has "lost" 22 years of his life. The temptation to get even must have been great. But this is how he summarizes the whole affair:

> I am your brother, Joseph, whom you sold into Egypt. And now do not be distressed or angry with yourselves because you sold me here, for God sent me before you to preserve life. For the famine has been in the land these two years, and there are yet five years in which there will be neither plowing nor harvest. And God sent me before you to preserve for you a remnant on earth, and to keep alive for you many survivors. So it was not you who sent me here, but God. He has made me a father to Pharaoh, and lord of all his house and ruler over all the land of Egypt. Hurry and go up to my father and say to him, "Thus says your son Joseph, God has made me lord of all Egypt" (Genesis 45:4-9 ESV).

There is enormous irony in his words. The very thing used against him (their betrayal) results in his exaltation so that he can now save the brothers who betrayed him. The central truth is in verse 8: "It was not you who sent me here, but God."

Those are the words of either a madman or a man of faith. He mentions God five times in his statement so his brothers won't miss the point. "I know what you did. I haven't forgotten your treachery, but that's not the issue. You did what you did because you wanted to hurt me, but God allowed it to happen so I would end up a ruler in Egypt, and so at the exact moment you would need me, I would be here to save you and your descendants." His vision of God was so great that it dwarfed his view of the sin of his brothers.

How God Involves Himself with Evildoers

Given Joseph's amazing words, we cannot help but ask: How does God involve Himself with evildoers? What did Joseph mean

54   THE HEALING POWER OF FORGIVENESS

when he said to his brothers, "It was not you who sent me here, but God"? After all, if not for their betrayal, he never would have ended up in Egypt. How does a holy God accomplish His plan for us through the deeds of evil people? It's easier to answer that question in the negative. God is not the author of evil, nor does He tempt us to do evil (James 1:13-15). What the brothers did to Joseph was unquestionably evil, but He does not dwell on that. There is a sense in which we must say that God is not the cause of evil or a partner in evil, but in some manner—which is hard to put into words—He is involved in the evil deeds of evildoers. He does not cause sinners to sin, but what they do fits into His ultimate plan.

1. He allows them to reveal what is in their hearts.

Joseph's brothers were motivated entirely by envy and malice. They couldn't stand the thought that their little brother would one day rule over them. God simply gave them a chance to reveal the envy that was already there. As long as they were under Jacob's direct control, Joseph was safe. But when they were out gathering the flocks, and Joseph came to find them, their latent envy boiled to the surface. At first they planned to let him die in the pit, but God interposed, and the Midianite traders came along. As the story unfolds, others enter the picture. First Potiphar, and then his wife. Later the baker and the cupbearer, and still later, the Pharaoh. They all acted according to their own inclinations, but all in accordance with God's plan. God didn't cause the brothers to envy nor Potiphar's wife to lust. The brothers and the wife did that on their own. He simply gave them a chance to act on their evil intentions. In so doing, He allowed them to reveal the evil that was already in their hearts. This is what Jesus meant when He said to Pilate: "You would have no authority over me at all unless it had been given you from above" (John 19:11 ESV).

2. He permits Satan to instigate them to evil.

Satan is a roaring lion who prowls the world, looking for those he can destroy (1 Peter 5:8). But though he possesses great power, he can do nothing without God's express permission. In Job 1, it is God who tells the devil to consider His servant Job. And Satan cannot afflict Job beyond the limits established by God. The devil is powerful, but he is not omnipotent. He has great knowledge, but he is not omniscient.

A few hours before Peter betrays Jesus, Jesus told Peter that Satan had requested permission to sift him like wheat—meaning that Satan could not tempt Peter to evil without God's permission (Luke 22:31). Satan operates within limits imposed by God. This is both a comfort and a warning. It is a comfort to know that our temptations do not happen by chance yet are permitted by our heavenly Father. The warning is that God still holds us accountable for how we respond. None of us can escape judgment by saying, "The devil made me do it." Satan may have tempted you, but you did the sinning all by yourself.

3. *He withdraws His restraining grace.*

Restraining grace simply means God doesn't let circumstances get as bad as they could be. But when God removes His hand of grace, things fall apart quickly. Romans 1 tells us God exercises judgment on unbelieving humanity by giving men and women over to further sin. Sometimes God's harshest judgment on sinners is to do nothing at all. He simply says, "If you want to destroy your own life, go ahead. If you want to destroy your own family, go ahead. I won't stop you. You've already rejected Me, so I will now respect your decision. If you wish to plunge off the cliff, go ahead, but you'll find out how sharp the rocks are at the bottom of the ravine."

If men despise God's mercy, they are left with nothing but His judgment. He blinds the eyes of those who choose not to see, and He hardens the hearts of those who prefer to go their own way.

4. *He uses the deeds of evildoers to accomplish His own purposes.*

Sometimes God uses the deeds of evildoers to further His own plans in the world. When Christ was born, the Father used the paranoia of Herod the Great to guide the magi to Bethlehem. Later, God used Herod's slaughter of the innocents to lead Mary and Joseph and the baby Jesus to Egypt so that the Scripture could be fulfilled that says, "Out of Egypt I called my son" (Matthew 2:13-15).

We see this even clearer in the events surrounding the death of Christ. Who killed Jesus? For 2,000 years men have argued that question. Did the Jewish leaders kill Jesus? Clearly, they wanted Him dead and plotted to make it happen. What about the Romans? They were the only ones with the legal power to put someone to death. How about the centurions? They were the ones who performed the literal act of crucifixion. And in a larger sense, is not the whole sinful world of humanity guilty of His death? Did not our sins put Him on the cross? There is plenty of guilt to go around in the death of Jesus Christ. But what about God? Though He cannot be "guilty" of the death of Christ, was not the death of Jesus part of the Father's plan from the beginning? The answer is yes. Jesus was the Lamb slain before the foundation of the world (Revelation 13:8). How do we reconcile the plan of God with human guilt in the death of Christ?

Here is Peter's answer as he preached in Jerusalem to some of the very men who participated in the death of our Lord: "This Jesus, delivered up according to the definite plan and foreknowledge of God, you crucified and killed by the hands of lawless men" (Acts 2:23 ESV). Jesus' death was not some afterthought with God, as if it happened because events suddenly spun out of control. He died according to the "definite plan and foreknowledge" of God, and He could not have died otherwise. But His death took place at the hands of "lawless men" who stand guilty before the Lord. Even though we may not fully see it, there is perfect harmony between God's predestination and the free moral choices of sinful men. In the case of Christ, God used the evil deeds of wicked men who crucified the Son of God in order to bring salvation to the world.

How Knowing This Helps Our Faith

So far, it may seem as if I am trying to impugn God by somehow making Him responsible for the evil in the world. But the truth behind Genesis 45 needs to be tattooed on our souls. We desperately need an infusion of good theology so that when trouble comes our way (and it comes to all of us sooner or later), we won't buckle under the pressure and watch our faith suddenly disappear. Understanding that God is intimately involved in even the worst things that happen relieves us from worry and doubt and fear. Does it justify sin? Not at all. Knowing this truth brings good to our soul and great honor to our God.

1. *We know our troubles did not happen by accident.*

When we focus on immediate causes, we end up in despair, anger, and bitterness. It's easy to think only of the people who have hurt us deeply—parents or children or grandparents or friends we thought we could trust, or church members who let us down, or people at work who stabbed us in the back. The list goes on and on. But as long as we focus exclusively on the people who hurt us, we are doomed to dwell in the swamp of bitterness. Far better it is to understand that our enemies (who often are our closest friends) are actually instruments in God's hands. They are His rod to correct us and to shape us into the image of Jesus Christ. Having said that, I hasten to add that God's purposes and theirs are vastly different. Our enemies mean to harm us, drag us down, hurt us deeply, and discourage us so we give up. Not so the Lord. He allows our enemies to taunt and torment us, but His purposes are higher and better and nobler. Ultimately, He allows their unkindness to humble us, to break us of our pride, and to cause us to cry out to Him for mercy and deliverance. What they intend and what God intends are two different things. Never forget that fact.

Charles Simeon said that when God is finished with our enemies, He will cast them into the fires of eternal judgment. Those who hurt us will end up in hell forever. He cites the fact this is how

God dealt with the pagan nations that brought judgment against Israel in the Old Testament. The major and minor prophetic books are filled with warnings to those nations that their own day of reckoning will someday come. And come it did—for the Assyrians, Babylonians, Edomites, Egyptians, and all the other nations used to chastise God's people.

How does this principle apply today—especially when those who torment us may themselves be born-again Christians? The answer is simple, though the precise application will vary. God knows how to discipline His children, and that includes believers who take unfair advantage of us or go out of their way to mistreat us. The day will come when they will be brought low before the Lord. Count on it. Those who misuse others will someday be called to account for it—if not in this life, then in the life to come. The scales of justice will be balanced in the end.

And in the end, we will be improved, our faith will be stronger, and our reliance on the things of this world will be lessened. The Lord will be our portion. A man told me that after going through a hard time, he finally came to the place where he had to say, "Lord, I am satisfied with you." Once he said that, he gained a new perspective on his troubles and his life began to change. When hard times come, we should say, "It is the Lord; let Him do what seems best to Him." After Job had lost virtually everything, he declared, "The LORD gave, and the LORD has taken away; blessed be the name of the LORD" (Job 1:21 ESV). This is true for all once we can view the hand of God in our trials.

2. We can see good where others can only see evil.

More than anything else, this was the secret of Joseph's willingness to forgive: *He saw God everywhere.* Because he had such a profound sense of God's presence, he understood that every event in his life must somehow be ascribed to the hand of God working behind the scenes. Thus he could say to his brothers, "It was not you, but God who sent me to Egypt." The same is true for his seduction by Potiphar's wife, the false rape accusation, and the years he spent in prison. All of it related back to God's purposes for his life. To make the point clearer, we should understand that Joseph means to say more than simply "God was there" when all the bad circumstances happened. That is true, of course, but it does not communicate the full sense of his words. Joseph means to say, "God was in charge of the whole process." It's not as if the brothers sold him into slavery and then God intervened to bring about a good result. Joseph's words demand something more than that. Joseph means that everything that happened—the good and the bad—was part of God's ultimate plan for his life. He was sent to Egypt to save the lives of his own family—the very brothers who had betrayed him. This was God's plan from the beginning, and that fact alone explains all that happened to him. What a profound view this is of the sovereignty of God.

Now, how much of God's plan did Joseph understand in the beginning? Zero. When he was in the cistern, he had no clue that one day he would be the number-two man in the most powerful empire in the world. When he was working for Potiphar, he had no clue that soon he would be in prison. When he was in prison, he had no idea he would one day interpret Pharaoh's dream. When the cupbearer forgot him, he had no reason to think he would ever be remembered again. Even during the "seven fat years" and the first part of the "seven lean years," Joseph had no idea God would use him to deliver his family. We can only imagine Joseph thought he would never see his brothers or his father again. He was in Egypt, they were in Canaan, and there was no reason for them to go to him, or for him to go to them. As the long story unfolds, Joseph had no more clue about the big picture of his life than we do about the big picture of our lives. As far as he knows, he was sold into slavery by his brothers, purchased by Potiphar, falsely accused by Potiphar's wife, thrown into prison, delivered from prison, and promoted by Pharaoh. Now he's virtually the prime minister of Egypt. By itself, it's an amazing story no one could have predicted. And until the first visit from his brothers, he had no clue about what God might be doing in his life.

That's the way life is for all of us. As I write this, I am sitting at my desk typing these words into my computer. Outside the sun is shining. It's a clear, cold day in Oak Park. So far the phone has not rung even once. Life is peaceful and good. As I look at my life, I'm not aware of anything major (either good or bad) that is about to happen to me. But my perception bears no relation to God's plan for me. God doesn't consult me in advance about His plans for my life. Looking back, I can see how circumstances and events have fit together in a certain way to bring me to where I am right now. But as I look into the future, I can't predict what might happen next week, or next month, or next year. Looking back, I can say that "all things work together for good." Looking ahead, I am trusting God will make my path straight and lead me in the way He wants me to go.

Years ago I spoke to a man whose wife had been in and out of drug rehab several times. Her struggles with drugs and alcohol (and his struggles with anger) had reduced their marriage to a shambles. It may have been the most hopeless marriage I ever saw. But through nothing less than a miracle from God, they somehow pulled through and survived a crisis that lasted for the better part of a decade. One day the man looked me in the eye and said, "I now understand that it had to happen the way it did." It takes great faith in God to make a statement like that, and it could only be said at the end of the ordeal, for in hindsight he could see that even the worst moments were leading to something much better.

3. We have a reason to forgive those who hurt us.

Of course, sometimes those "much better" moments never come. Not every story has a happy ending. Sometimes there is no reconciliation, and sometimes the mistreatment continues unabated. But if we believe in the sovereignty of God, we have a reason to forgive those who hurt us. I'm not saying we should forget what they did to us. We can't really forget because the memories are with us forever. But we *can* forgive even when we can't forget. To forgive means to choose not to remember. To pardon means to clear the record so we no longer cling to the hurts of the past. This is possible only when we come to see our enemies as agents of the Lord, sent by Him (or allowed by Him to come) for reasons that we may never fully understand. If this sounds impossible to do, please recall Jesus' words from the cross; "Father, forgive them, for they do not know what they are doing" (Luke 23:34).

4. *We have a new admiration for God's wisdom in all things.*

Life is like a giant jigsaw puzzle. And we are like children trying to put the puzzle together with only a handful of pieces and without the box that has the picture on the cover. We're left trying to fit our little handful of pieces together and trying to figure out the big picture at the same time. No wonder we struggle to figure out what life is all about. As the years pass we pick up more pieces to the puzzle, and things that once troubled us now seem to fit into place. And we have a new appreciation for the wisdom of God because nothing is ever wasted. Everything "fits" somewhere.

> *God is painting a masterpiece
> in your life, and before He is
> finished, He will use
> every color on His palette.*

Or we are like ants crawling across a painting by Rembrandt. When we come to the darker colors, it seems as if the entire painting is dark, somber, forbidding. Everything around us is dark brown or dark blue or midnight black. But if we could only stand back from the painting, we would see that the darker hues are offset by lighter colors—red, green, yellow, blue, and orange. It is the darkness of the darker hues that makes the brighter colors stand out so vividly. So it is with life itself. We may spend days or weeks or years in the dark tones of life. Sickness, heartache, tragedy, mistreatment, and betrayal may cause us to think there are no lighter tones. But God is painting a masterpiece in your life, and before He is finished, He will use every color on His palette. If you do not see the final product on earth, you will see it clearly in heaven.

During my college years I worked briefly at a carpet mill in Chattanooga, Tennessee. My job was fairly low-tech—mostly pushing a broom and keeping the walkways clean. In my spare moments I loved to watch the huge carpet machines at work. As you stood in the back of a machine, you could see huge spools of yarn—dozens of them, of every conceivable color—spinning rapidly as the yarn went into the machine. From the back side, the yarns and machine seemed to be a meaningless jumble of colors and noise. Nothing made any sense—all you could see was a mass of colored yarns making their way at high speed into the mechanical weaver.

But when you walked to the front of the machine, an entirely different sight greeted you. There you could see carpet slowly emerging—row by row, all the colors perfectly in place, arranged in order as if by magic. But it wasn't magic at all. Someone had programmed the machine to take that tangle of threads and transform it into a pattern of exquisite beauty.

In this life, we stand, as it were, at the back of the machine, looking at the multicolored yarns of circumstance. Some are the dark colors of sadness and confusion, others the bright tones of happiness and success. On this side there seems to be no pattern—only colors and noise. Now and again God gives us a peek at the finished product and we are aware that something beautiful is being produced in us by the Master Designer. *But in this life, we never see the big picture.* That will all change when we get to heaven. Then we will see that everything that happened to us had a purpose—even those things that seemed to bring nothing but pain and heartache. Those dark tones that seem so pointless now will become a vital part of a pattern so beautiful that if we were to see it now, it would take our breath away.

How can we live with hope in a world where tragedy is never far away? The answer is simple, though not easy to put into practice. We live this way by faith. We choose to believe that God is at work in everything that happens to us. And we choose to believe that even when nothing makes sense to us. Faith like that is made strong when it is based on the Word of God. And that's why the story of Joseph is so important.

The world says, "Seeing is believing." If I see it, I will believe it. But that principle is reversed in the spiritual realm. God says, "Believing is seeing." We will see God's hand once we believe it is truly there. First Peter 2:19 says we can endure unjust suffering when we are "conscious of God."

How can anyone submit to unfair treatment graciously? How do we continue to praise God when we (or our loved ones) are being mistreated? *We endure unjust suffering for one reason and one reason only: because we are conscious of God.* Let's flesh this out in a series of statements:

a. I am where I am right now by God's appointment.

b. If God wanted me to be somewhere else, I'd be somewhere else.

c. When God wants me somewhere else, I'll be somewhere else.

d. Because God is good, it must be for my good to be where I am right now.

e. The fact that I can't see any good in my present situation doesn't mean it isn't there. It just means I can't see it right now.

f. I don't have to understand the big picture in order to believe there is a big picture.

g. God's promises cover the details of my life even when the details seem random and out of control.

h. God sometimes allows things to happen to me that seem unfair and even harsh.

i. I won't understand those things while I am going through them.

j. The one thing I can do is endure them patiently, because I believe God is right there with me every moment of every day.

It all depends on whether or not you are conscious of God. Do you believe God has you where you are for a purpose—even if you can't see what that purpose is? If you answer yes, then you will endure suffering even though it is painful and frustrating. If you answer no, then you will almost certainly try to bail out of your situation and you will probably become bitter and angry in the process.

How This Applies to Us

Charles Simeon concluded his sermon with two points of application that bear repeating:

1. *How happy is the Christian in this world!*

The unsaved have no hope in this world. To those who don't know Christ, bad things happen with no ultimate purpose. Not so for those who know the Lord. As the Christian navigates a tempestuous ocean, he does so knowing that an all-wise, Almighty Pilot is at the helm. Even when the waves rise around him and threaten to cast him into the deep, he has no fear. Though he does not know what will happen in the short run, he is certain that in the long run God's plan for his life will be worked out perfectly. Therefore, he is satisfied and has perfect peace in his soul.

2. *How happy will he be in that future world!*

The Christian firmly believes that Romans 8:28 is true in every circumstance. He believes that all things work together for his good and for God's glory because God has said it is so. Thus he walks by faith, not by sight. He firmly believes that someday he will see all the links in the chain of circumstances that led him from earth to heaven. And in that day he will bless the Lord for His sovereign wisdom displayed in every circumstance of life. With that confidence, he can rest in the Lord now, knowing all will be well later.

The Costly Act of Forgiveness

Charles Simeon ended his sermon with these words: "Let us commit ourselves entirely to God, and be satisfied with His dealings toward us." And "what we know not now, we shall know hereafter." I am struck by the phrase "be satisfied with His dealings toward us." How many of us can say we are satisfied with the Lord and how He has dealt with us?

On Sunday, November 24, 2002, Gary Witherall spoke at a memorial service for his wife held at the church building that adjoined the clinic where she was murdered three days earlier. Addressing the 400 mourners who packed the chapel (and others who stood outside in the rain), he explained again why they had come to Lebanon and how he felt about what had happened:

> "So many people think my wife's death was a waste…but we believe that coming here with the message of Jesus would never be a waste. It is a message worth laying our lives down for," he said. Sobbing, he added, "Whoever did this crime, I forgive them. It's not easy. It took everything that I have but I can forgive these people because God has forgiven me."[11]

Forgiveness is never easy. In a situation like this, it would appear to be impossible. But Gary Witherall has discovered the truth of the sovereignty of God. Good theology has rescued his soul in a moment when most of us would give in to despair and bitterness. The road of forgiveness will seem like weakness to those who don't believe in God, but as hard as it is, it is far better than giving in to bitterness that corrodes the heart and destroys the soul. Those who believe in God's sovereignty can overcome bitterness through the costly act of forgiveness.

In the end, forgiveness is not about us, and it's not about those who hurt us. Forgiveness is all about God. Until we grasp this, forgiveness will remain a terrible burden we cannot begin to bear.

Four

A Lesson from the Lord's Prayer

—— ❧ ——

It is by forgiving that one is forgiven.

MOTHER TERESA

The fifth petition of the Lord's Prayer seems simple enough, but simple things can sometimes be very deep. In this petition, Jesus said, "Forgive us our debts, as we also have forgiven our debtors" (Matthew 6:12). Everyone agrees this is a difficult word from the Lord. It is hard to understand, and even harder to apply. Our basic problem is this: It appears that the Lord has drawn something into this prayer that does not belong there. We would understand this petition perfectly if it read, "Forgive us our debts" and just stopped right there. That would make sense. We all understand that we need to confess our sins and ask for forgiveness. We know that confession and repentance are part of what prayer is all about. But why does Jesus add "as we also have forgiven our debtors"? At first glance, there doesn't seem to be any connection between the first part of the petition and the second part.

Grace or Works?

It seems as if Jesus is saying, "The way you treat other people is the way God will treat you." On one level that thought is puzzling; on another it is profoundly disquieting. On still another level, it appears to present a major theological difficulty. Not long ago I was invited to appear before our high school youth group for an event called "Stump the Pastor." The teenagers were asked to write their questions ahead of time—and they were encouraged to be both creative and obscure. Several of the students excelled in the latter category by asking questions such as, "Who or what was Ziv?" and "Who is listed as the seventh-to-the-last ancestor of Joseph?" But one question dealt with this very petition. It read something like this: "Why does Jesus say we should pray to be forgiven as we forgive others? Why would Almighty God tie Himself to what we do on earth?" That's a good question, isn't it?

So this petition is puzzling, difficult, and one that bothers every sincere thinker. It makes you wonder what Jesus really meant. Is Jesus teaching that God's forgiveness is conditional? Is He telling us that *our* forgiveness from God is somehow predicated on *our* forgiving other people? It does appear, at first reading, that is indeed what He is teaching. If so, is this not teaching us that forgiveness is a work by which we gain God's favor? What, then, happens to the great biblical doctrine of the grace of God? When it comes to forgiveness, who takes the first step—God or man?

Indeed, this is a difficult text of Scripture. Because it is, let me state my conclusion at the very beginning of this chapter. This verse means exactly what it says. The teaching of this verse can be summarized in one simple sentence: *Unless you forgive, God will not forgive you.* I repeat, this verse means exactly what it says. There is nothing hidden here; there is nothing tricky here. Jesus *is* saying that unless you forgive, you will not be forgiven.

Signing Your Own "Death Warrant"

Augustine called this text "a terrible petition." He pointed out that if you pray these words while harboring an unforgiving spirit, you are actually asking God not to forgive you. Ponder that for a moment. If you pray, "Forgive us our debts, as we have forgiven our debtors" while refusing to forgive those who have wronged you, this prayer, which is meant to be a blessing, becomes a self-inflicted curse. In that case you are really saying, "O God, because I have not forgiven my brother, please do not forgive me." That is why Charles Haddon Spurgeon, the great English preacher, said that if you pray the Lord's Prayer with an unforgiving spirit, you have virtually signed your own "death warrant."

During one period of his life, John Wesley was a missionary in the American colonies—primarily in the area that would become the state of Georgia. There was a general by the name of Oglethorpe with whom Wesley had some dealings. General Oglethorpe was a great military leader, but he had a reputation as a harsh and brutal man. One day he said to John Wesley, "I never forgive." To which Wesley replied, "Then, sir, I hope you never sin."

I received an e-mail from a man who has wrestled at length with the issue of forgiveness in his own life. Looking back on his own life, he discovered a powerful connection between forgiveness and being set free from a debilitating addiction:

> Your sermon reminded me that forgiveness is an act of the will, a choice that I make each time someone hurts me. That choice also has nothing to do with my "feelings," whether or not I want to forgive, or "feel like" forgiving. Most alcoholics/addicts have a very hard time with this, and it has been proven in hundreds of clinical tests that most of us with this problem have resentment at the core of our drinking. A case in point: When I joined AA I discovered I had a fierce resentment against my ex-wife. As my sponsor used to say, "Boy, she's livin' rent free in your head."
>
> One of the other pearls that he cast before this swine was that "having a resentment is like drinking poison and praying for the other guy to die." The logic of that stupidity finally rang

home with me. I guess prior to that the cheese had slipped off my cracker, but good.

The great danger was that if I did not forgive her, I could not be released from this prison and might drink again. Christ ordered us to do this. "If you keep My commands, you are My disciples. *Then* you shall know the truth and the truth shall set you free." This promise is conditional and doesn't apply to me if I don't keep His commands. Period.

Solution: I was told to pray for her every day and every time during every day that I thought of her for 90 days and to report to him every day what I had learned from this exercise. I discovered that somewhere between the thirtieth and sixtieth days, the resentment left me and for the most part has been gone ever since. When I think of her now, it's mostly in gratitude for the good years and kids we had together and to remember how my own irresponsibility in drinking led to the demise of that relationship. Those were my own bad choices.

Since then, the Lord has restored what the locusts had eaten and then some. When the ugly specter of previous resentment returns, I have to pray for her again. Works every time…even though sometimes I have to pray for the willingness to be willing.

> *To refuse to forgive someone and then ask God for forgiveness is a kind of spiritual schizophrenia.*

The Key Word

When we pray, "Forgive us our debts, as we also have forgiven our debtors," we are asking God to forgive our sins according to the same standard we have used in forgiving the sins of others. There are 11 words in the text, but only one of them is important for our purposes. It's the little word "as." Everything hangs on the meaning of that word. "As" is the conjunction that joins the first half of the petition with the second half. When Jesus says "as," He is setting up a comparison between the way we forgive and the way God forgives us. This text says that we set the standard and then God follows the standard. We establish the pattern and then God follows that pattern in the way He deals with us. When we pray this prayer, we are really saying, "O God, deal with me as I deal with other people. Deal with me as I have dealt with others." More specifically, we are saying, in effect, "God, I did some favors for my neighbor, and my neighbor is ungrateful to me for all I have done. I am angry with my neighbor and will not forgive him for his ingratitude. Now deal with me as I have dealt with my neighbor." We set the standard, and God follows our lead.

To refuse to forgive someone and then ask God for forgiveness is a kind of spiritual schizophrenia. You are asking God to give you what you are unwilling to give to someone else. The fifth petition of the Lord's Prayer says you cannot have it both ways. Do you want to be forgiven? You must forgive others. Unless you forgive, you will not be forgiven.

Junk Food of the Soul

There is another way to say this. The way we treat others has a direct impact on our relationship with God. As long as we harbor relational sins and wrong attitudes, we will never grow spiritually. These relational sins are like junk food of the soul. They choke off our craving for the Word so that instead of growing, we stay just as we are. As long as you treat people unkindly and gossip about them and harbor bitterness, you will never grow spiritually—not even if you come to church four times a week and go to Bible study every other day. Your relational sins will choke off God's Word in your life. That explains why some people come to church for years and never get better. They're harboring a relational garbage pit on the inside. They make excuses for their envy, they ignore their gossip, they make light of their cutting comments, and they justify their meanness toward others. And they don't grow because they can't grow. When your horizontal relationships with others are messed up, your vertical relationship with God will never be right. God has wired us up so that the horizontal and the vertical go together. John says it very plainly in his first epistle: "If anyone says, 'I love God,' yet hates his brother, he is a liar. For anyone who does not love his brother, whom he has seen, cannot love God, whom he has not seen" (1 John 4:20). We cannot say, "I hate you" to a friend or family member and then say, "Lord, I love you. Please bless me right now." God says, "No deal." It doesn't work that way.

Snack food has a way of messing up our appetite. It happened to me twice recently. One Thursday afternoon, I drove out to a sporting goods store looking for some cold-weather gear for my bike riding in winter weather. I didn't find what I was looking for, but I wanted to make the trip to the store worthwhile, so I bought a bag of trail mix and ate it on the way home. For supper, my wife Marlene had fixed a wonderful meal, but I could hardly eat because I wasn't very hungry. Then the very next afternoon, I ate a late lunch. I'm not sure why I did this, but I drove up to a popular hot dog stand. I went alone, which I shouldn't have done because when you go by yourself, you are tempted to eat too much. And that's what happened to me. While I was standing in line I thought to myself, *You should order some extra fries.* The fries at this stand are fabulous—the workers slice the potatoes while you watch, and they throw the slices right in the hot oil. Then they put the fries on top of the hot dog and serve this greasy dish in a brown paper bag. It's a little bit of heaven. But they serve plenty of fries with the hot dog, so you don't really need extra fries. But I ordered them anyway…and ate every one of them. About an hour or two later, Marlene called and said she was preparing a special supper because it was Friday night and our son Mark was going to be gone for the evening. Marlene is a marvelous cook, and she wasn't happy to hear that I wasn't hungry. But that wasn't her fault. It was mine—for eating too many greasy French fries.

That's what happens when you eat too much junk food or too many snacks—messes up your appetite. And the same thing happens to you spiritually when you indulge in relational sins. When you're angry or upset or critical or mean or unkind or when you speak cutting words, that's a poison in your soul that chokes off your desire for God's Word.

When your horizontal relationships are out of whack, your vertical relationship is out of whack also.

Taste and See

Do you see how it all comes back to God once again? Loving your brothers isn't about you or them. Forgiving those who have hurt you isn't about you or them. It's about God.

When we are angry and bitter…
When we envy others…
When we criticize those who aren't like us…
When we pass along rumors…
When we cling to hurtful memories…
When we argue with those who call us to forgive…
When we respond harshly to those who bother us…
When we lose our temper…
When we answer hastily with foolish words…
When we judge others harshly…
When we answer our spouse with harsh, cruel words…
When we are impatient and irritable toward our children…
When we have no time to be kind to the less fortunate…
When we go through our day with a perpetual scowl…

When we act in these ways, it is always because we have forgotten the goodness of the Lord. Psalm 34:8 says, "Taste and see that the Lord is good." God tastes better than sin! Revenge is sweet, but God is sweeter. Sin brings pleasure for a moment, but with God there are eternal joys. You got a taste of God's goodness when you came to Christ. Do you remember what that felt like? Do you remember how wonderful it was to have the load of sin lifted off your shoulders? Do you remember what it felt like to finally be free? Some of us have forgotten what that felt like, and we have forgotten where we came from, and we have forgotten the pit we were in before Jesus rescued us. And when you forget God's goodness, it's easy to become critical and judgmental of others. Your bitterness will kill your appetite for His sweetness, or His sweetness will dispel your bitterness. You can't have both at the same time!

After I shared this truth with my congregation, a man said to me, "I need to go buy a broom." When I asked why, he said, "So I can sweep some junk out my life." I think a lot of us need to do some soul-sweeping. And if you've been eating too much spiritual junk food, you need to pray, "Make me hungry for you, O Lord!"

All in the Same Boat

Not long ago our church hosted a concert benefiting Breakthrough Urban Ministries. They do an incredible job of reaching people in the inner city of Chicago. Over the last few years, we've had a chance to partner with them and see firsthand the power of Jesus Christ to reclaim broken lives. The benefit featured the choir from Landmark Baptist Church in Chicago, plus our own Celebration Choir, plus the musical group Proclaim. Near the end of the concert, as Proclaim was about to sing its last song, Keith Johnson (a member of our church) gave a mini-sermon on the importance of caring about the hurting people of the world. He and a few others go out to the west side of Chicago every Friday night to witness to the prostitutes to bring them to Jesus. Some of the women who have been reached for Christ now attend our church. It's not easy for them to come here, but they do, and I'm glad they are here because their presence demonstrates the power of the gospel and helps us move one step closer to being a truly Christian church. Their presence reminds us that when it comes to salvation, we're all in the same boat. We're all sinners desperately in need of God's grace. It's just that some of us have more "respectable" sins, that's all. But apart from Jesus, we'd all be going to hell. During his little mini-sermon, Keith said, "I'm so glad to be part of this ministry that reaches out to people who don't look right or act right and sometimes don't smell right. But that's okay, because someone reached out to me when I was in need of a Savior."

And that touches a problem facing many evangelical Christian churches. We've forgotten what we smelled like before Jesus saved us. We didn't smell very good on the inside, and maybe we didn't smell so good on the outside, but someone came to us with the good news and led us to Jesus. We've forgotten how we used to stink in the eyes of the Lord. We've forgotten the pit we were in when God found us. We've forgotten what it means to be lost. It's time that we started remembering the goodness of the Lord.

When you remember the Lord's goodness to you, you won't have the time or the inclination to look down on others or harbor hatred or bitterness or envy or malice in your heart. What is the answer? Try harder? Be nice to each other? No, the answer is not in you at all. The answer is God! Every part of your life as a Christian is about God—who He is, and what He has done for you. Has the Lord been good to you? Have you tasted His goodness in your life? Has God rescued you? Did He answer your prayers when you cried out to Him?

If so, give thanks and remember His goodness. Rejoice in it, and let it be the foundation of your life. And you will find your anger and malice and envy and all those other junk food relational sins slipping away. So let me repeat the phrase I've used several times in this chapter, only this time with a twist: *The horizontal is the key to the vertical, and the vertical is the key to the horizontal.* It's all about God. We look down on others because we have forgotten how bad we smelled before we tasted God's goodness. Remember His goodness to you, and you'll start treating people with true brotherly love, and then you'll grow.

An "Unforgiven" Christian

But does the Bible really teach that God's forgiveness of us is somehow linked to our forgiveness of others? Yes, indeed it does.

Let's go back to the words of Jesus. The fifth petition, which we've already examined, is in verse 12. Now let's drop down two verses. The Lord's Prayer is over, but Jesus is still speaking:

> If you forgive men when they sin against you, your heavenly Father will also forgive you. But if you do not forgive men their sins, your Father will not forgive your sins (Matthew 6:14-15).

I want to call one crucial fact to your attention: Jesus had just given the Lord's Prayer, and the only part He singles out for additional commentary is the fifth petition. All the other petitions are left alone. I believe He offered further commentary because He knew we would feel uncomfortable with this part of the Lord's Prayer. He knew we would try to wiggle out from under it. That is why in verses 14-15 He spells it out so clearly—so that no one can doubt it.

What happens when a believer holds a grudge? What happens when he refuses to forgive? What happens when a Christian harbors anger and ill feelings toward those who have wronged him? Is he forgiven? Yes, in the sense that he is justified before God. Yes, in the sense that when he dies, he will go to heaven. No, he is not forgiven in the sense of having daily cleansing and sweet fellowship with the Lord. He is "in Christ" and "out of fellowship" with the Lord. He is walking in the flesh. He has given Satan a foothold in his life (Ephesians 4:26-27). He is walking in disobedience before the Lord, and he opens himself up to divine chastisement by the Lord (Hebrews 12:4-11).

As strange as it may sound, there is such a thing as an "unforgiven" Christian. This is not a statement about ultimate destinies. To be "unforgiven" in this sense means that the channel of God's grace is blocked from the human side. In particular, it means you have chosen to hang on to your bitterness and to forfeit your daily walk with the Lord. You would rather be angry than joyful. You have chosen resentment over peace. Your grudges have become more important to you than the daily blessing of God. You would rather live with the "hidden torturers" than experience the freedom of forgiveness.

If you are a Christian—a genuine believer in Jesus Christ—unless you forgive, you will not be forgiven. Why? Because God has already forgiven 100 percent of your sins by the blood of Jesus Christ. How dare you, then, be unforgiving to someone who hurt you. That's really the issue. How dare you be unforgiving after what Jesus Christ did for you on the cross.[12]

> *T*he more you see the seriousness
> of your sin before God, the less
> the sins of other people
> against you will bother you.

What happens when we refuse to forgive? Here are ten consequences of an unforgiving spirit (I compiled this list using material from R. T. Kendall, Waylon Moore, and Bob Leland):

1. Our fellowship with the Father is blocked.

2. The Holy Spirit is grieved.

3. Your prayers will not be answered.

4. God leaves you alone to face the problems of life in your own power.

5. The devil gains a foothold through your bitterness.

6. You force God to become your enemy.

7. You lose the blessing of God on your life.

8. You waste time nursing a wounded spirit.

9. You become enslaved to the people you hate.

10. You become like the people you refuse to forgive.

The Real Condition of Forgiveness

The real condition of the forgiveness of sins is a repentant heart. Would we not all agree on that? Before you can be forgiven, there must be true repentance before God. And what is the mark of a penitent heart if it is not a forgiving spirit toward other people? As John Stott puts it, "God forgives only the penitent and one of the chief evidences of true penitence is a forgiving spirit."[13] How can you even talk about wanting your sins forgiven if you're holding grudges against other people? You're asking God to do for you what you are unwilling to do for others.

Our real problem at this point is not theological, but personal. We don't see ourselves as very great sinners; therefore, we do not appreciate how greatly God has forgiven us. And when your own sins seem small, the sins of others against you will seem big indeed. The reverse is also true. The more you see the seriousness of your sin before God, the less the sins of other people against you will bother you. To paraphrase the Puritan preacher Matthew Henry, "He who relents is he who repents." Don't talk about repentance unless you are willing to forgive your brothers and sisters. Otherwise your repentance is just hot air and empty talk. True repentance starts with a change of mind that leads to a change of heart that leads to a change (in this case) in the way we view those who have sinned against us.

Many years ago I pastored a small church in Southern California. I went there two months after graduating from seminary, and stayed for about five years. In seminary we were told that it was typical for a church to grow for about six months after a new pastor arrives, and then the growth normally levels off. That's exactly what happened here. The church grew for a few months, and then the growth leveled off. And it stayed level. Very level. Extremely level. Nothing I did seemed to make any difference in the growth of the church. After a few years I began to think about leaving. One Wednesday afternoon I was in my office at church doing some work when the phone rang. The call came from the pastor of a very large church on the West Coast. His call was unexpected and unsolicited. It was "the call" that every young pastor dreams about. Someone had given him my name because he was looking for a pastor to join his staff and share in the preaching responsibilities at his church. It was a dream job in every way. He said he wanted to come and chat with me in person. Then he asked the size of my congregation. When I told him, there was a short pause. He asked me to send my resumé and then said, "I'll get in touch with you soon."

I couldn't wait to go home and tell my wife the good news. That very day I put my resumé in the mail along with some printed sermons. After mailing the material, I began to dream about all the possibilities. The sermons I would preach, the vast crowds that would attend, the doors that would begin to open. Even though several decades have passed since that phone call, I can still remember and even feel inside the incredible excitement, the euphoria I felt at the moment. My life was about to radically change for the better…or so I thought.

A few days passed with no word from the pastor, and I thought to myself, *He'll call me soon.* After a week or so, I decided he was probably busy but would get around to calling soon. After all, pastors of large churches have a lot to do, and he probably was busy. More days passed, and I began to get concerned. Every day I waited for the mail to arrive, and anxiously flipped through the junk mail, hoping for a letter that never arrived. Days slowly turned into weeks, and as time went on, my joy turned to concern, and my concern turned eventually into frustration. After a month had passed, my frustration turned to despair.

After still a few more weeks, the realization hit me: *He's not going to get back in touch with me even though he said he would.* And my despair turned to anger. Who did he think he was to treat me that way? Maybe I pastored a small church, but I hadn't asked him to call me. That was his idea. I didn't ask him to recruit me with promises of a bright future. He was the one who said, "I'll get in touch with you soon." The truth was hard to face:

He wasn't going to write.
He wasn't going to call.
He wasn't going to talk to me at all.

I sank into a deep depression. Looking back from the vantage point of many years' hindsight, it now seems silly that I was so concerned. But back then I felt betrayed by someone who had entered my life, made a promise, and then had not even bothered to call back to say, "I'm not interested." Even if he had decided I wasn't qualified, didn't I at least deserve the courtesy of a phone call?

I was inconsolable. My wife tried to encourage me, but to no avail. Worse, this wasn't the kind of problem I could share with anyone else. It was too embarrassing to mention to my friends in the ministry. And I felt used and useless. Plus, at that point in my life, I simply wasn't mature enough to understand that these things happen all the time.

People make promises they don't keep.
People say they will call you but they don't.
People intend to stay in touch but soon forget you.
People ask for help and then never say thanks.
People tell stories about you and then deny it to your face.
People fail all the time in a million different ways.

People are people. We all fail in many ways. We overlook it when *we* do it, but we're shocked when *someone else* (especially someone we thought we could depend on) turns out to be human.

Months went by, and I never heard back from the man. Eventually I got over the disappointment, but the anger stayed with me for a long time. It was a low-level sort of anger that made me short-tempered, snippy, cranky, and generally a miserable grouch. Looking back, I am amazed that my wife stayed so positive while I wallowed in my self-pity. And beneath it all was a deep reservoir of self-doubt. This whole episode made me wonder about my long-term prospects as a pastor. Perhaps I had been weighed in the balances and found wanting. The dejection from thinking I might be inadequate was even worse than the residual anger I felt.

The turning point came rather unexpectedly. One afternoon Marlene and I went to a dollar store to do some shopping. Even though I can't remember the name of the store, as I type these words I can clearly picture myself going up and down the aisles. Marlene was shopping, and I was idly looking at the shelves. And of course, I was still thinking to myself about what had happened months earlier. For the five-thousandth time, I was replaying it all in my mind. At that moment, God spoke to me. I can't think of a better way to describe this even though I didn't hear an audible voice. But in that dollar store, as I meandered through the aisles, the God of heaven and earth spoke to me. He said something like this: "Ray, wake up. You've been stewing about this for far too long. You've done the same thing yourself to other people a thousand times." There it was. That was the bottom-line truth that would set me free. What that big-church pastor had done to me wasn't so unusual. I had done the same thing over and over and over again to other people. God continued:

> "You've made promises you didn't keep."
> "You've started projects you didn't finish."
> "You've let people down who depended on you."
> "You've not made phone calls you said you were going to make."
> "You've led people to believe things you knew weren't true."
> "You're as bad as he is."

Then the thought came: "No, you are worse. He sinned against you once. You sinned twice. You've done the same thing he did. And you're bitter at him because he's a sinner just like you."

Just like that, I felt a massive weight lifting from my shoulders. Once I could face the truth, then I could be set free. And the anger and despair and depression left my soul. I started laughing and singing right there in the dollar store. It was a moment of self-revelation. I saw myself as the great sinner that I am, and that sight set me free. It was no burden for me to forgive the pastor of the large church when I realized that he might pastor a larger church, but in my eyes I was a larger sinner.

There is one more detail to this story. Two months later I received a letter from the pastor who had forgotten about me. He apologized for his oversight and offered a reasonable explanation. It truly was just "one of those things." I haven't had a negative thought about him since that day in the dollar store over 20 years ago. Once I saw myself as a sinner, it was easy to forgive him.

Needed: A Serious Moral Inventory

There is a vital link between the way you treat other people and the way God in heaven is going to treat you. Let's face it: We don't like that. We'd much prefer if we could just have our relationship with God insulated and encapsulated so we could treat other people any way we like. Jesus says, "No deal. You can't have it that way." *Unless you forgive, you will not be forgiven.* This is a hard word, isn't it? But it is a hard word of grace. Many of us desperately need to take inventory of our hearts and ask ourselves some serious questions:

> Am I up-to-date on my forgiving?
>
> Am I holding a grudge against anyone?
>
> Am I harboring any bitterness against any person?
>
> Am I talking too much about what others have done to me?
>
> Have I forgiven those closest to me who have hurt me so deeply?

Someone says, "But I can't forgive." No, don't ever say that. The word *can't* is a cop-out. The issue is deeper than that. You won't forgive. Don't make excuses and don't play games. If you are a true Christian, a genuine believer in Jesus Christ, your sins have been washed away, and you can forgive. What God has done for you, you can do for others.

As long as you refuse to forgive, you're better off not praying the Lord's Prayer. Because unless you forgive, you will not be forgiven. As long as you hold on to your resentments, you are still chained to the past. You only hurt yourself and block off the channel of God's blessing in your life. Although there is freedom in Christ, the unforgiving Christian knows nothing about it. He is still in bondage to the remembered hurts from the past. And until those chains are broken by a decisive act of forgiveness, he will remain a slave to the past.

I have said several times that this is a hard word, and indeed it is. But it is also a cleansing word that cuts through all our flimsy excuses and leads us to a fountain of grace where we can be healed, made whole, and restored to a right relationship with our Creator. Our God freely forgave us while we were His enemies. Can we not do for others what He has done for us?

The word of the Lord remains. Unless you forgive, you will not be forgiven.

Five

Seventy Times Seven

———— ✿ ————

*Forgetting is something that time takes care of,
but forgiveness is an act of volition, and only the sufferer
is qualified to make the decision.*

SIMON WIESENTHAL

*M*any years ago I preached a series of sermons called "The Marriage Clinic." Instead of picking the topics myself, I gave the church a ballot with a list of suggested topics and asked the people to choose the ones they wanted most to hear. The series was so popular that I decided to do it again the next year, only this time I called it "The Family Clinic." Once again I gave the congregation a ballot listing various topics relating to the family and asked the congregation to vote for the ones they most wanted to hear.

Interestingly, only one topic was selected both times. All the other topics were picked only once—either for the marriage series, or the family series. The topic was "How to Handle Anger and Bitterness." That puzzled me for a while. I hadn't expected it to be so popular. So I asked Marlene why so many of our people wanted to know how to handle anger and bitterness. She replied with characteristic wisdom, "It's probably because they have a lot of

85

anger and bitterness." She was right. In the years since then I have learned that most Christians struggle with these emotions. They want to know how to handle them because they have so much of them stored up inside.

This then brought to mind the lady who came to see me because her husband was an absolute bum. He wouldn't get up in the morning, he wouldn't get dressed, he wouldn't keep a job, he wouldn't help around the house, he wouldn't talk to his wife, and he wouldn't go anywhere or do anything. He just sat around the house all day long. "Pastor, I'm thinking about getting a divorce," she told me.

Then I remembered another woman who came to see me. She was one of the pillars of the church. After 35 years of marriage, her husband had an affair with his secretary, committed adultery, and carried in his wallet pictures of the child he fathered. She told me, "It's getting to the point where I may just blow up any day. I don't know how much longer I can take this."

Several years after that I received a letter from a dear friend in a distant state who was caught in a difficult marital situation. She wrote, "I surely need to review your forgiveness sermon. I try to keep up to date on my forgiving, but find my heart pretty cold and stony."

Can This Marriage Be Saved?

In the years since then, I have spent hundreds of hours talking with husbands and wives about their marriages. Usually by the time a couple goes to see a pastor, their marriage is already in a state of serious distress. They come with stories of marital unfaithfulness, emotional or physical abuse, financial mismanagement, verbal abuse, communication breakdowns, disagreements over childrearing, petty grievances that have become huge differences, lack of love, loss of respect, widely differing expectations, and a host of other problems. More than that, they come because those problems have built up to the point where they threaten the continued existence of the marriage.

Every couple has the same questions: Is there any hope? Can our marriage be saved? Should we give up and get a divorce, or is there a better way? The problems I just mentioned are notoriously difficult, and none of them lend themselves to easy or quick solutions. I have also learned over the years not to make promises I cannot keep. While I do not believe divorce is ever mandated, I also understand that sometimes it cannot be avoided. In today's legal climate, one person can file for divorce and there is little the other person can do to stop it. Sometimes marriages end, even the marriages of Christian people who at one time were both faithful in the church. There is no getting around that fact, and there is no use in pretending it is not true. Each case is different and each marriage has its own unique set of factors that must be carefully analyzed. But over the years I have discovered that whenever a couple has trouble in their marriage, they must eventually face the issue of anger and bitterness. If they refuse, they may make changes that work good on the surface, but the underlying problems will not go away.

Forgiveness is not some kind of miracle cure that can solve all the problems of your life. But it is a foundational issue we must deal with. When we have anger and bitterness stored up inside us, we must learn how to forgive. And we may even need to forgive over and over again. There is no escape from the need to forgive because on this side of heaven, there is no escape from living in a sinful world. Whenever sinners live together, they will sooner or later (probably sooner) do things that irritate, upset, and hurt each other. Forgiveness makes it possible for irritations to be overlooked and deep hurts to be healed.

"How Long Do I Have to Take It?"

In one of His most famous parables, Jesus told a story about forgiveness that makes it very clear how forgiveness is to be carried out. The story, found in Matthew 18:21-35, is the Parable of the Unforgiving Servant.

Here we see the apostle Peter come to Jesus with a question we have all asked at one time or another. Somebody had done him wrong, and Peter had forgiven him. The same fellow did it again, and Peter had forgiven him again. He did it again, and Peter forgave him again, but this time Peter got mad.

So he comes to Jesus with a question we can all understand. "Lord, how many times shall I forgive my brother when he sins against me?" Peter wanted to know how much guff he had to take from somebody. When do you quit turning the other cheek? When is it okay to blow your stack?

Now, Peter didn't wait for an answer. He was ready to suggest one. He asked, "Up to seven times?" We might think Peter wasn't being very generous, but in that place and time, he was. The rabbis taught that you had to forgive a man three times, and then you could retaliate. So Peter thinks to himself, *Well, I'll just double that and add one.* Seven, after all, is the perfect number. To be honest, forgiving a man seven times is commendable. Most of us get frustrated if we have to forgive someone twice. By human standards, Peter's suggestion to forgive seven times was extravagant.

No More Mr. Nice Guy

Peter's heart was in the right place, but his attitude was wrong. He wanted to put a legal limit on forgiveness. He wanted a number, a limit, a place where he could finally say, "No more Mr. Nice Guy." But look at Jesus' answer in verse 22: "I do not say to you seven times, but seventy times seven" (ESV). That clunk you hear is Peter falling over in a dead faint. He couldn't believe his ears. Seventy times seven? That's 490 times! Jesus said, "Peter, you've got it all wrong. You don't count the number of times you forgive someone. *Forgiveness is unlimited.*"

Now, 70 times seven does not mean we're to keep count. Rather, it means there is no limit to the number of times you should forgive someone else. By the time you've forgiven someone 490 times, you've gotten into the habit of continual forgiveness.

The truth of unlimited forgiveness is hard for us to grasp, so Jesus told a story in verses 23-35 to help illustrate that truth. The story begins: "The kingdom of heaven is like a king who wanted to settle accounts with his servants. As he began the settlement, a man who owed him ten thousand talents was brought to him." Here's a great king who one day decided to call in all his debts. So he sent out his soldiers, and back they come with this man. When the king asks, "How much does he owe?" his accountants check the books and answer, "Ten thousand talents, your majesty."

To give you some perspective, a talent was an enormous amount of money. A man might work all his life and make ten talents, or possibly 30 talents. But here's a man who's run up a debt of 10,000 talents. In today's terms, that might come to $25 million. How did he run up such a big debt? Perhaps he was the governor of a province and had skimmed off the tax revenues, secretly amassing a huge fortune. The day of reckoning has come, and the man is flat broke. He spent it all; he doesn't have a penny left. So the king says, "Sell his wife, his kids, his house, and while you're at it, sell him." Not that this man was worth that kind of money; the king merely wanted to get back whatever he could.

Rich Man, Poor Man, Beggar Man, Thief

At this point the servant does what any of us would have done: He falls on his knees and begs, "Be patient with me...and I will pay back everything" (verse 26). But this is no time to make excuses. Unless something happens fast, this man is dead meat. That's why he's begging. And he even makes the ridiculous promise to pay it all back. He couldn't do it in a million years! But somehow this touches the king's heart. The Bible says the king was moved with compassion. And he not only releases the man, he also forgives the debt. He wipes the slate clean and erases the book. Now the man owes him nothing. This is the great miracle of the story. The king forgave this enormous debt, this unbelievable amount of money. And the man walks away scot-free.

Soon afterward, this forgiven man spots a man who owed him some money—100 denarii. A single denarius was the average wage for a day's work, so a hundred denarii would equal about three months' pay for a workingman in the first century. If you translate that into modern terms, it might equal as much as $10,000. That's a substantial sum of money.

There are two crucial points to keep in mind at this point: First, 100 denarii was not a small amount, but it was not an impossibly large debt to repay. It is perfectly believable that the man borrowed the money in good faith and fully intended to pay it back over a period of months or years. Unlike the first man, when the second one said, "Be patient with me and I will pay you back," he wasn't being unrealistic. If the first servant would have patience, the second man would indeed pay him back in full.

Second, 100 denarii is not a small amount, but it pales in significance when compared to the debt of 10,000 talents. That's the real point of the story. The first man could never, ever, under any circumstances pay back his debt. Without the grace of the king, he would be in prison for the rest of his life. The first debt was enormous; the second debt was not.

So the forgiven servant sees a fellow servant who owes him $10,000, grabs him by the throat, and says, "Where's the money you owe me, buster? I want it right now." Verse 29 is almost a word-for-word replay of verse 26. Only this time the situation is reversed. The first servant is no longer begging; rather, he is demanding payment. Don't let this point slip by. He had every legal right to demand payment. No one could fault him for wanting his money. That's not the issue. The issue is that the first man wouldn't even give the second man a chance to pay the debt. He wanted his money then and there. Well, the second servant wasn't walking around with $10,000 in his pocket. It would take some time to get that kind of money together.

But the first servant is unwilling to wait. Verse 30 says, "He went off and had the man thrown in prison until he could pay the debt."

The first servant made a serious mistake—he did this in broad daylight. If you're going to be chintzy, it's better to do it behind closed doors. Someone who knew what the king had just done for the first servant saw this, too. Word got around, and soon everybody was talking about it. It wasn't the fact that the first servant would not forgive the second servant that shocked them. It was that he was so unforgiving after having found such mercy himself. Eventually the news gets back to the king. And boy, does he get mad. He sends out his soldiers and they haul the man in. This time there will be no mercy. The king says, "You wicked servant...I canceled all that debt of yours because you begged me to. Shouldn't you have had mercy on your fellow servant just as I had on you?" (verses 32-33). The king had forgiven the first servant a $25-million debt. Forgiven him when he could have enslaved him for life. Forgiven him when he was flat broke. Forgiven him when, by every law in the land, he could have destroyed him. The first servant deserved punishment, and instead found mercy.

Shouldn't that servant have shown the same mercy to the fellow servant who owed him a lousy $10,000?

Consequently, there's no forgiveness this time. The king won't be conned again. The Bible says he called for the torturers and handed the man over to them "until he should pay back all he owed" (verse 34).

The Hidden Torturers

That's the story Jesus told. And He didn't leave us to wonder about the application. He gives it in verse 35: "This is how my heavenly Father will treat each of you unless you forgive your brother from your heart." These words are for believers. Jesus said, "What happened to that man will happen to you unless you learn to forgive and forgive and forgive." The torturers will come and take you away. What torturers? The hidden torturers of anger and bitterness, which eat your insides out. The torturers of frustration and malice, which give you ulcers and high blood pressure and migraine headaches and lower back pain. The torturers that make you lie awake at night on your bed stewing over every rotten thing that happens to you. Why? Because you will not forgive from your heart.

Researchers have discovered the practical implications of Jesus' words. According to *Newsweek* magazine, forgiveness works in two different ways. First, it reduces the health problems associated with anger, hatred, and unforgiveness. "These have specific physiologic consequences—such as increased blood pressure and hormonal changes—linked to cardiovascular disease, immune suppression and, possibly, impaired neurological function and memory." Second, forgiveness promotes well-being because it allows you to build a strong social network. "Someone who nurses grudges and keeps track of every slight is obviously going to shed some relationships over the course of a lifetime." The article concludes by quoting a proverb by Confucius: "If you devote your life to seeking revenge, first dig two graves."[14]

"Pay Me Right Now!"

Too often we are like the unforgiving servant. We stand before Almighty God with our sins piled up like a mountain. The mountain is so tall we can't get over it, so wide we can't go around it. Our sins are like a $25 million debt we could never pay in our lifetime or in a thousand lifetimes. And God, who is rich in mercy, says, "I forgive all your sins. My Son has paid the debt. You owe Me nothing." Then we rise from the pew and leave the church humming, "Every day with Jesus is sweeter than the day before." Before we get to our car we see a person who has done us wrong and we want to grab him by the throat and say, "Pay me right now!"

No wonder we are tormented. No wonder we are so angry and bitter. No wonder we have problems. No wonder our friendships don't last. No wonder we can't get along. No wonder Christmas is such a difficult time of the year. We have not learned the secret of unlimited forgiveness. Verily, the hidden torturers have done their work.

> *Forgiveness is wonderful because the forgiver always has the last word.*

If you want the theme of this chapter in one sentence, here it is: *The way to become great in the kingdom of God is to become a great forgiver.* Mark Twain said it this way: "Forgiveness is the fragrance the violet gives to the heel that has crushed it." Forgiveness is wonderful because the forgiver always has the last word. Someone hurts you, and you forgive that person. He does it again, and you forgive again. He does it a third time, and you forgive again a third time. And so it keeps going. But you always have the last word. Why? Because a person can't wrong you more than you can forgive him.

Difficult, But Not Impossible

We must not lose sight of what Jesus was teaching in the parable. He was not suggesting that forgiveness is easy. It's not. To pay back a debt of $10,000 would take weeks or months or possibly years. But it could be done. Forgiveness is difficult. It requires patience and a gentle spirit. After a relationship has been torn open, healing will not come overnight. *But it is possible.* That's the crucial point. If two people are willing to work at it, healing and reconciliation can take place. With humility on one side and patience on the other, the hurt can be healed and the breach repaired.

But as long as we focus on the wrong people have done to us, forgiveness is impossible. Their sins against us will always look mountainous in our eyes. How could we ever trust anyone who hurt us like that? The only hope of lasting forgiveness is to shift your focus from the sins of others against you to your own sins against God. That changes the equation because it forces us to look inside, to see in horrific clarity the depths of our own depravity. No matter what others have done to us, what we have done to God by sinning against Him is infinitely worse. Therefore, whatever it costs us to forgive someone else will be infinitely less than what it cost God to forgive us.

Finally, the parable brings home the point that whatever forgiveness costs us, unforgiveness costs far more. We pay a far higher price when we're bitter than when we forgive. Worse, we keep on paying and paying and paying, which is why some people carry grudges all the way to the grave. They are still paying for their refusal to forgive.

I Can't Go Back

Let's wrap up this chapter with a principle I call "The First Rule of Spiritual Progress." This principle is comprised of three sentences that have four words each—words which, when taken together, give you the key for moving forward with your life.

> I can't go back.
> I can't stay here.
> I must go forward.

You can't go back to the past—not to relive the good times, or to seek revenge for the bad times. And you can't stay where you are right now. Life is like a river that flows endlessly onward. It matters not whether you are happy in your present situation or whether you seek deliverance from it—you can't stay. The only way to go is forward. *Forgiveness is God's means of letting go of the past and moving forward with God.*

When I said earlier that forgiveness is simple, I wasn't saying it is easy. If you have been deeply hurt, nothing will be harder for you than letting go. But the message of the Bible is clear: Unless you let go of the past, you are doomed to live there forever.

Here are two stories to ponder. One comes from the Civil War, the other from the Vietnam War.

Charles Bracelen Flood, in his book *Lee: The Last Years*, tells of a time after the Civil War when Robert E. Lee visited a woman who took him to the remains of a grand old tree in front of her home. There she cried bitterly that its limbs and trunk had been destroyed by Union artillery fire. She waited for Lee to condemn the North or at least sympathize with her loss. Lee paused, and then said, "Cut it down, my dear madam, and then forget it."[15]

Good advice from a man who knew the horrors of war and suffered the pain of defeat.

The second story comes from an interview with Pete Peterson, the first postwar American ambassador to Vietnam. Mr. Peterson's appointment was ironic because he served six years as a prisoner of war in the dreaded Hanoi Hilton. He returned to the land where he was held captive—not for revenge, but to represent the United States. When asked how he could do this after years of starvation, torture, and inhuman brutality, he replied, "I'm not angry. I left that at the gates of the prison when I walked out in 1972. That may sound simplistic to some people, but it's the truth. I just left it behind me and decided to move forward with my life."

At some point we all have to decide to move on with life. Toward that end, I wish to put forward a novel idea. *You ought to forgive those who have hurt you—not for their sake, but for yours.* I suppose that's why we don't want to forgive. We hope that by nursing our anger we can somehow strike a blow for justice against those who have hurt us. In the end, we hurt ourselves at least as much as we hurt the other person. And often, the person who hurts us ends up winning twice—once when he hurt us, and again when we dwell on the incident.

That's why Jesus' parable must be understood as teaching continual forgiveness—the kind you practice over and over and over again. Remember, forgiveness isn't—or shouldn't be—a tool for manipulating people into having a good relationship with you. No one can force another person to be reconciled to you. That must come from a heart prompted by God's Holy Spirit.

For God's Sake...and for Yours

Ultimately, there are two very good reasons to forgive that have nothing to do with the other person:

- You should forgive because God has commanded it.
- You should forgive because forgiveness is good for your own soul.

Any other benefits are like ice cream added to a piece of apple pie—nice, but not necessary.

In short, we should practice forgiveness for God's sake and for our own sake. That ought to be enough to motivate any of us.

Many of us need this truth because we've been living for years under the burden of remembered hurts. Some of them go back to our childhood. Some of them involve people we haven't seen for a long time. We need to take a trip out to the Cemetery of Forgiveness, make a list of the faults, sins, and failures of those who hurt us, dig a hole in the ground, and bury those faults forever. And *never* dig them up again.

Forgiveness *Is* Possible

I once knew of two women in the same church whose husbands had committed adultery. Neither man seemed more or less likely to do such a thing. The circumstances were different, the incidents far separated in time and place. One man confessed to his wife with tears and later sought counseling. The other man admitted his sin but never sought forgiveness. Not long afterward he died, and then she died. There was bitterness and enormous sadness on both sides. He went to the grave unforgiven, partly because he would never ask for it, partly because she never gave it. What of the other couple? Theirs was not an easy road back. But they decided together to walk the path of forgiveness. More than

20 years had passed when they told me the story. You could hear a whisper of sadness in their voices, but the bitterness was long gone. I should add that I was totally surprised when they told me about what had happened, for they had a radiant and happy relationship. I would never have imagined what they had been through if I hadn't heard it directly from them.

Another story comes to mind: A Christian man had a long-term affair that lasted for years. When the truth came out, he denied it at first, but then admitted his adultery. With great difficulty, he confessed his sin to his wife who apparently had never suspected a thing. To say she was devastated would be putting it mildly. She wept for days. How could the man she trusted betray her so deeply? How could she ever trust him again? I will never forget sitting in her home listening to her pour out her heart. Even as I write these words, I can picture the anguish etched on her face. Most of what she said I have forgotten. But one statement still echoes across the years. She had decided to forgive him. Exactly what that decision cost her, I do not know, but I do know it did not come cheap. Her soul agonized over her husband's sin as she tried to gauge the sincerity of his repentance. Was he truly sorry? Was the affair really over? How could he have been so stupid? What if he did it again? How could she forgive him for years of adultery? The answers took weeks and months to formulate in her heart. But eventually she saw clearly the path she needed to take. She would forgive her husband, take him back, and try to make the marriage work. When she tried to explain this to me, it all boiled down to one sentence: "How could I not forgive him when the Lord has forgiven me of so much?" She said it not with joy (that would be asking too much), but with a resigned faith. This was the foundation of life for her.

I remember thinking to myself that I wasn't sure I would be as generous as she had been. But then, I wasn't in her shoes. And I suppose, looking back, that I was angry with the man for his brazen deception of so many people for so long. But he hadn't committed adultery against me. And his wife, who had been so greatly sinned against, found the strength from the Lord to forgive him. And she did it because of a profound sense of God's forgiveness in her own life. What she had received, she now gave to her unfaithful husband.

> *Forgiveness is difficult, but it is not impossible.*

Back then, I would not have held out any hope for the marriage to survive. That was many years ago. They are still married and they seem happy together. I say that from a distance because they moved away and I haven't talked to either of them in a long time. But theirs seems to be a case where love truly covered a multitude of sins. She could not have done it by herself. Only God can give that sort of grace. What she freely received, she freely gave.

Forgiveness *is* possible. Healing *is* possible. That which was so carelessly broken *can* be restored. But it takes patience, and loving hands, and a full dose of the grace of God. *Forgiveness is difficult, but it is not impossible.* Where the hurt runs very deep, or goes back many years, you will be wise to seek the counsel of other Christians at certain points along the way. Forgiveness is not a magic potion that will suddenly take the shadows out of your life. Nor is the work of forgiveness done quickly or easily. Forgiveness is not an event; forgiveness is a highway you walk every single day. But there is freedom and healing and wholeness for those who dare to make the journey.

Many of us have lived far too long with unresolved hurts going back many years. We've been angry and bitter all that time. The hidden torturers have done their work. No wonder our marriages are so unhappy. No wonder divorce seems like a good alternative. No wonder we determine to shut a friend or co-worker out of our lives, or to seek vengeance.

But it's time to forgive.

Where should we begin?

- Perhaps forgiving from your heart means writing a letter of forgiveness to the one who hurt you.

- Perhaps it means confessing to a friend that you are struggling with issues of forgiveness.

- Perhaps it means asking God to forgive someone for what he or she did to you.

- Perhaps it means memorizing Psalm 103:12, Ephesians 4:31-32, and Hebrews 10:17 in order to get God's viewpoint on forgiveness.

- Perhaps it means listing the other person's offenses one by one and writing over them "Forgiven" and then offering the list to God in prayer.

- Perhaps it means meditating on the fifth petition of the Lord's Prayer—"Forgive us our debts, as we also have forgiven our debtors" (Matthew 6:12).

- Perhaps it means confessing your sins to your spouse or friend—especially your sin of harboring an unforgiving spirit toward him or her—and asking for forgiveness.

- Perhaps it means confessing your anger toward God for allowing terrible things to happen to you. Your struggle with forgiveness toward another person may ultimately be caused by unresolved anger toward God. If you are angry at God, it is possible you have never yielded to Him the right not to know why someone has hurt you so deeply. Until you yield that right to God, you will find it almost impossible to forgive that someone.

- Perhaps it means asking God to bless, in every way, the person who hurt you—emotionally, mentally, spiritually, and physically.

- Perhaps it means taking a step of active love toward the offender—loving him or her in spite of what he or she did or the way he or she is.

Forgiveness will mean different things to different people. The cost will differ depending on the magnitude of the offense. But the result is always the same—liberating freedom from the past and a new foundation on which to build a healthy marriage or friendship.

Whatever you need to do in order to forgive, go ahead and do it.

How many times should you forgive? Jesus said, "Seventy times seven."

Six

Judge Not!

*There is no man so good, who, were he to submit
all his thoughts and actions to the laws, would not
deserve hanging ten times in his life.*

MICHEL DE MONTAIGNE

hey called him "Daddy King." When Martin Luther King, Sr.
died in 1984, he was eulogized as the father of the civil rights
movement in America. One black leader said, "If we started our
own country, he would be our George Washington." In his 84
years he endured more than his share of suffering and hatred.
During his childhood in Georgia, he witnessed lynchings. The
first time he tried to register to vote in Atlanta, he found that the
registrar's office was on the second floor of City Hall—but the
stairwell was closed, the elevator for blacks was out of order, and
the one working elevator was marked "Whites Only."

King, Sr. is mostly remembered for the accomplishments of his
eldest son, Martin Luther King, Jr.—the leader of the nonviolent
civil rights movement who was cut down by an assassin's bullet in
1968. One year later, his second son drowned in a backyard swim-
ming pool. The crowning blow came in 1974 during a church

service. As his wife played "The Lord's Prayer," a young man arose in the congregation and began shooting. Mrs. King collapsed in a hail of gunfire, while Dr. King watched in horror from the pulpit.

Near the end of his life, reflecting on the loss of his wife and oldest son, he spoke of the policy of nonviolence he had come to embrace. "There are two men I am supposed to hate. One is a white man, the other is black, and both are serving time for having committed murder. I don't hate either one. There is no time for that, and no reason either. Nothing that a man does takes him lower than when he allows himself to fall so low as to hate anyone."

> *A*s costly as it is to forgive, there is only one consolation— unforgiveness costs far more.

But how can a man not hate someone who kills his wife or oldest son? It seems natural and even proper to hate killers, doesn't it? The answer comes back, "There is no time for that." To hate is to live in the past, to dwell on deeds already done. Hatred is the least satisfying emotion, for it gives the person you hate a double victory—one in the past, one in the present.

No time to hate? Not if you have learned how to forgive. Forgiving does *not* mean whitewashing the past, but it does mean refusing to live there. Forgiveness breaks the awful chain of bitterness and the insidious desire for revenge. As costly as it is to forgive, there is only one consolation—unforgiveness costs far more.

I wonder how many of us have gotten in trouble because we gave in to our anger. Perhaps we have said words in a moment of tension that we later came to regret. Marriages and families have been broken, friendships ended, careers destroyed, and churches split because we lost our temper and said words or did actions we later regretted.

The Sin of Judging Wrongly

Behind our anger lies a problem we rarely talk about and therefore rarely face. *We have wrongly judged another person and have sinned in the process.* In our rush to judgment, in our haste to make sure someone else takes the blame, in our zeal to find the guilty party, we have violated the words of Jesus in Matthew 7:1: "Judge not, that you be not judged" (ESV). The words are simple and clear. They are plain and unambiguous. Because they are familiar, we tend to forget about them. Or worse, we find a way to explain them away. Perhaps it will help to hear this verse worded differently. Listen to the words as found in The Message by Eugene Peterson: "Don't pick on people, jump on their failures, criticize their faults—unless, of course, you want the same treatment." And this is Peterson's version of verse 2: "That critical spirit has a way of boomeranging." That's not really a translation, but it is entirely faithful to the meaning of the text.

There are several ways we can approach a text like this. We could spend a lot of time talking about the illustration Jesus used in which He referred to the speck in your brother's eye and the log in your own eye. It's funny and ironic, and when Jesus spoke these words, I'm sure His hearers laughed out loud. I'll return to that illustration shortly, but first, let's focus on verse 1. What exactly did Jesus mean when He said, "Judge not"?

For starters, it helps to know what He did *not* mean. Jesus is not saying we should never pass any sort of judgment. Every day we make hundreds of judgments about the world around us. It is not wrong, for instance, to sit on a jury and render a verdict. Nor is it wrong for an admissions committee to decide which students to accept and which to reject. Nor is it wrong for an employer to decide who gets a promotion and who doesn't. Nor is it wrong for schools to judge certain students worthy of high honor at graduation. We all have to make decisions every day that involve other people. We pass judgments on appearance, behavior, speech, deportment, attitude, work ethic, productivity, keeping or breaking a promise, guilt or innocence, which we believe and which we do not believe.

Condemnation Condemned

What, then, did Jesus mean when He said, "Judge not"? The word translated "judge" often means "to condemn." It means to come to a negative conclusion about another person and then to condemn him. That is what Jesus is forbidding. Let me be a little more specific about this.

First, we are not to pass final judgment on any person. Final judgment belongs to the Lord. We are not in the condemning business. If anyone needs to be condemned, God Himself can take care of that. We should have no part in it.

Second, we are not to judge the motives of others. The Bible says, "Man looks at the outward appearance, but the LORD looks at the heart" (I Samuel 16:7). Often we are quick to come to negative conclusions about others based on why we think they did something. But try as we might, we see only the outside. God alone sees the heart.

- We can judge what people *do;* we cannot judge *why* they do it.
- We can judge what people *say;* we cannot judge *why* they say it.

Only God can judge the hidden secrets of the heart; leave such judgments to Him. You don't even know your own heart, much less the heart of anyone else. "The heart is deceitful above all things, and desperately sick; who can understand it?" (Jeremiah 17:9 ESV). Sometimes when little children have been caught disobeying and you ask them why they did it, they will reply tearfully, "I don't know." That's not a cop-out; it's a profound theological truth. We are so wicked by nature that we don't know why we do what we do. All of us can remember times when we did or said something foolish, and looking back, we can honestly say, "I don't know why

I did something stupid like that." If we can't understand our own heart, how can we ever presume to understand anyone else's?

Third, we are not to be faultfinders. One source (www.Word smyth.net) defines a faultfinder as "one who finds much to criticize or complain about, esp. of a petty nature," and lists these synonyms: malcontent, scold, nag, and critic. Related words include grouch, grumbler, and bellyacher.

Proverbs 11:12 tells us, "It is foolish to belittle a neighbor; a person with good sense remains silent" (NLT). The Message is even more pointed: "Mean-spirited slander is heartless; quiet discretion accompanies good sense." Faultfinding is the "venom of the soul." It destroys our joy, drains our happiness, and prevents us from having close friendships. No one likes a faultfinder because no one likes being around a nitpicking critic. This sin comes partly from spiritual pride and partly from disguised envy. We criticize others in order to bring them down to our level. Or worse, we tear them down in an attempt to prove they are beneath us.

Faultfinding is a deadly disease because, if not kept in check, it turns us into cynics who persistently expect the worst from others. The faultfinder expects failure and secretly gloats when he finds it. Is it any wonder that the faultfinder almost always is a gossip and a talebearer? When he spots the flaws of others, he can't wait to spread the news. Such a person is a spiritual vulture. Like the vultures of the air that live off dead, rotting flesh, these sad individuals thrive on the mistakes and sins of others. They fly across the landscape, keeping a close eye out for the failures of others. Then they swoop in for their daily feast.

Each Sunday morning I pray with a group of men in my church office before the first worship service. Over time, we have gotten to know each other very well. To an extent, we've become accustomed to each other's prayers. I know what they are going to say, and they know what I am going to say. But one Sunday while we were praying, one of the men broke through to transparent honesty when he said, "Lord, too often I am so hard on the people closest to me." Many of us could say the same words. Husbands are hard on their wives. Wives criticize their husbands. Parents tear down their children and strip away every vestige of self-esteem. Friends attack friends, Christians belittle each other, and many families are held together by the glue of mutual disdain. Why is it we are so hard on those whom we say we love the most? And why are we so lenient when the person who offends us is someone we don't know? That makes no sense.

Breaking Jesus' Command

Jesus said, "Judge not." There are so many ways in which we break this command. Here are some examples:

Blowing small infractions or mistakes all out of proportion.

Maximizing the sins of others and minimizing our own.

Coming to quick, negative conclusions.

Making mountains out of molehills.

Getting involved in situations in which we should not be involved.

Passing along critical stories to others.

Having a strong bias toward finding others guilty.

Being too harsh even when speaking the truth.

Adding aggravating remarks when telling a story.

Dismissing an unkind remark by saying, "I was only joking."

Being critical, and then trying to cover up our words.

Being unkind, and then quickly changing the subject.

Telling too many people about how others have hurt or offended us.

Taking pleasure in condemning others.

Telling the truth in order to hurt, not to help.

Putting others down in order to make ourselves look better.

Note that it's quite possible to have a judgmental spirit even while telling the truth. Some people use the truth as a club to beat others over the head. Simply saying, "Well, it was the truth, you know" does not get you off the hook.

Our judgment is wrong when it is

- needless,
- unfounded,
- hasty, or
- severe.

In the course of thinking about this topic, one fact kept bothering me: *I see far too much of this in my own life.* If I am honest with myself, I know that I'm far too quick to pass judgment on others. I see too much of myself on the aforementioned list, and that makes me feel uneasy.

Eating in Total Silence

Here is a simple guide to help guide our speech. It's an acrostic based on the word *need*.

> N—Is it necessary?
> E—Will it encourage?
> E—Will it edify?
> D—Will it dignify the other person?

When I shared that with my congregation, one person told me that when his family eats dinner, they observe the TKN rule.

> T—Is it true?
> K—Is it kind?
> N—Is it necessary?

If a statement doesn't meet the rule, it doesn't get said. It would be a good idea if every family adopted that rule for their mealtime conversations—although it might mean most of our meals would be eaten in total silence! But silence is preferable to breaking the Lord's command regarding how we speak.

And that brings me back to the speck and the log. It's easy to see a speck in your brother's eye, and much harder to see a log in your own. When we deal with the faults of others, our greatest need is for clear vision. That's why Jesus said, in Matthew 5, "You hypocrite, first take the plank out of your own eye, and then you will see clearly to take the speck from your brother's eye." First, we must see clearly. And we cannot do so until we have removed the impediment from our own eyes.

First Things First

Christian love is not blind. God never says, "Ignore the faults of others." But He does say, "Take care of your own faults first." Look in the mirror! Ask God to show you your sins. The familiar words of Psalm 139:23-24 come to mind: "Search me, O God, and know my heart; test me and know my anxious thoughts. See if there is any offensive way in me, and lead me in the way everlasting." If we would pray that way and mean it, we would do a lot more confessing and a lot less judging.

The order in which we do things is crucial. We are to judge ourselves first by asking God to show us our sins. We are to say, "Lord, show me the truth about myself." That's a dangerous prayer because if you mean it, God will definitely answer it. Go someplace quiet and ask the Lord to reveal to you the truth about yourself. When you pray that way, the answer will come. Sit and wait for the Holy Spirit to show you your weaknesses, faults, mistakes, bad attitudes, foolish words, pride, arrogance, need to be in control, need to run the world, need to tell others what to do, desire to have your own way, anger, bitterness, lack of mercy, lack of love, lack of compassion. I can say from personal experience that if you offer up such a prayer and wait long enough, the Lord will always give you the answer you need.

"Lord, I'm the One"

During a trip to Haiti several years ago, I got up early every morning and took a long walk down the rutted dirt road that led from the camp to the village. No matter how early I got up, I always ran into Haitians walking one way or the other. Every morning I saw at least one woman carrying a container of water on her head. I saw students walking several miles each morning to go to school, and I saw old men with machetes getting ready to cut the sugar cane. Being in another country has a way of changing your perspective and helping you see things more clearly, and that's what happened to me. The Lord spoke to me about many things—especially about my life and my relationship to Him.

Also, almost every morning I would sing as I walked along the road. Usually I sang hymns, but one morning I started singing a song that I learned over 30 years ago. In fact, it was the theme song of the greatest revival I ever took part in. In May 1970, just before I graduated from high school, God visited the First Baptist Church of Russellville, Alabama, with life-changing power. There are men in the ministry today whose hearts God first touched during those amazing days. I was the song leader for the revival. Almost every night the choir sang a song by John R. Rice called "Lord, I'm the One." Almost every night the choir sang a chorus that contained the phrase, "Lord, I'm the one." For some reason (I think I know why), the Lord brought that little song back to my mind during our trip to Haiti.

Here is the background to all this: Sometime earlier a friend had said some very unkind words to my wife. The details don't matter, except to say that casual comments can sometimes cut very deeply. And as we all know, comments from friends generally hurt more than comments from total strangers. If you are married, you understand that you are probably quicker to forgive a comment made about you than a comment made about your spouse. I was angry, and my wife was both angry and deeply hurt, and that made the offense that much worse in my eyes. But for various reasons, there wasn't much I could do about it. We all understand that some interpersonal issues are not easily solved. So I got angry, stayed angry, and kept the matter mostly to myself. I tried to be friendly when I saw this person, but with mixed success.

Months after the incident, I didn't think about it much, but it was still unresolved in my heart. And I didn't deal with my feelings of anger until that week in Haiti. Something about walking along that rutted dirt road and seeing the Haitians who didn't know me or my wife and had never heard of the person who said those unkind words caused me to take stock of my heart. I was harboring anger, and I didn't want to face that fact. But the Lord would not let me rest until I did.

I didn't know it at the time, but the Lord was working in the same way in my wife's heart. Marlene told me later that during those weeks of being hurt, God spoke to her and said, "You are a sinner, too." And so little by little, the Lord led us to forgiveness and letting go of the hurt by showing us our sin.

When you can finally say, "I am a sinner, too," then you are set free to forgive those who have hurt you. As long as you set yourself on a moral plane above the rest of humanity, and especially above those who sinned against you, you cannot and will not forgive. It is liberating to finally say…

> I have been unkind to others.
> I have spoken hurtfully to my friends.
> I have told lies.
> I have repeated gossip.
> I have spoken harshly to my loved ones.
> I have broken promises.
> I have held grudges.
> I have been inconsiderate.
> I have demanded my own way.
> I have trampled on the feelings of others.

It is hard to face the truth about ourselves. Yet it's also the only way to be set free.

Years ago a friend sent me a sheet of paper from a counselor that had a saying based on the famous words of Jesus, "You will know the truth, and the truth will make you free" (John 8:32). The counselor had taken the last phrase and reworded it to say, "The truth will set you free...but it will hurt you first."

The words startled me, and then it was as if someone had turned on a light in my head. Yes, of course—it makes perfect sense! The truth *will* set you free, but it *will* hurt you first.

This is why many people have trouble growing spiritually. It's not because we don't know the truth. We hear the truth at church, on the radio, from our friends, from books and tapes and seminars and concerts. And we get it straight from the Bible. That's *not* our problem. If just knowing the truth were all we needed, we'd all be candidates for permanent sainthood. No, the problem runs deeper than that. We know the truth but we don't want to let it hurt us so we deflect it, ignore it, deny it, attack it, argue with it, and in general avoid it in any way we can. We're like a spaceship being attacked by aliens: We put up the force field so we can deflect the incoming bullets of truth. After a while, we get so good at deflecting the truth that it no longer gets to us at all.

We hear the truth...we know the truth...but we deflect the truth so it never gets close enough to hurt. Therefore, we are not set free.

And that's why...

> We're still angry.
> We're still stubborn.
> We're still bitter.
> We're still greedy.
> We're still arrogant.
> We're still filled with lust.
> We're still self-willed.
> We're still unkind.

A Sunday school teacher finished her lesson on forgiveness and decided to review it with the children in her class. "Can anyone tell me what you must do before you can be forgiven of sin?" After an uncomfortable silence, one child volunteered an

answer; "We have to sin." I'm sure we've all fulfilled that requirement—I know I have. And precisely to the extent that I see my
own sin will I be willing to forgive the sins of others.[16]

Judge Yourself First

Did you notice what Jesus called the judgmental person in
Matthew 7:5? A hypocrite. What a terrible word that is! And that's
what we are when we judge and condemn others without first
judging ourselves. The order is crucial here: First, we are to judge
ourselves. We are to be hard on ourselves. We are to ask the Lord
to show us our sins. Until we do that, the speck in our brother's
eye will look like a log to us. And we won't even see the log in our
own eye. Once we have allowed the Holy Spirit to do His painful
surgery within, once we have confessed and repented and
mourned over our own sin, then and only then are we ready to do
surgery on someone else. This is how you will know you have
reached that point: Your sins will bother you a lot more than the
sins of others. And the failures of others won't seem so big to you.
You'll know you're ready to talk to a brother or sister when you
don't want to do it anymore. The person who has judged himself
will display these character qualities:

- humility
- godly sorrow
- gentleness
- reticence
- patience
- discretion

Delicate Eye Surgery

To simply gaze on the sins of others is vain and empty and
wrong. It turns us into judgmental Pharisees who are quick to
condemn. But once we are cleansed and humbled by the Lord,
then we are ready to remove the tiny speck from a brother's eye.

And that brother will be glad for us to do it because he knows we are not there to condemn but to help.

The eye is a very sensitive organ. I know that because I've had six eye surgeries over the past few years. It takes a compassionate hand and a delicate touch to do surgery in the eye. When you have eye trouble, you need a doctor who knows what he is doing because even the slightest mistake can have catastrophic consequences. Sometimes in our haste to help others, we can cause more damage than the original speck of dirt caused.

There is a difference between someone who loves you and wants to help you and someone who puts you under a microscope only to find fault with all you do. I have found that those most critical of others tend to have the most sins in their lives. And those closest to God tend to be the most charitable. They are the quickest to forgive, quickest to restore, and the quickest to help someone who is struggling with sin.

Where do we go from here? "Daddy King" was right. We have no time to hate, no time to condemn, no time to live in bitterness and anger. How will we get from here to there? We need the help of God to do a supernatural work in our hearts. May God deliver us from a judgmental spirit.

We can judge others or we can forgive, but we can't do both at the same time.

Seven

Overcoming a
Judgmental Spirit

———————— ✤ ————————

*It is a terrible thing for a sinner to
fall into the hands of his fellow sinners.*

F. B. MEYER

Christians love to fight over their deeply held beliefs. Unfortunately, sometimes we fight over issues that don't matter much.

Once upon a time a man took a walk and came to a bridge. When he got to the middle of the bridge, he saw another man standing on the rail, obviously about to jump. The other man was distraught, so the first one said, "Don't jump. I can help you." "How can you help me?" asked the man on the rail. The first man replied with a question of his own: "Are you a Christian?" "Yes, I am." "That's wonderful. So am I. Are you Catholic or Protestant?" "I'm Protestant." "That's great. So am I. What sort of Protestant are you? Are you Baptist, Methodist, Lutheran, Presbyterian, or something else?"

"I'm a lifetime Baptist," said the man on the rail. "Praise the Lord," came the reply. "So am I. Let me ask you this. Are you Northern Baptist or Southern Baptist?" "I'm Northern Baptist."

"Are you Northern Conservative Baptist or Northern Liberal Baptist?" "I'm Northern Conservative Baptist." "Well, call Ripley's. This is amazing. So am I. Are you Northern Conservative Baptist Fundamental or Northern Conservative Baptist Reformed?" The man on the rail thought for a moment and then declared, "My father raised me as a Northern Conservative Baptist Reformed." "It's a miracle," said the first man. "Put 'er there, pal. So am I."

Then the first man asked, "Are you Northern Conservative Baptist Reformed Great Lakes Region or Northern Conservative Baptist Reformed Great Plains Region?" The man on the rail said, "That's easy. My family has always been Northern Conservative Baptist Reformed Great Lakes Region." "This is a miracle of miracles. I don't often meet a brother who shares my own heritage. One final question: Are you Northern Conservative Baptist Reformed Great Lakes Region Council of 1855 or Northern Conservative Baptist Reformed Great Lakes Region Council of 1872?" The man on the rail replied instantly, "Since the days of my great-grandfather, we have always been Northern Conservative Baptist Reformed Great Lakes Region Council of 1872." This statement was followed by an awkward pause. Looking up, the first man cried out, "Die, heretic!" And he pushed the other man off the bridge.

We laugh at that story because in many ways it is so close to the truth. If two Christians agree on 79 out of 80 points, they will usually focus a disproportionate amount of their attention on the single point on which they disagree. And often, the smaller that final point, the more likely they are to argue about it. I don't know what compels us to do that. Maybe its just human nature that leads us to focus on the trivial issues that don't matter while ignoring the major topics on which we agree 100 percent.

This chapter is about the dangers of a judgmental spirit. Even though this problem exists both inside and outside the church, my focus is strictly inside the church. I want us to think about the tendency we all have to criticize fellow Christians who don't do or say things the way we think they ought to be said or done. I want us to think about the terrible results that can occur when we are too quick to offer personal judgments on believers who don't meet our personal standards. And I would like to offer some suggestions on how we can overcome the impulse to wrongly criticize our brothers and sisters in Christ.

As we begin, let's note that this problem is neither isolated nor new. Churches have struggled with this issue for 2,000 years. The New Testament makes it clear that the earliest Christians had difficulty accepting new or different people into their assemblies. When Paul wrote to the church at Rome, he devoted almost two full chapters in his letter to this difficult issue. Romans 14 teaches us an important truth about accepting other believers; let's begin with a brief look at the historical background of this text.

Historical Background

Rome was the center of the world in Paul's day. It was the capital of the empire and the seat of the Caesars. You've heard it said, "All roads lead to Rome." In the first century, that statement was very true. All roads did lead to Rome. The city had become a melting pot where people from many different cultures mingled together. As ambassadors and envoys from the various provinces came to Rome, they settled in the city, creating a complex mix of races and ethnic groups. Add to that the foreign slaves and prisoners of war who lived in Rome. When the gospel came to Rome (not long after the resurrection), it crossed many of those racial and ethnic lines. As a result, the church at Rome reflected the diverse makeup of the city itself.

This fact helps us to understand Paul's words in Romans 14. He was writing to a growing church with a wide variety of people in the congregation. Human nature being what it is, it's not surprising the various groups within the church were having trouble getting along. Romans 14 reveals conflict in the church in five different areas:

- new converts and longtime believers
- converted Jews and converted Gentiles

- vegetarians and meat eaters
- observers of special days and those who observed no special days
- total abstainers and wine drinkers

We should not assume from this list that there were only two groups in the church with these "opposite" characteristics. For example, a person could be a new believer who was a converted Gentile, a vegetarian, a Sabbath keeper, and a wine drinker. Each church member in Rome could possess a variety of these characteristics or preferences, meaning there were a lot of different possible makeups within the congregation. Evidently these believers had difficulty getting along. The meat-eaters didn't trust the vegetarians, and the vegetarians thought the meat-eaters were compromisers. The converted Jews kept kosher, but the converted Gentiles thought that was a waste of time. The wine drinkers felt drinking wine was permissible so long as you didn't get drunk. The total abstainers thought that was merely a convenient excuse for drinking alcohol.

In short, the church at Rome was anything but one big happy family. It was big, it was a family, but it was far from happy. Paul understood the conflict. After all, he had been raised in the womb of Orthodox Judaism. He knew all about keeping kosher, following the strict dietary laws, and living under the Law. No doubt he had struggled with many of these issues in the years following his conversion to Christ. Now he writes to help others who were wrestling with these same issues.

Biblical Exhortations

Romans 14:1-12 contains three basic exhortations:

1. *Accept one another—God has accepted you!*

The first verse gives us the theme of the entire chapter: "Accept him whose faith is weak, without passing judgment on disputable matters." The word "accept" means to open your heart and your home to other people. "Disputable matters" are issues such as eating meat, drinking wine, and keeping special days. These matters—while important—should not stand in the way of our relationship with other believers. "Passing judgment" means to come to a negative conclusion about other Christians on the basis of their outward behavior in disputable areas. We could paraphrase verse 1 this way: "Make friends with everyone in the church without stopping to worry about whether they agree with you on everything or not."

> *God accepts people solely on the basis of their faith in Jesus Christ, and so should we.*

Consider this situation: It's time for a birthday party, and you're wondering what to serve. Maybe your idea is to cook some rib-eye steaks, lobster tail, a nice casserole, some homemade rolls, baked potatoes, and a nice dessert. (That sounds good to me!) Or maybe you prefer to buy some premium tofu, put it in a bowl, pour gravy on it (or whatever it is you do to tofu), and serve it with some bean sprouts and soy milk. For dessert you decide to take some bean curd and dip it into chocolate. That's not exactly my preference, but it doesn't matter at all. Here is Paul's point: If you want to cook some steaks, cook some steaks. If you want to have tofu and chocolate-covered bean curd, have at it. It doesn't matter to God—He's not up in heaven checking your menu to see if it passes muster. Eat whatever you like. And don't feel you need to explain yourself to anyone else.

The danger addressed here in Romans 14 is that the meat-eaters will look down on the vegetarians and the vegetarians will condemn the meat-eaters. But we must not fall into that trap.

The last phrase of verse 3 explains why we are to accept those whose lifestyle may be different from ours: "For God has accepted him." God's grace has nothing to do with eating meat, drinking wine, or keeping special days. But neither does it extend only to vegetarians, total abstainers, or those who observe no days at all. God accepts people solely on the basis of their faith in Jesus Christ, and so should we. Or to put it another way, who are we to reject the person whom God has accepted? If God has accepted him, how can we reject him?

2. Have your own convictions—Jesus is your Lord.

Verse 5 tells us plainly: "Each one should be fully convinced in his own mind." To be fully convinced means that after looking at all the evidence and considering the various views on a given issue, you have come to a settled conclusion in your own mind. *It assumes an honest investigation coupled with an open mind.*

Notice how many times Paul mentioned the Lord Jesus Christ in these verses: "He who regards one day as special, does so to *the Lord.* He who eats meat, eats to *the Lord…*he who abstains does so to *the Lord…* If we live, we live to *the Lord;* and if we die, we die to *the Lord.* So, whether we live or die, we belong to *the Lord.* For this very reason, Christ died and returned to life so that he might be *the Lord* of both the dead and the living." Seven times in these verses Paul relates our lifestyle choices directly to our relationship with Jesus Christ. If we are fully surrendered to His lordship in our lives, then we are free to make up our own minds in these disputable areas.

Do you want to eat meat? Eat it, for Jesus is your Lord. Do you prefer to be a vegetarian? Have your bean sprouts and give thanks to God. Are you a total abstainer? If so, rejoice that you know Jesus Christ. Do you drink wine with your dinner? Give thanks to God that Jesus is your Lord. If He is your Lord, you can make your own decisions, knowing that He alone will be your judge.

Note that in this passage, Paul mentions a particular area of contention. One group at Rome observed certain days as holy (perhaps the Sabbath or possibly the various Jewish feast days), while another group said that all days were alike because every day belongs to the Lord. That has many practical ramifications. If you want to go to church on Tuesday night, go ahead. Nothing wrong with that. But don't judge those who prefer to go to church on Thursday morning. When I was growing up, there was no flexibility in this regard. We "knew" that all Christians went to church three times a week—Sunday morning, Sunday evening, and Wednesday night. And Sunday morning was always the same—Sunday school at 9:45 AM and morning worship at 11:00 AM. We never heard about having multiple worship services. Sunday evening was Training Union at 6:00 PM and evening worship at 7:00 PM. Wednesday night was a supper followed by a prayer meeting at 7:00 PM. None of this new-fangled having classes on Wednesday night. That was just the way we did it, year after year. But now churches have changed greatly, and they have services and programs at every possible hour and on different days of the week.

We see the same principle at work every year at Christmastime. At our church in Oak Park, we decorate the sanctuary and the hallways with garlands and with beautiful wreaths. We have a Christmas concert with our orchestra and choir. And we often have a Christmas caroling outreach, plus two Christmas Eve services. Normally we start singing Christmas carols soon after Thanksgiving. I'm very happy about that because Christmas has always been a favorite time of the year for me. But consider these facts: Nowhere in the New Testament are we told to celebrate the birth of Christ with a special season of the year. Nowhere are we told to have concerts and Christmas Eve services. For that matter, we don't even know for certain the precise day of Christ's birth. Scholars even argue about the exact year. And the word *Christmas* isn't found anywhere in the Bible. There is no command to sing "Hark, the Herald Angels Sing" or "Angels We Have Heard on High" or "Away in a Manger." Nor is there a command to recreate the manger scene. Most of what we do at Christmastime stems from long-held (and deeply felt) traditions handed down across many generations. They are noble and worthy traditions that go far back in church history, but they don't come directly from the New Testament.

My point is, we don't have to celebrate Christmas. We could just cancel it. I am not suggesting that we could stop believing in the incarnation or the virgin birth, because those facts are among the nonnegotiables of the Christian faith. But we aren't compelled by the Bible to do all the activities we usually do. If a church somewhere decided not to observe Christmas, that church would not be doing anything wrong. And a church should not be despised for that choice any more than we should be judged because we choose to make a great emphasis in celebrating the birth of Christ each year. There is room in the body of Christ for significant differences in the way we approach the traditions of our faith.

3. Don't judge others; we will each answer to God.

Paul asks two pointed questions in verse 10: "Why do you judge your brother? Or why do you look down on your brother?" To "judge" in this context implies coming to a negative conclusion about the way someone lives. This kind of judging leads to "looking down" on other believers—i.e., believing that you are better or superior to others because a) you do things they don't do, or b) you don't do things they routinely do. Either way, you end up seeing yourself as better than your brothers or sisters in Christ. Three different times, Paul reminded the Christians in Rome that each of them will stand individually before God. No one will answer for anyone else. God will not judge you according to how someone else lives. When you stand before the Lord, He won't quiz you about what Mr. Jones did or how Mrs. Johnson lived. You'll answer for yourself, and no one else.

Also, if God is going to judge your friends someday, why should you get involved? He knows them better than you do; He loves them more than you do; and He can read the thoughts and intents of their hearts, which you can't read at all. We're all called to focus on our own lives—and that should leave us very little time to be concerned about other people.

With all that in mind, let's now look at five important principles we can glean from Romans 14.

a. Christians Often Disagree with Each Other

This statement always comes as a surprise to new believers, but those of us who've been around for a while accept it as a given. Sometimes new Christians come into the church thinking that at last they've found paradise on earth, where everyone always agrees with everyone else and we're all happy together all the time. *It doesn't take long for that balloon to burst.* We're just normal people with a wide range of opinions, and we're joined by our common allegiance to Jesus Christ. Here's a short (and very incomplete) list of some matters that conservative evangelicals argue about:

movies	drinking wine
interracial marriage	women wearing jewelry
hairstyles	raising children
seeker services	faith-promise giving
politics	dating standards
smoking	pledging
ecumenical movement	liberal churches
borrowing money	Christian psychology
fishing on Sunday	mode of baptism
divorce and remarriage	worship styles
women ushers	timing of the rapture
pipe organs	school choice
Rush Limbaugh	age of the earth
men wearing beards	birth control

Regarding this list, keep in mind that 1) some issues that appear "silly" to you are very serious to other Christians, and 2) if we asked ten Christians to divide this list into "silly" and "serious" categories, we would get ten different answers.

b. Disagreement Is Not Always Wrong or Sinful

Many of us have a hard time with this point—especially when we feel passionately about some secondary issue. If you have strong feelings about men wearing beards or about Rush Limbaugh, you'll have a hard time accepting those who either disagree with you or simply don't care about "your" issue one way or the other. Disagreement often reflects cultural differences more than biblical principles. Your particular set of standards may tell more about your upbringing than about what God approves or disapproves. In any case, we should not automatically assume the worst about people who disagree with us.

c. We Must Distinguish Between Primary and Secondary Issues

A primary issue is one that deals with a central doctrine of the Christian faith. This category includes the inspiration and inerrancy of the Bible, the deity of Jesus Christ (including the virgin birth, the miracles, His death and bodily resurrection, His ascension into heaven, and the reality of the personal, visible, bodily return of Christ to the earth), salvation by grace through faith, the doctrine of the Trinity, the importance of the church as the body of Christ, the truth of eternal life with Christ, the resurrection from the dead, and the reality of heaven and hell. There are also foundational doctrines dealing with basic sexual morality that must be upheld. These things are primary because they describe central, defining truths of the Christian faith. To deny these matters is to put yourself outside the realm of true Christianity.

When we discuss these issues, there can be no compromise. Ultimately, you either believe in the virgin birth or you don't. If you don't, you have denied a clear teaching of the New Testament, which involves your whole view of the Bible as God's Word and ultimately calls into question your belief in Jesus Christ as the Son of God.

Regarding, primary truths our *manner* must always be kind, and our *convictions* must be rock-solid. In the end, there can be no Christian fellowship with those who deny the key doctrines of the Christian faith. As Edward John Carnell said, "It is better to divide over truth than to unite around error."

Having said that, we must admit that many of our debates have nothing to do with primary issues. By definition, evangelical Christians already believe the core truths of Christianity. Our debates generally focus on secondary issues, which I would define as issues about which the Bible does not clearly speak. For instance, the Bible says nothing about fishing on Sunday. There is simply no verse that addresses that particular issue. Whatever you believe about that will have to be decided by a) inferences drawn from biblical principles, b) your personal preference, c) a combination of a) and b). The same is true for homeschooling. While the Bible has much to say about education in general, and while it clearly lays the burden of teaching children upon the parents, it doesn't tell us precisely how that responsibility must be discharged. Is it wrong to send Christian children to a public school? Since there were no first-century equivalents of either public or Christian schools, we aren't sure how to answer those questions.

Or take the hot issue of contemporary versus traditional worship. The New Testament gives us a few general guidelines for worship, but they are quite sketchy. If Paul were alive today, would he prefer Fanny Crosby over Point of Grace, or would he embrace Steven Curtis Chapman over P. P. Bliss? I know of no sure way to answer that question. Since nearly the entire corpus of Christian hymnody had yet to be written in A.D. 50, we may assume that even if they could understand the words, the first-century Jerusalem Christians would be mystified by all forms of Christian worship today. A similar analysis could be done for each debatable item on the list. Either the Bible says nothing at all, or what it does say is difficult to properly interpret. In such cases, we are free to have our own convictions, but we must hold them lightly lest we blur the line between primary and secondary issues and end up elevating fishing on Sunday to a level equal with the resurrection of Jesus.

d. Accepting Others Requires Humility Above All Other Virtues

I define *humility* as understanding that God is God and you are not. Truly humble people are free from the burden of having to play God for other people. Once you decide that you can let God be God, then you can also relax and let Him deal with other Christians regarding these secondary issues. That doesn't mean you can't discuss these matters openly. Open discussion is a mark of a healthy relationship. Let the meat-eaters and vegetarians challenge each other's position—but only if they can do so in love and with deep respect. Humility doesn't mean no discussion; it does mean no animosity, no name-calling, no unfair accusations.

Over the years I've learned that...

- God blesses people I disagree with.
- God sometimes blesses people I wouldn't bless if I were God.

Sometimes I'm frustrated by those facts, especially when I see God blessing someone who seems to be profoundly wrong in some area. But humility forces me to admit that if God is God, He is free to bless anyone He chooses—and He doesn't have to ask my permission before doing it. A friend who led a Christian ministry told me he was having trouble with people in his organization who seemed to delight in offering negative comments on everything and everybody. He solved it by instituting this simple rule: If it doesn't apply to you personally, feel free to have no opinion about it. I have found this to be a liberating principle that has helped me a number of times over the years. Sometimes we simply have too many opinions on too many topics. Many times I have helped myself by saying, "I feel free to have no opinion about that." And I sleep well at night when I follow that rule.

e. We Can Let Jesus Deal with Those Who Disagree with Us

This is the logical conclusion of everything we have learned thus far. Paul says, "Don't judge another believer." Why? Because God will judge him. If your friend who eats meat has made a bad choice, God can make that clear to him better than you can. If he smokes, God can convict him or his doctor can convince him. If he has some strange view of the rapture, God can deal with him if he needs to be dealt with. Don't get in God's way. Let Him deal with people who disagree with you. And in the meantime, don't forget to treat them as brothers and sisters in the Lord.

Practical Application

As I come to the end of this chapter, I'd like to leave you with one very practical word of application. The next time you are tempted to criticize someone—especially someone close to you, such as a friend, a family member, a co-worker, a colleague, a church member—before you utter a word, stop and say a prayer for that person. Before you criticize, pray. Ask God to bless that person. Pray that God will guide him or her. And yield your heart to the Lord.

If you pray first, you may end up saying nothing at all. As someone has said, "Miss no opportunity to keep your mouth shut." Or if you do speak, what you say will likely be changed because you prayed first. Pray more, and talk less...and your words will have a greater impact.

Eight

How to Behave in a Cave

— ❧ —

*When a deep injury is done to us,
we never recover until we forgive.*

ALAN PATON

When the phone call came, I knew it would be bad news. The chairman of the elder board called to say that two of the elders had put forward a motion asking for my dismissal as pastor. The vote failed, 4-2. I found out later that the two dissenting elders thought another elder would vote with them, but he didn't. Since they lost the vote, the two elders immediately resigned from the board and announced they were leaving the church. The remaining elders sent a letter to the congregation explaining what had happened. Such letters are never easy to write because you don't know how much to say, and you can't control how people will respond, no matter how you say it. The letter was a bit ambiguous because the charges against me were not of a moral nature. A few days later the chairman showed me a notebook containing pages of comments that were made about me. But there were no charges of immorality, heresy, false doctrine, or any sort of financial impropriety.

I never saw all of what the chairman had documented in his notebook, and now that 18 years have passed, I'm glad I never saw it. So much has happened in my life—both good and bad, happy and sad—so much water has gone under the bridge, and my life has taken so many turns I never expected that I'm glad I didn't have to read those charges against me. But I know the essence of what they said, know what those two elders wanted. They wanted me gone because I wasn't the kind of pastor they preferred.

That experience was very personal and painful. It was a rejection of me and my leadership and my personality and my style and everything about me. And the whole church ended up knowing about it. Even though the letter was veiled in what it said, the picture was still clear for everyone to see. Two of the elders wanted the senior pastor gone. When they failed, they resigned and left the church, taking a number of families with them.

The following months would see three waves of families leaving the church as a result. The first wave left with the two elders. The second wave left a few months later in sympathy with the first group. It was the third group that broke my heart. They left months later not because they agreed with the two elders, but because the church had changed and, to them, didn't feel the same anymore. They believed in my leadership, but left anyway. That was hard to take.

Eighteen years later I still don't fully understand all that had happened. The whole episode took an enormous toll on my wife and on our three children. And it left me feeling unclean, vulnerable, angry, confused, and scared. There's no fight like a church fight. When things grow ugly in the family of God, they can spiral downhill very fast. As I look back, I don't see much good from what happened during the year before the crisis and the year afterward. It was a hard, sad, difficult time.

When the two elders lost the vote and left the church, I happened to be preaching through the early years of the life of David

(1 Samuel 16–31). The Sunday after the resignations took place, I was scheduled to preach on 1 Samuel 24. I had entitled my sermon "How to Behave in a Cave." It could not have been more appropriate. My sermon began with these words:

> What a week it's been. There's never been one quite like it before. And I must confess that I've never had one like it in my years as a pastor. There were times this week when I thought the phone was going to ring off the wall.
>
> I would also like to say a word of appreciation for all the acts of kindness, the phone calls, the notes, the words of encouragement. On Friday, an anonymous friend placed a little refrigerator magnet on my desk. It reads, "Lord, if there's any more trouble coming, send it now while I'm used to it." Someone even sent over a Pick-Me-Up bouquet. It worked, just like Merlin Olsen said it would.

Here's the background of 1 Samuel 24: David is on the run from King Saul, who is trying to kill him. Motivated by anger and envy, the king knows God intends to replace him with young David, and he decides to kill David rather than give up his throne. David and his men—some 600 strong—come to a place called En Gedi, an oasis on the western shore of the Dead Sea. There, the barren mountains rise almost straight up from the shore. The mountains are limestone, laced with steep ravines, honeycombed with caverns. It was made to order for a man running from the law.

At En Gedi, David and his men found a cave large enough for all 600 of them. They were able to hide in passageways far back from the entrance. With that in mind, let's pick up the story in verses 1-3: "After Saul returned from pursuing the Philistines, he was told, 'David is in the Desert of En Gedi.' So Saul took three thousand chosen men from all Israel and set out to look for David and his men near the Crags of the Wild Goats. He came to the sheep pens along the way; a cave was there, and Saul went in to relieve himself. David and his men were far back in the cave." Saul hears the call of nature and steps inside the nearest cave. Little does he know that the man he seeks is only a few yards away, hidden by the rocks and the darkness.

The Encounter in the Cave

While Saul attends to his business, 600 pairs of eyes watch from the darkness. A whisper spreads though the men. Here's a chance for David to attack Saul. The men tell this to David, covering their desire for revenge with a thick coat of religious varnish: "This is the day the LORD spoke of when he said to you, 'I will give your enemy into your hands for you to deal with as you wish'" (verse 4). They believe it is God's will for David to kill Saul. After all, Saul's been trying to kill David. "Do God a favor and get him right now," they tell David.

But David did something that must have seemed funny at the time. While Saul was preoccupied, David crept up and cut off the corner of his robe. Just a practical joke, really. No harm done. When Saul puts his robe back on, it's going to be shorter. But "afterward, David was conscience-stricken for having cut off a corner of his robe" (1 Samuel 24:5). And here is David's explanation to his own men in verse 6, "The LORD forbid that I should do such a thing to my master, the LORD's anointed, or lift my hand against him; for he is the anointed of the LORD." David's action was wrong because it made the king look bad. It was wrong because it showed a lack of respect. It was wrong because it wasn't David's place to get even. It was wrong because cutting Saul's robe was the first step toward murder. It was wrong because Saul was still the Lord's anointed. Cutting off a corner of the royal robe was an act of physical and spiritual vandalism. It was an attack on Saul and his right to be king.

While David was feeling bad, his men were mad. They wanted him to kill Saul. Meanwhile Saul left the cave to rejoin his men. He had no clue that anything unusual had happened—not until David called it to his attention. The rest of 1 Samuel 24 documents two speeches—one by David in verses 8-15 and one by Saul in verses

16-21. Verse 22 ends the chapter with these words, "Then Saul returned home, but David and his men went up to the stronghold." (The "stronghold" is most likely a reference to Masada.)

> *We have no control over how people treat us.... But we do have control over how we respond.*

A Crucial Question About David's Choice

The most important fact in the whole story is that David refused to kill Saul even when he had a golden opportunity. Why didn't David get revenge while he had the chance? Chuck Swindoll calls revenge "life's most subtle temptation," and indeed it is. For who has not felt the sting of unfair criticism? Who has not been surprised at some time or other by unexpected conduct from one's friends? Who has not been disappointed by someone close to them? Maybe you have been denied a promotion for which you were clearly qualified. Maybe a coach passed you over for a starting role even though you deserved it. Maybe your husband or wife has walked out on you. Maybe you have had your friends turn on you.

We have no control over what other people do. We wish we did—we wish no one would ever let us down, disappoint us, or turn against us. Yet it happens, and it happens to all of us. That's a fact. We never know when the hammer is going to fall.

Again, this is a key principle: We have no control over how people treat us—what they say or what they do. But we do have control over how we respond.

How should we respond when we've been hurt? There are two options, and only two. *We can try to get even, or we can do*

what David did in 1 Samuel 24. From the first part of 1 Samuel
24, we know what David did—or more specifically, what he
didn't do. When he had a chance to kill Saul, he didn't. In verses
8-15, he tells why.

Reason #1: David did not seek revenge because he respected Saul's authority over him.

In verse 8, David called Saul, "My lord the king!" He recognized Saul was still the king no matter what he did or how he did
it. It was not an issue of whether or not Saul treated David right.
As long as Saul was the king, he deserved respect by virtue of his
position. In particular, that meant that David was not free to get
even or take revenge in any form.

In the army you'll hear the saying, "You don't salute the man;
you salute the rank." The colonel may be an absolute jerk, but that
doesn't matter. You salute him by virtue of his position. That's precisely the principle here. David owed Saul his respect by virtue of
Saul's position as king. The matter is stated in another way in
verse 10: "I will not lift my hand against my master, because he is
the LORD's anointed." Who chose Saul to be king? God did. By
whose authority did Saul occupy the throne of Israel? By God's
authority. Therefore, to attack Saul is to indirectly attack God
Himself. If a man is God's anointed—good or bad—he is not to
be touched.

Please understand that David had every reason to get even
with Saul. The man was a killer, a psycho on the throne, a malev-
olent madman whose fits of rage and paranoia drove him over the
edge. David would have been doing the world a favor and no one
would have blamed him for it. But still, David didn't do it. Why?
Because he recognized Saul's authority over him.

Reason #2: David did not seek revenge because he was willing to wait for God to vindicate him.

David's second reason is stated plainly in verses 11-12: "Now
understand and recognize that I am not guilty of wrongdoing or

rebellion. I have not wronged you, but you are hunting me down to take my life. May the LORD judge between you and me. And may the LORD avenge the wrongs you have done to me, but my hand will not touch you." There are two interesting facts here: *First, David was not shy about pointing out the truth.* He plainly says Saul had wronged him. Sometimes in our hurry to reconcile with someone we overlook the fact that wrong was done. It's rarely true that "we're both right and we're both wrong." That implies a kind of neutrality that cancels the need to make moral judgments. Such a position is useful only for those who live in a fantasy world. Saul was wrong, David knew it, and he plainly said so.

David also understood a second fact many of us never grasp: *When it comes to revenge, God is much better at it than we are.* That's because He looks down from heaven and sees all sides of every issue. He knows who is right and who is wrong. So often our perspective is clouded and our judgment faulty. We see our side only. But God knows all, and He will not forget to avenge the wrongs done to His children.

James Russell Lowell wrote these famous words: "Truth forever on the scaffold, wrong forever on the throne. Yet that scaffold sways the future, and, behind the dim unknown, standeth God within the shadow, keeping watch above his own." That's the way it often seems these days: Truth forever on the scaffold, wrong forever on the throne. In this topsy-turvy world, the bad guys seem to keep on winning. But it is true, and you can count on it: God stands in the shadows keeping watch above His own.

David understood that God was ready, willing, and able to take care of him. And in God's timing, Saul would be out of the way and David would ascend to the throne. If God had wanted Saul removed sooner, He would have done it. There were 10,000 ways He could do it. God didn't need David's help. Even when David was clearly the better choice for king and Saul had gone nuts, and even when God had rejected Saul, He still didn't need David's help.

How many sins are committed because we are in a hurry? Because we're under pressure to give in to our passions? Because in the crunch we cut corners we would never cut otherwise? How many stupid decisions do we make because we aren't willing to wait for God? We can take great personal comfort in knowing that God will take care of matters when we suffer for doing what is right, God sees, and He remembers. That's a promise you can count on.

Reason #3: David did not seek revenge because he did not want to descend to Saul's level.

In verse 13 David said: "As the old saying goes, 'From evildoers come evil deeds,' so my hand will not touch you." David was saying, "If I attack him, I'm only sinking down to his level." I've heard it said this way: Never wrestle with a pig. You're bound to get dirty, and the pig loves it. There are times when you need to walk away from an argument because if you open your mouth, you'll soon be wrestling with a pig. The saddest part about trying to get even is it makes you a perpetual victim of the person you hate. Revenge makes you go through the hurt over and over again. You never really get over it. Ultimately, it drags you down to the sewer where your enemies dwell. And the moral filth that covers them soon covers you as well. And while you are staying up late at night seething in anger, they are oblivious to what you're going through. As we learned earlier, when you give in to the temptation to get even, your enemies have won twice: When they first hurt you, and when you can't get the offense out of your mind.

Three Steps in the Right Direction

Put it all together and what do you have? David didn't take vengence for three reasons: First, because he recognized Saul's authority over him. Second, because he was willing to wait for God to vindicate him. And third, because he did not want to descend to Saul's level. Let me repeat what I said earlier: We cannot control what people say about us or do to us. We're going to be hurt again and again. People are going to fail us, misunderstand us, doubt our integrity, and judge us a threat. For every David, there's a Saul lurking somewhere in the shadows. While we can't control our enemies, we *can* control our response. How we respond makes all the difference in the world between walking beneath or above our circumstances.

So how should we respond to mistreatment and the temptation to get even? Here are three practical suggestions:

Watch your words

Angry people usually make statements they later regret. Under pressure, we may blurt out words that will end a friendship forever. Or we may say words that inflict a wound out of proportion to the original offense. Or we may cause the problem to escalate to the point of blowing up.

You will rarely regret the comments you *don't* make. It's only the careless comments you *do* make that you regret. When you are angry, take to heart the words of Proverbs 10:19: "When words are many, sin is not absent, but he who holds his tongue is wise."

Focus on the Lord Jesus Christ

We are called to be like our Master, who, when He was reviled, reviled not again, when He was cursed, cursed not in return; when He was abused, refused to repay in kind; when He was mocked, did not retaliate; when He was hung between two thieves and crucified for crimes He did not commit, prayed for those who killed Him: "Father, forgive them, for they do not know what they are doing" (Luke 23:34). Of all people, He had every right to seek revenge, but He chose instead to submit to the Father's will. When you feel tempted to give in to anger and bitterness, remember the words of 1 Peter 2:21: "To this you were called, because Christ suffered for you, leaving you an example, that you should follow in his steps."

Lay your burden down

Sooner or later you have to stop fighting the battle. Sooner or later you have to put down your weapon. Some people are chained to the past because they will not let go of remembered hurts. In the end, the desire for revenge hurts you more than it hurts anyone else. It's an all-consuming emotion that destroys you from the inside out. I read a story about a wise, older monk and his young apprentice, who were walking together along a forest trail. Their monastery had a rule forbidding all contact with women. Coming to a river with a fast-flowing current, they saw an old woman weeping near the shoreline. She asked for help, saying that she couldn't cross the river on her own. Without a word, the older monk picked up the woman and carried her to the other side. She went on her way while he and his young colleague continued on their journey. Two-and-a-half hours passed without a word being spoken, but the young monk was seething on the inside. When he could contain himself no longer, he blurted out, "My Lord, why did you carry that woman across the river? You know that we are not supposed to touch a woman." The wise, older monk looked down at the young man and said, "I put her down hours ago. Why are you still carrying her?"

Good question. Why are you still carrying the burdens from the past? Isn't it time to put them down once and for all?

Let me say frankly that it's not easy to return good for evil, to refuse retaliation when it lies within our power, to refrain from bitter words, and to appeal to our adversary's nobler side even at the cost of our own dignity. *It's not easy or natural, but we are called to exactly that kind of supernatural life.* And there's no guarantee it will work out. Sometimes our enemies remain our enemies until the day we die. That may not be good news, but it is reality.

Looking back on my experience 18 years ago with those two elders, I can't say that I perfectly followed my own advice. Sometimes in my frustration, I made comments about those two elders that I regretted later. And sometimes I focused all my attention on the crisis in the church instead of letting it go. I do remember that one of the elders had loaned me a book much earlier. When I returned it many months later, I wrote a note wishing him well.

And several weeks later, I happened to meet him while doing hospital visitation, and we had a brief but pleasant conversation. It's the only time I saw him after his departure. Looking back, I can say that walking the path of forgiveness was a journey of many months that never led to any final reconciliation. But I can testify that by the grace of God, I came to the place where what happened to me no longer filled my heart and mind. And now, after 18 years, it all seems like a distant dream. The bad feelings vanished long ago.

Time to Lay That Burden Down

Some of us are walking around with a heavy load of bitterness and frustration. Perhaps you're angry at someone who hurt you. Or maybe you are carrying a burden of third-party resentment—that is, you are angry about how someone else you care about was mistreated. It's time to lay that burden down. God never meant for you to carry it around or to think about getting even.

Right now, focus on someone you want to get even with. Think about a specific person, if you can. *It's time to let go of the matter and let God take over.* It's time to be set free from bitterness. You have to call your anger or bitterness what God calls it: sin. If you are willing to do that, then you can be set free.

Here's a simple prayer that may help you lay your burden down. I have included a space for you to insert the name of the person or persons who have hurt you in some way.

> *Heavenly Father, I thank You that Jesus Christ took my sins upon Himself when He didn't deserve them. I confess to You that I am resentful toward _____. Father, I ask You to do what You know is best in this situation. Please forgive me for harboring anger and bitterness. Set me free from this bondage, and please keep me from it for the rest of my life. Teach me to forgive as Jesus, did. I pray this in the name of Jesus who forgave me all my sins. Amen.*

Nine

Hot Coals ·

*The best way to destroy an enemy
is to make him a friend.*

ABRAHAM LINCOLN

ecently I came across a thoughtful quote from Booker T. Washington, founder of the world-famous Tuskegee Institute in my home state of Alabama. As a black man growing up in the segregated South, he experienced more than his share of hatred, prejudice, and unfair treatment. But as a Christian, he also knew that a man is not judged by what he goes through, but by how he responds to it. He expressed his credo in one powerful sentence: "I will not let any man make me lower myself by hating him." Is it any wonder that we remember Booker T. Washington as one of the greater Americans this country has ever produced? You can't always stop people from hating you, but you don't have to hate them back. You can't always make people love you, but you can always love them back.

Jesus gave us the principle that we call the Golden Rule. It goes like this: "Do to others what you would have them do to you" (Matthew 7:12). Treat people as you would like to be treated. Speak to them as you would like to be spoken to. Grant them the honor that you wish they would grant to you. Give them the respect you desire for yourself. Offer them the kindness you wish they would offer you.

In Romans 12:17-21, Paul expands upon the Golden Rule and applies it to the hardest of all hard cases. How do you respond to those who badly mistreat you? Or to say it another way, what do you do when you've been done wrong?

The answer comes in two parts: When we've been done wrong, 1) we are to live in peace with our enemy if at all possible, and 2) we are not to seek revenge. In fact, we are to reach out to those who have hurt us by doing practical deeds of kindness to them. In so doing, we are overcoming evil with good (see Romans 12:21).

The Call to Peace

Romans 12:17-18 contains one negative and two positive statements. The negative is, "Do not repay anyone evil for evil." That speaks of retaliation and seeking revenge. And the first positive statement involves personal responsibility: "Be careful to do what is right in the eyes of everybody." That is, don't give people a reason to treat you unkindly.

This has many practical applications. It affects how we dress and act, the way we treat others in public, common courtesy, honesty at work, having a cheerful heart, being a team player, and not being a troublemaker, grump, whiner, constant complainer, or hypochondriac. Live in such a way that no one can make an honest accusation against you. Live so that if they are going to accuse you, they have to tell a lie to do it.

Then there is the second positive statement: "If it is possible, as far as it depends on you, live at peace with everyone." I like this statement because it strikes me as utterly realistic. In a fallen world, it isn't always possible to live at peace with everyone. Sometimes, despite our best efforts, we'll rub people the wrong way. Sometimes you are thrown into a situation at school or at work with people who are grade A, board-certified, 100 percent jerks—and you can't do anything about it. Such people don't want peace; they want to make trouble.

A friend of mine once mentioned a colleague at work who yells at everyone all the time for no particular reason. She just yells and yells and yells. He called her a "rageaholic." That's a great word to describe a very sick person. Unfortunately, she's not the only one out there. You can find at least one person like that in every school, business, and neighborhood. Paul's advice regarding such a person is simple: Live at peace with him or her. If that doesn't work, make sure you aren't part of the problem. Note that little phrase, "as far as it depends on you." The only person you can take care of is you. Do you remember the saying, "It takes two to tango"? We could rephrase the words to "It takes two to tangle." If you refuse to tangle, at least you can't be blamed for causing the problem. So be a peacemaker to the point that, if someone makes trouble for you, no one can legitimately blame you.

The Warning Against Revenge

Paul clearly rules out all attempts at revenge: "Do not take revenge, my friends" (verse 19). There are no exceptions—no maybes, ifs, or buts. Revenge and retaliation are forever ruled out for the believer in Christ. The next few verses give us three reasons for this.

1. *Revenge is God's work*

"Leave room for God's wrath, for it is written, 'It is mine to avenge; I will repay'" (verse 19). President John F. Kennedy liked to say, "Don't get mad, get even." That represents the wisdom of the world. And that's the way most people, even many Christians, operate. With one slight revision in some cases: We get mad, then we get even. By contrast, Paul says, "Let God handle the revenge. That's His special ministry." Have you ever thought of vengeance as a "ministry" of God? Well, it is. Vengeance is one aspect of God's justice. It's His way of balancing the scales of life.

What happens when we try to take vengeance into our own hands? We almost always mess it up. We're either too harsh or too soft, we strike too fast or too late, or we attack the wrong person or say the wrong words, or we end up making matters worse and not better. Too many times we're like Bruce Willis in one of those *Die Hard* movies. We load up our guns, run into the room, and start firing. Our motto is "Kill 'em all and let God sort 'em out later." And if we accidentally hurt some innocent people, we rationalize our actions by saying, "Well, it's a tough world, and sometimes people get hurt."

The most important reason not to take revenge is that by our clumsiness we may block God's work in another person's life. We typically just want to get even, but God wants to bring that person to a place of repentance and reconciliation. God has a better view than we do, and He has a higher goal. Vengeance is His specialty.

When we talk about God, remember that He's the one who kicked Adam and Eve out of the Garden, and who caused the Red Sea to dry up for the Israelites and close up to drown the Egyptians. He's the one who opened up the ground and swallowed the sons of Korah and who struck Miriam with leprosy. He's the one who delivered Goliath into David's hands and who caused David's infant son to die because of his affair with Bathsheba. He allowed Peter to walk on water, and then Jesus rebuked him to his face and said, "Get behind me, Satan!" He worked miracles in the early church but killed Ananias and Sapphira when they lied about their giving.

He's God. He sees what we don't see; He watches the motives of the heart. He knows our thoughts before we think them, our words before we speak them. He knows what we're going to do before we do it, and He knows the reason behind it. Revenge is His special ministry to mankind. You can never do it as well as He can. Instead, you'll just mess things up. So leave vengeance to the Lord. He's far better at it than you will ever be.

2. *There is a better way to get even*

"On the contrary: 'If your enemy is hungry, feed him; if he is thirsty, give him something to drink. In doing this, you will heap burning coals on his head'" (verse 20). This is one of the most unusual verses in the New Testament. What does Paul mean when he talks about heaping hot coals on your enemy's head? Paul is quoting from Proverbs 25:21-22, and the statement has three parts: the command, the result, and the reward.

The command is, "If your enemy is hungry, give him food to eat; if he is thirsty, give him water to drink" (Proverbs 25:1). Needless to say, this flies in the face of common sense. You shoot enemies; you don't feed them. After all, if you feed your enemies, they will get stronger and stronger and then attack you. But God says to feed them. You are to act contrary to your natural tendencies when you respond to your enemies.

---

*T*hose who are close to you are sometimes used by God to expose the weak areas of your life.

Who is the "enemy" in Romans 12:20? He or she is almost always a friend, colleague, or family member who has hurt you in some way. My enemy, by definition, will usually be someone close to me. I don't have any enemies in Iran because I don't know anybody over there. But it's not hard for me to have enemies in Oak Park because I live there and know many people there. Let me give you this definition: *An enemy is any person God uses to reveal your weaknesses.* An enemy is like a chisel God uses to chip away at the rough spots in your life. That's why if you are married, your husband or your wife will be your enemy some of the time. No one knows your weaknesses like your spouse. He or she knows the hidden blemishes, secret sins, and bad habits the rest of the world never sees. But they know your faults because they live with you every day.

Can a husband be your enemy? Yes, and you can still love him even when you can't stand him. Can a wife be your enemy? Yes, because she knows your weaknesses and sees the real you that the rest of us never see. You may put on a front at church, but your wife knows the real story. And, if she loves you, she'll have to be your enemy from time to time. Otherwise, how are you ever going to get better? That's why you have to feed your enemy. You can't let your wife or husband starve to death. That's why you have to give your boss or your teacher or that obnoxious person in the next office something to drink. Those who are close to you are sometimes used by God to expose the weak areas of your life.

Now, there's a happy result from treating your enemies kindly—you heap burning coals on their head. Many Bible commentators think Paul was referring to an Egyptian custom in which a person would actually put burning coals on his head as a sign of repentance for his sin. If that is the case, then Paul is suggesting that we can win our enemies to our side by deeds of love and kindness. "The coals of fire this may heap on him are intended to heal, not to hurt, to win, not to alienate, in fact, to shame him into repentance."[17] You may have heard the statement, "Killing 'em with kindness." That's what Paul is talking about here. Through deeds of love shown to those who have hurt us deeply, we may actually change their hearts and lead an enemy to become a friend. Someone has said that the best way to get rid of an enemy is to turn him into a friend. The apostle Paul would certainly agree.

What would qualify as "hot coals"? A kind word, a phone call, a brief note, a flower, a meal, a small gift, a letter of recommendation, running an errand, offering a ride, helping complete a project, rewriting a report, stepping in to save a failing project, putting in a good word to the superiors, helping clean the classroom, going bowling, and so on. The list is endless, because "hot coals" refers to any act of kindness you do for an enemy. Your only limit is your creativity.

Then Proverbs 25:22 tells us the good result: "And the LORD will reward you." God rewards those who show kindness to their enemies. How? It's hard to say. One obvious answer might be to cause your "hot coals" to turn your enemy into a friend. Or, God might promote you or pour out new blessings or grant you answers to your prayers or new spiritual growth.

A woman wrote me to say she realized she needed to forgive her husband, who left her for a younger woman after 26 years of marriage. She found out later that he had been having an affair over the previous year. To make matters worse, she discovered that some of her friends not only knew about the affair, they were aiding her husband and helping him cover up his infidelity. When she wrote her note to me, she said she realized she had never truly forgiven those friends for what they had done. Here is her story:

> Today I wrote to four people the Lord brought to my mind and let them know I was praying for God to bless them. I felt the need to write to them and tell them I had asked for them to receive a blessing from God. At first it was the hardest thing I had done in sooooooo long, but then I started writing the quick message and telling them that after hearing a sermon (didn't say on what) I was writing to tell them I'd asked God to give them a special blessing. Three of the four people have claimed to be a Christian, but they all contributed to my ex's infidelity and adultery. Yet, after writing the e-mails, I felt better and more at peace.

This is an especially good example because she did not mention the way these people had hurt her. She simply wrote to say she was praying for them to receive a blessing from the Lord. How did they respond to those notes? I don't know, and it doesn't matter. She did what she needed to do, and it set her free. By pouring hot coals on those who betrayed her, she was set free, and now God can deal with those people any way He chooses.

With that truth firmly in mind, we now come to the third reason revenge is ruled out for the children of God.

3. *Revenge destroys you, but good overcomes evil*

Our text ends with a pithy little motto that sums up Paul's teachings in this passage: "Do not be overcome by evil, but overcome evil with good" (verse 21). When Paul says, "Do not be overcome with evil," what he means is, "Don't let revenge destroy your life." Too often, we look at life as a kind of competition. "He hit me, so I had to hit him back." "Sure, I said some awful things to him, but he said them to me first." This happens in marriages all the time. We play games of tit-for-tat. You hurt me, so now I'm going to hurt you. You cheated on me, so now it's okay if I cheat on you. You slapped me, so I can slap you back. You raised your voice, so now I'm going to raise mine just one decibel louder. And on it goes. We may even enlist the Bible in an attempt to support that kind of behavior. You know, the passage about an eye for an eye, a tooth for a tooth (see Deuteronomy 19:21). It's called evening the score.

Why Revenge Doesn't Work

Getting even doesn't work. All it does is unleash a whole cycle of retribution and violence. And the cycle never ends because someone else always wants to have the last word. Paul tells us not to do that because it's destructive. You may win the battle, or say the last word, or strike the last blow, but in the end, you've destroyed your spiritual life. In the process of hurting another person, you've hurt yourself, too. Anger has done its dirty work on the inside. You seethe with malice, rage, hurtful feelings, and horrible thoughts that keep you up late at night. That's one reason many people are sick today. They aren't sick, because of some bug or strange virus. No, their soul is sick, and as a result their body is sick. The list is long, but it includes high blood pressure, heart problems, back problems, tension headaches, nightmares, ulcers, stomach problems, weight problems, blurred vision, a stiff neck, and insomnia.

Paul then said, "Overcome evil with good." This is the bottom line. Although we live in a world where evil seems to win out, more often than not, that's only a temporary situation. Dr. Martin Luther King, Jr. said, "The arm of the universe is long, but it bends toward justice." While evil may do well in the short run, in the end, good always wins. If life were a 100-yard dash, you would bet on evil. But life is a marathon, and because it is, good will win out in the end. It might not win out in the course of one lifetime or in one generation, but eventually, God does move to bring justice into the world. And if justice doesn't come in this life, it will definitely come in heaven. Justice *will* be done. Evildoers *will* be punished. And those who follow the way of Jesus *will* be rewarded. That's the promise of God.

The Brother of the Faith

A while back I read a sobering book titled *Against All Hope,* by Armando Valladares.[18] The book tells the story of the author's 22 years in a Cuban prison. I do not have the words to tell you what his experience was like. The brutality was beyond belief. Suffice it to say that the Nazis had nothing on the Cubans. They only did it on a larger scale. Truly, the Cubans treated pigs better than they treated prisoners. During the author's early years of imprisonment, over 6,000 people were kept in a massive prison on the Isla de Pinos. Most of them were political prisoners whose only crime was opposing Castro. In the book, Valladares describes how men were left naked to wallow for months in their own excrement, beatings, food unfit for barnyard animals, and systematic attacks by the prison guards.

The men in this prison were organized into forced-labor teams and sent to work in rock quarries. When the men returned from the quarry, they were tired, hungry, and exhausted. They were dirty, some of them barefoot, with their clothes hanging in tatters.

As they entered the compound, the guards screamed for them to move faster. When the men didn't respond, the guards began beating them with machetes. As the beatings increased, something strange happened. As he was being beaten, one prisoner raised his arms and face to the sky and shouted, "Forgive them, Lord, for they know not what they do!"

The other prisoners called this man the "Brother of the Faith." He was a Protestant minister who had dedicated his life to spreading the Word of God. He spent his days and nights going through the cells, finding sick men, and washing their dirty clothes for them. He started a prayer meeting and even preached sermons standing behind a pulpit improvised from an old salt-codfish box. The soldiers tried to break up the meetings by beating the prisoners, but they never succeeded. If a prisoner became sick or fell behind in his forced labor, the Brother of the Faith would show up to help and encourage him to keep going and not to give up. He would help the other man do his work so he wouldn't be brutally beaten. Sometimes the guards would come up from behind and hit him for no reason. Instead of cursing or retaliating, he would stand up, face the guard, look him in the eye, and say, "May God pardon you." He constantly reminded the other prisoners not to hate.

Eventually the men were transferred to an even worse prison—Boniato. Torture went from unspeakable to unimaginable. One day a riot broke out and the guards moved in with machine guns. Total slaughter ensued.

> But suddenly, as though to protect them, there appeared a skeletal figure with white hair and flaming blazing eyes, who opened his arms into a cross, raised his head to the invisible sky, and said, "Forgive them, Lord, for they know not what they do." The Brother of the Faith hardly had time to finish his sentence, because as soon as he appeared, Lieutenant Raul Perez de la Rosa ordered the guards to step back, and as the Brother of the Faith was speaking he fired his AK submachine gun. The burst of

fire climbed the Brother of the Faith's chest, up to his neck. His head was almost severed, as though from the blow of an ax. He died instantly.[19]

Jesus said, "The good shepherd lays down his life for the sheep" (John 10:11). We wonder, *Is it possible to live that way?* The answer is yes, even in the most desperate circumstances, even in the midst of the most unspeakable brutality. Yes, you can...if you are willing to lay down your life.

Learning What God Is Like

In 1849, Frederick W. Faber wrote a hymn called "Workman of God." The hymn speaks of what it means to overcome evil with good in a world where evil often seems to win the day:

> Workman of God! O lose not heart,
> But learn what God is like;
> And in the darkest battlefield
> Thou shalt know where to strike.
>
> Thrice blest is he to whom is giv'n
> The instinct that can tell
> That God is on the field when he
> Is most invisible.
>
> Blest too is he who can divine
> Where real right doth lie,
> And dares to take the side that seems
> Wrong to man's blindfold eye.
>
> Then learn to scorn the praise of men,
> And learn to lose with God.
> For Jesus won the world through shame,
> And beckons thee his road.
>
> For right is right, since God is God;
> And right the day must win;
> To doubt would be disloyalty,
> To falter would be sin!

When we read the story of Armando Vallardares, we are entitled to wonder if we could ever have that sort of courage. We'll never know until we're put in a similar situation. But the secret of his faith is not hard to find. We see it in the first verse of Frederick Faber's hymn: "Workman of God! O lose not heart, *but learn what God is like.*" It's all about God all the time. It's not about us, and it's not about the people who have hurt us. You will never pour hot coals of kindness on your adversaries until you "learn what God is like."

And how do you do that? Study His ways. Memorize His Word. Ponder His character. Remember His goodness to you. Think about His compassion for sinners. Examine His justice. Fix your mind on His holiness. Consider His wisdom. Meditate on His mercy. Delight in His decrees. Obey His commands. Believe His promises. Give thanks for His salvation. Rejoice in His faithfulness.

The Reformers often used the Latin phrase *Coram Deo,* which means "before the face of God." It's a reminder that God is always watching everything we do. His eye is always on us, nothing escapes His notice, and all of life must be lived for His approval. World-renown organist and composer J. S. Bach carved the words *Soli Deo Gloria* on his organ at Leipzig to remind him that all his music be composed and performed for the glory of God. That's why the initials SDG appear at the end of his compositions.

The only way to be delivered from a spirit of revenge is to be so filled with God that a desire for revenge finds no place in your heart. When God Himself fills your heart, you will find a new strength to love your enemies, no matter what it takes. Learn what God is like, and you will overcome evil with good.

Ten

Questions
and Answers

— 🌿 —

The Bible tells us to love our neighbors,
and also to love our enemies; probably because
they are generally the same people.

G. K. CHESTERTON

Archbishop Desmond Tutu once said, "Without forgiveness, there is no future." He was speaking not just of personal pain, but also in the larger context of South Africa in the aftermath of apartheid. What is true of individuals is true of families, and what is true of families is true of cities and states. And what is true for states is true for nations as well. Without forgiveness, there is no future. We could add to the archbishop's statement in several ways without changing its basic meaning:

> Without forgiveness, there is no freedom.
> Without forgiveness, there is no recovery.
> Without forgiveness, there is no healing.

But in a world with so much pain, hatred, and animosity between races, tribes, clans, and nations, is forgiveness realistic? Or is it just a distant dream, a theory that can never become reality?

The question is fair and honest and deserves an answer. In an attempt to provide one, we might end up saying, "Yes, forgiveness is the best way, but it is so far beyond us that we must settle for something much less." We could say that, and indeed we may think that, but we would be wrong. Forgiveness may be beyond us, but that doesn't mean it is impossible. It just means we have fallen short of God's goal for us.

Let's begin with the observation that the forgiveness of sins is a major biblical doctrine. The Bible has a great deal to say about God's forgiveness of our sins because that is where salvation really begins.

- "As far as the east is from the west, so far has he removed our transgressions from us" (Psalm 103:12).
- "If you, O LORD, kept a record of sins, O Lord, who could stand? But with you there is forgiveness" (Psalm 130:3-4).
- "You have put all my sins behind your back" (Isaiah 38:17).
- "I—yes, I alone—am the one who blots out your sins for my own sake and will never think of them again" (Isaiah 43:25 NLT).
- "You will trample our sins under your feet and throw them into the depths of the ocean!" (Micah 7:19 NLT).
- "Everyone who believes in him receives forgiveness of sins through his name" (Acts 10:43).
- "In him we have redemption through his blood, the forgiveness of sins, in accordance with the riches of God's grace" (Ephesians 1:7).

Salvation begins with our forgiveness by God. If God did not forgive us, we would have to shoulder our sins forever, and be weighed down under a load of guilt that could never be removed.

But the Bible also has a lot to say about *our* forgiveness of the sins of *others* against *us*. Here are two examples:

- "When you stand praying, if you hold anything against anyone, forgive him, so that your Father in heaven may forgive you your sins" (Mark 11:26).

- "Be kind and compassionate to one another, forgiving each other, just as in Christ God forgave you" (Ephesians 4:32).

There are several points we should observe from these two verses on forgiveness:

First, Christianity is supremely a religion of forgiveness. It begins with God and comes down to us.

Second, God has only one solution to the problem of human sin—the act of forgiveness. If we do not accept His solution, no other will be offered.

Third, God Himself has shown us how to forgive others. We are to do for others what He has done for us.

Fourth, there is a direct connection between our own spiritual health and our willingness to forgive those who have sinned against us. When we have a "root of bitterness" springing up within us, we cannot be truly healthy.

I'm sure we would all agree that forgiveness is of the Lord in the sense that forgiveness starts with God, comes down to us, and then goes out to other people. This is what Ephesians 4:32 plainly says. We are to forgive as God has forgiven us. In his massive commentary on Ephesians, Harold Hoehner points out that the word translated "forgive" in the NIV Bible is part of a Greek word meaning "be gracious." It includes forgiveness, but is a much broader concept. We are to extend grace to others as God has extended grace to us. We, the undeserving who have been showered with God's grace in Christ, are to give to other undeserving sinners (who have sinned against us) the same outpouring of grace. From God to us to others. Grace to us, grace to others. This is God's plan.[20]

But is it realistic to live this way? Is the standard too high? Can anyone really practice this in a fallen world? What would a "grace full" lifestyle look like? When Paul uses the words, "forgiving each other," what does he mean? Several practical questions arise at this point.

Practical Questions About Forgiveness
1. *What is forgiveness?*

The various authors of the Bible used a number of different Hebrew and Greek words to communicate the concept of forgiveness. One word means "to blot out" in the sense that God erases the record of the sins we commit. A common Hebrew word means "to lift and carry away," speaking of the complete removal of our sins from us, as if a heavy load were lifted from our shoulders. Still another word means "to release from debt," indicating the punishment for sin has been canceled. And one Greek word means "to show grace to one who has sinned greatly," speaking of the undeserved nature of forgiveness. Indeed, forgiveness is truly a gift from God. In their book *Forgive and Love Again*, John Nieder and Thomas Thompson point out that the Bible uses at least 75 different word pictures of forgiveness. Here are a few of them:

- "To forgive is to turn the key, open the cell door, and let the prisoner walk free."
- "To forgive is to write in large letters across a debt, 'Nothing owed.'"
- "To forgive is to pound the gavel in a courtroom and declare, 'Not guilty!'"
- "To forgive is to shoot an arrow so high and so far that it can never be found again."
- "To forgive is to bundle up all the garbage and trash and dispose of it, leaving the house clean and fresh."
- "To forgive is to loose the moorings of a ship and release it into the open sea."
- "To forgive is to grant a full pardon to a condemned criminal."

- "To forgive is to relax a stranglehold on a wrestling opponent."

- "To forgive is to sandblast a wall of graffiti, leaving it looking like new."

- "To forgive is to smash a clay pot into a thousand pieces so it can never be pieced together again."

- "Or think of yourself as a banker. In your hand is a note detailing a huge debt owed to you. What debts of others does your note list? Slander? Fraud? Rape? You carefully take the note and look at it once more. But instead of putting it back in the file, you tear it into a thousand pieces. That's forgiveness."

- "When we forgive, we consciously, before God, cancel the debt. We discard the note. We pardon the prisoner. We release the offender."[21]

We can also find it helpful to know what forgiveness does *not* mean:

- Denying the evil that was done.
- Excusing sinful behavior.
- Pretending it never happened.
- Glossing over the pain you suffered.
- Removing all consequences for wrong behavior.
- Overlooking criminal behavior.
- Approving of evil.
- Condoning abuse.
- Acting as if the sin never happened.
- Letting others continually abuse you.
- Pretending you weren't hurt.

Forgiveness is not the same as reconciliation or restoration. It's not a magic trick we can use to force others to become our friend again. It's not a tool designed to manipulate others into confessing what they did that hurt us so greatly.

What, then, is forgiveness? It is a choice, not a feeling. God never says, "Forgive them if you feel like it." Forgiveness is not about your feelings. If you have been deeply hurt, you will probably never "feel" like forgiving someone. Forgiveness is a choice, a decision you make in your heart. It is a choice to release others from their sins against you. That's why 1 Corinthians 13:5 tells us that love keeps no record of wrongs. Forgiveness means letting go of the anger and the desire for revenge. Seen in its true light, forgiveness is an act of mercy toward the offender.

> *Forgiveness is not about fairness. Rather, it's about grace.*

Sometimes we hear people say, "He doesn't deserve to be forgiven." Of course he doesn't. No one "deserves" forgiveness. Forgiveness isn't earned, and if a person could "earn" forgiveness, he wouldn't need it in the first place. It is a gift of mercy that you give to someone who has hurt you. But note this qualifier: The gift is extended to the other person, but the action remains between you and God. The other person might never know about it. When you forgive, God knows and you know—and that's all that matters. And the end result is a change in the way you feel and act toward that other person.

A friend wrote and said, "I'm looking for fairness, but can't seem to find it." And you won't find it, because forgiveness is not about fairness. Rather, it's about grace.

2. How do I know when I have truly forgiven?

The answer will vary depending on the person involved and what he or she did to you. Here are a few helpful guidelines (taken partly from Kendall and also from a list by the Puritan author Thomas Watson).

- Face what they did and forgive them anyway.
- Don't keep bringing it up to them.
- Don't talk about it to others.
- Show mercy instead of judgment.
- Refuse to speak evil of others.
- Choose not to dwell on it.
- Pray for them.
- Ask God to bless them.
- Do not rejoice at their calamities.
- Help them when you can.

In giving this list, I do not mean to imply we must carry out all ten guidelines before we can say we have truly forgiven another person. The presence or absence of repentance plays a role as well. We would do well to take this list and dwell on it, pray over it, and ask ourselves some hard questions.

3. Is forgiveness an event or a process?

The answer is it's both. Forgiveness is an event in the sense that you must, at some point, decide to forgive. And it is a process that must be repeated often over time. I spoke with a woman whose husband abandoned her for a younger woman, leaving her with a very young child to raise alone. As she told me the story, she said, "I guess I've forgiven him a million times. I forgive him over and over again every day." "You'll probably have to forgive him a million more times before it's over," I replied. That may not seem like a word of hope, but, in fact, it is. Remember, forgiveness isn't a tool for manipulating people into having a good relationship with you. No one can force another person to become reconciled with you. That must come from a heart prompted by God's Holy Spirit. As we've noted earlier, there are two very good reasons to extend forgiveness that have nothing to do with the other person:

- You should forgive because God has commanded it.
- You should forgive because forgiveness is good for your soul.

Any other benefits are like ice cream added to a slice of apple pie—nice, but not necessary. We should practice forgiveness for God's sake and our own. That ought to be enough to motivate any of us.

Sometimes we will struggle with forgiving a certain person for years. As a child, C. S. Lewis suffered greatly from a teacher who was a bully. This teacher made life a living hell for his students. Lewis never forgot the pain and humiliation he suffered at his hands, and he never felt able to forgive him. Near the end of his life, however, he wrote to a friend in America:

> Do you know, only a few weeks ago I realized suddenly that I had at last forgiven the cruel schoolmaster who so darkened my childhood. I'd been trying to do it for years; and like you, each time I thought I had done it, I found, after a week or so it all to be attempted over again. But this time I'm sure it's the real thing.[22]

That strikes me as an entirely honest statement. Forgiveness is a journey toward freedom that sometimes requires multiple steps before we reach our goal. Do not despair if your first few steps must be repeated again down the road. Keep walking, and eventually you will get there.

4. Does forgiveness always lead to reconciliation?

The answer is no. Forgiveness is one thing, reconciliation is another. Reconciliation requires forgiveness, but forgiveness does not demand reconciliation. Forgiveness depends on you. Reconciliation depends on you plus the other person. It implies confession, repentance, forgiveness, restoration of trust, the passage of time, and a mutual desire to reconcile. Often it is not possible; sometimes it is not wise:

The former friend we forgive may not be good for us. A former husband may be still addicted to abusing women. A former partner may be a crook—a forgiven crook, but still a crook. Being forgiven does not qualify a person to be a friend, a husband, or a partner. And if he does not qualify, we are better off to walk away and heal ourselves alone.[23]

5. What about the person who says, "I can forgive but I can't forget"?

This is a common problem and a common statement. I must confess I have changed my answer to this question over the years. If you go back and listen to my sermon tapes on forgiveness from a few years ago, you will hear me say something like, "If you haven't forgotten, you haven't forgiven." I'm smiling as I write these words because that statement is so obviously wrong I wonder what made me ever think that way. We all understand that God "forgets" our sins when He blots them out, puts them behind His back, and casts them into the depths of the sea. He can "forget" our sins because He's God and has the power to do that. But we're not God, and our painful memories often return to haunt us.

In pondering this problem, my mind ran to a scripture in the book of Hebrews that speaks of God's forgiveness of our sins. Surely if we have trouble forgetting, what about God, who never forgets anything? Hebrew 10:17 quotes God as saying, "Their sins and lawless acts I will remember no more." According to the phrase,"I will remember no more," God chooses not to remember our sins.

That's helpful, isn't it? *Forgiveness is a choice we make.* It is not a feeling or a mood or a passing notion. Forgiveness does not mean we somehow wipe out of our mind the record of what happened. Forgiveness means we choose not to remember it. There is a big difference between remembering a painful event and dwelling on it. We can all remember (if we try hard enough) events in the past that hurt us deeply. Forgiveness means we choose not to dwell on those events. It also means we choose not to hold a grudge against someone who has wronged us. Clara Barton, founder of the Red Cross, was talking with a friend one day when the name of a person they both knew came up. Years before, that person had acted meanly toward Clara. The friend asked Clara, "Don't you remember when she did that to you?" "No," Clara replied, "I distinctly remember forgetting that."

6. Does forgiveness mean I have to let people walk all over me?

When I was preaching on forgiveness at a conference center in Colorado, a young man in the audience asked, "I know we are supposed to forgive, but does that mean you just lie there and take it?" Does forgiveness mean letting someone keep hurting you over and over again? How does forgiveness apply to an abusive marriage relationship? How does it apply to unethical situations in your workplace?

> *Forgiveness does not cancel all the consequences of sinful behavior.*

When it comes to injustice, there is a big difference between *how* you respond and *why* you respond. There are many times when the only proper response to injustice is confrontation. Such confrontations are rarely easy or pleasant, and sometimes they lead to the breaking of a friendship. But that's not really the issue. The issue is *why* we confront injustice. That's where forgiveness comes in. If we confront injustice out of anger and bitterness or out of a deep desire to get even with someone who has hurt us, then we ourselves are guilty of sin and God will not bless our efforts. Why? Because, as James 1:20 says, "Man's anger does not bring about the righteous life that God desires." Thus, forgiveness is *always* appropriate, even in cases where we are deliberately and repeatedly wronged. In those cases, it is imperative that before we take a step of confrontation, we rid ourselves of the venom of bitterness and the acid of resentment. Otherwise we will be guilty of carrying out a righteous action in an unrighteous way, and God will not bless us.

Forgiveness and justice are different, and we do well to keep them separate. The same is true for forgiveness and reconciliation. No wife needs to stay in an abusive relationship. And when you see the law being broken, you have a moral obligation to call the police. Forgiveness does not cancel all the consequences of sinful behavior. Even when we forgive someone who harms us, that person may still end up going to prison.

7. *Do I need to tell the person, "I forgive you"?*

Not necessarily. Obviously, if a person asks for forgiveness, and if you intend to forgive him or her, then of course you should say, "I forgive you." But most of the time, the people who hurt us are not seeking forgiveness or reconciliation. Sometimes it isn't helpful to say, "I forgive you," for then you end up picking a fight because the person responds, "I didn't do anything that needs to be forgiven." Remember, your forgiveness doesn't depend on them. You don't need their permission to forgive them. You don't need their agreement that they were wrong. Just forgive them. Choose forgiveness in your heart, and then move on with your life.

8. *How do you forgive if they do not confess?*

How do you forgive those who do not, will not, or cannot own up to what they did? If they don't ask for forgiveness, how can you forgive them? This is a painful problem for many people because we live in a cruel world filled with mean people. There are individuals who will stomp on your face and walk away laughing. And they'll do it again and laugh again. You might work with someone like that, or be married to someone like that. You may have a relative who sexually abused you and has never admitted it. And how do you forgive someone who has died? What about people who have moved out of your life and you have no way of confronting them? What does it mean to forgive in such situations?

Writing over 450 years ago, John Calvin addressed this very question by saying there are two kinds of forgiveness. One is when the person who did the wrong admits it, comes to you asking for forgiveness, and you grant it—and the relationship is restored. That's the best kind; that's the ideal. There is confession, forgiveness, reconciliation, and healing. Unfortunately, however, sometimes people who have wronged us will not admit their guilt no matter what we do. In fact, sometimes they will lie to cover up the truth. Sometimes they will cut off the relationship rather than face the hard work of reconciliation. Sometimes they will keep right on hurting us on purpose.[24]

How can you forgive in a situation like that? Calvin said you can forgive even in that situation in the sense that you let go of your anger and bitterness and refuse to let the hurt dominate your life. True, the relationship remains broken. It may never be healed. But you can choose not to remember the sins of the other person. You can choose to wipe the slate clean so your life is free from bitterness. That's not easy, but it's far better than living in the past and nursing a wounded spirit. It's also biblical, for in this we have the example of Jesus Himself, who, when He hung on the cross, prayed, "Father, forgive them, for they do not know what they are doing" (Luke 23:34).

9. What about the feelings of anger that keep coming back?

This common problem confirms that forgiveness is often a process and a journey, not just a one-time event. It's a choice we must continue to make over and over again. In one of her writings, Corrie ten Boom tells of some Christian friends who wronged her in a public and malicious way. For many days she was bitter and angry, until she forgave them. But during the night she would wake up thinking about what they had done, and she would get angry all over again. It seemed the memory would not go away.

Help came from her pastor, to whom she confessed her frustration after two sleepless weeks. He told her, "Corrie, up in the church tower is a bell that is rung by pulling on a rope. When the sexton pulls the rope, the bell peals out ding-dong, ding-dong, ding-dong. But if he doesn't keep pulling on the rope, the sound slowly fades away. Forgiveness is like that. When we forgive someone, we take our hand off the rope. But if we've been tugging at our grievances for a long time, we mustn't be surprised if the old angry thoughts keep coming for a while. They are just the ding-dongs of the old bell slowing down."

So it's not surprising if, after forgiveness, the memories keep coming back for a while. If you refuse to dwell on them, they will slowly fade away. Why? When you forgive, you let go of the rope, and the force is gone out of your anger.

Supernatural Help From God

God makes forgiveness possible

That brings me back to the original question: Is forgiveness realistic? On a purely human level, the answer is no. In our own strength, we will never be able to forgive others as God forgives us—completely, absolutely, freely, immediately, graciously, with no strings attached. As long as we live on the human level, complete forgiveness will be beyond our grasp. But once we bring God into the picture the answer changes, because with God, all things are possible.

On the supernatural level, forgiveness is not only realistic, it's the "supernatural" way of life. Forgiveness is nothing less than a miracle of God. It is a miracle we receive the moment we put our trust in Jesus Christ. And it is a miracle we give to others when, in

Jesus' name, and by His power and for His sake, we forgive those who sin against us.

"Without forgiveness, there is no future." So said Archbishop Desmond Tutu. His words ring true because they are based on the truth of God. Without forgiveness, there is no future, no freedom, no hope, and no healing. But where there is forgiveness, there is grace and mercy and a future as bright as the promises of God.

God moved the fence for us

During World War II, as the Allied soldiers fought their way across France, a soldier died during a bloody firefight. After the battle was over, his buddies wanted to find a way to give him a decent burial. The only cemetery in the closest village was a Catholic cemetery, so they approached the priest and asked for permission to bury their fallen comrade there. "Is he Catholic?" the priest asked. "No, he's Protestant," came the reply. With great regret, the priest said, "He cannot be buried here. This cemetery is reserved for baptized members of the Catholic Church." The soldiers found a suitable place outside the fence bordering the cemetery and with great sorrow, buried their friend. The next day the soldiers returned to the tiny village, hoping to add some flowers to the grave. To their surprise and consternation, when they came to the burial spot, they could not find the grave. Not knowing what else to do, they asked the priest if he knew what had happened. He told them that after they had buried their friend, he could not sleep during the night. So he got up early in the morning and moved the fence to include the body of the much-loved soldier who had died.[25]

That's what God did for us. He could not rest while we were on the wrong side of the fence. He wanted so much to bring us into His family that He sent His Son, the Lord Jesus Christ, who through His death on the cross, "moved the fence" so we would have a place in God's family.

If God "moved the fence" for us, can we not do the same for others? If God found a way to include us in His love, can we not reach out to include those who have sinned against us? This is the very heart of the gospel. What God has freely done for us, we are called to do for others. The heart of God is filled with love, and at its center stands a cross. Through that cross, we have been forgiven. May God give us the grace to "move the fence" for others in the same way that He "moved the fence" for us.

Eleven

The Final Step

--- ❦ ---

Forgiveness is setting a prisoner free,
and then realizing the prisoner was you.

Lewis Smedes

t was 3:00 AM and as the fleet moved through the darkness of
the Pacific Ocean, men on every ship began to stir. This was the
hour, this was the moment of truth. The waiting was over. The
battle was about to begin. From headquarters came the signal:
"Climb Mount Nataka." That meant the attack was on.

For one man, it was the greatest moment he had ever known.
The long years of training were about to pay off, the countless
hours of drills repeated over and over again. He was the man
chosen to be the leader. When Mitsuo Fuchida woke up, he
dressed, ate breakfast, and then pulled on his heavy, fur-lined
flight jacket. Then he went to the operations room for a last-
minute intelligence briefing. Tying a white headband with a red
circle around his flying cap, he jumped into his plane. At 5:30 AM
he took off, the first plane in a squadron of 200. From the carrier
decks of the *Hiryu*, the *Soryu*, and the *Atsugi*, plane after plane

followed him in two waves until the total reached 350, the largest airborne naval assault in history. As the planes sped across the 230 miles that separated them from the island of Oahu, not a word was exchanged among the pilots. The die was cast, the decision had been made. And as Mitsuo Fuchida came across the final mountain that separated him from Pearl Harbor, he cried out the prearranged code word that meant total surprise had been achieved. In his excitement he repeated the word three times: "Tora! Tora! Tora!"

The first bombs fell at 7:55 AM Pearl Harbor time. As battles go, it was over quickly. Within an hour and a half, the second wave of planes had returned to the carriers. The damage was done. Behind them, the Japanese pilots left a sea of flaming wreckage. Before it was all over, the death count would reach 2,403. To this day it remains the single greatest naval defeat in American history.

The End of Innocence

That day—December 7, 1941, a day that lives in infamy—one world died and another world was born. It was the end of the Age of Innocence. In one tragic moment, America was jerked into the modern era. Up until that hour, America had basically been a sleeping giant, taken for granted by the other nations of the world. After Pearl Harbor, we would never be taken for granted again. But from that day, and from what followed after that day, America became and still remains a superpower. Seen in that light, the attack on Pearl Harbor was the single most important event in America in the twentieth century.

Because Pearl Harbor dominated the press at the time, and has gotten so much attention since, many people don't realize there were two other epochal events that took place that same week. One took place on the outskirts of Moscow, when, after a desperate battle, the Russians decisively turned back the German army. The Russians stopped the Nazis at the very edge of the city. Little noticed at the time, that German defeat changed the course of World War II. Up until that moment, Hitler's grand design had been to quickly defeat Russia, sue for peace with England, and thus keep the United States out of the war. Once Hitler knew he could not conquer Russia, he knew his only choice was to go west, even though that meant America would eventually enter the war. Thus the course of history was changed two days before Pearl Harbor.

But that's not all. The other great event, totally unnoticed and unreported at the time, took place in Washington, D.C., the day before Pearl Harbor. On December 6, 1941, a new U.S. government committee, code named S-1, met in Washington, D.C. Its subject: the feasibility of constructing a weapon called the atom bomb.

These two events—bunched into a short three-day window of time—not only galvanized a nation, but also changed the balance of power and ultimately redirected the course of human history.[26]

From Pearl Harbor to Baghdad

What happened at Pearl Harbor led directly to the U.S. involvement in World War II, the bloodiest war in world history. By the time it was over, some 25 million people had died. If you take the long view of history, you can see that what happened at Pearl Harbor led eventually to Hiroshima and Nagasaki, and that in turn set the stage for the Cold War, which itself led us into the Korean War, and ultimately to the war in Vietnam and to the ongoing crisis in the Middle East. To put it another way, there is a dotted line that stretches from Pearl Harbor to Baghdad. What started over 60 years ago has ramifications that are still with us.

According to an article in the *Canadian Army Journal*, a former president of the Norwegian Academy of Science, aided by historians from England, Egypt, Germany, and India, came up with some amazing figures: Since 3600 B.C. the world has known only 292 years of peace. During all the other years there have been 14,531 wars, large and small, in which 3,640,000,000 people have been killed. The value of the destruction would pay for a golden belt around the world 97 miles wide and 33 feet thick. In addition, since 650 B.C. there have been 1,656 arms races, only 16 of which have not ended in war. The remainder ended in the economic collapse of the countries concerned (as happened in the disintegration of the Soviet Union). To put it another way, in world history we have seen 13 years of war for every year of peace. Since the beginning of time, more than 8,000 peace treaties have been agreed upon. Although meant to last forever, the average time those treaties remained in force was two years.[27]

God intends to bring peace on earth by moving from heart to heart to heart. His plan is not to reach people by the masses, but one by one. In that sense, there is no such thing as institutional peace or national peace. There are only men and women who love peace, and men and women who love war. Unfortunately, there still seem to be a lot more people who love war than people who love peace.

This works itself out on a very personal level. We all have to live with the choices we make. If we choose to be angry or bitter or critical or mean-spirited, then we have to face the consequences of our behavior. That's why the message of peace doesn't come through peace conferences, as good as those might be. The message of peace is spread one heart at a time, one person at a time. Someone may object, "That's an awfully slow way to bring peace on earth. Isn't there a better plan?" The answer is simple. It *is* a slow plan, but God's way is the only way that works.

From Heart to Heart to Heart
Jake DeShazer

We're back now at Pearl Harbor. It's a few months after the attack, and America is trying to come back from the great defeat. The military is re-arming and getting ready for all-out war in the Pacific. General Jimmy Doolittle is chosen to lead a daring daytime bombing raid over Tokyo. Militarily the bombing raid has little affect on the war, but it has a profound impact on both the

Japanese and American mindsets. It boosts American morale, and sends a signal to the Japanese that they are not safe on their island fortress. Unfortunately, the bombers run out of fuel and are unable to make it to friendly Chinese airstrips. Most of the pilots are forced to bail out over hostile Japanese-held territory.

One of the men who bailed out was Jake DeShazer. Held in a prisoner-of-war (POW) camp for nearly four years, he was beaten, mistreated, and nearly starved to death. He spent 40 months in Japanese prisons—including 34 months in solitary confinement. Three of his buddies were executed, and another died of slow starvation.[28] By his own admission, Jake hated the Japanese with a fierce and passionate hatred. He hated their appearance. He couldn't stand their language. When the Americans in the POW camp asked for some reading material, they were given an English-language Bible—14 months later. The Bible was given to the officers first, but eventually was passed on to Jake DeShazer. For the first time in his life, he read the Bible. As he read the story of Jesus, the message of forgiveness overwhelmed him. On June 8, 1944, in a Japanese POW camp in China, Jake DeShazer gave his heart to Jesus Christ.

> How my heart rejoiced in my newness of spiritual life, even though my body was suffering so terribly from the physical beatings and lack of food! But suddenly I discovered that God had given me new spiritual eyes and that when I looked at the enemy officers and guards who had starved and beaten my companions and me so cruelly, I found my bitter hatred for them changed to loving pity. I realized that these people did not know anything about my Savior and that if Christ is not in a heart, it is natural to be cruel. I read in my Bible that while those who crucified Jesus had beaten Him and spit upon Him before He was nailed to the cross, on the cross He tenderly prayed in His moment of excruciating suffering, "Father, forgive them for they know not what they do."[29]

In that one transforming moment, all the anger, hatred, and animosity was gone. Jake even started loving his Japanese guards. And after the war was over, Jake DeShazer came back to America, enrolled in Seattle Pacific University, and later returned to Japan as a missionary, where he preached and wrote gospel tracts.

Mitsuo Fuchida

The year is 1945. The Japanese people are trying to put their lives back together. Mitsuo Fuchida was discharged from the army and returned home to work on the family farm. His fighter pilot days were over—forever. For a while he thought he would be tried as a war criminal, but instead he was called as a witness and was never accused of any war crimes. Shortly after the war he spoke with a friend who spent time in American POW camps. The friend told him about an 18-year-old volunteer named Peggy Covell, who had been especially kind to the prisoners.

> When the prisoners asked her why she had been so helpful, she replied, "Because Japanese soldiers killed my parents." She explained that her parents were missionary teachers in Japan at the beginning of the war. They fled, only to be captured later in the Philippines. They were judged to be spies and, while kneeling in prayer, they were beheaded. When Peggy heard about this three years later in the States (she had been evacuated), she was filled with hate. But she concluded that her parents must have forgiven their killers. Now God asked her to forgive—and show it.[30]

Hearing that story caused Mitsuo Fuchida to conclude that the real hope for peace could come only from a supernatural source. In 1950, Mitsuo Fuchida rode the train to Tokyo. As he was walking across the station platform, someone handed him a little piece of paper. He glanced at the title—"I Was a Prisoner of Japan"—and stuffed it into his pocket. He thought it was another story of Japanese atrocities. It wasn't. It was Jake DeShazer's story of how he had come to Christ. As Mitsuo Fuchida read the story, he was captivated. It told of a man who once hated the Japanese but now gave his life to reach them for Jesus Christ. The tract caused Mitsuo Fuchida to find a Bible and to begin reading it. As a Buddhist, it was all new to him. He was enthralled by the story of Jesus Christ, especially by the story of the crucifixion, and most especially by the words from the cross: "Father, forgive them, for they know not what they do."

These are the words of Mitsuo Fuchida:

> I was impressed that I was certainly one of those for whom He had prayed. The many men I had killed had been slaughtered in the name of patriotism, for I did not understand the love which Christ wants to implant within every heart.
>
> Right at that moment, I seemed to meet Jesus for the first time. I understood the meaning of His death as a substitute for my wickedness, and so in prayer, I requested Him to forgive my sins and change me from a bitter, disillusioned ex-pilot into a well-balanced Christian with purpose in living.
>
> That date, April 12, 1950, became the second "day to remember" of my life.[31]

As the news of Mitsuo Fuchida's conversion spread, his friends and family members were shocked. There were huge newspaper headlines that read, "Pearl Harbor Hero Converts to Christianity." Mitsuo's old war buddies visited him, attempting to convince him to give up this crazy idea. But they couldn't. And so the man who led the attack on Pearl Harbor became a Christian and a fervent evangelist for the gospel of Jesus Christ.

Joe Morgan

The story is not yet over. We're back in 1941 again. This time we are on the ground with a 19-year-old young man from Brockton, Texas, named Joe Morgan. He was raised as a Baptist and, at one point, felt God was calling him to be a preacher. But those plans were set aside when he joined the navy in order to see the world. When the attack descended upon Pearl Harbor, he was paralyzed with shock at first, but then grabbed a gun and started firing wildly at the attacking planes. He stayed at his position all day and all night, waiting for the planes to come back—but they never did. After the war Joe Morgan went to seminary and he, too, became a preacher. Where do you suppose his first church was? In Hawaii. He struggled for years with hatred for the Japanese. He simply couldn't forgive them for what they had done at Pearl Harbor. He hated them for all the atrocities in the Pacific. "When we dropped the atomic bomb on Hiroshima, I cheered. I was happy that we had finally killed so many of them," he said. Years passed, and he was still a pastor on Oahu, eaten up with anger and bitterness. Then in 1956, a friend told him about an unusual guest speaker who was coming to a local Methodist church. It was a man from Japan named Mitsuo Fuchida, the man who led the attack on Pearl Harbor. With great skepticism, Joe Morgan went to hear him. Afterward he confronted Fuchida and told him he had been on the ground at Pearl Harbor. Fuchida bowed slightly, then very gently said, "Gomenasai," which means, "I'm sorry." Then the man who led the attack reached out his hand to one of the men he had tried to kill on that day. Joe Morgan's response?

> As he reached out to shake my hand, I experienced the miracle of my lifetime. The anger and hatred were gone. God had let me forgive.[32]

From Enemies to Friends

What a story of the grace of God! It started on the deck of a Japanese aircraft carrier. It led to a Japanese POW camp in China. It continued on the platform of a Japanese rail station. It climaxed at a Methodist church in Hawaii 11 years later.

- Jake DeShazer, who hated the Japanese, found Christ in a POW camp.
- Mitsuo Fuchida, who led the attack at Pearl Harbor, found Christ after reading Jake DeShazer's tract.
- Joe Morgan, who was on the ground at Pearl Harbor, found freedom from hatred when he met Mitsuo Fuchida.

That these former enemies became friends is a testimony to the power of Jesus Christ to bring reconciliation between even the worst of adversaries. And whatever happened to Joe Morgan? In his later years he became a chaplain for the Pearl Harbor Survivors Association. On December 7, 1991, on the fiftieth anniversary of the attack, when President George H. W. Bush spoke at the National Cemetery of the Pacific, Joe Morgan gave the invocation.

Is there such a thing as peace on earth? The answer is yes. But the peace Jesus came to bring is not won around a conference table or at the point of a bayonet. His peace goes from heart to heart to heart. It *is* possible for former enemies to be reconciled, and for people who once hated each other to love each other and to forgive.

It is against that backdrop that we consider the words of Jesus in Luke 6:27-36 (ESV).

> I say to you who hear, Love your enemies, do good to those who hate you, bless those who curse you, pray for those who abuse you. To one who strikes you on the cheek, offer the other also, and from one who takes away your cloak do not withhold your tunic either. Give to everyone who begs from you, and from one who takes away your goods do not demand them back. And as you wish that others would do to you, do so to them. If you love those who love you, what benefit is that to you? For even sinners love those who love them. And if you do good to those who do good to you, what benefit is that to you? For even sinners do the same. And if you lend to

those from whom you expect to receive, what credit is that to you? Even sinners lend to sinners, to get back the same amount. But love your enemies, and do good, and lend, expecting nothing in return, and your reward will be great, and you will be sons of the Most High, for he is kind to the ungrateful and the evil. Be merciful, even as your Father is merciful.

"Love your enemies."

That may be the most difficult command Jesus ever gave. Even when we read it in the Bible, it is extremely difficult to believe that Jesus really meant what He said. But in case we have any doubts about this, consider the way this command is explained:

Do good to those who hate you.

Bless those who curse you.

Pray for those who abuse you.

As if that were not enough, Jesus gave us some additional commands so we can't weasel our way out:

If someone strikes you, turn the other cheek.

If someone takes your shirt, give him your jacket, too.

If a beggar comes to you, give him something.

If someone in need takes something from you, do not demand it back.

And in the middle of all this we have Luke's version of the Golden Rule: "As you wish that others would do to you, do so to them." Jesus also said it's not enough to love those who love you. As Frank Burns said on the TV show *M*A*S*H*, "It's nice to be nice to nice people." Sure it is, but that doesn't win any points with the Lord. Even sinners are nice to nice people.

Then like any good preacher, Jesus repeated His main point just in case we didn't get it the first time around: "Love your enemies" (verse 35). And do good even to people whom you know will treat you rudely in return. Be willing for others to take advantage of you. Don't go around thinking you deserve something in return. That's not why you forgive others, and that's not why you love your enemies. After all, you may forgive someone who was a jerk, and that person may still be a jerk after you forgive him. And you may love your enemies, and they may still be your enemies tomorrow morning.

> *L*ove and hate cannot coexist in
> the same place at the same time.

Why Live Like This?

Let's stop for a moment and observe these truly radical sayings by Jesus. A friend once commented to me that everything the world teaches us about human relationships is wrong. Compared to what most of us have heard, the words of Jesus are (literally) out of this world. That is, they come from another place altogether. If we take these words seriously (as we should), we will often find ourselves at odds with the conventional wisdom most people hold to regarding relationships. Why, then, should we live this way? What's in it for us? Jesus gives us two answers:

1. *You will receive a great reward.* I believe Jesus is referring primarily to a great reward in heaven. But there are also rewards even in this life when we love our enemies. Perhaps the greatest reward is that we are set free from bitterness and anger. Love and hate cannot coexist in the same place at the same time. If we love our enemies, we will not hate them. It's really as simple as that.

2. *You will demonstrate you are a true child of God.* God specializes in being kind to the unkind and showing mercy to mean people. He specializes in showering grace upon sinners, and He loves to turn enemies into friends. When we love our enemies, we're showing forth the character of God to the world and proving that we are part of God's family. There ought to be a family resemblance that even the unsaved can spot.

That's why the text ends with these words: "Be merciful, even as your Father is merciful" (verse 36 ESV). Did you get that? "Your Father." If we say God is our Father, then we have obligation to show forth His character to the world. And what better way to do it than by the way we treat our enemies?

Who Are My Enemies?

That leads to a very practical question: Who are my enemies? *In the broadest sense, an enemy is anyone who turns against me.* The dictionary defines an enemy as "one who feels hatred toward, intends injury to, or opposes the interests of another." It's important as we think about what Jesus said that we not restrict the term *enemy* to people such as Saddam Hussein and Osama bin Laden. Jesus was talking not about enemies in general, but personal enemies. Our personal enemies tend to be much closer to home. In fact, home is the first place to look for our enemies. Jesus said, "A man's enemies will be the members of his own household" (Matthew 10:36). In that surrounding passage, Jesus specified three very close relationships that can go sour:

A father and his son,

A mother and her daughter,

A mother-in-law and her daughter-in-law.

We can easily extrapolate from that list to other close relationships, including the husband-wife relationship and relations with grandparents, uncles, aunts, and other more distant relatives. These are the people we go home to every day or interact with on more or less a regular basis. Every week we work with or go to school with people who may dislike us. We may even come to church and see people we would rather not see. Many of our enemies are found in our immediate sphere of influence. If this teaching of Jesus about loving our enemies is going to work, it must work first in the relationships closest to us. You have to learn to deal with the people closest to you before you can impact the world around you.

God's Call to Forgiveness

I received a very honest e-mail from someone who read one of my sermons on forgiveness. I have never met this person and, as far as I know, the person has never attended the church I pastor. Here is part of the e-mail:

> I am in the depths of unrelenting and what appeared to be immovable unforgiveness due to serious wrongs and abuse committed against me by a very close believer. I have read anew the "forgiveness" scriptures. I have been receiving counsel. I have bought ALL of the forgiveness books. But nothing has touched my heart, spirit, and understanding like this message. Even as I write, I am crying, as I know God is calling me to forgive this person for HIS sake, even as He has forgiven me. And as I do, as I stop dwelling on the pain and hurt of it all, the years of anger, bitterness, and resentment will subside in me.

Those words have the ring of truth about them. Christians can hurt each other deeply and repeatedly. Sometimes we do it deliberately. Our feet are made of clay because we are sinners, too. In a fallen world, the people we thought we could trust will often let us down. Sometimes the people we love the most will turn against us. And sometimes it will happen over and over again, and we will discover that our loved ones have become our enemies.

Let me be more specific:

- Your children could be your enemies.
- Your husband could be your enemy.
- Your wife could be your enemy.
- Your ex-spouse could be your enemy.
- Your parents could be your enemies.

That's why the words of Jesus are so difficult to obey. We are instructed to love those who have hurt us deeply—even those who despitefully use us and abuse us and victimize us again and again. And that's very hard to do when the attacks come from someone close, someone whom we should be able to trust.

Yet the command remains: "Love your enemies." We cannot escape it. *This is the final step in forgiveness.* We have not totally forgiven until we can bless those who have hurt us.

Seven Ways to Love Your Enemies

So the question then becomes both personal and practical: How do we love our enemies? Here are some suggestions:

1. *Greet your enemies.* This is a simple step we often overlook. One part of loving our enemies is to greet them graciously when we see them. Sometimes (often, perhaps) instead of turning the other cheek, we turn our whole body away so we won't have to say hello to someone who has hurt us. Some of us have been quite adept at looking the other way, ducking into a room, crossing the street, or even using Caller ID to keep from greeting those who have hurt us. But if we greet only our friends, what benefit is that? Do not even sinners greet each other? One part of loving your enemies is to greet them instead of avoiding them.

2. *Disarm your enemies.* That's what you do when you turn the other cheek or go the second mile. You disarm them by doing what they least expect, which includes speaking well

of them. General Robert E. Lee was once asked his opinion of a fellow officer who was widely known as one of Lee's greatest detractors. The general said he thought the man was a very fine officer. "General," his questioner replied, quite perplexed, "I guess you don't know what he's been saying about you." "Oh, yes I do," replied Lee. "But I was asked my opinion of *him*, not his opinion of *me*."[33]

> *A*s long as we talk over and over again about how others have hurt us, we will never find the strength to forgive.

3. *Do good to your enemies.* It's fascinating that in Luke 6, when Jesus said, "Love your enemies" (verses 27,35), both times He immediately added, "Do good to them" so that we wouldn't miss the point. Doing good to your enemies means seeing beyond your pain and their meanness to their humanity. It means seeing them as people made in the image of God and understanding that there is something twisted inside that causes them to do what they do. Doing good means doing what will promote their healing despite the way they have treated you. The idea is for you to make the first move. You send the e-mail. You pick up the phone. You make the contact. You bridge the gap. You set up the appointment. I once met a businessman who is greatly gifted in sharing Christ with others. He has a knack for saying the right thing at the right time so that people are eager to know Jesus. What's his secret? He said there are four keys to being used by God to help others: Show up, hang loose, trust God, stay alert. Those four keys will work for you if you want to help those who have hurt you.

4. *Refuse to speak evil of your enemies.* That's what Jesus meant when He said, "Bless those who curse you." It means you refuse to think evil thoughts or speak evil words against those who have wronged you. The book of Proverbs has a great deal to say about the power of words. For example, "The tongue has the power of life and death, and those who love it will eat its fruit" (Proverbs 18:21). Every time we open our mouth, life or death comes out. I am increasingly impressed with this thought: Forgiveness in many cases is not possible because we will not stop talking. As long as we talk over and over again about how others have hurt us, we will never find the strength to forgive. At some point, we have to stop talking and start forgiving.

5. *Thank God for your enemies.* If you believe in the sovereignty of God, you must believe your enemy is sent to you by God's design and with God's approval. Your enemy could not torment you apart from God's permission. Behind your enemy stands the hand of God. And God would never permit this if he did not intend to bring good out of the situation.

6. *Pray for your enemies.* When Martin Niemoller, a German pastor, was arrested by the Nazis in World War II, he prayed daily in his prison cell for his captors. His fellow prisoners asked why he prayed for his enemies. "Do you know anyone who needs your prayers more than your enemies?" he replied. But what if you hate the person you are praying for? Tell that to the Lord. He won't be surprised. Then say, "Lord, I hate this person, but You already know that. I ask You to love this person through me because I can't do it in my own power. I ask You for a love I don't have and can't begin to produce." God will not turn you away when you come with an honest heart, admitting you need His love to flow through you.

As I was working on this chapter, I thought that I should take my own advice and begin to pray for some people who have been difficult for me to interact with. So I bowed my head and began to pray. When the first name came to mind, immediately (in less than three seconds!) I sensed strongly that I should contact that person. I didn't want to do it, but I couldn't shake the impression. At one point, I looked up and started laughing because I knew this was from the Lord. I couldn't just keep on praying. I had to make the contact. We'll see what happens next. This particular person is unhappy with me (and with others) for a variety of reasons. Perhaps I can make a difference. Perhaps not. But I know I have to make the effort. The rest is in the Lord's hands.

7. *Ask God to bless your enemies.* Here's a simple way to do that. When faced with someone who has mistreated you, ask God to do for him or her what you want God to do for you. Seek the same blessing for that person that you want God to give to you. Think of it this way: The greater the hurt, the greater the potential blessing that will come when we totally forgive, and by God's grace, bless those who curse us.

Your Enemy, a Gift from God

Let me offer one final word: *Your enemy is a gift from God to you.* Though you probably can't see how that is possible, remember, that enemy is present in your life only with God's permission. To say that is not to excuse evil or to condone mistreatment. It is to say exactly what Joseph meant when he said to his brothers, "You meant evil against me, but God meant it for good" (Genesis 50:20 ESV). Our enemies humble us, they keep us on our knees, they reveal our weaknesses, and they expose our total need for God. Just as David needed King Saul to pursue him, persecute him, and repeatedly attempt to kill him, we need the enemies God sends to us. If we didn't need them, He wouldn't send them. Therefore, we should thank God, who knows best, and we should love our enemies the best way we can. Often God raises up an enemy to see if we really want to be like Jesus. He will keep our enemies alive and well as long as we need them.[34]

Unfinished Business

We often wonder what it means to love our enemies. That seems such a hard thing to do. If it means that we have to feel affection for them, most of us can never do that. But love is more than just an emotional feeling. In this case, loving our enemies means seeing a good opportunity and putting ourselves at personal risk to help someone who doesn't like us. Most of us would be perfectly happy if we didn't have to mess with our enemies at all. We prefer to leave them alone, and hope that they will leave us alone. How neat, how tidy, how convenient. But loving our enemies means more than putting them in some airtight, hermetically sealed compartment where they won't bother us anymore. It means more than saying, "Good riddance." If we are going to love our enemies, then we are going to have to take some risks and lay ourselves on the line for the sake of those who are trying to hurt us.

That might mean making phone calls we don't want to make; it might mean writing letters we don't want to write. It might mean some face-to-face confrontations we would rather avoid. It will certainly mean some difficult moments. But that is what God is calling us to do. And to be perfectly frank, I cannot guarantee you success because I cannot guarantee how your enemies will respond. I do guarantee that God will bless you when you dare to obey His word. Jesus never said, "Love your enemies as long as they love you back." No, He simply said, "Love your enemies." No strings attached.

It may be that you've cut someone out of your life because he hurt you and God is saying, "You need to take care of some unfinished business." Maybe you've gloated while your enemies have suffered, and now God is saying, "You need to reach out to them." Perhaps you need to begin praying for a good opportunity to show love to someone who has turned against you. When I shared this with my congregation, I mentioned in passing that most of us will have more than one enemy. A woman came up afterward and said with a smile, "You were talking to me when you said that. I needed extra room on the paper to make my list."

The decision about what to do will be different for each of us. Some of us know exactly who we need to see and what we need to say. Is there someone in your life you need to talk to? Someone who would be easier to simply leave alone? If the answer is yes, then the question God is asking is, What are you going to do about it?

Jesus said, "Love your enemies." It won't be easy, but we have no other choice. And if we love them, who knows? Someday they may become our friends once again.

> *If you forgive,*
> *you will be set free.*

The Power of Forgiveness

When Nick, our youngest son, graduated from high school, we hosted a party for him at our home. During the party, someone came up to me and said, "I took a walk this evening with two friends." She meant that during the party she and two friends had taken a walk half a block from where we live in Oak Park. "We walked to the place where your van was wrecked, and we stood there looking at the tree the van hit." That was over ten years ago. I hadn't thought about the wreck in a long time. So much had happened since then. That night, four people got in our van and took a joy ride. Less than a block from our house, it spun out of control and hit a tree at approximately 55 miles per hour. All four people were injured, and the van was totally destroyed. Looking back now, I see clearly that hitting the tree was a mercy from God.

If the van had not hit the tree, it would have hit a house 50 feet farther, and someone would likely have been killed. The person who spoke with me at the party was in the van that night, as were the other two people. She said they stood and talked about the wreck for a while. Then she said, "I asked them to forgive me for my part in it. And they said, 'We forgave you for that a long time ago.'" Then they spontaneously hugged her. "This is going to help me in so many ways," she told me. She is right. Forgiveness always helps us because it sets us free from fear, guilt, anger, and bitterness so that we can get on with life. It is a transforming gift from God.

The next day I walked up the street myself and looked at the tree. You can still see the scars where the van hit. But when you look up, you can see green leaves everywhere. The tree, though once badly injured, is healthy once more. Though it still bears the scars of the past, you can't see the scars unless you look for them.

The tree is a parable of the power of forgiveness. Though we have been badly injured, by the grace of God we can be healed and made healthy once again. The scars might remain with us till we die, but they will not be the first thing people see. Through the grace of forgiveness, the green leaves will flourish once again and become more prominent in our life.

You don't have to stay chained to the past forever. Is God calling you to forgive? Do it. Do it now. Do whatever it takes for as long as it takes. Do it for your sake. Do it for the Lord's sake. Don't focus on the other person. It's not about him or her anyway. It's all about you and the Lord. If you forgive, you will be set free. That's the whole message of this book. Now it's time to do something about it.

Notes

1. R. T. Kendall, *Total Forgiveness* (Lake Mary, FL: Charisma House, 2002), pp. xix-xxii.

2. Many of the ideas in this section come from Scott Hoezee, "Out of the Depths," www.calvincrc.org, September 14, 2003.

3. J. R. Grider, "Forgiveness," *Evangelical Dictionary of Theology*, ed. Walter Elwell (Grand Rapids: Baker Book House, 1984), p. 421.

4. Lewis Smedes, *The Art of Forgiving* (New York: Ballantine Books, 1996), pp. 5-12.

5. Bruce Larson, *There's a Lot More to Health Than Not Being Sick* (Garden Grove, CA: Cathedral Press, 1991), p. 15.

6. Chuck Colson, "The Enduring Revolution," www.iclnet.org, January 1, 2004.

7. Ibid.

8. James Montgomery Boice and Philip Graham Ryken, *The Heart of the Cross* (Wheaton, IL: Crossway Books, 1999), p. 17.

9. *Atlanta Constitution* online, December 9, 2002.

10. Charles Simeon, *Expository Outlines of the Whole Bible*, vol. 1 (Grand Rapids: Baker Book House, 1988), pp. 286-91.

11. Edward E. Plowman, "Bullets Won't Stop Us," www.worldmag.com, December 7, 2002.

12. John McArthur offers an excellent discussion of this issue in chapter 3 of his book *Forgiveness* (Wheaton, IL: Crossway Books, 1998), pp. 53-74.

13. John R. W. Stott, *Christian Counter-Culture* (Downers Grove, IL: InterVarsity Press, 1978), p. 149.

14. Jordana Lewis and Jerry Adler, "Forgive and Let Live," www.msnbc.com, September 27, 2004.

15. Charles Bracelen Flood, *Lee: The Last Years* (New York: MacMillan, 1952), pp. 52-53.

16. Dave Burchett, *Bring 'Em Back Alive* (Colorado Springs, CO: Waterbrook Press, 2004), p. 189.

17. John Stott, *Romans* (Downers Grove, IL: InterVarsity Press, 1994), pp. 336-37.

18. Armando Valladares, *Against All Hope,* trans. Andrew Hurley (New York: Alfred A. Knopf, 1986).

19. Ibid., pp. 325-26.

20. Harold Hoehner, *Ephesians: An Exegetical Commentary* (Grand Rapids, MI: Baker Book House, 2002), pp. 639-40.

21. John Nieder and Thomas Thompson, *Forgive and Love Again* (Eugene, OR: Harvest House Publishers, 1991), pp. 62-63.

22. Cited by Lewis Smedes in *Forgive and Forget* (San Francisco: HarperCollins Publishers, 1984), p. 95.

23. Lewis Smedes, *The Art of Forgiving* (New York: Ballantine Books, 1996), p. 28.

24. John Calvin, *Commentary on a Harmony of the Evangelists, Matthew, Mark and Luke,* tr. William Pringle, vol. XVI (Grand Rapids, MI: Baker Book House, 1979 reprint ed.), pp. 364-65.

25. Warren Jones, "Grace Is Flexible Fences," www.bethelumc.us, December 31, 2004.

26. George Will, "Surprise Attack Backfired on Japan," *Chicago Sun-Times,* December 6, 1991, p. 41.

27. Paul Lee Tan, *Encyclopedia of 7000 Illustrations* (Rockville, MD: Assurance Publishers, 1979), p. 1571.

28. Chuck Colson, "Forgiving Our Enemies," www.townhall.com, December 7, 2004.

29. Jacob DeShazer, "I Was a Prisoner in Japan," www.bli.org, January 3, 2005.

30. David Seamands, "The Kamikaze of God,"www.christianitytoday.com, January 2, 2005.

31. Dean Merrill, "30 Years from Pearl Harbor," *Moody Monthly,* December 1971, p. 29.

32. Richard Price, "The Terror of Pearl Harbor," *USA Today,* December 6, 1991, p. 2A.

33. Daniel D. Meyer, "Crime and Punishment," www.cc-ob.org, August 4, 2002.

34. R. T. Kendall, *Total Forgiveness,* pp. 157-58.

Special Note

If you would like to contact the author, you can reach him in the following ways:

By letter:

Ray Pritchard
Calvary Memorial Church
931 Lake Street
Oak Park, IL 60301

By e-mail:

PastorRay@calvarymemorial.com